A handbook of dispute resolution

'This handbook contains an authoritative and extremely helpful analysis of the facilities for resolving disputes by third parties.'

Lord McCarthy

A Handbook of Dispute Resolution examines the theoretical and practical developments that are transforming the practice of lawyers and other professionals engaged in settling disputes, grievance-handling and litigation. The book explains what distinguishes ADR from other forms of dispute resolution and examines the role ADR can play in a range of contexts where litigation would once have been the primary option, for example in family law and business law. In some areas, such as industrial relations, ADR is not an alternative, but the main method of conflict-intervention, as a chapter by ACAS demonstrates. A wide variety of methods is open to the non-litigious, including resort to ombudsmen, negotiation, small-claims courts, mini-trials and mediation; these and other options receive detailed attention.

Given that ADR is a relatively new discipline, questions about both the training of mediators and the role of government and legal institutions have not yet been resolved. The final sections of the book touch on these issues, drawing on case studies from the international arena. Examples from China, Canada, Australia and West Germany place ADR in a cultural and historical perspective.

A Handbook of Dispute Resolution offers an excellent introduction to a rapidly growing field, which is likely to make a great impact on future legal training and practice. Lawyers, law students, academics and 'dispute professionals' will find this book an invaluable resource.

Karl Mackie is a barrister and psychologist and practising arbitrator and mediator. He is Senior Lecturer in Law and Social Psychology and Director of the Centre for Legal Studies at the University of Nottingham. He is also Chief Executive of CEDR (Centre for Dispute Resolution), a new organization formed to promote the development of ADR methods in commercial disputes in Europe.

A handbook of dispute resolution

resolution

ADR in action

Edited by Karl J. Mackie

Routledge and Sweet & Maxwell

London and New York

First published in 1991
by Routledge
11 New Fetter Lane, London EC4P 4EE
in association with Sweet & Maxwell

Simultaneously published in the USA and Canada
by Routledge
a division of Routledge, Chapman and Hall Inc.
29 West 35th Street, New York, NY 10001

Printed and bound in Great Britain by Mackays of Chatham PLC, Kent
Typeset by LaserScript Limited, Mitcham, Surrey

British Library Cataloguing in Publication Data

A handbook of dispute resolution: ADR in action
    1. Arbitration. Law
    I. Mackie, Karl
    342.79

Library of Congress Cataloging in Publication Data

A handbook of dispute resolution: ADR in action/edited by Karl J.
    Mackie
    p. cm.
    Based on papers presented at a workshop held at the University of
    Nottingham in 1988.
    Includes bibliographical references and index.
    1. Dispute resolution (Law) – Great Britain. 2. Dispute resolution
    (Law) I. Mackie, Karl J., 1947–
    KD7644.A75H36 1991
    347.41'09–dc20   90-8988
    [344.1079]   CIP

ISBN 0-415-04124-4

Contents

Tables and figures

Tables

Figures

Contributors

Advisory, Conciliation and Arbitration Service (ACAS) is a statutory agency in the field of industrial relations (see Chapter 8).

George Applebey studied law at Glasgow University and Tulane Law School in New Orleans. He has been lecturer in the Faculty of Law at Birmingham University since 1973, and has also taught at the University of Kent at Canterbury and the University of Colorado. Since 1981 he has been assistant editor of the *Civil Justice Quarterly*. He is currently a member of the Industrial Injuries Advisory Council.

John Birds is Dibb Lupton Broomhead Professor of Commercial Law and Head of the Department of Law at Sheffield University. He has written widely in the areas of company law and insurance, including *Modern Insurance Law* (1988, Sweet & Maxwell) and contributions (with A. Boyle and G. Penn) to Gore-Browne on *Companies* (1987, Jordan) and MacGillivray and Parkington on *Insurance Law* (1988, Sweet & Maxwell).

Patrick Birkinshaw is Reader in Law at Hull University, and author of *Grievances, Remedies and the State* (1985, Sweet & Maxwell), *Open Government: Freedom of Information and Local Government* (1986, Local Government Legal Society Trust), and *Freedom of Information: The Law, the Practice and the Ideal* (1988, Weidenfeld and Nicholson).

Professor David A. Cruickshank is the Director of the Professional Legal Training Course, Continuing Legal Education Society of British Columbia, and Adjunct Professor at the Faculty of Law, University of British Columbia. As a law professor at UBC and the University of Calgary, he has developed curricula in many aspects of clinical legal education. He is a practitioner with experience as a litigator and negotiator.

Dorothee Eidmann is a sociologist and research assistant. She has conducted research and published in the fields of family and legal sociology. Since 1986 she has been based at the Zentrum für Europiäsche Rechtspolitik, University of Bremen.

Dr Tony Gibson is Director of the Neighbourhood Initiatives Foundation, and the Department of Environment's Consultant on 'Working Neighbourhoods'. His books include *People Power* (1979, Penguin); *Counterweight: the Neighbourhood Option* (1984, TCPA); *Us and Them – How to use the Expert to get What People really Want* (1986, TCPA).

Neil Gold is Head of Professional Legal Education at the City Polytechnic of Hong Kong and was formerly Dean of the Faculty of Law in the University of Windsor, Ontario, and Director of the Commonwealth Institute for Legal Education and Training. His publications include *Essays on Legal Education* (ed., 1982, Butterworths) and *Learning Lawyers' Skills* (co-editor with Mackie and Twining, 1989, Butterworths).

Cosmo Graham is Head of Professional Legal Education at the City Polytechnic of Hong Kong and was formerly a Lecturer in Law at the University of Sheffield. He is the co-editor with T. Prosser of *Waiving the Rules: The Constitution under Thatcherism* (1988, Open University Press), and joint author with T. Prosser of *Privatizing Public Enterprises* (forthcoming, Oxford University Press). His current research interests are complaints procedure in the insurance industry and the regulation of privatised enterprises.

Karl J. Mackie is a barrister/psychologist, Director of the Centre for Legal Studies and Senior Lecturer in the University of Nottingham. Recent publications are *Lawyers in Business and the Law Business* (1989, Macmillan) and *Learning Lawyers' Skills* (co-editor with Gold and Twining, 1989, Butterworths). He is an arbitrator and mediator with the Advisory, Conciliation, and Arbitration Service. His current research interests include commercial ADR, international negotiating skills and business strategy.

Tony F. Marshall is Director of the Forum for Initiatives in Reparation and Mediation. Previously a Principal Research Officer for the Home Office, he is author of *Counselling and School Social Work* (with G. Rose), (1974, Wiley), *Alternatives to Criminal Courts* (1985, Gower), *Bringing People Together* (1985, Home Office) and other publications.

David A. Newton is Secretary-General and Chief Executive of the Australian Commercial Dispute Ltd and formerly a corporate lawyer for a large Australian-owned multinational company. He is a solicitor and mediator, and Chairman of the Council of Asia Pacific Commercial Dispute Resolution Centers.

Michael Palmer is Director of the East Asian Law Centre and Lecturer in Law at the School of Oriental and African Studies, University of London. He has conducted long-term field research among the Chinese people of the New Territories of Hong Kong, and published a number of essays on traditional Chinese law and society and recent developments in modern Chinese law. He is currently working on a general study of law in the People's Republic of China.

Dr Konstanze Plett is a Senior Research Associate and lecturer at the Zentrum für Europiäsche Rechtspolitik, University of Bremen. She has held research posts in Hamburg and been Visiting Research Fellow at the Institute for Legal Studies, University of Wisconsin-Madison. She has published in the fields of copyright law, insolvency law, legal sociology and legal theory.

Richard Thomas has been Director of Consumer Affairs at the Office of Fair Trading since March 1986 and has written and broadcast extensively on consumer and legal matters. He qualified as a solicitor in a City of London firm in 1973 and subsequently worked as a lawyer for the Citizens' Advice Bureaux and for the National Consumer Council. He was a member of the Lord Chancellor's Advisory Committee on the Civil Justice Review.

Bonita J. Thompson QC practised law in Saskatoon in the early 1970s and became Assistant Professor of Law at the University of Saskatchewan. After receiving an LL M from Yale in 1977, she practised in British Columbia before joining the Ministry of the Attorney-General. She was appointed Queen's Counsel in 1986, and became the first Executive Director of the British Columbia International Commercial Arbitration Centre. She has since joined the law firm of Singleton Urquhart Macdonald as counsel.

Tom R. Tyler is Professor of Psychology and Political Science at Northwestern University and a Research Fellow at the American Bar Association. He has written two books on conflict resolution, *The Social Psychology of Procedural Justice* (with Allan Lind) (1988, Plenum) and *Why People Obey the Law* (1989, Yale University Press).

Janet Walker co-directed the Conciliation Project Unit set up by the Lord Chancellor's Department as a major research programme into family conciliation services. She is Director of the Family and Community Dispute Research Centre and Senior Lecturer in Social Policy at the University of Newcastle upon Tyne, England. She is a practising mediator and family therapist and has published a number of studies on dispute resolution and social policy.

R.E. Wight was educated at Aberdeen University, then worked as a researcher at Leicester Polytechnic and Birmingham University. After a period as a lecturer in the Centre for Commercial Law Studies at Queen Mary College, he is currently a Lecturer in the Department of Law, University of Essex.

Acknowledgements

The concept for this volume was fashioned as a consequence of a Workshop held at the University of Nottingham in 1988, probably the first Workshop in the UK to consider Alternative Dispute Resolution (ADR) in depth across a range of fields of dispute. A number of the chapters were first presented in an earlier version at the Workshop while others have been commissioned and written since in an attempt to provide a comprehensive introduction to developments in ADR. Inevitably there are many who contributed to the Workshop and others who influenced this book and my thinking on dispute resolution, and my thanks go to them; my apologies go to those whose work would have appeared in this volume had I been producing an encyclopaedia rather than a more limited text. In particular I wish to thank Professor William Twining and Dr Sally Lloyd-Bostock, who consulted on the development of the Workshop, and Jane Rudge for her committed help and support in the organization and administration both of the Workshop and later with the process of putting together this volume. In the United States Tom Colosi and Robert Coulson of the American Arbitration Association and James Henry of the Center for Public Resources helped me understand the American scene, an understanding which was deepened by participation in the American Bar Association 1989 conference on dispute resolution; David Newton, Howard Ambrose and many others in Australia helped me sense the possibilities of dispute resolution systems. Finally, I should thank my mother and father for giving me an early insight into disputes domestic and international; Ann, Karen and Alan for their various tough lessons in negotiation and disputes management outside the world of theory; and ACAS for their support for my development as an arbitrator and mediator.

A number of more formal thanks are also appropriate:
To the *Civil Justice Quarterly* (Sweet & Maxwell), which originally published in earlier versions Chapter 9 by John Birds and Cosmo Graham and Chapter 12 by Richard Thomas.
To *Arbitration*, the journal of the Chartered Institute of Arbitrators, which published part of the final chapter of this volume.
To the American Arbitration Association for permission to reprint the AAA Mediation Course Outline and Observers' Sheets.

To Little, Brown & Co. Publishers, for permission to reprint pages 8–9 of S.B. Goldberg, E.D. Green and F.E.A. Sander (1985) *Dispute Resolution*.
To the National Institute of Law Enforcement and Criminal Justice, US Department of Justice, Washington, DC, for permission to reprint the table of Dispute Processing Options from D. McGillis and J. Mullen (1977) *Neighborhood Justice Centers*.

Karl J. Mackie

1 Dispute resolution: the new wave

Karl J. Mackie

THE ADR MOVEMENT

While much of Eastern Europe rediscovered the 'rule of law' in 1989, in the same year a less newsworthy, but in its own way still extraordinary, event took place on Hawaii for a nation well experienced in the rule of law. The American Bar Association, representative of some 800,000 US lawyers in the world's most 'sue-conscious' society, devoted its annual convention there to the theme of 'Resolving Disputes in Pacific Ways'. The choice of theme, leaving aside its geographical aspirations, reflected the remarkable success within some two decades of the concept of 'Alternative Dispute Resolution', a concept that has now established its acronym, ADR, as a term of art. 'ADR' – alternatives to litigation as a means of dispute resolution – was being explored not only in the substantive debates amongst the lawyers attending the convention, but also in reports of new dispute resolution legislation, mechanisms, projects and services taking place within many of the states (Hawaii itself a very active participant in this) – not to mention the posters, badges, T-shirts and fortune cookies promoting the concept.

> ADR has quietly slipped into the mainstream of legal practice. For some, the mention of ADR signals debate over whether some means for dealing with conflict is faster or better than litigation, while for others, ADR represents a reminder of traditional notions of legal negotiation and settlement. Both views miss the point. Over the past two decades ADR has become a cornucopia of processes, procedures and resources for responding to disputes, all of which supplement rather than supplant traditional approaches to conflict. Contrary to its label, ADR is not an alternative or substitute at all; it adds useful tools to an attorney's existing professional tool box.
>
> (Dispute Resolution First Aid Kit for Attorneys,
> ABA General Practice Section, 1988, Introduction)

As the chapters in this handbook demonstrate, however, the United States is not alone in its interest in developing or improving alternatives and supplements to litigation. Nor is it alone in a revival of interest in the theory and processes of dispute resolution generally. And 'revival' is the most appropriate term in this context since too much can be claimed for ADR as a modern movement. Many of the techniques adopted in ADR, such as mediation, have an ancient history (Stein 1984) or have been used for decades in some fields such as labour relations or international affairs (Merrills 1984). Similarly the concern with reforming the delays and costs of the legal process have a long pedigree (e.g. Pound 1906) and can be seen as part of the historical ebb and flow of managing the conflicting and competing concerns within legal processes (Tomasic and Feeley 1982: Introduction). The forces behind the development of administrative tribunals in the UK, for example, share many of the characteristics of the concerns of the ADR movement, promising 'cheapness, accessibility, freedom from technicality, expedition and expert knowledge' (Franks 1957: para. 406).

However, the ADR movement stands out for its success in crystallizing the concerns of a range of constituencies interested in reform of legal practice as well as of those keen to re-examine the wider potential of varied forms of dispute resolution. In turn it has stimulated experimentation, provided new models of dispute resolution, new applications of older methods, new forums for dispute resolution, and a new emphasis in lawyer education. Thus this handbook surveys some of that American experience as well as exploring developments in the UK and other countries.

The explosion of interest in dispute resolution in the late twentieth century should perhaps come as no surprise. Dispute resolution is clearly a 'growth industry' in a modern world that can generate disputes or social conflict (and, through the communications media, heightened community awareness of such problems) as fast as it generates new technologies, new forms of relationship, and new social problems to take their place alongside many well-trodden dispute contexts. As the chapters in this handbook demonstrate, pressure for reform and expansion of dispute resolution mechanisms has been building up in the UK and other countries, sometimes stimulated by the 'ADR movement' *per se*, but more often by the internal dynamic of pressures to manage areas of social conflict in more 'effective', 'efficient' and 'appropriate' ways. One of the beneficial side-effects of the ADR debate has been to expose for scrutiny many of the assumptions and criteria behind such labels.

The philosophical roots of the movement lie in a patchwork of concerns generated by the philosophical and professional aftermath of the 1960s' generation: concern with peaceful resolution of disputes from community to global contexts; recognition of the failure of many traditional social mechanisms to respond to the new challenges of a consumer-led society; a renewed emphasis on a search for community living and a community justice to match it; an undermining of the concept of professional expertise and status in favour of client self-direction; a wave of anthropological studies which brought attention to the roots of community dispute resolution mechanisms, forms which were simpler in meaning and structure and less tainted by bureaucratization and professional monopoly. The development of these ideas has also struck a sympathetic chord amongst those faced with the practical difficulties of how to ease the increasing caseload and logjams of the courts.

Many disciplines and interests have therefore contributed to the motive force of dispute resolution growth. The ADR movement as such, however, has received its most specific expression in legal scholarship, arising from the increasing dominance of law and legal or quasi-legal institutions as vehicles to achieve social justice and social control simultaneous with a deepening concern (particularly in the United States) with 'the pathology of litigation' (Henry and Lieberman 1985). Nevertheless the varied nature of the philosophical roots of ADR can be gauged by the different concerns which still guide ADR developments. Goldberg *et al.* (1985: 5), for example, identify four separate goals discernible within the movement, goals which may overlap and conflict:

1 to relieve court congestion as well as undue cost and delay
2 to enhance community involvement in the dispute resolution process
3 to facilitate access to justice
4 to provide more 'effective' dispute resolution.

They define an effective dispute resolution mechanism as 'one that is inexpensive, speedy and leads to a final resolution of the dispute. At the same time it should be procedurally fair, efficient (in the sense of leading to optimal solutions), and satisfying to the parties' (Goldberg *et al.* 1985: 7).

This convergence of interests has given a new energy and focus for experimentation, whether through the use of established dispute resolution methods (such as mediation and ombudsmen) in new contexts, or in the development of relatively novel methods of dispute resolution (such as the 'mini-trial' and 'med-arb') and novel dispute resolution institutions and practices (such as the 'Multi-Door Courthouse'). Finally, the ADR movement has been instrumental in renewing the challenge to the prevailing approach to legal education; an approach which continues to emphasize case-law, appellate trial judgments and adversarial professional philosophy disproportionately to the many other contexts of dispute resolution involving legal rules and practice, to the many skills of dispute resolution effectiveness other than black-letter law interpretation, and to the diverse professional role-models available other than that of lawyer as intellectual and procedural gladiator.

ADR OR DR?

The concept of mechanisms that are appropriate to assist the resolution of disputes can be said to run parallel to the existence of human community. Systems of dispute resolution in early societies gave rise in turn to the (ultimately) sophisticated and elaborate system of dispute resolution represented by modern law and legal processes (Stein 1984). Proponents of ADR have claimed, putting the concept in its simplest terms, that there are other and often 'better' routes to settle disputes than available through this developed framework of 'traditional' litigation procedures. Thus the adjective 'Alternative'. However, as debate and practice have developed, this simple approach has been refined.

Paradoxically most proponents of ADR are now agreed that the expression 'alternative' is an inappropriate one, although their reasons or emphases for this may differ. First, there are many areas of social dispute which have not been associated with litigation as a dispute resolution mechanism, so that the issue of finding an alternative to litigation is not a relevant or helpful starting-point. (Indeed the problem may be in some cases how to encourage and improve access to litigation.) Neighbour or consumer disputes, for example, are often seen by an aggrieved party as too 'minor' to contemplate litigation. On the other hand, potential business partners may reach an impasse in negotiations over a contract, but the alternative may be to do business elsewhere, not to litigate.

Second, it is well known that most disputes for which the litigation system is a recognized forum never reach a trial. Even amongst those which are formally entered into the litigation process by writ or summons, the pattern is similar – some 90 per cent or more typically are settled out of court or withdrawn before trial. In these cases it is therefore litigation which is the minority 'alternative' method to other major dispute settlement processes. (This is even more true of many Asian and other societies, where there is historically greater emphasis on social harmony and avoidance of conflict rather than the American-style individualistic pursuit of rights. From this perspective what the Americans call alternative dispute resolution methods can be seen rather as an attempt to return to earlier community models of dispute settlement – 'back-to-basics' dispute resolution.)

Third, there has been an emerging recognition that the value of ADR is in its emphasis on thinking of a *spectrum* of dispute resolution mechanisms which can be judged by how *appropriate* they are to a particular dispute and its substance, context and parties. There is a 'universe of disputes' and a spectrum of dispute resolution mechanisms which may be designed to match the various elements within this universe. Within this spectrum, litigation – dispute settlement before a judge in a public forum in accordance with recognized legal rules – has a valid place as appropriate to many types of community disputes. The term 'alternative' has, from this perspective, an unfortunate connotation of a rebel movement, an attempt to oust the courts and lawyers from dispute resolution mechanisms. Most proponents of ADR are seeking not to oust the courts and lawyers but to make them more aware of, and more skilled in selecting from and using, the range of possible dispute resolution processes appropriate to settling a dispute. Finally, many of the developing ADR processes are in fact being incorporated into court procedures or adopted by legislation as recognized adjuncts to settlement mechanisms through the courts.

Thus there has been a growing tendency to omit the expression 'alternative' from titles of textbooks on dispute resolution (e.g. Goldberg *et al.* 1985; Riskin and Westbrook 1987). Despite a number of attempts to find a new adjective and/or acronym, however, 'Alternative Dispute Resolution' and its acronym remain the most widely recognized terms of art to describe the range of processes, other than litigation, used to settle disputes. They are used as such in this book. It is important to bear in mind, however, that a full understanding of dispute resolution methods needs to encompass the role of litigation practice and management of litigation. Also, that the pressures which have spawned ADR developments are also transforming traditional litigation practice (see Chapter 3 by George Applebey in this handbook). These topics are, however, the staple diet of standard legal textbooks, and so do not form a major part of this handbook.

THE CRISIS IN DISPUTE RESOLUTION

The use of the term 'alternative' and the fact that the concept of ADR has been taken more on board by American legal scholars and lawyers do help to demonstrate an important source for the revival of interest in dispute resolution. There is a crisis in many countries in terms of overload of the litigation system, reflected in extensive delays before court hearings and judgment, particularly but not exclusively in civil matters. Alongside this, and often seen as a contributory cause of it, is a social structure of legal practice which has proved difficult to change and is a major element in the costs of bringing a legal action and in public perceptions of the difficulties of enforcing or defending rights or advancing disputes through the courts. That crisis and the accelerating costs of using lawyers are most advanced in the United States although they are also well recognized as demanding reform in the UK.[1] (See Mackie 1989; Lord Chancellor's Department 1988.)

Also under attack by the ADR movement are the assumptions that form part of the lawyer's 'standard philosophical map' derived from legal education and the conventions of the profession (Riskin 1982) that is that within an 'adversarial' system of law, the lawyer's responsibility is to seek to 'win' for the client using every tactic that is professionally allowable (or not explicitly prohibited); and that the object of the process is victory in relation to a carefully defined question of principle as applied to (usually) a definite past incident or incidents. Thus trials issue narrow win–lose outcomes rather than problem-solving solutions which take into account the context of the dispute, the merits on both sides and the wider relationship of the parties, past, present and future; law firms handle cases in 'litigation departments' rather than 'settlement departments' – although most of the time they settle rather than go as far as trial (but often for negative reasons of cost considerations and uncertainties of trial judgment rather than positively negotiated mutually satisfactory outcomes); relations between clients and client attitudes to legal action become soured by legal wrangling and procedural hurdles motivated by lawyer obsession with technical victories.

This backcloth philosophy to disputing is seen as damagingly restricted in its purpose and vision.[2] Parties tend to lose control of the process and become forced into narrow, adversarial positions to fit the professional framework. Client problems and the solutions to such problems, however, more often than not fail to fit into such a narrow strait-jacket but are complex and interactive in nature, whether in terms of neighbourhood disputes or crime, marriage relations, labour–employer concerns, or in terms of commercial activity and transactions in the world of business. Reappraisal of dispute resolution methods has therefore often been directed at finding ways to return to more socially harmonious procedures and to methods which will get to the roots of a problem more creatively and effectively or which will better enhance transactional bargaining. This new emphasis has also led to reconsideration of basic negotiation skills.

Nor is this desire to discover new approaches fuelled only by motives of altruism or philosophical exploration. It also reflects concern amongst lawyers that costs, delay and unsatisfactory service are driving potential or existing clients away, either to forgo their rightful claims against other parties or into the arms of other professions and dispute resolution businesses. (Unlike the USA, however, the idea of private sector dispute resolution agencies has not yet caught on in the UK although some attempts are being made to establish them in the field of commercial disputes.)

DISPUTING – PROCESS AND CONTENT

One can speak of ADR as a movement in the United States, without exaggeration, because of the extent to which study and debate have focused on procedural mechanisms as such, that is on *processes* of negotiation, mediation, conciliation, and so on. This theoretical emphasis has not been so strongly reflected in other countries. Interest in the UK has primarily been *context*-based. Energies, intellectual debate and experimentation have primarily concerned the *substantive* area of dispute e.g. family conciliation and mediation, consumer arbitration and ombudsman schemes, commercial arbitration reforms, final-offer arbitration developments in industrial relations.[3] (Significantly the area where there has been most interest in 'ADR', commercial business-to-business relations, is also the most US-influenced.)

While it may be possible to separate process and context issues at the level of concept and theory, in practice the two are often inseparable, if only by reason of the fact that the history and culture of a dispute arena are inevitably enmeshed in any dispute. Nevertheless the act of exploring the varied forms and contexts of dispute resolution may be a vital stimulus in enhancing awareness of other options and thereby encouraging flexibility and creativity in decision-making over dispute resolution mechanisms. This handbook therefore attempts to bring together these different emphases in a comprehensive introduction to the world of dispute resolution, drawing both on substantive debates and on international and UK perspectives on the processes of dispute resolution.[4] It has three aims:

1 to enhance awareness within the UK and elsewhere of the concept and potential of ADR
2 to provide a comprehensive introduction to ADR developments within the UK and therefore help 'bridge the gaps' in knowledge which exist between practitioners and scholars engaged in different sectors and institutions
3 to explore some of the issues raised by ADR for research and education, and for future policy initiatives.

Part I focuses on recent developments in procedural mechanisms, looking at negotiation and mediation, grievance mechanisms, reforms in litigation procedure for small claims, arbitration reforms and other ADR developments. It begins with a research-based justification for making a distinction between process and substance in considering the meaning of justice as viewed by actors in the system. Part II looks at dispute resolution in a range of studies which draw out the emphasis on the social contexts of a dispute: neighbourhood, consumer, family, industrial relations, ombudsmen and financial services. Part III provides some examples of comparative developments outside of the UK and USA. Part IV of the handbook explores the research and education and training needs created by ADR perspectives, and the possibilities for future developments in ADR.

NOTES

1 There are of course important differences in the two legal systems and therefore in terms of how reformers apportion responsibility for the crisis e.g. the US retains the jury system in civil trials while facing a crime explosion, has a more troublesome discovery of evidence system, and a system which encourages litigation by reason of allowing cases often to be taken by lawyers on a contingency fee basis (the lawyer is paid on a percentage of the damages or settlement outcome) while not requiring a loser to pay the other side's costs. In the UK concern has more often focussed on the question of the restrictive practices attributed to the legal profession, in particular the retention of a divided profession of solicitors and barristers with their own restricted spheres of activity.

2 A similar divergence can be found in scholarship over the topic of 'regulation' (see Mackie 1989: ch. 10).

3 To avoid further restrictiveness, the terms 'conflict', 'grievance' and 'dispute' are used in this handbook without an attempt to differentiate them by definitions. Although differentiation between the concepts is useful for some purposes, it is less so in the context of a work seeking to advocate creativity, flexibility and depth of approach in handling varied forms of dispute, and one warning of the over-narrow view of disputes often take in litigation and case-law.

4 The one area I am conscious of omitting is that of disputes between nations. For a useful introduction to this, see Merrills (1984). The United Nations Charter Article 33 (1) provides for a range of dispute resolution methods in encouraging the peaceful resolution of international disputes.

Part I
Dispute resolution
mechanisms and
procedural justice

Introduction

In designing mechanisms appropriate to disputes, a principal claim of ADR scholarship is for the need to acknowledge and respond to diversity – diversity in the types of disputes that may justify intervention, in the parties to a dispute and their interests and values, in the forms that dispute resolution may take, in the need or demands for community involvement in dispute resolution processes and outcomes. At the same time one can recognize that distinctive patterns and traditions of dispute resolution emerge. Perceptions of grievances and bases for conflict are interpreted through societal, group and individual attitudes as well as by legal rules. So also are understandings of which dispute resolution processes and interventions are valid, useful and accessible. The interplay of these perceptions and understandings of what makes for a grievance or conflict and the means available for dealing with them can be said to form the dispute resolution 'system' in any community. The result of this interplay is to define what disputes are valid, which dispute resolution processes applicable and valid, and how disputes are managed. The outcome of this process may be ultimately to enhance the role of law and lawyers or to exclude legal rules and processes either inadvertently, by custom, or even explicitly as in certain forms of arbitration (see Macaulay 1963; Beale and Dugdale 1975; Ferguson 1980).

Many grievances and disputes, probably a majority, are never 'resolved' as such, but only allowed to die by one party 'lumping it' or by the unilateral action of another party exercising power. (They are an important category, however, for ADR developments in terms of arguments over access to justice. This accounts in part for the reform pressures behind civil justice reform, and the emergence of tribunals, administrative review mechanisms, and complaints and consumer redress systems.) In others the parties may reach an accommodation by negotiation without outside intervention. In other cases, there may be assistance from third parties to reach an agreement, through expert advice or fact-finding or by means of conciliation and mediation efforts. Finally, the outcome may be adjudicated by a third party. The legal significance of the process or outcome (for example whether the outcome is legally binding) is again variable, depending on the process, the dispute and the parties to the dispute. Dispute resolution processes can therefore be more or less within the 'shadow of the law' (i.e. reliant on legal rules or predicted legal outcomes) and more or less within the 'shadow of the court' (i.e. court-initiated).

The spectrum of types of dispute resolution processes can be classified in many ways. In a simple form (excluding unresolved or unilaterally resolved disputes, and dispute prevention systems) it could be classified in terms of the *dominant formal emphasis* in the role of the third party as:

Representative	Facilitator	*Investigator*	*Adjudicator*
(client adviser, advocate)	(conciliator, mediator)	(complaints bureau, ombudsman)	(trial judge, arbitrator)

The processes may in practice overlap or may be applicable at different phases of a dispute or to different parts of the same dispute, or be found in formal or informal 'hybrid' forms. (Thus the need to refer to the dominant emphasis ascribed to the role.) For example the commercial client who employs a solicitor adviser in a business contract dispute may be described as 'negotiating' with the other party, but the lawyer is likely to be assisting the negotiation by means of expert advice, by acting as advocate for the client, by mediating between the client's stated desires and the other party's interests (or the legal rules limiting the client's position), by investigating the history of contract negotiations, by occasionally adjudicating in collaboration with the other party's professional adviser where the parties hand over the decision on details of an agreement to the lawyers. Or a collective agreement between a union and company may allow a form of 'med-arb', that is the parties may invite a third party to seek to settle the dispute by mediating an agreement but give that party power to arbitrate on any issues on which the parties remain in disagreement after mediation. Or the parties may agree to be bound by an expert opinion on one aspect of their dispute, but to use this as the basis for further negotiations. And so on. (Note also the more established investigatory role for the judges within the civil law inquisitorial system than in the common law adversarial tradition.)

Intersecting through the conceptual dimension of the type of mechanism, or *third-party role*, run a number of other dimensions of context, process and outcomes that are also relevant to an appraisal of dispute resolution processes in any particular situation: the *type of dispute* – is it grievance-based (usually reflecting an imbalance of power), rights-based (e.g. seeking to enforce the terms of a contract or a legal rule), or interests-based (i.e. reflects an impasse which has arisen over the attempt of one party to establish a new relationship such as a pay increase or a contract negotiation); *relationship of the process to legal rules* and *to the legal system* (in the shadow of the law or in the shadow of the court?); *relationship between the parties* (including the third party) and of the parties to *the community* and *other sources of power and influence*; opportunities for *access to other dispute resolution mechanisms*; whether there is *compulsion* to enter the process or whether it is voluntary; *extent of powers* given to the third party by way of managing the process, the parties and others; degree of *formality*; whether the proceedings are *private or public*; questions of *confidentiality* of information obtained in the process; the mode of *communication* involved (hearing or documents only?); *rules of evidence* and of *representation*; *whether the outcome is binding or non-binding* (some forms of adjudication may be non-binding);

whether the outcome is subject to a *right of appeal, review or renegotiation*; *enforceability* of outcome; etc. Despite the attempt to present a simple classification of types, therefore, it should be remembered that there are a remarkable number of ways of conceptualizing, classifying and analysing disputes and dispute resolution mechanisms. Goldberg *et al.* (1985) have attempted to chart a number of these characteristics in relation to the wider range of processes reviewed by ADR writers in the United States (see Table I.1).

The complexity of conceptualizing and classifying ADR is at the heart of the robustness underlying ADR theory and practice, and casts doubt on attempts to suggest that any one method, even formal litigation, should have a declared monopoly on claims of superiority as an effective dispute resolution mechanism or instrument of 'justice' (itself a multi-faceted concept). (In this context see, however, the critique of ADR by Fiss 1984.)

The thrust of the ADR critique of dispute resolution has been to reawaken interest in particular in the domain of facilitation of settlement or assisted negotiation. Some definitions of ADR in fact exclude adjudication. However, as stated in Chapter 1, this is to ignore the fact that similar pressures for more responsive dispute resolution have led to important changes in systems of adjudication and arbitration; also the fact that the courts have in a number of instances taken the lead in fostering settlement mechanisms as an adjunct to trial processes. Thus it is unhelpfully narrow to exclude consideration of adjudicative mechanisms. Equally, alongside a reawakening of interest in non-adjudicative third-party intervention, there has come a revival of interest in negotiation itself, a technique long associated with legal settlement and one which appears to form an important element within conciliation and mediation techniques.

The chapters in Part I of this handbook are selected in the main to highlight aspects of process or procedural justice in the main forms of ADR in the UK, exploring the major methods in the system, the nature of the criticisms of these methods, the arguments for reform, and the influence of ADR on the debates in the area. However, the part begins with a more fundamental question – to what extent is procedure a relevant issue? The debate over ADR has given a new emphasis to questions of process in evaluating fairness, justice or effectiveness. But to what extent is this in any case a relevant consideration? Many lawyers might argue that only clients who 'win' are likely to feel satisfied with a process. Tom Tyler's summary (Chapter 2) of recent research work in the United States, assessing the attitudes of litigants exposed to varying processes, suggests that disputants are well able to distinguish procedure from outcome in terms of their evaluation of dispute resolution. Indeed, and perhaps not surprisingly, clients seem to place greatest weight on fair process rather than on outcome fairness or on winning. This client judgment has long been reflected of course in legal (and lay) jurisprudence in emphases on due process, on agreed procedures in private justice systems, and on the rules of 'natural justice'. However, the research evidence provides further useful confirmation of the importance of regularly reviewing dispute resolution processes in *process* terms. The 'professionals' in the system are likely to become so used to dealing with processing of clients that

Table 1.1 Primary and hybrid dispute resolution processes

| Characteristics | 'Primary' dispute resolution processes | | | |
	Adjudication	Arbitration*	Mediation	Negotiation
Voluntary/ involuntary	Involuntary	Voluntary	Voluntary	Voluntary
Binding/ non-binding	Binding, subject to appeal	Binding, subject to review on limited grounds	If agreement, enforceable as contract	If agreement, enforceable as contract
Third party	Imposed, third-party neutral decision-maker, generally with no specialized expertise in dispute subject	Party-selected third-party decision-maker, usually with specialized subject expertise	Party-selected outside facilitator, usually with specialized subject expertise	No third-party facilitator
Degree of formality	Formalized and highly structured by predetermined, rigid rules	Procedurally less formal; procedural rules and substantive law may be set by parties	Usually informal, unstructured	Usually informal, unstructured
Nature of proceeding	Opportunity for each party to present proofs and arguments	Opportunity for each party to present proofs and arguments	Unbounded presentation of evidence, arguments and interests	Unbounded presentation of evidence, arguments and interests
Outcome	Principled decision, supported by reasoned opinion	Sometimes principled decision supported by reasoned opinion; sometimes compromise without opinion	Mutually acceptable agreement sought	Mutually acceptable agreement sought
Private/public	Public	Private, unless judicial review sought	Private	Private

Table 1.1 Continued

Characteristics	Private judging	'Hybrid' dispute resolution processes			
		Neutral expert fact-finding	Mini-trial	Ombudsman	Summary jury trial
Voluntary/ involuntary	Voluntary	Voluntary or involuntary under FRE 706	Voluntary	Voluntary	Involuntary
Binding/ non-binding	Binding, subject to appeal	Non-binding but results may be admissible	If agreement, enforceable as contract	Non-binding	Non-binding
Third party	Party-selected third-party decision-maker, may have to be former judge or lawyer	Third-party neutral with specialized subject matter expertise; may be selected by the parties or the court	Party-selected neutral adviser sometimes with specialized subject expertise	Third-party selected by institution	Mock jury impanelled by court
Degree of formality	Statutory procedure but highly flexible as to timing, place and procedures	Informal	Less formal than adjudication; procedural rules may be set by parties	Informal	Procedural rules fixed; less formal than adjudication
Nature of proceeding	Opportunity for each party to present proofs and arguments	Investigatory	Opportunity and responsibility to present summary proofs and arguments	Investigatory	Opportunity for each side to present summary proofs and arguments
Outcome	Principled decision, sometimes supported by findings of fact and conclusions of law	Report or testimony	Mutually acceptable agreement sought	Report	Advisory verdict
Private/public	Private, unless judicial enforcement sought	Private, unless disclosed in court	Private	Private	Usually public

Source: Goldberg *et al.* (1985: 8–9) Reprinted with permission of Little, Brown and Company.
Note: *Court-annexed arbitration is involuntary, non-binding and public.

they may forget the value clients place on having their say on what they regard as a just procedure, or they may get out of touch with the need to fit the process to new (or newly articulated) social needs or economic demands. The outcome may be a long-delayed civil justice review! (See pp. 40–41.)

The evidence is also encouraging in finding a popular consensus rather than a diversity of views on what is meant by fair procedure, albeit a consensus sophisticated enough to recognize the need to adjust procedural considerations in the light of the type of dispute involved and relationship of the parties for example marital versus criminal. Four key dimensions of evaluation, which tend to recur across different settings, are what Tyler terms *representation* (an opportunity to participate in the process), *interpersonal respect* (being treated by authorities with respect), *neutrality* of the third party, and *fairness of outcome*. Such judgments are not necessarily based on formal definitions of fair procedure however.

George Applebey (Chapter 3) describes ADR developments (illustrating at the same time the inadequacy of the adjective 'alternative'), in the context of reforms in the civil courts in the UK, and relates this to ADR advances in the USA. Complaints of formality, complexity, delay and expense have fuelled attempts at reform of the litigation system, as much as they have been a driving force for a reconsideration of dispute resolution processes in general. He argues that the changes have been substantial, if ponderously slow, and that they reflect in part a continuity of tradition as well as novel developments. The 'success' of such reforms however, as he demonstrates in the context of small claims procedures, are problematic, given such factors as the varying attitudes of adjudicators to their role, the disparities of power and experience between 'repeat-players' and 'one-shotters' in the system, and the inertia of conservatism in the adversarial tradition. 'Simple justice' appears by no means simple to achieve. ADR experiments to find a more satisfactory procedure for small claims are, however, more advanced in the United States, principally with experiments in conciliation or mediation.

Also widespread in the USA are experiments with alternatives to civil trials, often as a means of reducing backlogs of cases or reducing cost and delay – court-annexed arbitration schemes, mini-trials, summary jury trial (trial by a mock jury as a quick guide for the parties), and 'rent-a-judge' for the more affluent. As the recent Civil Justice Review report (Lord Chancellor's Department 1988) reminds us, the civil trial system itself would break down were it not for the extensive presence of pre-trial settlement. Although major reforms of the civil justice system may to some extent reduce the case for alternatives, Applebey argues in support of a multiplicity of avenues for the resolution of disputes.

An area of dispute, which traditionally has been difficult for the court system to handle in any substantial sense (other than by the blunt instrument of judicial review) and yet a central concern of modern societies, is that of citizen grievances against public bodies and the state. Patrick Birkinshaw (Chapter 4) surveys complaints mechanisms in administrative law and indicates that a decade of 'deregulation' has by no means restricted this field. Rather, the boundaries of the mechanisms created for this process are also extending and diversifying as new forms of government intervention and privatization confuse the boundaries of public and private sectors (perhaps nowhere more so than in the system developed by the Financial Services Act 1986?). The model of the ombudsman for example has been transferred into the private sector (its more typical locus in the United States). Other forms of intervention have been developed which can sometimes be similarly classified as dispute intervention by a 'neutral fact-finder', but which may also have added (or reduced) powers in comparison to the ombudsmen system – the '*Almost Ombudsmen*' in Birkinshaw's terminology, such as the Police Complaints Authority, Data Protection Registrar and Commissioner for the Rights of Trade Union Members. Other variants that Birkinshaw explores are the creation of formal internally based grievance mechanisms (e.g. in social security claims procedures), and mechanisms which are targeted primarily at remedying *systems* rather than redressing individual grievances such as the Comptroller and Auditor-General Reports or prisons inspectorate reports. Given this background of expansion, it is perhaps not surprising that Birkinshaw can report a growing number of requests for judicial review of the grievance-handling institutions themselves.

As in other forms of dispute resolution, the courts being a prime example, one's analysis of dispute resolution mechanisms should go beyond the direct case-law and caseload of such mechanisms. The presence of a grievance-remedying third party may also indirectly influence their fields of jurisdiction in important ways – in terms of reforms of the internal procedures of organizations investigated, or they may act more widely in a sector as 'architects of procedure', for example to encourage (or perhaps if ineffective, discourage) avoidance of red tape, speedy procedures, keeping complainants fully informed of progress. The extent to which an agency achieves this will relate to a number of factors, not least the powers, prestige and publicity that underpin its actions (cf. the debates in recent years over the Press Council's effectiveness).

Arbitration has often been categorized alongside litigation as a traditional form of adjudication with limited relevance to ADR. This is somewhat ironic given that arbitration has been seen in the commercial sphere as an important mechanism to *avoid* litigation in favour of speedier, simpler, more expert and more private judgement. Its failure to live up to this promise deserves of closer study from those who now advocate alternative means as instruments to the same ends. For the last few decades, the arbitration world has struggled with this paradox, a debate which has led to more legislation freeing the process from close supervision by the courts, not to mention fierce debates on the role of lawyers as representatives in arbitration proceedings. Robert Wight (Chapter 5) explains the nature of arbitration and the issues that are being confronted in this process in domestic and international arbitrations. The care attached to describing the elements of a valid arbitration is, however, indicative of how judicialized in form and philosophy commercial arbitration has become. (In the British context, this forms a striking contrast with industrial relations arbitration, which has remained relatively free from legal intervention and is binding in honour rather than in law – see Chapter 8 by ACAS in Part II.)

Tony Marshall (Chapter 6) provides a useful introductory summary of the key motivations behind ADR, as against the use of law, in approaching the settlement of community disputes. The rationale for action in this area has been the need to develop broader and 'better' goals of settlement than are provided within the standard philosophical map of the legal justice approach. Even within the criminal justice system, studies of typical criminal cases suggest that they are often more accurately regarded as 'neighbour' disputes in their underlying character. Dispute settlement therefore has to be targeted to reconciliation and a sense of future problem-solving rather than a legal rule-based analysis of the causes of a past event. Marshall outlines the development of mediation approaches, and draws a distinction between two types of mediation used, principally deriving from the extent to which mediation processes are an outcome of justice system referrals (the 'stronger' version of mediation) or centred in voluntary community work. The former account for the largest proportion of mediation cases even in countries where the neighbourhood justice movement has been more dynamic than in the UK. (See Tony Gibson's Chapter 11 in Part II for a practical example of a creative dispute resolution process applied outside the justice system-type dispute.) Marshall concludes his review with the insightful remark that the differences between ADR processes may be more important than the original differentiation between ADR and law.

Karl Mackie (Chapter 7) is concerned to give a more detailed account of the nature of the processes and techniques underlying 'successful' negotiation and mediation. He explores negotiation through three recent major works relevant to negotiation skills, and highlights the importance of levels of analysis in evaluating the success or otherwise of negotiated settlements and the nature of the processes involved. While negotiation is frequently regarded as a context separate from third-party intervention, the presence of a lawyer acting for a client on both sides adds to the dynamics of the dispute, a point which the work of both Genn and Williams (reviewed in the chapter) highlight. Mackie picks up the theme introduced by Marshall of mediation, and explores the processes taking place in mediation, its function and skills, and relationship to adjudication.

2 Procedure or result: what do disputants want from legal authorities?

Tom Tyler

This chapter examines research on customer satisfaction.[1] The customers studied are the clients who come to lawyers and judges for help with their problems or disputes. A key concern in such studies is what determines how satisfied clients feel with the third parties, that is the lawyers and judges with whom they deal and with the various dispute resolution forums used to settle their problem. In other words, what do people want from third parties and how do they evaluate them?

Imagine a typical civil case for a lawyer – a divorce. Think of three possible things that clients could care about. The first is winning and getting as many assets as possible for themselves. The second is getting a fair settlement, that is 'having things come out right'. The third is having the dispute resolved in a fair way: this includes issues such as being allowed to participate in the process and being allowed to present one's side of the story. While all of these things may matter somewhat, what do clients care *more* about?

Lawyers and judges often regard the answer to this question as obvious: clients want to win! Lawyers typically believe that clients evaluate them based on the size of the outcome they deliver when the case is settled, while judges think that they are evaluated based on the favourability of the verdict they reach. Neither group thinks that clients are particularly concerned with how the problem is solved. They believe that formal trials, settlement conferences and negotiation in courtroom halls are similarly satisfying to clients if they lead to a favourable case disposition. As a consequence, cases are frequently settled in private conferences between lawyers or among lawyers and a judge.

Interviews with clients suggest a different conclusion about the basis of client satisfaction with lawyers and judges. Clients care most strongly about the procedure by which their problem or dispute is resolved. In particular, people place great weight on having their problem or dispute settled in a way that they view as fair. The second most important issue to clients is achieving a fair or equitable settlement. The least important factor is the number or value of the assets which they end up winning.

Procedural judgments are especially important in clients' evaluations of the third party – the lawyers, the judge and the court system. In other words, no one is happy about losing his or her case. People will, however, evaluate lawyers and judges more positively after losing their case if their case is resolved in a way that they view as fair (Tyler 1984; 1990).

An example of people's reactions to the courts is provided by interviews with defendants in traffic court in Chicago (Tyler 1990). In Chicago traffic court cases are often automatically dismissed if the defendant shows up in person for a trial. The theory is that the defendant has already paid a fine by missing work to come to court. It is not unusual, therefore, for cases to be dismissed in large groups. Consider a woman who came to court with pictures she had taken to show that the sign telling her that her driving was illegal was obscured from the road. When she arrived in court her case was dismissed. From an outcome perspective this was a victory. She paid no fine and has no criminal record. Was she pleased with this victory? No! She was upset and gave a very negative evaluation of the judge. Why! She viewed the procedure as unfair. She was not listened to and did not have an opportunity to present her evidence. In other words, she was not allowed to participate in the procedure through which her case was settled.

We might expect that people would lack clear procedural preferences and have unclear views about procedural fairness since people typically have had little experience with either the dispute resolution procedures used in their case or with possible alternatives. On the contrary, however, people seem to have very clear and strongly held views about the fairness of different types of procedure, however those views are derived.

The importance that people attach to feeling that their problem or dispute was settled using fair procedures emerges clearly in studies of defendants in mis-demeanour and small claims courts (Tyler 1984), as well as in studies of citizen–police interactions. It has also been found to be important in studies of civil litigation conducted at the Institute of Civil Justice of the Rand Corporation (Adler *et al.* 1983; Lind *et al.* 1988; MacCoun *et al.* 1988). Other work has found that fair procedures matter a great deal to felony defendants (Casper *et al.* 1988; Tyler *et al.* 1989). Concerns about procedural justice are widespread.[2]

Issues of procedural fairness are likely to be especially key when clients have unrealistic outcome expectations. In divorce cases, for example, both parties often begin without any real awareness of the extent to which their life-style will be affected by the division of marital assets. Both parties imagine themselves unrealistically well-off after the settlement. In such a situation both are likely to end up receiving less than they expect and feel that they deserve in the settlement. Satisfaction with and acceptance of such negative results is enhanced by feelings that the settlement procedure was fair.

One obvious question is whether procedural issues influence behaviour, in addition to affecting outcomes. If a client is asked to choose between winning or having a fair outcome, for example, what would they choose? Several types of evidence suggest that concerns about procedural fairness also affect clients' behaviour. Studies of mediation, where client acceptance of third-party decisions is voluntary, have suggested that people are more likely to accept decisions if they are made in a way that the client thinks is fair (McEwen and Maiman 1984).

In other words, the same outcome is more acceptable if it is reached in a way that those involved view as fairer.

These findings have important implications for practising attorneys and for judges. The satisfaction of disputants can be enhanced by using 'fair' procedures to deal with client problems. Of course, to make this approach work legal authorities need to show clients that they are using fair procedures.

WHY IS PROCEDURAL FAIRNESS IMPORTANT?

Procedural justice is not always of equal importance to disputants. Studies typically find that procedural fairness has at least some influence. What varies is whether it is the crucial issue to parties or whether other issues also matter. Perhaps the most interesting finding of recent research is that, in legal settings, procedural fairness does not decline in importance as the issues involved become more important to the parties (Casper *et al*. 1988; Tyler 1990). Concern about fair procedures is not simply found with trivial disputes. People care even more strongly about procedural justice when the stakes are high.

WHAT IS A FAIR PROCEDURE?

The suggestion that people care about the fairness of procedures raises the question of what people mean by a fair procedure. It is first important to note that procedural justice judgments are multidimensional, involving the consideration of a wide variety of issues. For example Sheppard and Lewicki (1987) used an open-ended response format that allowed decision-makers to indicate why a procedure they had experienced was unfair and found sixteen different types of criterion used to make procedural fairness judgments. People used a wide variety of issues to make their assessments about the extent to which a procedure is fair or unfair.

Ideally the same procedural issues would always be key to understanding what people mean by a fair procedure. In such a situation the same procedural issues would matter irrespective of the personal characteristics of the disputants or the nature of the dispute.

Recent research suggests that personal characteristics do not influence how people define the fairness of decision-making procedures. For example Tyler (1988; 1990) found that a random sample of citizens of Chicago, who varied widely in ethnic background and economic status, held a common definition of what a fair procedure meant within a given situation. This finding suggests that legal authorities can generally expect that the various parties to a dispute will have similar ways of evaluating whether or not they were treated fairly.

Research also suggests that laypeople are able to distinguish between different types of procedures and do not think that the same procedure is fair in all settings (Tyler 1988). People do not, for example, think that an adversary trial is the way for a husband and wife to settle a marital quarrel. Similarly they do not think that felony cases ought to be settled by informal discussion. The meaning of a fair procedure changes depending on both the nature of the dispute and the relationship of the disputants. As a consequence, there is no such thing as a universal fair procedure for solving all problems and disputes. Since the legal system handles a wide variety of types of problems, ranging from accident claims to child custody cases, no single set of concerns will apply to all legal problems.

Although people's concerns will not always be the same, there are some general suggestions from research concerning the meaning which clients give to fair procedure (for a discussion of people's views in non-legal settings, see Lind and Tyler 1988). Four issues generally dominate disputant assessments of procedural fairness: representation, ethical appropriateness or interpersonal respect, neutrality, and outcome quality.

Representation

One important element in feeling fairly treated is feeling that one has had an opportunity to participate in the settlement procedure. This includes having the opportunity to present one's side of the case, being listened to, and having one's opinions considered by the third parties involved. Research suggests that clients who feel that they have participated in the settlement process are much more accepting of settlement outcomes, irrespective of what those outcomes are.

Two aspects of participation can be distinguished: control over the decision made (decision control) and control over opportunities to present evidence or make arguments (voice or process control). An instrumental perspective on participation suggests that people focus on the extent to which they are influencing the final outcome. An alternative is the value expressive view, which suggests that people value the opportunity to present their case, independently of the effects of that presentation on the outcome of their case.

The original research of Thibaut and Walker (1975) focused on direct or indirect control over decisions. People were viewed as valuing the opportunity to present their case only to the extent that they felt such a presentation influenced the outcome of the case. In contrast, subsequent studies have found that first, having process control is more important to people's feelings of being fairly treated than is having decision control, and second, people value process control even when it is not linked to decision control (Lind *et al.* 1983; Tyler *et al.* 1985; Tyler 1987). These findings suggest that the benefits of process control are value expressive, not instrumental. Those with problems value the opportunity to present their problems to authorities. By allowing disputants to bring their problems to them, authorities are reaffirming the disputants' social standing and their right to call on the authorities for help. Tyler (1987) supports this interpretation by finding that the opportunity to address authorities is valuable only if people believe that what they say has been considered by the authorities. People's standing in the group is not validated by being ignored, nor would being ignored suggest that an organization is responsive to appeals for help.

Interpersonal respect

A second important aspect of feeling fairly treated is not directly related to the process of solving the problem. It is connected to the interpersonal context created by dealing with third parties. People have been found to place great weight on being treated politely and having respect shown for their rights and for themselves as people (Tyler and Bies, 1990).

Interpersonal issues are particularly important in dealings with public authorities (Tyler, 1989b). Consider an example from research on the police. If a home is burgled, the likelihood that the police can solve the crime and get citizen belongings back is very low. Fortunately for the police, citizen evaluations of their performance are not linked to whether they solve the crime. Such evaluations are linked to how the police treat the citizen when they come to the citizen's home to write out a burglary report. If they are polite and treat the citizen's concern as legitimate and deserving of serious attention, people feel better about the police (Parks 1976). In other words, it is interpersonal issues that dominate reactions to the experience, not the handling of the burglary which is the original reason for the call to the police. Similarly the way that lawyers and judges treat citizens has an important impact on their views that is unrelated to how their case is handled.

The conclusion that interpersonal issues matter in dispute resolution parallels an earlier finding in the literature on negotiation. Studies of the prisoner's dilemma game have found that issues of 'face' and 'face saving' often over-whelm bargainers, leading them to make choices not in their self-interest. As in that literature, the literature on procedural justice suggests that disputants place great emphasis on the interpersonal climate within which the dispute resolution process occurs.

Neutrality

People also value evidence of neutrality in authorities. This includes evidence that the authorities are not biased, that they are honest, and that they make decisions based on factual information about the case.

Outcomes

Finally, as would be expected, people feel more fairly treated if they receive a fair outcome. In other words, procedural issues are not independent of outcome issues. To some extent procedures are judged by the outcomes they produce.

Tyler (1990) directly compared the magnitude of the effects of outcome favourability and non-outcome-based criteria of procedural fairness (representation, interpersonal respect, neutrality) on procedural fairness judgments. He found that non-outcome-based procedural justice criteria explained 47 per cent of the variance in procedural justice judgments which could not be explained by outcome judgments, while outcome judgments explained only 1 per cent of the variance in procedural justice judgments which could not be explained by non-outcome-based procedural justice criteria. In other words, outcome favourability had almost no influence on procedural justice judgments. On the other hand, outcome fairness judgments are typically highly related to procedural justice judgments. Tyler (1990) found that the average correlation between indices of the two concepts was $r = 0.62$. Hence, receiving a fair outcome and viewing the process as fair were highly interrelated.

FORMAL VERSUS INFORMAL JUSTICE

An interesting finding of research on lay conceptions of fair process is that people often focus on informal aspects of the situation, not on the formal structure of justice represented in institutions such as the courts. People may not, as a result, feel more fairly treated if they are in a situation that is formally defined as involving a fairer process (Tyler 1989a).

An example of the formal/informal distinction is found in people's reactions to the alternative dispute resolution movement. The past decade has seen an enormous expansion in the use of informal dispute resolution procedures such as mediation and court-annexed arbitration. Many legal scholars have raised questions about the use of such procedures, citing a number of valid concerns about the lack of procedural safeguards in informal justice. From a legal scholar's perspective such procedures may not be 'just'.

While informal alternative dispute resolution procedures may not be 'just' when judged against formal legal criteria of justice, studies interviewing disputants whose cases are handled using such procedures generally find that disputants like ADR procedures and that this is true irrespective of the outcome of those procedures. Why? People typically feel that they have had more opportunity to participate in settling the problem in an informal mediation session.

Another example of the divergence between formal and informal conceptions of fairness can be found in studies of felony case dispositions. Such cases are frequently disposed of through plea bargaining. The practice of plea bargaining has been widely attacked by legal scholars, as has ADR, for lacking procedural safeguards that are the essence of formally defined 'fair procedure'. On the other hand, several recent studies have found that defendants do not necessarily feel more unfairly treated if their case is disposed of through the plea bargaining process. Why? Again, defendants *think* that they have more opportunity to participate in informal plea bargaining than in a formal trial.

This discussion is not intended to suggest that client judgments about fairness ought to replace the judgments of legal experts in designing legal procedures. Clients may lack sophisticated knowledge about the legal system and about both the alternative legal procedures which might be used to solve a problem and the general system-level consequences of using a particular procedure for settling cases. Hence, client judgments may be 'uninformed' and should be used with caution. The point is to highlight that the client's perspective is different from that of the third parties.

The distinction between clients and third parties suggests one important qualification to the previously outlined findings. Most of the research described has focused on people who have infrequent dealings with lawyers and other legal authorities, that is on typical citizens. It is not clear whether 'repeat-players' in the legal game, that is businessmen with frequent legal problems or lawyers themselves, also care about procedural justice.

SUMMARY

The goal of this chapter is to make three basic points. First, that issues of procedure matter to clients. Second, there is more to fair procedure than achieving a fair outcome. Third, people's conceptions of fair procedures often differ in important ways from the formal structure of fair procedure in the American legal system.

NOTES

1 I would like to thank Karl Mackie for comments on a draft of this chapter.
2 Studies demonstrating procedural justice effects have utilized a variety of methodologies, including laboratory experiments, scenario studies, field experiments and surveys. For an explanation of these different types of methodologies and an examination of the relationship between the methodology used and the results obtained, see Lind and Tyler (1988).

3 Alternative dispute resolution and the civil justice system

George Applebey

WHAT IS ALTERNATIVE DISPUTE RESOLUTION?

The purpose of this chapter is to describe briefly some of the developments in and around the civil courts which have occurred over the last few years, which could, broadly, be described as alternative dispute resolution.

Quite what is meant by alternative dispute resolution, a topic so familiar that it has acquired its own acronym (ADR), is nevertheless open to discussion. 'Alternative to what?' 'What do we mean by a dispute?' 'How do we distinguish a dispute from a problem, a grievance, or a claim?' 'What does "resolved" mean, in this context?' 'Are settlements of disputes to be encouraged, whatever the final outcome?' These and many other questions have to be addressed in order to give a clear picture of what ADR means. Obviously no answer can be entirely definitive. Chapter 1 of this handbook has already discussed many of these matters.

For practical purposes a wide view of ADR will be taken as anything resembling a legal or para-legal process, arbitration, negotiation or conciliation plus several of the ordinary rules of civil procedure currently in operation in the courts, which provide for any alternative to formal adjudication. This chapter will concentrate on ADR in the civil justice system of England and Wales, with references to the United States, where ADR has developed at a far faster rate.

WHAT ARE THE LIMITS OF 'FORMAL ADJUDICATION?'

ADR has to begin with the courts. What sort of matters do courts do well, and what do they do badly? Where should the limits of adjudication be? Most important of all, what are the faults in ordinary civil procedures which call for alternative solutions?

In determining the appropriateness of adjudication or one of the newer alternatives, many factors may be relevant. First, the *relationship between the parties* is important. This might be an ongoing one, for example between spouses, or based on a single incident between strangers, for example a road accident. Where the relationship is to continue, then a solution brought about or agreed by the parties themselves is thought to be more likely to be acceptable then one imposed by a court of law.

Second, Fuller (1978) points out that *the nature of the dispute is important*, certain matters being better left to the courts. The Report of the Council on the Role of Courts (published in 1984) discusses the criteria for determining the fitness of cases for courts:

> Which types of cases are and which are not fit for courts? There is no single answer to this question; rather, a number of criteria dictate various axes of inclusion and exclusion. Two sets of criteria – functional and prudential – are used to examine how cases fit on five axes set forth below. The functional criteria are those factors that make a court peculiarly suited (or unsuited) to hear the matter in controversy. These include objectivity, the necessity for authoritative standards, and the need to determine past vs. future events. Prudential criteria are those factors that make a court more or less suited than other institutions to hearing and resolving a dispute, given that a court is competent to adjudicate the issue in controversy. Prudential criteria include costs, the need for particularized consideration, the preference of the parties, the vitality of another institution (including the family), the need for immediate resolution of a specialized problem, and the ability to act indirectly.
>
> (Council on the Role of Courts 1984)

The last point, 'ability to act directly', is explained in the following paragraph of the report.

> Courts need not always adjudicate directly. They may perform best in some cases by hovering in the background, standing ready to decide if the litigants cannot settle their differences. These cases include child custody disputes, in which considerable harm can be anticipated from a court's involving itself directly in ongoing familial relations. Courts can also play a backup role by shunting or diverting cases initially to another form of dispute resolution, like public arbitration or private fact-finding. Finally, courts can serve as architects of process, fashioning the procedures that other institutions should use to arrive at an acceptable decision in order to obviate the need for court participation.
>
> (Council on the Role of Courts 1984)

Third, there may be a distinction between *new disputes* which require a decision (and therefore adjudication) and recurring examples of the same issue which might be handled less formally.

Fourth, *the amount at stake* is often cited as a major factor in seeking alternatives. The cost of paying a solicitor was often disproportionate to the amount involved in most consumer cases and this led directly to the setting up of a litigants-in-person policy for small claims in England and Wales in 1973. Not every small claim is simple, however, and for this reason there are usually rules for the transferring of complex cases for trial in the county court.

Fifth, *the need for speed and the reduction of cost* is a paramount factor in many of the ADR system which have been set up.

Finally, *the strength of bargaining power and availability and quality of legal services* can have a considerable impact on the outcome of disputes and therefore on any alternatives designed to equalize these factors.

It is worth bearing in mind that ADR is a response to formality, complexity, inadequacies and expense in the ordinary courts. These problems are increasingly being discussed and reform is in the air. The creation of the Civil Justice Review (CJR) in 1985 by the Lord Chancellor is but the latest attempt to deal with many of these problems. As the proposals of the CJR are implemented over the next few years, hopefully efficiency will increase and the need for ADR may be reduced, but not extinguished.

One final comment. There is of course a large amount of writing on dispute resolution generally, much of it coming from sociologists and cultural anthropologists. Interesting and illuminating as this is, and of great comparative value, it should be borne in mind that ADR is primarily a search for legal solutions to the problem of mass litigation and dispute. This is not to say that other societies cannot offer a great deal of insight. The writings of Danzig (1973), using the example of tribal Kpelle moot of Liberia, greatly influenced the establishment of Neighbourhood Justice Centres across America.

THE BACKGROUND TO ADR

ADR has its roots in the United States in the late 1960s; most of the interesting developments and studies came from there in the 1980s. In the United Kingdom it is even more recent. This obscures the fact that many such alternatives are not new phenomena. Arbitration of commercial disputes goes back to the late seventeenth century. The modern treatment of small claims is not a new alternative for such disputes at all, but merely a return to earlier ways of dealing with cases involving small amounts as originally envisaged when the county courts were first set up in 1846, and even earlier in the old Courts of Requests and further back still in the Piepowder Courts of the late Middle Ages. Of these it has been said 'these Courts materially attracted merchants because of the speed and simplicity of procedure and because the law administered in the Courts gave effect to their own customs which formed the basis of their dealings' (Abel-Smith and Stevens 1970). Instead of being a novel development therefore, or an aberration, the present treatment of small claims may be no more than a continuation in twentieth-century guise of a long-standing tradition of resolving the everyday problems of the market-place, of buying and selling faulty merchandise and goods without the cost and inconvenience of handing over such matters to the formal machinery of the courts of law. In this sense, ADR has simply been one aspect of a wider process, of reforming the courts and bringing them slowly into line with modern needs, a task which may appear ponderously slow to the outsider, but one which has been continuous and substantial.

What is alternative depends on what is traditional. In England and Wales this would mean the court structure and rules of civil procedure which followed the reform of the Supreme Court of Judicature Acts 1873–75. This provided for a division of civil matters between the High Court and county courts each with their own set of rules. Criminal cases went to Assizes, Quarter Sessions and Magistrates' Courts, with the last mentioned using mostly lay judges. Procedure denoted formal written pleadings, an adversarial system, a single hearing, the principle of orality (or reliance on oral evidence rather than written), strict limitations on what could be regarded as evidence, a 'passive' judge who did not take a major part in cross-examining witnesses, a jury to determine questions in fact (though this has now atrophied in civil cases, with defamation cases being a notable exception) and the court's judgment being on a winner-takes-all basis. The rule also developed in England that the successful party usually had all the costs paid by the losing party.

In the twentieth century the situation has changed rapidly and out of all recognition. Most obvious is the emergence of the tribunal as a forum for dispute resolution for everything from mental health to dealing with quotas for dairy produce. Some of the earliest, such as national insurance tribunals set up in 1911, still survive in an amended form, as Social Security Appeal Tribunals. Others are much more creatures of the last few decades, perhaps the most significant being industrial tribunals. The unplanned growth of tribunals led to the setting up of the Franks Committee in 1955. The Franks Committee made an attempt to impose some kind of uniformity on them by insisting that they should observe basic principles of openness, fairness and impartiality and by recommending the establishment of an independent Council of Tribunals to supervise their activities. Tribunals were to remain free to regulate their own procedures (subject to judicial review on points of law, or breach of the rules of natural justice). Some so-called tribunals, such as the Employment Appeal Tribunals, are actually courts of law, but most tribunals differ markedly from courts in terms of informality, rules of evidence and cost. It is better, however, to regard most of these as less formal adjudication, rather than ADR.

At the same time as tribunals were developing, a whole range of non-judicial remedies were also coming into being for dealing with complaints of one sort or another, for example the Police Complaints Authority and the Broadcasting Complaints Authority. The most famous of these statutory remedies for complaints was the establishment in 1967, of the Parliamentary Commissioner for Administration, or Ombudsman. In 1974 this system was extended to appoint two new Ombudsmen, for Local Government. Implicit in all this is the fact that the majority of disputes involving the state and the citizen and between individuals go not to courts of law but to tribunals or special bodies set up for a particular purpose. This says something about the way courts operate and have been perceived in recent years. A perception which has led to a search for alternatives, even for matters traditionally within the courts' jurisdiction.

ARBITRATION OF SMALL CLAIMS

The development of small claims procedures in this and many other countries is a product of developing consumer awareness seeking to find fairer and more effective means of enforcement of complaints than could then be obtained through the courts. Consumers were often parties in the civil courts but almost invariably as debtors and therefore defendants, from which our county courts derived, as they still do, a huge volume of business. Those who advocated small claims courts were arguing for a better means of dealing with private individuals' complaints, bringing the consumer into the legal system as plaintiff. When called upon to adjudicate such cases the county courts at that time were said 'to lack the right approach, were too formal, too awe-inspiring for ordinary people and too weighed down with procedural rules' (Consumer Council 1970).

The first alternative to emerge in this country were the two arbitration schemes for small claims in Manchester and London. The jurisdiction of both these independent 'small claims courts' was based on agreement, arbitrators were non-judges (often lawyers or technical experts) and a range of less formal practices and procedures were employed. Dependent on private funding, both schemes ran out of money by the end of the 1970s but nevertheless created enormous interest, while acting as a spur to further changes in the courts themselves (Applebey 1978).

To what extent then can the present county courts' rules pertaining to small claims be said to be alternatives to ordinary civil procedure? The first separate small claims court opened in Cleveland, Ohio, as long ago as 1913. In England and Wales the key changes took place in 1972 and 1973. In 1972 pre-trial reviews were introduced in the county courts and a year later a Practice Direction was issued based on the existing section 92 of the County Courts Act 1959 providing for arbitration by the registrar of small consumer claims. This formed the basis of the new procedure. The Practice Direction was aimed at a less formal hearing, where strict rules of evidence would not apply, cases could be decided on documents only, hearings could be held in private, and procedure at hearings was to be at the registrars' discretion who nevertheless were encouraged to adopt an inquisitorial role whether parties were appearing in person or not. Lawyers would be allowed to appear at a small claims hearings (unlike for example, California, where they are barred) but in order to discourage their use a 'no costs' rule was introduced whereby, except in exceptional circumstances, legal costs could not be recovered where the amount of claim was below the small claims limit. This package, it was thought, would encourage consumers as litigants in person to feel confident enough to take more cases to the county court and get a quick and informal outcome. Such matters as right of appeal etc. were left deliberately vague. The importance of the pre-trial review introduced at this time should not be ignored. Here was the possibility of resolving disputes through conciliation or settlement by bringing the parties face to face, before the hearing. The pre-trial review was of course primarily to prepare cases for their eventual hearing and sadly it now appears in neither respect do they seem to have worked as well as hoped.

The small claims procedure was altered again in April 1981 when the financial limit was raised from £200 to £500, automatic referral to arbitration was introduced, subject to a new set of grounds for rescinding the arbitration. There were also new procedural rules for arbitration, and a simplified 'no costs' rule, as well as reforming the pre-trial review and calling it the 'preliminary consideration'.

These measures were some way short from what some were calling for at that time, particularly those involved with the voluntary arbitration schemes at Manchester and London. The Lord Chancellor rejected then, as he still does, the idea of a separate system of small claims courts independent or separate from the county courts, manned by people other than full-time judges. However, one result of the recent Civil Justice Review may be that in addition to increasing the jurisdiction of the procedure to £1,000 the term 'small claims court' may come to be employed and a 'free-standing' code for small claims will be introduced, separate from the other county court rules.

How have these changes worked in the county court? In 1986, as part of the Civil Justice Review, the management consultants, Touche Ross, were asked to provide a 'factual basis' on which any reforms of small claims might be based. The bulk of the management consultants' study was based on a sample of 876 cases taken from the court records of twenty selected county courts which were set down for arbitration during 1984 and the first half of 1985. Interviews took place with 247 of the plaintiffs and 161 of the defendants in the cases studied, and also with 29 County Court Registrars. A number of interesting points emerged.

1 From an admittedly weighted sample, Touche Ross found that private individuals were plaintiffs in 38 per cent of cases, but defendants in 58 per cent of cases. There were 'relatively few cases of large organizations being sued'. The image of small claims arbitration as being the private individual against the business defendant was therefore inaccurate.
2 The 'no costs' rule had not deterred the use of solicitors: 23 per cent of plaintiffs and 13 per cent of defendants were represented at hearings by solicitors and overall 48 per cent of parties were assisted by lawyers at some stage of the proceedings.
3 The outcome depended little on whether parties were represented or not. Of all plaintiffs 67 per cent 'won' their cases at arbitration hearings, as against 70 per cent for represented plaintiffs alone. Hearings took longer when solicitors were present. Only 50 per cent of litigants had someone other than a solicitor accompanying them.
4 The average small claim was for £216, the consultants calculated, and 67 per cent of claims were for less than £250. The average award was £186. Overall the survey indicated a broad measure of satisfaction with the present procedures among those interviewed, though there were also a fair number of criticisms.
5 The number of arbitrations rose from 5,915 in 1974 to 44,700 in 1985. This amounted to a fairly large increase; however, to put these figures in perspective it might also be noted that in 1985 in one county court alone (Birmingham), over 60,000 summonses were issued for non-payment of water rates by Severn Trent Water Authority.

These findings were recently criticized in the Civil Justice Quarterly by Whelan (1987). The two major problems with the study were first, that it omitted to analyse the fundamental question of accessibility, and second, that the way in which the sample was selected and the analysis presented was biased in two respects, in the collection and preparation of data. Whelan concluded that neither the study undertaken by the management consultants nor the findings reported in the Consultation Paper gave a fair picture of the operation of the small claims procedure.

A number of problems have been identified with small claims in the county courts (Applebey 1978; National Consumer Council 1979). One is lack of uniformity. Different registrars took quite different attitudes to small claims not only in terms of their approach to the rules, but also in their enthusiasm for, as one American survey described it, 'the adjudicative callisthenics' of small claims hearings, bearing witness to the fact that the task of conducting hearings between litigants in person could be both arduous and time consuming. There were therefore wide differences from one county court to another. Many users of the procedure thus found it slow moving, overcomplicated and frustrating and not quite the system of 'simple justice' they had been led to expect.

In the United States there have been a number of major studies of small claims (see e.g. National Center for State Courts 1978). The main problems identified have included the following.

1 Domination of small claims procedure by business plaintiffs has led to some states limiting the number of claims which can be filed in any one year or month. For example California limits use of the court to six per day, Colorado a total of five per year and Nebraska to ten per year.
2 Inequality between parties in terms of representation and experience of the procedure: the difference between so-called 'repeat-players' and 'one-shotters' may be crucial. There is continuing debate over whether lawyers be allowed to appear in small claims courts.
3 Role-conflict problems on the part of judges and arbitrators: as in England and Wales, this has sometimes led to lack of uniformity between courts.
4 Should there be a pre-trial stage to help settle the case, or prepare litigants in person for the hearing?

Litigants in person also had problems learning their legal rights, filling out forms, finding the right court, serving the complaint (a greater problem in the USA than here) and knowing what evidence and witnesses were necessary to prove their case. As with other types of ADR most would say that the goals of any small claims procedure should be to provide speedy, inexpensive and simple justice in consumer type cases involving small amounts of money. A subsidiary goal might also be that small claims procedure should set the pace for other procedural reforms, providing the chance to experiment, and perhaps ultimately find a model which might be an alternative to the adversarial approach to court adjudication. However, this is easier said than done.

Yngvesson and Hennesey (1975) referred to the conservatism of lower courts and the legal profession when they said

> Empirical studies of the small claims process as it functions today reinforce the impression of an underlying conservatism. Most small claims hearings follow the adversarial model. Although the process is speedy and inexpensive, it remains too complex for many litigants to handle on their own. In spite of the goal that lawyers should not be necessary, they are present in most courts, a factor which seems to increase rather than reduce complexity. In spite of the goal of a radical change in the role of the judge, he remains a judge in the traditional sense in most courts, although this role is unsuited to proceedings in which one or both parties may be unrepresented and may need judicial assistance.
>
> (Yngvesson and Hennesey 1975: 219)

In the USA some major procedural alternatives to adjudication for small claims have been tried. One of these is the 'conciliation model', variants of which have been implemented in several cities (Cleveland, Minneapolis, Philadelphia, New York and Washington, DC).

> The main feature distinguishing conciliation from adjudication is that the 'judge' is not a judge, but an active agent in eliciting the true nature of the dispute and in bringing the parties toward a mutually acceptable resolution. The process is meant to be therapeutic rather than judgmental, and with this in mind the parties to the dispute are encouraged to express their feelings as well as telling the facts of the matter in dispute, with a view to increasing mutual understanding.
>
> (Yngvesson and Hennesey 1975: 256)

According to the research (Yngvesson and Hennesey 1975: 257; quoted in Goldberg *et al.* 1985: 172), there are two main advantages of the conciliation model for small claims. First, it aims at amicable resolution of a dispute rather than at fault-finding and an either-or decision, an important consideration when ongoing relations are at issue. Even when there is no ongoing relationship, compromise may be the most satisfactory solution for both parties since the outcome of litigation is unpredictable and each party risks total loss; time and trouble involved may be more than the chance of winning is worth. Second, parties to the dispute are provided an opportunity for settling which may be an important factor in resolving the dispute. Judges often feel uneasy about the conflict of role in acting both as judge and as conciliator.

Some states, the most notable being Maine, have attempted to operate a system of conciliation or mediation for small claims. The results have been described by McEwan and Maiman (1981; 1984).

In the United States there are also a number of ombudsman-type processes for handling consumer grievances. Many states have consumer protection divisions where claims are mediated by telephone (or sometimes in person). There are also a number of 'media action lines' that seek to mediate consumer disputes. A key feature of these schemes is said to be the presence of a powerful ally on the side of the consumer. A consumer using mediation in these settings is likely to have far more influence. Another means of increasing consumer power is through organization and aggregation in the form of class actions, common in the USA but not yet a feature of British law.

In the United Kingdom, the Office of Fair Trading has for some time encouraged arbitration of complaints by traders and industries as an alternative to the county courts (see Thomas 1988: 206). Thomas sees the advantages of these schemes as giving the consumer greater choice, commitment to make the schemes work by their sponsors, scope for innovation, specialist jurisdiction, and the fact that private arbitration schemes are better placed to observe and systematically draw attention to trends and practices revealed by individual disputes. However, there are also weaknesses such as giving the consumer a bewildering multiplicity of different schemes, that they may draw attention away from the more urgent task of improving the courts themselves, their limited jurisdiction, dependence upon private sponsorship, degree of actual and apparent independence, and lack of adequate resources given to the scheme.

SOME RECENT ALTERNATIVES TO CIVIL TRIAL IN THE USA

A large number of alternatives have appeared in the USA over the last few years. Some are mainly aimed at speeding cases through the system. Examples of this are California's Economical Litigation Project and the Kentucky Caseflow Management Program. Many of the experiments are local. For example in Rochester, New York, a system of compulsory but non-binding arbitration was introduced in the city court, to deal with a backlog of cases. The result was a fall in pre-trial settlements from 83 per cent to 33 per cent (Weller *et al.* 1981).

Several ADR examples are now quite widespread. First, there is *court-annexed arbitration*. These have been studied by the Institute for Civil Justice (Rolph 1984: Ebener and Betancourt 1985; Adler *et al.* 1983; Hensler 1984). Under such schemes defended civil cases have been referred to an arbitrator, who is usually a lawyer or a person with a skill or experience in a particular area. The reference to arbitration is usually with consent but may be compulsory, with the object of reducing cost and delay. Some of the evidence suggests these objects may not always be achieved, though the use of court-annexed arbitration is increasing.

Second, there is the *mini-trial*. This is described by Henry and Lieberman (1985: 427–8, n. 1; see also Goldberg *et al.* 1985: 271–80).

The mini-trial is not in fact a trial at all, but a highly-structured settlement process. Because it is a flexible device that can be tailored to the precise needs of the parties, no single procedural model of the mini-trial has yet prevailed. But in general, the known mini-trials share many of the following characteristics:

1 The parties negotiate a set of procedural ground rules (a protocol) that will govern the non-binding mini-trial.
2 The time for preparation is relatively short – between six weeks and three months – and the amount of discovery is relatively limited.
3 The hearing itself is sharply abbreviated – usually no more than two days.
4 The hearing is often conducted by a third-party neutral, typically called the 'neutral advisor'.
5 The case is presented to representatives of the parties with authority to settle; there is no judge or jury.
6 The lawyers present their 'best' case; they do not have time to delve into side issues.
7 Immediately after the hearing, the party representatives meet privately to negotiate a settlement.
8 If they cannot reach a settlement, the neutral advisor may render an advisory opinion on how he thinks a judge would rule if the case were to go to court.
9 The proceedings are confidential: the parties generally commit themselves to refrain from disclosing details of the proceedings to any outsider.

(Goldberg *et al.* 1985: 282–3)

A third alternative is the *summary jury trial*. The credit for this goes to a particular judge, US District Judge Thomas D. Lambros of Ohio. The summary jury trial is the courtroom equivalent of the mini-trial. A case is presented during the course of a single day to a mock jury consisting of jurors drawn from the real jury panel. The jurors do not know until after they have rendered their verdict that it is not binding. In thus giving the parties a 'real' verdict, the procedure creates an incentive for them to settle their case privately. The record to date suggests a high settlement rate. The summary jury trial has also been adopted in a number of federal courts.

Finally, there is the system known as *'rent-a-judge'* (Goldberg *et al.* 1985: 280–1). This is becoming increasingly popular with those who can afford to do so. A judge, usually retired, is hired at commercial rates to hear a case and the parties by contract agree to abide by the judgment. Hearings are private and the procedure can be adapted to the needs of the case. There have been a number of well-publicized examples. One was the actress Valerie Harper suing Lorimar television production company, claiming that she had been wrongly dismissed from her television series. Rather than wait five years for the case to reach court, both sides agreed to pay £32,000 to hire their own judge, bailiff, clerk and court reporter for a trial held in a rented public courtroom before a jury selected from the public rolls. The jury awarded Miss Harper £1,100,000 damages and a share of Lorimar's future profits that could be worth more than £9 million. It was also reported that the actors Clint Eastwood and Sondra Locke had 'rented a judge' to hear their contested 'palimony' dispute (*Daily Telegraph*, 2 June 1989).

CONCILIATION IN DIVORCE

The development of conciliation in relation to divorce proceedings is of course a recent phenomenon since collusion acted as a bar to divorce prior to the Divorce Reform Act 1969. In 1974 the Finer Report defined conciliation as

> assisting the parties to deal with the consequences of the established break-down of their marriage . . . by reaching agreements or giving consents or reducing the area of conflict upon custody, support, access to and education of the children, financial provision, the disposition of the matrimonial home, lawyers' fees, and every other matter arising from the breakdown which calls for a decision on future arrangements.

Conciliation was seen at the time as necessary because of the perception among many that litigation exacerbated the hostility between the parties to divorce and that this had a particularly harmful effect on the children involved. Litigation in matrimonial matters was also expensive, involving over half the civil legal aid expenditure. Conciliation could therefore reduce the human and financial costs of divorce.

The current schemes may be divided into in-court procedures and out-of-court conciliation services (Wikeley 1988). In-court schemes exist in the majority of divorce county courts, the first having been established at Bristol county court in 1977. Under these schemes the registrar orders a conciliation appointment, after proceedings are filed. This is attended by the parties and their legal repres-entatives, and the registrar or divorce court welfare officer then seeks to resolve the matter in dispute. If successful, a consent order is made, if not, the registrar gives directions for trial. Problems have arisen over the role of a judge, the registrar in this context, and also of the divorce court welfare officer, who is basically a probation officer attached to the divorce county court whose principal function is to prepare reports on custody or access arrangements where the court so requests. The Report of the Inter-Departmental Committee on Conciliation (Booth Committee), published in 1985, recommended that a welfare officer should not both conciliate in a case and later report on it. There have also been doubts expressed by the judges on this potential conflict.

Pre-trial reviews were also tried in the High Court Principal Divorce Registry for property applications but these were abandoned. A conciliation scheme has, however, now been introduced for various proceedings involving children.

Out-of-court conciliation schemes are very diverse. The conciliators are usually part-time volunteers, and the majority belong to the National Family Conciliation Council. These services have developed in an *ad-hoc* way because of the absence of a clear lead from government. The Booth Committee Report concluded that out-of-court schemes were less cost effective than in-court ones, and would not lead to savings in overall costs. Nevertheless, these schemes were appropriate to matrimonial proceedings and were to be encouraged, the main reasons being that it placed the responsibility on the parties to seek agreement, emphasized joint responsibility for the consequences of marriage breakdown, and forced the parties to face issues which might only later emerge as contended legal issues. The Booth Report has not yet been implemented. Since then the Report of the Conciliation Project Unit, an interdisciplinary team based at New-castle University, has been published. This is an evaluative study of different conciliation schemes examining their scope, methods, cost and effectiveness (Lord Chancellor's Department 1989b).

It is not only in the area of family law that conciliation has been employed. In relation to individual employment law and collective disputes, the Advisory, Conciliation and Arbitration Service (ACAS) has developed a role in con- ciliating and mediating disputes since its inception in 1974. Conciliation of cases going to industrial tribunals relating to unfair dismissal as well as claims for sex or racial discrimination has now become an accepted practice, though again doubts have been expressed as to the effectiveness and even the correctness of this approach.

In October 1990 the Bar Council proposed a pilot scheme for conciliation in civil cases in the county courts. It was envisaged that lawyers be used as conciliators for claims up to the limit of the county court jurisdiction.

NEGOTIATION AND SETTLEMENT OF CLAIMS FOR DAMAGES

Personal injuries account for a large part of the business of the civil courts. The Pearson Commission (1978) estimated that somewhere in the region of 300,000 claims were made each year by an injured victim against another person on the basis of negligence or breach of statutory duty. Of these 85 per cent were concluded without any court proceedings. The Civil Justice Review considered personal injuries as part of its remit, and using figures for 1984, which would still be typical, out of 55,000 cases in which proceedings were initiated (31,000 in the High Court, and 24,000 in county courts) only 3,650 cases actually went to trial. The rest were either settled or withdrawn. Of the remainder, personal injury cases still form the majority of all types of civil cases tried by High Court Judges.

With regard to settlements the Civil Justice Review commented:

In practice it is recognised universally that the functioning of the system of Civil Justice depends on the propensity of most cases to settle. Were it otherwise, the burden on the system, and the resulting delays, would become intolerable. It is perhaps for this reason, and notwithstanding the importance of settlements, that the formal procedures laid down in the Rules of the Supreme Court and the County Court Rules focus hardly at all on specific measures aimed at achieving settlement. Involving itself directly in the settle-ment process would defeat the need of the system to minimise its work-load.

Making a virtue of necessity, it is often argued that settlement is in any case superior to trial as a method of resolving disputes. Consensual arrangements, it is said, are to be preferred to imposed adjudication. The correctness of this view depends of course on the satisfaction of a number of conditions, the most important of which are the availability of full information to both parties and freedom from pressures unrelated to the merits of the case. Possibly with a view to satisfying these conditions, some jurisdictions have established procedures, such as settlement conference and conciliation arrangements, for effecting settlements under the aegis of the court. Without ruling out the possibility of introducing formal settlement procedures in England and Wales it is suggested that it will be best to concentrate limited court resources on those changes most likely to offer useful results. As will be seen from what follows, the procedural changes proposed are mainly directed towards achieving better preparation for trial. At the same time steps which encourage better pre-trial preparation ought also to contribute towards earlier, and better informed settlements.

(Lord Chancellor's Department 1987: 51–2)

The majority of settlements are a result of negotiations between solicitors on a 'without prejudice' basis and are more or less informal, though they do become binding once agreed, as a contract. Strictly speaking, informal settlements are not ADR, although the study of negotiation and settlement processes is now a part of the curriculum in a number of American Law Schools. The usual starting-point is the work of Fisher and Ury (1982).

Settlements were recently studied and evaluated by Genn (1987). The goal of ADR that such settlements are likely to be in the best interests of both parties is not entirely borne out. The main reason for settling cases at all has to do with the deficiencies and dangers of civil litigation, and in particular the problems of delay and enormous expense. The current enthusiasm of ADR for settlements is challenged by Owen Fiss (1984).

As an example of a more formalized settlement process, a large number of cases involving occupational diseases, have been taken out of the system, by means of agreed compensation schemes between trade unions and the employers' insurers. The largest group involves deafness cases, Britain's largest single claim for damages to date, a great majority of which have been processed through compensation schemes.

So far about a dozen illnesses or diseases are covered. The settlements involve an agreed scale of damages for degrees of disability once a person is diagnosed as suffering the condition in question. Negligence does not have to be proved, and the time of waiting for an award and the risk of costs are dramatically reduced. The Trades Union Congress (TUC), which helped to set up these schemes, sees advantages as well as pitfalls.

1 The need to establish employer's liability where an eligible person contracts a disease covered by the scheme is removed.
2 The avoidance of legal rules and court proceedings means that the costs, delays, and uncertainty in obtaining compensation are usually cut down.
3 Because the legal rules on fault liability, causation and contributory negligence do not specifically apply, some work people can recover compensation who may not have succeeded in a legal action.
4 Compensation schemes can enable a large number of outstanding claims to be dealt with relatively quickly on an agreed, uniform basis.

5 Any possible problems with the law of limitation, imposing time limits for claims by individual litigation, can be avoided.

However, negotiated compensation schemes can normally be agreed only because the employers concerned, and/or their insurers, see advantages to themselves as well. These advantages include the reduction of costs, and avoidance of repeated negotiations or litigation, which also benefit unions and their members. But employers and insurers may also seek other benefits from compensation schemes, which may be disadvantageous to unions and their members.

1 The provisions of compensation schemes, such as date of earliest liability or levels of compensation, may not be as good generally as the rules which would apply in a legal action. Employers may argue that some 'discounting' is justified because of other advantages from having the scheme.
2 Settlement of claims under a compensation scheme may restrict the development of further case law, which might have improved or clarified the legal position and hence the basis for the terms of compensation. This is particularly so where scheme rules provide that unions will not support legal actions in respect of cases covered by the scheme.
3 Pressure upon employers to improve health and safety standards may be reduced. This is because claims under compensation schemes may attract less interest and concern than litigation, which tends to get more publicity and exposes the employer's behaviour.

PAYMENT INTO COURT

Some of the long-standing rules of civil procedure have been designed to avoid the need for a trial, and as such can be said to be alternative. One at least is by no means a recent development. This is called 'payment into court'. As early as 1834, by statute, a defendant could pay money into court in actions of contract; in 1875 this was permitted in all actions for debt or damages. Payment into court is not in fact a defence, rather it is an attempt to force a compromise. A plaintiff who persists in an action, after payment of the sum into court, runs the risk of costs. The courts, in their discretion over costs may, and ordinarily do, order that plaintiffs who insist on continuing their action and do not recover more than the amount paid in, shall pay the costs of both sides incurred after the payment into court. The plaintiff who persists after a payment into court runs a considerable risk, and is therefore likely to think seriously about settling. The system of payment into court not only applies where the case concerns a damages claim but also can now apply to other types of cases by a device known to lawyers (after the case which established it) as a 'Calderbank letter' (*Calderbank* v. *Calderbank* [1975] 3 All E.R. 333).

The dangers and disadvantages of payment into court are well illustrated by a recent case which received a good deal of publicity (see *New Law Journal*, 10 March 1989: 319, 392). Two sisters, Ann Chastell and Frances Warby, sued Tesco for wrongful arrest, false imprisonment, libel and slander after the company had accused them of switching the price tag on a toaster. The women won their case but the damages awarded of £800 fell short of Tesco's payment in of £1,500. The plaintiffs therefore became liable to costs, estimated at £16,000. (The level of damages awarded was subsequently raised on appeal to the Court of Appeal so that Tesco became liable for costs.)

The outcome of the case prompted calls that the case be investigated by the Lord Chancellor, on the unusual ground that the jury's award was too low, and also that the payment into court system should be changed. The National Consumer Council (1989) has recently issued a report entitled *Ordinary Justice*. In it there is dissatisfaction that the Civil Justice Review recommended no change to the rule as to payment into court which put

> unacceptable pressure on plaintiffs to accept low offers. The rule effectively asked plaintiffs to play 'double or quits' with their compensation money, whether they accept an offer which appears to be considerably less than the court would award, or they go ahead in the knowledge that there is a small chance that the court may award less.

The Council recommended that successful plaintiffs should be liable only where payments-in exceed the eventual award by at least 25 per cent. In small cases involving less than £2,000 it should exceed the award by at least £500. Plaintiffs should not have to decide whether to accept payments until after they have seen defendants' witness statements.

Finally, it is worth mentioning a change in the rules of civil procedure introduced in 1980, aimed at expediting settlements and indeed allowing parties to avoid the courts altogether. Order 42, rule 5A introduced a radical change in practice with regard to the settlement of actions in the Queen's Bench Division. The rule makes it possible for the parties to an action, provided they are legally represented and not under a disability, to consent to the settlement of their dispute and to a judgment being entered embodying the terms of the settlement without the necessity of the settlement being approved by a judge, master or other judicial officer. The new procedure is intended to save time – of the parties and of the court – as well as costs. Before any judgment or order to which the rule applies may be entered, it must be drawn up in the terms agreed and expressed as being 'by consent' and it must be endorsed by solicitors acting for both parties. A consent judgment or order under rule 5A has the same effect and all the consequences of a court judgment or order despite the absence of approval or even scrutiny by any judicial officer.

THE CIVIL JUSTICE REVIEW

In February 1985 the then Lord Chancellor, Lord Hailsham, announced he was setting up a Civil Justice Review 'to improve the machinery of civil justice by means of reforms in jurisdiction, procedure and court administration and in particular to reduce delay, cost, and complexity'. Five types of cases were included in the review – personal injuries, the commercial court, enforcement of debt, housing, and small claims.

The review of procedure was designed to avoid consideration of alternative dispute resolution since it was required to proceed on the basis of the 'existing machinery for bringing claims', neither were changes in substantive law to be considered. Nevertheless alternatives to trial, such as arbitration, were discussed. As we have seen extension of the small claims limit to £1,000 is now a likelihood, and paper adjudication of certain types of housing cases is also proposed. Consideration is also given to a system of court-annexed arbitration which we have seen exists in a number of jurisdictions in the United States. The Civil Justice Review does not propose a system of court-annexed arbitration, although it does envisage as a next stage that a pilot scheme may soon be set up. There is a proposal, however, to devise a system of in-court arbitration for claims between £1,000 and £5,000 and, in all those types of business in which individuals tend not to be represented, a suggestion that judges act on a more interventionist basis.

Major changes in jurisdiction and court management are likely as a result of the Civil Justice Review, the most important being the transfer of a large number of High Court actions to the county courts as the ceiling of the latter's jurisdiction is raised from £5,000 to possibly £50,000. As well as the small claims limit going up to £1,000, debt enforcement will be streamlined to allow payments directly to creditors, rather than through the county courts. In housing cases, tenants will have faster and cheaper access to the court system and landlords will be able to recover rent arrears without seeking possession of the property. Some of these proposals could lead to reforms which would greatly streamline civil procedure, as well as increasing access to the public, thereby decreasing the pressure for alternatives.

CONCLUSION

Alternative dispute resolution is not new in the legal system but it has received a tremendous impetus as a means of dealing with the huge increase in different types of disputes over a range of matters, undreamt of even a few years ago. Much research still has to be done on the effectiveness of these alternatives and on civil procedure generally to find out how successful many of these new solutions to disputes really are.

Even though ADR is still to some lawyers and judges a radical idea, most civil proceduralists now recognize that it is wrong to regard formal adjudication as the only or even the norm for dispute resolution. Trying to fit all types of disputes within the confines of the 'ordinary' civil process proved to be a strait-jacket and has been shown to be by no means the most successful means of dealing with many types of actions. Efforts have to be made to divert many types of cases from ordinary litigation and find other cheaper, quicker and more efficient methods of resolving them. As we have seen this has led to a search for less formal alternatives, such as negotiation, mediation and arbitration, for a range of matters.

It is concluded that there ought to be a multiplicity of avenues of dispute resolution, hopefully complementing one another, the choice of which avenue to take ideally being in the hands of the parties themselves, and with the added availability of so-called 'exits' by which a party may opt out or change in the course of proceedings if he chooses. The promotion of such a heterogeneous collection of processes is the aim of those interested in reforming civil justice, one of the most urgent tasks facing the legal system today.

4   Complaints mechanisms in administrative law: recent developments

Patrick Birkinshaw

Grievances are endemic to the social system. The inability of the judicial and political processes to cater adequately for the multiplicity of grievances generated by an interventionist state has been well observed, even in those jurisdictions where the expectations for redress from those processes are greater than in Britain (Stewart 1984; Taylor 1986).[1] One might expect that after ten years of policies aimed at getting the state off the citizen's back and encouraging the citizen to opt out of public provision of services, there would have been a corresponding decrease in complaints mechanisms and the need for them in the public sector. The reality defies such a simple analysis.

OMBUDSMEN

First of all, the ombudsmen established in the 1960s and 1970s for central government, local government and the health service still thrive – to varying degrees. The Barlow-Clowes fiasco in 1988, involving allegedly inadequate supervision by the Department of Trade and Industry (DTI) over an investment company which defaulted on 18,000 investors, brought the Parliamentary Commissioner for Administration (PCA) rare publicity and prominence when he decided to investigate complaints of maladministration against the DTI. However, complaints to the PCA declined in 1986 and 1987.[2] The Commission for Local Administration (CLA) conversely reported an increase of 4 per cent in complaints for 1987–88. With the introduction of the right of direct access to the local ombudsman, removing the need to go via an elected representative, a significant increase in complaints has taken place. For complaints concerning health authorities, the Hospital Complaints Procedure Act 1985 required the Secretary of State to issue directions on the complaints procedure for hospital patients before the Health Commissioner is invoked, as well as the necessary steps for publicity. The Department of Health published a code in June 1988 (HC (88) 37). It is an interesting confirmation of good practice provisions for complaints procedures emphasizing easy access to designated officers, an absence of red tape, speedy investigation and keeping complainants fully informed of progress. Also recommended as a mandatory practice is the supply of a report of investigation to the complainant, the monitoring of complaints and full publicity for the existence of procedures. Those dealing with complaints about 'clinical judgment' – which the health ombudsman cannot investigate – are subject to an agreement appended to the back of the code.

ALMOST OMBUDSMEN AND DEVELOPMENT ON A THEME

Second, in those parts of the state that have not been privatized, the statute book has witnessed a wide variety of grievance remedial devices. The Police Complaints Authority, established in 1984 for England and Wales, is not a fully fledged ombudsman; rather the authority has the duty to supervise those complaints made to the police which it must receive on a mandatory reference from police authorities, and which involve death or serious injury or which are specified in regulations, as well as additional complaints.[3] The authority has power to direct that disciplinary proceedings be brought against officers, to be kept informed of complaints and to approve the appointment of an investigating officer by the chief officer, or authority concerned, to investigate a complaint against an officer.[4] In 1987, 4,148 cases for consideration for supervision were received (418 on a mandatory reference; of the remainder 333 were accepted for super- vision). The overwhelming majority of complaints will be dealt with through the police force itself, either by the informal conciliation procedure or by a formal investigation. The lack of the authority's powers to identify wrongdoers acting in concert, and the limitations imposed on the use to which it may put information in an investigation have been identified (Police Complaints Authority 1987–88: ch. 2). There has also been acute criticism of prosecutions by the police on complainants which suggested revenge, and the adequacy of internal police investigations has been questioned.

The Data Protection Registrar serves, *inter alia*, as an ombudsman for those with complaints about holders of computerized data concerning the complainants. The registrar's remit covers *all* holders, whether in the public or private sector subject to a variety of statutory exemptions. The Interception of Communications Act 1985 and the Security Service Act 1989 have established Commissioners as well as tribunals to oversee the operations of the state in telephone tapping, interception of communications or 'anything' done to an individual or their property by the security service. Neither procedure applies to actions taken without warrants where one is required, so that potentially the worst abuses, that is those perpetrated without authority, are not covered although under the latter Act a variety of additional matters may be investigated and reported on.[5] An internal ombudsman has also been created for members of the security services who feel that their conscience dictates that they behave other than in accordance with their official duties.[6] The Employment Act 1988 introduced a Commissioner on a statutory basis to assist complainants claiming victimization by their trade unions. The provision is similar to those existing in Equal Opportunities and Race Relations legislation.

PRIVATIZATION, REGULATION AND GRIEVANCE REDRESS

Third, it has been argued elsewhere that Thatcherism has not so much re-introduced a cleavage between the public and private sectors to unleash market forces in an expanded private sector, rather it has acted as a catalyst for a confusion of the public and private sectors (Birkinshaw 1988; Harden *et al.* 1990). A wide range of policy programmes indicate the growth of joint enterprise initiatives between public agents and private actors in the provision of employment training, city technology colleges, greater commercial involvement in the allocation of university funds, student grants, in commercial enterprise and major developmental projects. There has been increased public regulation of private and privatized markets, and the courts themselves have acknowledged the com-penetration of the public and private sectors (Poggi 1978).[7] What has been notable has been the extension of public law forms of redress into the private or privatized world.

In 1984 OFTEL (Office of Director-General of Telecommunications) was created to act as a regulator, and grievance-remedying device for customers, of the telecommunications industry. The Director-General (DG) is assisted by advisory bodies and monitors the quality of service.[8] There is provision for disputes involving more than £1,000 to go to arbitration. The DG has emphasized that he should not act as British Telecom's (BT) 'Complaints Department' and that complainants coming directly to him are told to write to BT, and to return if still dissatisfied. The DG has acknowledged that complaints from customers assist the DG 'to judge what reshaping of the regulatory arrangements may be needed' (Director-General of Telecommunications 1988: para 1.31) while also recognizing that clearer objectives may be required for BT's *internal* handling of complaints (1988: para 1.32). Under the Gas Act 1986, OFGAS (Office of Director-General of Gas Supply) regulates the gas industry, but it accepts only complaints dealing with licence-enforcement issues. Other complaints are dealt with by the Gas Consumer Council, which has eleven regional offices. To confuse an already complicated picture, complaints from non-tariff customers (industrial users) on non-enforcement issues may be referred to the Office of Fair Trading.[9] Under both schemes, licence modification proposals may be referred to the Monopolies and Mergers Commission.

The regulation of the City was, until 1986, a largely private affair, propped up by criminal investigations and loose regulation by the DTI, the Bank of England and a variety of domestic bodies including the Stock Exchange and the Panel on Take-Overs. The Financial Services Act 1986 provided that in return for self-regulation under a statutory umbrella, the regulatory body recognized by the Secretary of State and the five self-regulatory organizations (SROs) would have to publish their rule-books, which would contain details of their practices and standards and also provide for independent investigation of complaints against themselves and their members.[10] The Securities and Investment Board (SIB), the regulatory body and a limited company, had intended originally to implement an ombudsman scheme that would cover all the SROs but desisted from this proposal when it reasoned that it lacked the statutory power to establish such a model. The Act provides that SROs establish similar protection for investors as the SIB rules,[11] but there are 'interesting differences' between the schemes (Birds and Graham 1988: 324) a situation described as a 'bugger's muddle' by the ombudsman for unit trusts on his resignation (Guardian, 23 March 1989). Under the Act, recognized professional bodies dealing with investments will use existing grievance procedures for clients such as, in the case of solicitors, the Solicitors Complaints Bureau. In his proposals for the reform of the legal profession, the Lord Chancellor advocated the introduction of an independent ombudsman (Lord Chancellor's Department 1989a) which has now been enacted.

An ombudsman for insurance companies was established on a voluntary basis in 1981 by five major companies. By 1988 over 180 companies belonged to the scheme. In 1986 an ombudsman for banking was established – again on a voluntary basis. The Building Societies Ombudsman (BSO) was introduced by an Act of Parliament in 1986 for private sector business.[12] For the insurance and banking models, boards of directors play an important part in the financing and terms of reference of the schemes, yet only in the statutory BSO is there independent oversight of the terms of reference of the ombudsman (Birds and Graham 1988: 324). Annual reports are published, but not decisions of individual cases. Little is known about public awareness of such procedures; only the BSO can *insist* that it obtains information from the body investigated. Whether an ombudsman exists at all is often fortuitous. For company pensions there is an Occupational Pension Advisory Service for complainants. It received 2,000 calls in 1987, and advises complainants on investments totalling over £200 billion held on trust. It is not an ombudsman and possesses no investigatory remit.

FORMAL GRIEVANCE PROCEDURES

Fourth, we have witnessed the introduction of a large number of formal grievance procedures for public programmes possessing a wide range of objectives and methodologies. One of the most important came with the introduction of the Social Fund in 1988. Out of this fund will be paid a variety of discretionary and cash limited loans and grants to meet certain needs.[13] Meeting needs depends upon the state of the local Department of Social Security (DSS) office's budget, so needs in the loan and grant category are prioritized separately with greater needs being met first. There is some, but far from complete, similarity to the pre-1980 system of special needs payments (Mullen 1989). Certainly discretionary payments have replaced legal entitlement in statutory rules. Discretionary payments are made by Social Fund Officers (SFOs), who must have regard to a variety of statutory provisions and administrative guidance and directions. A Social Fund Manual for SFOs has been published. Where a payment is cash limited, appeal to an independent tribunal under statute has been abolished. Instead, a disappointed applicant has the right to have the decision reviewed by the same or another SFO. Further review may be made by an SF Inspector.

Directions and guidance address the manner in which reviews are to be made (see Mullen 1989 for details). SFIs are to be 'independent' of the DSS and are appointed by the SF Commissioner who monitors decisions and offers advice and assistance to improve decision-making. Under regulations a review is provided for on a written application.[14] Where the decision is not revised 'wholly in the applicant's favour' an opportunity for an interview with the SFO must be offered with the right to be accompanied by a friend or relative. At the interview, an explanation of the reasons for the decision will be given and representations may be made and new evidence presented. Where a decision is not revised 'wholly in the applicant's favour' a higher official will make the decision, keeping a written record of it. Review by the SFI allows for an interview but it is meant to be a paper review. It is 'likely that there will be minimal scope for reconsideration of the discretionary element in decision-making' at this stage (Mullen 1989: 88), nor is there provision for any broader lessons from SFI involvement to be publicized to achieve greater consistency and better practice. The internal review procedure has little to commend it as a legitimizing device and has to be seen in the context of the government's professed objective of extirpating the 'dependency culture'. The discretion of SFIs – former government officials in the DSS – is highly structured by ministerial guidance of which they must take account and which seems to aim to keep local offices within their budgets rather than to expose the unarticulated criteria employed in the exercise of subjective discretion as K.C. Davis (1971) advocated. Decisions will be subject to the investigation of the Parliamentary Commissioner for Administration (PCA 1987: paras 11–12) and the process of judicial review. Successful challenge has taken place in the courts, only for the decision to be nullified by regulations.

For complaints concerning school allocation and special educational need, appellate procedures have been introduced under the Education Acts 1980 and 1981 respectively. Appeal committees are established by education authorities and, in the latter case, there is a further appeal to the Secretary of State. Under the Education Reform Act 1988 (section 16(3)) authorities, after consulting governing bodies of aided and special agreement schools, are to establish formal arrangements for dealing with complaints that authorities or governing bodies have exercised powers unreasonably, or have failed to discharge duties, under the Act (basically concerning the National Curriculum) or cognate legislation. Arrangements are to be approved by the Secretary of State and will be concerned with complaints made on or after 1 September 1989. A Circular has been issued to authorities on the procedures (DES Circ. 1/89). Under section 23(2), the Secretary of State must not deal with a complaint until the local procedure is exhausted.

Elsewhere in local government, special committees were established under statute to deal with rent and rebate appeals; the Local Government Finance Act 1982 maintained the provisions allowing complaint and objections to be made to the auditor at the time of audit. Under the Local Government Act 1988 (section 30 and sched. 4) auditors are given powers to issue prohibition orders to stop unlawful expenditure or conduct leading to a loss or deficiency, and increased powers to seek judicial review of decisions and failures to act by a body whose books he is accounting. In his report on the *Conduct of Local Authority Business* Widdicombe (1986) suggested that the local ombudsman should be empowered to assist those seeking judicial review where an authority had persistently broken the law, or where there were implications for the council as a whole and its procedures or where legal clarification was required.

The Broadcasting Complaints Commission (BCC) was established by the Broadcasting Act 1981. It describes itself as a 'quasi-judicial body' and has jurisdiction over complaints of unfair and unjust treatment and unwarranted invasions of privacy by the BBC and independent broadcasting sector. It believes it is 'insufficiently known and understood by the public' and in 1987–88 it received 152 complaints, 93 of which were outside jurisdiction and 26 were subject to full adjudication. Confusion in the public eye is likely to be increased by the government's decision to establish a Broadcasting Standards Council, initially on a non-statutory basis, which will be a deliberative body issuing codes on subjective matters of taste and decency. The BCC is critical of broadcasters for not giving sufficient publicity about its existence to viewers. It was particularly scornful of the BBC. It is worth noting that at least the BCC represents a statutory commitment to a grievance procedure: an analogue for the Press was resisted, and a self-regulatory framework was preferred under a much criticized Press Council. Its chairman asked the public to participate in reviewing its role (*Guardian* 22 February 1989). Following the Calcutt Report (Cmnd. 1102, 1990) a non-statutory complaints commission has been established. Whether the commission will remain non-statutory depends upon how successfully the Press can reform its operations. Complaints about advertising have been affected by a European Directive on Advertising, which relies heavily upon the self-regulatory bodies, the Advertising Standards Authority and the Code of Advertising Practice, to implement its provisions. These are to be spelt out in regulations and empower the Director General of Fair Trading to seek, ultimately, an injunction in the courts against a misleading advertisement.

OVERSIGHT, SYSTEM-INSPECTION AND GRIEVANCE REDRESS

Finally, it is well not to overlook those bodies whose responsibilities are not the redress of individual grievance, but the investigation into systemic operations such as the economy, efficiency and effectiveness of government, governmental agencies' and local government expenditure, inspection of the prison system, mental health system, education and social services, and so on. All of these assist in identification of failures in the delivery of, or proper performance of, various programmes, or of malfunctioning that will, if it has not already, emerge as grievances to be redressed. The investigation by the Comptroller and Auditor General (CAG) and his reports for the Commons Public Accounts Committee on a variety of topics – such as *Quality of Clinical Health-Care in NHS Hospitals* (NAO 1987–88a), *Quality of Service to the Public at DHSS Local Offices* (NAO

1987–88b; PAC 1987), *Management of Family Practitioner Services* (NAO 1987–88c), and *Incorrect Payments of Social Security Awards* (NAO 1986–87) – are excellent reports in areas where grievances are rife and which help to highlight administrative breakdowns in a wider context than an individual dispute. CAG reports also examine the special procedures operating between producers and government agencies to regulate prices and to act as grievance or appellate bodies on terms which appear extremely beneficial to the producers e.g. the Pharmaceutical Price Regulation Scheme and the Review Board for Government Contracts.[15] The reports of the Prison Inspectorate not only allow us to peer into the dreadful conditions in our prisons or to assess controversies such as the report on prison suicides in September 1986, but also have built up sufficient anxiety for former inspectors to advocate more effective grievance procedures for prisoners, including a prison ombudsman. The Mental Health Act Commission does hear inmates' complaints and has also recommended the establishment of effective grievance procedures within individual institutions or over such institutions (Mental Health Act Commission 1987: ch. 6). Such a recommendation has equal validity for private institutions catering for the old or for the mentally retarded, subjects gaining recognition because of programmes of 'community care' or off-loading on to private enterprise of tasks previously undertaken by public authorities.

One agency with a broad remit, some of which falls within this category, others elsewhere, is the Office of Fair Trading (OFT). Much of its work on consumer affairs involves licensing, agreement on codes with trade associations and seeking judicial orders against persistent offenders under Part III of the Fair Trading Act 1973.[16] On the competition side, its work involves investigation, negotiation and advice on monopolies, mergers, anti-competitive practices and the investigation of certain complaints under the Gas Act 1986 (relating to industrial users). However, like the DTI and its Companies Investigations Branch, it relies heavily upon complaints from individuals to launch investigations into allegations of unfair practices by traders or anti-competitive practices or abuse of monopolies.[17] Complaints come directly, via local trading standards offices and otherwise. Complaints are used by the OFT as a source of information from which investigations and negotiations may ensue: the OFT is not established to pursue each complaint to a conclusion with redress or rejection; nor does it possess the resources for such. There is the risk, of course, that the complaints it receives will be tendentious and unreliable; they will certainly be one-sided. Nevertheless, they are an essential source of information necessary for the promotion of the collective weal.

TRIBUNALS AND INQUIRIES

As well as the above developments, we have witnessed the creation of new tribunals, especially in banking and financial services, data protection, community charge/poll tax and security where it was felt that certain grievances lend themselves to an adjudicatory process. The rules for environmental planning inquiries were amended to allow for pre-inquiry hearings although the vast majority of inquiries are now dealt with by a single inspector on a written procedure who determines the appeal: far more like the functional equivalent of a tribunal. The purpose of an inquiry is to allow objections to be raised and heard before a decision on a policy is taken. One of the most controversial inquiry decisions involved a non-inquiry decision to allow the proposal to build the railway link to the Channel Tunnel without a public inquiry but under the private bill procedure. This allows for the raising of objections and legal representation at the Committee stage of the Bill. This is daunting and expensive.[18] A Select Committee heard objections into the proposal to build the Tunnel. Under the Act authorizing its construction, planning permission was both deemed to be given and an extensive resort was made to use classes provisions which allow a change of use of land without planning permission. These devices have been a prevalent feature of planning policy in the 1980s, as has the 'call in' procedure whereby the Secretary of State calls in a planning decision from a local planning authority to centralize the ultimate decision-making process.

Inquiries in the planning field are meant to be as informal and accessible as possible so that parties should be able to participate without fear of financial penalty. Recent changes in the guidance for the award of costs have facilitated the scope for the award of costs at inquiries against parties (Purdue 1987; Cocks 1988) and seem directed against both the reluctant planning authority and the appellant. Costs for and against third parties 'will be made only in exceptional circumstances' (DoE Circ. 2/87 1987).

The apprehension exists that the sum effect of these developments, as well as changes in rules for nuclear power inquiries,[19] is to ease the planning process for commercial interests and developers and to reduce the efficacy of local opposition, either via elected representatives or local objectors.

More generally, easing the regulatory burden upon the public is geared towards unleashing enterprise and initiatives. As a practical issue those who wish to avail themselves of such deregulated opportunities are small in number and by no means representative of the public interest or at least, more importantly, few appropriate safeguards exist to ensure that they are representative of the public interest. They simply happen to coincide with the policy preferences of the government of the day. While we have witnessed increased demands for more participation in decision-making and greater openness and information, we have not developed on a formal basis the 'planning cells' which exist in some German Länder and cities. These produce citizens' reports which are based upon provision of information, time off work and remuneration for participants selected randomly in areas and whose selection is supervised by a judge. It aims for *a priori* avoidance of grievances, rather than *a posteriori* resolution. Whether through this process the 'silent majority is able to participate in making decisions that affect everyone' would be open to debate (Dienel 1989: 66). But it is an interesting theme.

INFORMAL PROCEDURES

So far, the emphasis has been largely upon procedures that are statutory and, to varying degrees, formal. Alongside the statutory schemes there exist informal mechanisms, invariably, though not solely, attending more obvious statutory schemes. The existence of such procedures may be *ad hoc* or interest specific and can result from privileged access or regularized lobbying. There may also be more coherent internal procedures developing as a matter of practice but which are not publicized. Or there can be regular ways of responding to complaints, especially on referral from an elected representative, particularly MPs (see Rawlings 1986), to streamline the response procedure to a complaint or request for a review. US Federal Agencies and government departments have widespread experience of informal and internal resolution of grievances before a formal complaint is made to an outside or independent body. The subject of the complaints in one study concerned freedom of information disputes and the role of the Department of Justice (Birkinshaw 1989). US agencies have emphasized the importance of complaints to obtain information about their delivery of regulatory programmes and feedback of public feeling to obtain data from which performance may be enhanced.[20]

In local government in England and Wales research has shown the existence of informal grievance procedures: very often they are triggered off as internal mechanisms against ombudsman involvement after a councillor's complaint. However, within authorities exemplary models of complaint handling have been noted. In some service areas an awareness of efficient and responsive mechanisms has been observed although there has not been the necessary degree of agreement to settle upon a particular process (Lewis *et al.* 1987; Birkinshaw 1987). Such seems to be true with complaints about social services, where there has been more agitation over the distinction between the terms: complaint, grievance (an unresolved complaint), request for assistance that cannot be met, etc. Social services' complaints have featured many of the national *causes célèbres* in local government, and support for parental rights has been on the upsurge since the Butler-Sloss inquiry after large numbers of children were placed in care following medical reports alleging sexual abuse (Butler-Sloss 1988).[21]

JUDICIAL OVERSIGHT, GRIEVANCE PROCEDURES AND EFFECTIVENESS

One effect of the growing number of requests for judicial review has been an increased judicial intervention into bodies created by Parliament to attend to grievances in particular areas. The Commission for Racial Equality, for instance, had an unhappy passage at the hands of the courts in the 1980s, which caused it to seek more informal methods to achieve its objectives of eradicating discrimination, for example more negotiation on codes and increasing assistance for individuals before courts and tribunals. It turned away from new formal investigations as these had proved a minefield.[22] The local ombudsman has also encountered hostile decisions and an increased propensity for judicial interference.[23] This is an office where many have agreed that its lack of enforcement powers has been a severe impediment to an effective complaints procedure. We shall have to see whether the successful applications for review add significantly to those authorities which have been reluctant to accept its decisions. Proposals before Parliament will provide for greater duties upon authorities, and greater powers for the local ombudsmen to publicise his decisions and their failure to accept them (Housing and Local Government Bill 1988–89).

A reluctant customer of the Parliamentary Commissioner has been the Lord Chancellor's Department (LCD). This has involved complaints about the administration of the courts, not about judges, it should be noted. None the less, the LCD has insisted that any such investigation would constitute an unwarranted trespass into judicial independence. The PCA refused an informal compromise and was still awaiting a response after eleven months (PCA 1988: para. 54). The PCA has himself been the subject of accusations of maladministration concerning delay over his investigations (PCA 1985–86: 42 *et seq*) although the office has managed to reduce the period of investigation and report to ten months eighteen days. In 1987 there were none the less forty-six late responses from departments to his initial communication; a period of six weeks had been set down by the Select Committee on the PCA. Although the PCA publishes examples of improvements in administrative procedures in his reports, the actual record is difficult to establish. This partly relates to the insistence on 'maladministration', rather than a broader concept or catalogue of woes relating to defective administration. It is interesting to compare the much wider remit of the ombudsman for Ireland (Ombudsman Act (Ireland) 1980) and indeed that laid down by a judge of the Supreme Court of Canada, who held that administration 'encompasses everything done by governmental authorities in the implementation of government policy' excluding the legislature and the courts. Commercial affairs, excluded in the UK, were therefore included.[24] In fact, the Australian ombudsman has recommended an ombudsman for judicial administration (Australian Commonwealth Ombudsman 1985: 226–7). For the CLA, while its existence has 'markedly improved the performance of local government' there is 'overwhelming evidence that many authorities have failed to respond adequately to its suggestions' on, for example, its code of practice on complaints 'and have ignored significant aspects' of the code (Lewis *et al.* 1987: 7). High on the priorities of the PCA and CLA should be investigations on their own initiative as is common elsewhere.

SOME CONCLUDING COMMENTS

The motivations for establishing a grievance procedure are virtually as limitless as the procedures that exist: they might arise from a desire to increase captious resentment against certain areas or tiers of government; to encourage a shallow consumerism; to court political popularity; to divert attention away from the real problems; to downplay the courts; or to act as a necessary adjunct to controversial political reform. The procedures that exist rarely have the necessary armoury or inclination to act effectively as the citizen's protector or champion unless it suits government's designs so for them to act. But this can be counter-productive for a government's intentions. With nationalized industries, the lack of effective grievance procedures, still a contemporary problem (Birkinshaw 1985), helped to isolate such industries from popular and lasting acceptance. Today, privatization of monopolies has led to increasing complaints about lack of adequate service (*Which?* 1988) and inability of the regulatory watchdogs to obtain necessary information to set appropriate pricing policies. Yet as the Public Accounts Committee has said (*vis-à-vis* consumer consultative committees): the pursuit of a business-like approach 'is not inconsistent with conducting business in public'.

What function ought grievance procedures to fulfil? They should allow members of the public an opportunity to make a complaint about, or objection to, a proposal, action or inaction that affects their lives. The fact that a grievance may 'objectively' be deemed *de minimis* goes to the kind of procedure, not its existence. It would be foolish to deny that too much concentration upon grievance redress may deflect attention away from other legitimate objectives: clearer and better regulation; greater participation in decision-making; law enforcement by agency and specialists rather than reacting to individual complaints; or wider dissemination of information and public education. All of these are in fact cognate issues to grievance redress. Complaints must be effectively and fairly dealt with. Their resolution is a component of a larger theme involving accountability and responsiveness for the exercise of power. The desiderata for such processes involve: enjoying the confidence of the participants, being open and accessible, speedy, cheap, fair and just, independent and adequately resourced. Also involved is the formulation of the best procedure or process to cater for widely different complaints while avoiding unnecessary duplication of procedures. But so too are public involvement in decision-making, openness and feedback to decision-makers as part of a learning process.

The era of opting out of public provision of services and privatization has seen no slackening in awareness of the need for effective and fair redress of grievance.[25]

NOTES

1 Nor is this inability a recent phenomenon. In 1666 judges were given special appointments to sit on tribunals to deal, in a more expeditious and informal manner, with an anticipated plethora of disputes arising from the rebuilding of London after the Great Fire.

2 In 1986 – 719 complaints referred; 1987 – 677. It was anticipated that complaints would increase by 100–150 per cent after the addition of a wide range of non-departmental bodies to the PCA's jurisdiction: PCA Annual Report 1986 (HC 248, 1986–87). Applications for leave for judicial review for 1985–87, were 1,169, 816 and 1,529.

3 Those specified in regulations and referred by police authorities, chief constables or the Metropolitan Police Commissioner.

4 Disquiet has been voiced about the adequacy of police investigations and serious charges subsequently brought against complainants (Police Complaints Authority, *Triennial Report*, HC 446, 1987–88).

5 The security service tribunal may investigate activities where no warrant is required and may make recommendations following such investigations.

6 For other civil servants an internal procedure can end up with the Cabinet Secretary and the Prime Minister.

7 *R. v. Panel on Take-overs ex p. Datafin* [1987] 1 All ER 564.

8 As well as the mandatory ones, 165 telecommunication advisory committees have been recognized.

9 The DGFT exercises powers under the Fair Trading Act 1973 or the Competition Act 1980, Gas Act 1986 s. 32(2)(*b*) and (6). Electricity and water have their own procedures.

10 Financial Services Act 1986, Sched. 7, para 4(2).

11 Financial Services Act 1986, Sched. 2, para 3.

12 Building Societies Act 1986, ss. 83-84 and Scheds. 12 and 13. See also Jack Committee (1989), Appendix H on 'Commercial Ombudsmen'.

13 Social Security Act 1986, Part III, and see Mullen (1989) for an interesting account.

14 S.I. 1988, No. 34.

15 See PPRS, Oct. 1986, DHSS; RBGC (1987) *Fifth General Review of the Profit Formula for Non-Competitive Government Contracts*, London: HMSO.

16 Seeking orders against those who have persisted in a course of conduct detrimental to the interests of consumers in the UK regarded as unfair.

17 In one year the CIB received 441 complaints, 40 per cent of which were from private individuals, i.e. more than from the Stock Exchange or the DPP (*Guardian* 21 December 1988).

18 A joint committee of the Commons and Lords has recommended a greater use of public inquiries, where the Private Bill Procedure is currently employed.

19 NB the reduction of objectors' rights by the Electricity Generating Stations and Overhead Lines (Inquiries Procedure) Rules 1987.

20 Committee of Government Affairs *Study of Federal Regulation* Vol. III, 95th Congress, No. 95-71.

21 Increased protection for one group (parents) may well act to the detriment of another group (children). The Children Bill 1988–89 makes the child's welfare the court's 'paramount consideration'.

22 Federal and provincial governments in Canada have provided very interesting procedures and bodies to tackle discrimination: see the Canadian Human Rights Act and the Ontario Human Rights Code 1981.

23 *R v. Commissioner for Local Administration ex p. Eastleigh BC* [1988] 3 All ER 151; *R v. Ibid ex p. Croydon LBC* [1989] 1 All ER 1033.

24 J. Dickson in *Br. Columbia Development Corporation* v. *Friedman* [1985] 1 WWR 193, S.Ct.

25 On increased access to lawyers and the courts, and notwithstanding any such increase the need for grievance procedures as described above will remain, see Lord Chancellor's Department (1988); National Consumer Council (1989); Lord Chancellor's Department (1989a).

5 Developments in commercial arbitration

R.E. Wight

In view of the fact that business people have come to regard arbitration as their favoured means of catering for dispute resolution, commercial lawyers have recently been giving considerable thought to providing an appropriate legal setting within which arbitration can operate and so assist trade and commerce to flourish. Indeed, in the context of international arbitrations involving large sums of money, the provision of an acceptable legal framework can bestow significant economic benefits upon a state anxious to attract arbitration business. While there has been something of a renaissance in the study of arbitration law and practice, arbitration as a means of resolving disputes must not be thought of as a new phenomenon by any means; it has long been incorporated into most legal systems and stands alongside litigation as a legal means of resolving differences.

In view of its lengthy pedigree, it is perhaps surprising that no statutory definition of arbitration exists and no judicial attempt at a definition has met with universal approval.[1] This has, however, left the field open for academic lawyers to fill the gap. My favoured definition is that set out by Professor D.M. Walker.[2]

> [Arbitration is the] adjudication of a dispute or controversy on fact or law or both outside the ordinary civil courts, by one or more persons to whom the parties who are at issue refer the matter for decision.

This definition underlines what must be regarded as the four essential features of arbitration.

1 It is a procedure for handling *disputes*. In the absence of a dispute, procedures which in effect avoid disagreements between parties, such as valuation and certification under which, for example, some expert is required to certify that work on a building contract has been satisfactorily completed, cannot be classed as arbitration and so do not fall within the ambit of our discussions.

2 The outcome of an arbitration will be a *decision* on the matters in dispute referred to as an award. Although such awards may embody an agreed settlement between the parties, it must be stressed that (subject to any right of appeal) an arbitrator's award is binding on the parties to the arbitration, and that is so even if one of the parties fails to participate in the proceedings.

3 Arbitration stands alongside the ordinary court structure but is not part of that structure. This is a difficult concept to grasp in that ultimately arbitration can never be totally divorced from the court structure since the court's authority must be invoked, for example to give effect to arbitration agreements or to enforce an arbitration award against a recalcitrant respondent.

4 Inherent in (3) is the concept that resort to arbitration is a voluntary process being based on a contract first between the parties in dispute and second between those parties and the third-party arbitrator who has agreed to resolve the matter.

THE ARBITRATION AGREEMENT

The foundation for the arbitral process is to be found either in an arbitration clause forming part of a wider contract between the parties or in a submission agreement. The distinction here is that an arbitration clause is normally drafted at a point in time when no dispute has actually arisen whereas a submission agreement is entered into after a dispute has arisen and so those involved in drafting the latter can do so in the light of that particular dispute. Extremely laconic arbitration agreements have been upheld by the courts,[3] who merely require that the agreement records the intention of the parties that their disputes be resolved by arbitration and that there is a consensus on the appointment or method of appointment of the arbitrators. It is then for the courts to implement such agreements by staying any actions taken by the respondent in defiance of the agreement. One point which remains rather unclear is the relationship between the submitters and their arbitrators. Clearly it flies in the face of settled contract law for an agreement between the submitters to impose any obligations on a third-party arbitrator. It could be argued that an arbitrator, once approached, offers to accept office provided his or her appointment is satisfactory as to remuneration etc. More likely, it is the submitters who offer to appoint the person upon whom they are agreed as arbitrator and that person then accepts the appointment. Either way, there is clearly a contractual relationship between the submitters and the arbitrator and the remedies for any breach of the respective obligations of submitters and arbitrators would be the same as for any other breach of contract. An interesting question which awaits resolution is whether an arbitrator owes any duty of care to the submitters so as to render him or her liable in the tort of negligence.[4]

ARBITRABILITY

Although we are discussing commercial arbitration here, the view that arbitration is *only* appropriate for the resolution of commercial disputes should be noted.[5] However, most states, including the UK, do not restrict the role of arbitration to commercial matters. Essentially, all rights relating to purely private matters can be submitted to arbitration, whereas matters public in nature can not e.g. the field of family law and criminal issues. Some states, e.g. France, provide that arbitration clauses are valid only in relation to commercial transactions but do not impose the same restrictions on international agreements.[6] Although there are grey areas caused by varying conceptions of what the term implies, it is accepted that international commercial arbitration is subject to public policy limitations e.g. generally, disputes dealing with competition law, bankruptcy and intellectual property rights are deemed non-arbitrable. One point awaiting clarification is the attitude of an arbitral tribunal when asked to enforce contracts for payment of a bribe which are accepted as endemic in the commercial life of some parts of the world. It is probably the case that such contracts violate international public policy and cannot be enforced by arbitrators but this rather begs the question of the true nature of international public policy.[7]

WHO MAY ACT AS ARBITRATOR?

Restrictions on who may act as arbitrator are either legal or conventional. On the one hand arbitrators are appointed by contract and are therefore bound by the terms of the prior agreement and by ordinary contract law as to capacity; on the other hand arbitration awards are enforceable by the state which has an implicit interest that arbitrators must be credible. Legal disqualifications which cannot be waived by the parties are narrowly circumscribed and probably do not extend beyond infancy and insanity. Other disqualifications serve only to protect the interests of the parties and can therefore be waived by the submitters. Basically any factor which has a tendency to bias an arbitrator in favour of one of the parties would be a ground for the arbitrator's disqualification. A close family relationship would disqualify an arbitrator (by analogy with judges); some personal interest in the outcome of the proceedings, financial or otherwise, would serve (basically an application of the maxim *nemo iudex in rem suam*, no one may be a judge in his own cause).

As a matter of practice, the nature of the dispute clearly determines the appropriateness of the choice of arbitrator. Disputes of a factual nature are best dealt with by appropriate experts; disputes of a legal nature, such as the interpretation of a clause in a standard form contract, are best dealt with by lawyers.[8] In international commercial arbitration it is often more appropriate to appoint lawyers even where the dispute seems relatively uncomplex in that only a lawyer is likely to have the competence to deal with the questions of procedure and conflicts of law which may arise. Again, pragmatically, the choice of arbitrator in international commercial arbitration requires careful consideration so as to avoid unnecessary complications. For example, if a dispute involves parties of different nationalities, it is clearly desirable for the arbitrator to be fluent in the language in which the arbitration is to be conducted and so avoid the necessity to appoint an interpreter. Similarly those involved in appointing arbitrators should always bear in mind the nationality of a sole arbitrator or presiding arbitrator. Whereas such neutral nationality may seem to be mere pandering to party sensibilities, it may well serve to ensure more willing compliance with the eventual award. Again, with the hefty onus placed on the arbitrator in international commercial arbitration, it is desirable not only that an experienced lawyer be appointed, but also one experienced in the law and procedure of arbitration, which need not be the same thing.

On the other side of the coin, in order to retain their credibility amongst the arbitration community, arbitrators would be well advised to disclose all conceivable facts constituting grounds for their disqualification, both those existing at the outset and those which arise during the arbitration. Arbitrators should also take care to ensure that there is nothing in the submission which debars them from acting.

Finally, arbitrators must be replaced if they resign, die, become incapable of acting or become disqualified after a successful challenge.[9] It is to no one's credit that whereas challenges to arbitrators were formerly a rare event, with the development of commercial arbitration involving large sums of money, lawyers employed by the parties have been prepared to challenge arbitrators solely in order to procure a tactical advantage for their clients. Provisions do exist to limit such behaviour. The UNCITRAL arbitration rules state:[10]

10.1   Any arbitrator may be challenged if circumstances exist that give rise to justifiable doubts as to the arbitrator's impartiality or independence.

10.2   A party may challenge the arbitrator appointed by him only for reasons of which he becomes aware after the appointment has been made.

Similar provisions appear in other sets of rules, the Model Law and national legal systems. According to Redfern and Hunter (1986: 175), such challenges are usually based on some connection with one of the parties which brings into question the arbitrator's independence. It would seem that such challenges which seek to achieve a tactical advantage by causing delay and inconvenience are becoming increasingly common, although rarely successful in having the arbitrator removed. Nevertheless, the mere fact of challenge is hardly satisfactory for an arbitrator's reputation, particularly because the onus is on arbitrators to disclose circumstances which give rise to doubt as to their impartiality or independence. Of course, arbitrators ought not to accept an appointment if they have any reason to believe that one or other party will genuinely feel that they are not independent. When there has been a successful challenge, the new appointment will usually be made in the same way as the original appointment although national systems of law unusually confer powers of appointment upon courts if there are difficulties.[11]

THE CONDUCT OF ARBITRATION PROCEEDINGS

Arbitration procedure is regulated publicly by legal provisions and privately by contract. In England and Wales the Arbitration Acts 1950–79 contain various procedural powers available to an arbitrator which essentially comprise all those necessary to enable proceedings to be effectively conducted. The actual procedure used in the arbitration is basically such as the parties agree upon and the degree of formality or informality will depend largely on whether issues of fact or of law are pre-eminent in the case, for example counsel or solicitors may be instructed, there may be written pleadings or oral argument, there could be physical inspection of the premises or subject matter of dispute; there may be consultations with experts by the arbitrator if necessary; the arbitrator may submit a draft award/proposed findings to the parties and allow them to make representations on the proposed findings; the arbitrator may also make an interim award if this is deemed appropriate.

When deciding upon the appropriate procedure to be followed, the arbitrator must act within a fundamental three-cornered framework:

1 the arbitrator must ensure fairness as between the parties
2 the arbitrator must act within the terms of the submission
3 the arbitrator must proceed expeditiously.

The obligation of fairness is fundamental to the nature of arbitration and is not something which can be contracted out of by the parties, however informal the proceedings. The consequences of any serious failure in this respect could lead to the arbitrator being removed by the court or the award being rendered un-enforceable. It is, however, not easy to establish conclusively the meaning of fairness (frequently described as the equally vague concept, natural justice) in the context of arbitration proceedings.

One aspect of the duty of fairness is summarized in the maxim '*audi alterem partem*' (hear both sides) but some arbitrations may not require a hearing as when a skilled person is appointed to determine a dispute. Another feature of the obligation of fairness is to ensure that the parties are treated equally, for example intimation of an arbitrator's decision to inspect property must be given to both parties. Another practical obligation on the prudent arbitrator is to beware of accepting hospitality from one person where it could give rise to the suspicion that the case is being discussed in the absence of the opponent.[12]

The second basic duty of arbitrators is to act within the terms of the sub-mission. If they proceed '*ultra fines compromissi*' (beyond the scope of the reference to him) or fail to exhaust all the questions submitted to them, the courts may be called upon to intervene, either at the end or during the course of proceedings.[13]

The third basic duty of arbitrators is to exercise reasonable dispatch in the execution of their duties. While the precise meaning of this requirement is not clear it probably does not require an arbitrator to push ahead with proceedings in the absence of either party pressing for action.

As a back-drop to these fundamental duties, an arbitrator's award may be attacked if the arbitrator is guilty of misconduct. In addition to the more obvious examples of misconduct, such as bribery or corruption, English law treats as misconduct 'to behave in a way regarded by the courts as contrary to public policy',[14] which certainly seems to give the courts a broad discretion and clearly goes beyond moral wickedness.

THE AWARD

The whole purpose and rationale behind arbitration proceedings lies in the production of a valid and enforceable award. The primary features of an arbitral award are twofold:

1 its contents should finally dispose of all matters with which it deals
2 it is binding upon the parties to the arbitration, at least, subject to any right of appeal which may exist.

A third feature of international arbitration is that the award should of course be enforceable beyond national frontiers.

There is no statutory definition of an award but a decision of a tribunal which has the status of an award carries with it certain consequences, for example any legal time limits for challenging an award will begin to run and only an award qualifies for recognition and enforcement under international conventions. The contents of an award should be final, certain, consistent, unconditional and unambiguous, so in the course of drafting an arbitrator must exercise precision in language although no technical requirements need be met and laconic awards are common.

Formerly, because an award which had reasons on its face could be set aside by a court, arbitrators anxious to avoid this would simply omit reasons from their awards. Today, under the Arbitration Act 1979 s1(1), the court has no juris- diction to remit or set aside an award on the ground of errors of fact or law on the face of the award. It was thought that this provision would encourage arbitrators to include reasons in their awards.

COURT CHALLENGES TO AWARDS

One of the most important features of arbitration has always been the finality of the award. The cost and delay of court proceedings following on a form of arbitration deprive it of its essential point. Against that, the victim of a real or imagined miscarriage of justice may feel justifiably aggrieved if deprived of recourse to a higher tribunal.

The most recent legislation affecting arbitration in England and Wales is the Arbitration Act 1979, which specifically sets out to delimit the right of appeal to the courts. The prior special case procedure abolished by s1(1) was particularly unpopular amongst foreign parties to arbitration in England. Foreign govern- ments, for example, saw no reason why they should submit to the jurisdiction of English courts if an award was challenged. The consequence was a marked diversion of much large-scale arbitration business to other jurisdictions to the economic detriment of the United Kingdom arbitration community.

The present position under the Act[15] is that appeal lies to the High Court on any question of law arising out of an award on an 'arbitration agreement', when the court may

1 confirm, vary or set aside the award, or
2 remit the award to the reconsideration of the arbitrator or umpire together with the court's opinion on the question of law which was the subject of the appeal.

An appeal cannot be made unless either all the parties to the reference consent or one of the parties applies to the court and the court grants leave for the appeal to be made (s1(3)). Leave for an appeal will not be granted unless the High Court considers that, having regard to all the circumstances, the determination of the question of law concerned could substantially affect the rights of one or more of the parties to the arbitration agreement.

The first opportunity the courts had for discussing s1 occurred in *Pioneer Shipping Ltd and Another* v. *BTP Tioxide Ltd (The Nema)* 1980,[16] when Lord Diplock established guidelines as to how this discretion was to be exercised. His judgment emphasized that it had been Parliament's intention to promote finality of awards and so judicial interference with awards was tenable only if it was shown that the arbitrator had misdirected himself in law or had reached a decision which no reasonable arbitrator could have reached.

In the light of its origins, the Act also provides for exclusion agreements excluding both this limited right of appeal under s1 and the right to apply to the court for the determination of a preliminary point of law under s2. The Act distinguishes between three types of exclusion agreement: domestic, non-domestic and non-domestic falling within one of three special categories.[17]

A domestic agreement is defined as

an arbitration agreement which does not provide expressly or by implication, for arbitration in a State other than the United Kingdom and to which neither

1 an individual who is a national of, or habitually resident in, any State other than the United Kingdom nor
2 a body corporate which is incorporated in, or whose central management and control is exercised in, any State other than the United Kingdom, is a party at the time the arbitration agreement is entered into.

Exclusion clauses in domestic arbitration agreements are effective only if entered into after the commencement of the arbitration. Those included in non-domestic agreements falling within the special categories (questions within Admiralty jurisdiction, disputes arising out of contracts of insurance and those arising out of commodity contracts) take effect only where the exclusion agreement is entered into after the commencement of the arbitration or the award relates to a contract expressed to be governed by a law other than English Law. There are no restrictions placed on the operation of exclusion agreements contained in non-domestic agreements which fall without the special categories, such as large-scale international development contracts.

A LEGAL FRAMEWORK FOR INTERNATIONAL COMMERCIAL ARBITRATION

As previously mentioned, the arbitral process operates alongside the court system but is ultimately dependent upon it for support. This is clear in the context of the recognition and enforcement of awards. The production of an enforceable award is the rationale behind the arbitration process and when discussing international commercial arbitration this obviously requires the production of an award capable of enforcement wherever a respondent has assets. As Redfern and Hunter (1986: 341) say, the award must be 'transportable', meaning that it can be taken from the state in which it was made, under that system of law, to other states where it will qualify for recognition and enforcement under their system of law. For reasons already outlined arbitrations frequently occur in states to which the parties have no connection but when it comes to enforcement this must, of course, take place in a state in which the losing party does have some connection, in the sense of assets. The main thrust of international conventions in the arbitration field has been in the area of recognizing and enforcing awards, thus implicitly recognizing the importance of international commercial arbitration.

The first major development recognizing the importance of international commercial arbitration as an adjunct to international trade and commerce was the adoption of the Geneva Protocol of 1923 and the Geneva Convention on the Execution of Foreign Arbitral awards of 1927, both promulgated under the auspices of the League of Nations.

The Geneva Protocol 1923 contained two key elements. Under Art(4) contracting states were obliged to ensure that parties to an arbitration agreement did indeed resolve their disputes by arbitration rather than by resort to the courts. Under Art(3) states were to grant recognition and enforcement to arbitration awards made in their own territory. The importance of this measure lay not so much in its intrinsic worth but rather as a first step towards the recognition and enforcement of international arbitral awards. It applied only to arbitration agreements 'between parties subject respectively to the jurisdiction of different Contracting states' and it imposed an obligation on a state to enforce awards made in its territory only pursuant to an arbitration agreement covered by the Protocol.

The Geneva Convention 1927 built on the foundation of the Protocol and provided that an award would be recognised as binding and enforceable in the territory of any contracting state provided

1 the award was made pursuant to an agreement to which the 1923 Protocol applied
2 that the award was made in the territory of one of the contracting states
3 that the parties to the award were subject to the jurisdiction of one of the contracting states.

The Convention was subject to a number of rather clumsy requirements. In order to be recognized and enforced an award must have become 'final in the country in which it has been made' and the award must not have been contrary to 'public policy or the principles of the law of the country in which it is sought to be relied on'.[18] This latter requirement was always contentious in that it is perceived as reasonable for states to decline to enforce an award which contravenes its public policy but unreasonable to take into account its own legal principles when the award has been made in another state in accordance with its legal principles.

In the light of the problems encountered with these two conventions, the International Chamber of Commerce (ICC) took up the challenge and promoted perhaps the most significant single instrument dealing with international commercial arbitration. The ICC proposals were taken up by the United Nations Economic and Social Council and gave rise to the New York Convention, adopted in 1958 and given effect in the UK by the Arbitration Act 1975.

The New York Convention has met with widespread approval and has certainly assisted in the development of arbitration as a favoured method of resolving international trade disputes. The Convention does deal with the enforcement of arbitration agreements but its primary objective was to establish a more effective method of ensuring the recognition and enforcement of foreign awards. The New York Convention replaces the Protocol and Geneva Conventions as between parties to both agreements.

As far as recognition is concerned, states party to the Convention agree to accept the binding effect of awards to which the Convention applies, which can then be used as a defence in any legal proceedings which concern the subject-matter of the award commenced in the courts of the state involved.

Turning to enforcement, states party to the Convention undertake to enforce awards to which the Convention applies in accordance with their own procedural rules. The actual procedure for securing recognition and enforcement of the awards is very simple. All that a party seeking enforcement is required to produce before the court is (1) the award and (2) the arbitration agreement under which it is made.

The New York Convention lays down five grounds on which recognition and enforcement of awards may be refused at the request of the party against whom it is sought (upon whom the burden of proof lies), plus two additional grounds for refusal which may be raised by the relevant court of its own volition. The grounds are as follows:

1 incapacity of the parties or invalidity of the arbitration agreement
2 denial of a fair hearing
3 excess of authority or lack of jurisdiction
4 procedural irregularities
5 invalid award.

The two additional grounds on which the court may act are on arbitrability or public policy.[19]

There have been a number of cases in various states dealing with the interpretation and application of the New York Convention and one of the reasons for the current enthusiasm amongst the arbitration community for the Model Law project was the perceived lack of uniformity in the approach of national courts to the enforcement of awards.

The Model Law on International Commercial Arbitration, proposed by the United Nations Commission on International Trade Law and adopted in 1985, sets out to unify the laws of arbitral procedure in eight chapters dealing variously with the arbitration agreement, the tribunal, the proceedings, together with provisions relating to awards.

Probably the prime significance of the Model Law, whether or not it is implemented by many states, lies in the fact that it is a sort of state of the art treatise on the law of arbitration, the product of over four years' thought on the subject. Clearly any state embarking on amendments to its arbitration legislation will do so with regard to the text of the Model Law.

The Model Law and the New York Convention have laid down the foundations for a unified approach to international commercial arbitration which is likely to increase in popularity as a favoured means of resolving disputes in the international trade sphere.

NOTES

1 There has been a long series of cases involving the distinction between arbitration and valuation or certification. See *Sutcliffe* v. *Thackrah* [1974] A.C.727, *Arenson* v. *A* [1977] A.C.405.
2 Prin. I. 60.
3 For example 'Arbitration, Disputes to be settled by arbitration in Glasgow'.
   United Creameries Co. Ltd. v. *David T. Boyd & Co.* 1912 S.C. 617.
4 See Mustill, Comm. Arb. 190.
5 The commercial reservation appears in the New York Convention (see post) and nearly one-third of states who are parties to the Convention have taken advantage of it.
6 French Commercial Code Art. 631.
7 Ultimately the search for a definition of international public policy may amount to little more than the identification of a standard based on the lowest common denominator.
8 In Spain, where the matter in dispute is of a legal nature, a lawyer *must* be appointed.
9 s7 Arb. Act 1950.
10 UNCITRAL arbitration rules 1976.
11 s7 Arb. Act 1950.
12 A diktat which can cause difficulties during lunch intervals, for example. Anecdotally it has even been extended to the consequences of sharing a lift!
13 s2 Arb. Act 1979.
14 Mustill, Comm. Arb. 494.
15 s1(2) Arb. Act 1979.
16 [1981] 3 WLR 292.
17 s3 Arb. Act 1979.
18 Art. 1(d) and (e).
19 Art. V.

6 Neighbour disputes: community mediation schemes as an alternative to litigation

Tony F. Marshall

THEORY

Before discussing alternatives to litigation, it is as well to be mindful of the advantages that law offers and which may be lost in its replacement by another system of dispute resolution.

There appear to be six main types of benefit that stem from formal legal procedure:

1 Law itself, and its enforcement, are declaratory. Law prescribes minimum standards of acceptable behaviour.
2 Law, with its explicit threat of sanctions in the breach, is able to act as a general deterrent to misbehaviour.
3 The adversarial structure of the courtroom promotes clear and precise logical argument, with a potential for formulating the best cases to be made for and against the respective parties.
4 Law and its processes are public, visible and impressive.
5 Law offers predictability and certainty through its set procedures, along with the guarantee, ultimately, of a resolution.
6 Law provides professional support and representation for those who may be variously adept at making their own case.

These are powerful reasons for invoking the law. Nevertheless, in its operation, law also entails a number of disadvantages and limits to its effectiveness. I shall list nine of these.

1 Law can enable the policing of only a minimum level of morality – a sort of lowest common denominator. People may desire higher standards of civility in their neighbourhood, for instance, than the law prescribes, but they cannot obtain the aid of police, solicitors, etc. to support the eradication of behaviour which is rude or impolite or inconsiderate but not actually illegal. Ray Shonholtz (founder of San Francisco Community Boards) has used this argument for giving communities a role in local social control (e.g. Shonholtz 1987).
2 The deterrence provided by law is much less effective once the law has been breached. Those persons who have experienced sufficient internal or

external pressure to break the law and risk its sanctions are unlikely to find the equation much altered by the application of those sanctions. Law is thus preventive rather than rehabilitative.

3 Although the adversarial structure supports sound debate at an academic level, it is not a realistic model for producing good solutions in the everyday world. It assumes a right/wrong polarity that is rarely applicable to actual conflicts. It also prevents collaboration of the parties on trying to reach a solution acceptable to both. (In actual practice, lawyers spend a great part of their time on private negotiations outside the court to try to effect an agreed settlement, but this is not part of legal procedure. The fact that such extra-legal negotiations are commonplace demonstrates the limitations of law as a dispute-settlement instrument.)

4 The public nature of legal disputation, valuable for its openness, also re-inforces the adversarial process by forcing parties into entrenched and extreme positions.

5 A component of legal processes that aids resolution is the focus on very specific issues, at the expense of over-simplifying the conflict. For instance, a court case limits relevant considerations (a) to the past, and usually a narrow time-span within the past; (b) to the immediate parties involved; and (c) to the immediate causal circumstances only.

6 In practice the law can be said to set a bad example – the use of socially condoned violence. Law is perhaps the most civilized way we have of fighting; but it is still fighting. It is unfortunate that law has become the predominant representation of conflict resolution in modern society.

7 Law, in preserving its disinterest and integrity, is withdrawn from the real world in esoteric ritual that decides issues on the basis of academic argument and the minutiae of legislative documents, rather than on the potential of a particular settlement for resolving the problem in future, or in effecting reconciliation or mutual understanding.

8 Legal justice is based on correctness of procedure. The public conception of justice is in terms of the suitability of the outcome for resolving the practical problems and the feelings surrounding them. The two are often in opposition.

9 The law is costly; it cannot be used for every little conflict. There must be other processes and these need to be prevalent. Given their importance they should be as carefully planned and provided for, and be governed by proper standards (cf. Marshall 1985).

In an attempt to deal with the real disadvantages of the law, alternative dispute resolution (ADR) would seek to have such characteristics as the following.

1 ADR should be able to promote positive standards of behaviour (not just penalize prohibitions).

2 ADR should invoke interpersonal and community ties that are more meaningful to parties and act more effectively as a deterrent than the distant threat of sanctions. Ultimately the desire to live in society and to receive the

benefits of such association is the only positive motivation for reasonable behaviour (apart from strongly held moral beliefs).

3 ADR should be forward-looking towards settlement of ongoing conflict. It should be oriented to better relationships in the long run rather than a decision over one round. Losers are always looking for chances to become winners, so that a conflict is never really settled until both parties are satisfied.

4 The processes of ADR should in themselves create and maintain mutual respect, commitment, civility and creativity. They should reflect the ideals of a well-functioning society and provide a model for managing social relations.

5 ADR should relate closely to everyday life. Practical, feasible solutions should be sought, rather than abstract declarations of principle or fault. Processes should incorporate knowledge of the complexity of circumstances surrounding a specific conflict that is available in full only to the participants themselves, who should therefore play a major role in resolution.

6 To the extent that blame is relevant, it should be limited to particular events and not implicate the totality of a person's character. Maximum opportunity should be left for voluntary reconciliation.

7 ADR may well be cheaper, but cost should not be the dominant criterion, as this may jeopardize the maintenance of quality and standards. Rather, ADR should seek to offer better resolution than the law at no greater cost.

There are many strands and varieties of ADR offering some of the above features – rarely all at once. Different processes need to be adopted in relation to context and type of dispute. ADR is not to be defined – as is the law – by singular procedure but by reference to certain principles that may be put into practice in different ways.

The informing philosophy of ADR is that of co-operative problem-solving. The principles of this are as follows.

1 Parties should collaborate on resolving their conflict. Their conflict is to be seen as a shared problem that both need to resolve, but that they can resolve only with the aid of each other. The procedure should integrate the parties, not divide and oppose them as does the adversarial dynamic of law.

2 The conflict should be left in the hands of the parties (with whatever outside assistance, of say a mediator, they might need). Only the parties can decide whether they are willing to abide by a particular settlement. Only by being involved with the resolution process will they be fully committed to the outcome as their joint property.

3 The parties should be allowed to apply their own agendas – bringing into the discussion whatever observations and feelings they consider relevant, defining the issues that need resolution and deciding on the range or type of outcome that would be acceptable. In contrast, the law sets others' conflicts into its own set agenda, deciding whether or not it fits the wording of the established codes.

4 The process should be forward-looking – problem-solving, rather than assigning blame.

5 Like any problem, such as a crossword or a mathematical conundrum, conflict can be 'solved' only by the use of imaginative ideas, the ability to take a different perspective and the avoidance of 'thinking in a groove' or entrenched positions.

Co-operative problem-solving can be promoted in a number of ways. People can be trained in the necessary attitudes, techniques and skills themselves to negotiate directly with adversaries. Some community-based British projects, for instance, teach conflict resolution in schools so that children learn how to handle disputes more constructively. In other cases, parties may be able to negotiate directly while receiving third-party advice on how they might proceed. Lastly, the third party may be asked to facilitate the process more directly by acting as mediator.

Mindful that legal procedures have certain theoretical benefits, it has to be recognized that ADR may lack some of these. It is important to be able to evaluate these possible drawbacks. The limits of ADR can be summarized as follows.

1 ADR may not be publicly visible. It can give rise, therefore, to problems associated with the abuse of discretion by public officials or to accusations of private pacts that are not in the interest of the commonweal.

2 ADR outcomes are idiosyncratic and case-specific. There is no way of standardizing outcomes or avoiding local variation.

3 Participants in ADR may lack professional (i.e. legal) advice and representation.

4 ADR can be time-consuming because more issues may have to be subsumed: on the other hand, much knowledge can be taken for granted because the parties share it already.

5 ADR does not guarantee that a resolution will ultimately result. A judge, by comparison, will always make a decision eventually.

6 ADR will succeed only in so far as parties really want it to (although involvement can often affect their attitudes in such a way that settlement comes to be seen as better serving their interests than continued resistance).

If both law and ADR have their pros and cons how do we resolve this theoretical conflict? The balance of advantages depends on the type of issue at stake. The law works best in those circumstances for which it was essentially designed:

1 where the motivation of one party is clearly anti-social (criminal law)

2 where the behaviour in question was a single past occurrence without wider ramifications or future implications for the parties involved

3 where serious violations of basic human rights are involved

4 where the issue is at the forefront of changing morality – for instance the need to make public denunciation of domestic violence in order to counteract widespread chauvinist acceptance of male domination.

No single procedure can be perfect for every case, but in the above circumstances a formal system of adjudication is probably better than any alternative. The essential difference between the applicability of the law and ADR is that the former is best suited to those cases where basic rights are involved and the latter where the preservation or improvement of social relations are more prominent. An examination of the average court caseload would, however, almost certainly show that relationships were generally a prevalent issue in the majority. Even in the criminal courts, where many parties are strangers, the relationships between each and the community (in terms of rehabilitation and re-acceptance) are probably more important in their preventive potential than declarations of people's rights not to be victimized. In Marshall (1985) it was calculated on such a basis that over 80 per cent of the caseload of criminal courts in England and Wales would be more suited to an ADR approach than a strictly legal/judicial one.

One should not fall into the trap of assuming opposition between ADR and law, however. The two are, and always have been, interdependent. Often the success of ADR is predicated on the latent threat of legal action or knowledge of what the legal position would be. Good ADR implies good law and vice versa.

There are several unclear areas, too, where it is difficult to decide whether formal adjudication or ADR is the better approach. Complex social problems (not ideally suited to judicial process on the basis of conditions 1 and 2 above) may also involve important human rights or contentious moral issues for which the law is more relevant (conditions 3 and 4). A current example is that of domestic violence, where ADR would be best suited to the resolution of the underlying interpersonal problems (and therefore offer a better service to the individuals involved), but would not meet the need to publicize the existence of violence used by men to control women (which might have some effect in changing cultural mores and furthering general deterrence). The ambivalence this situation creates is well represented in the common phenomenon of wives reporting such crimes and then withdrawing from prosecution. In current social conditions the needs of individuals may have to be sacrificed to the social ones, but this should be a temporary phenomenon dependent on changes in public attitudes. Even so, it should be possible to supplement formal prosecution by other processes aimed at resolving interpersonal relationships.

Many of these kinds of dilemmas can really be resolved only by practical experimentation with procedure and modification of practice guided by growing experience. One area of such experimentation can be seen in the growth of community mediation schemes to deal, by and large, with neighbour disputes, which commonly otherwise reach the courts for a variety of 'offences' such as nuisance, assault, vandalism, harassment, threat or even murder.

PRACTICE

The most influential models for community mediation in modern times originated in the United States in the 1970s. The variety of schemes there have all tended to share certain principles of resolution. Generally one party will refer their problem to the mediation centre (or they will be referred, with their agreement, by some other agency) and the centre will attempt to contact the other party. If the latter is not willing to participate, the centre may give general advice or information to the complainant, but will normally not be able to take the issue any further. If the second party is willing, a time will be fixed for both parties to meet together with a mediator (or two co-mediators, or even a panel of mediators) at a 'neutral' venue. For a couple of hours or so, the parties will discuss the problem under the guidance of the mediators, whose main job is to set up ground rules and control the process, while trying to stimulate a free and fair exchange of views. Although the mediator will guide the parties through a series of stages[1] aimed at eventuating in an agreement, reaching such an outcome remains always under the control of the parties, as does the substance of the settlement. More than one mediation session may need to be scheduled to complete the process, and even after agreement, the centre will generally contact both parties again a few weeks later to check on whether it is working.

Although all schemes employ this core model, there are variations among them, of which one of the major distinctions is whether the bulk of referrals come directly from the community (self-referral or via neighbourhood agencies – e.g. San Francisco Community Boards) or from justice agencies (under a provisional stay of prosecution – e.g. Neighbourhood Justice Centres). The latter referrals tend to be associated with much more obvious pressure to settle. They are much more likely to get to mediation and to come to some agreement. The mediation procedure itself also tends to vary as a consequence either of the type of case or of the larger caseloads of centres taking referrals on diversion from legal process, in that sessions tend to be quicker, with less prior preparation with the parties, and with a more interventionist approach by the mediators. Ray Shonholtz (e.g. 1988) makes the distinction between conciliation (where the process focuses on the relationship and involves maximum party control or participation) and mediation (where the third party is more controlling, the process is more formal, and the focus is on getting to an agreement). The latter process tends to have fewer of the desirable ADR characteristics listed on pp. 66–7, e.g. less forward-looking, less account taken of feelings, less reconciling. Shonholtz's terminology, however, is confusing for people in Britain, where conciliation has traditionally been used to describe a process more akin to his own 'mediation'! I shall therefore use the terms M1 for the more formal version of mediation (his 'mediation') and M2 for the other (his 'conciliation').

The US 'Neighbourhood Justice Centre' model, using M1, has been successfully copied in Australia, initially by the New South Wales Community Justice Centres. In Britain, none of the projects takes referrals from the courts; their process is much more akin to M2.

Present community mediation centres in Britain, of which there are over twenty in operation or about to begin, are all independent community-based organizations existing on the basis of charitable funding and providing a free service for neighbour disputes. Some of the projects, particularly those in Northern Ireland, also aim at reconciliation between local groups (e.g.

Protestants and Catholics, or black and white). Most, however, spend the great majority of their time on interpersonal quarrels (which may, of course, also reflect broader social divisions). All the schemes are the result of local initiatives, many of the more recent ones stimulated and assisted by the national association for promoting mediation in the British Isles (FIRM).[2] The initiative may come from ordinary residents, a church group, a formal voluntary organization like Citizens' Advice Bureau (CAB), or a statutory authority (such as Environmental Health). Once started, however, the mediation centre will be an autonomous community organization able to present itself credibly as having a neutral position *vis-à-vis* different local groups and agencies. Such credibility is enhanced by recruiting lay volunteers to train as mediators, attempting to obtain a representative cross-section of the local population in terms of sex, ethnicity, social class, age and so on.

Each centre takes cases primarily from their local neighbourhood – which may be defined as anything from a single housing estate to a municipal borough, a whole town or even a whole city. Potential clients may be recommended to approach the centre from a wide range of agencies – CAB, local authority departments, community groups, the police, solicitors, etc. Local publicity also leads to direct approaches from people with disputes. Most will be neighbour disputes (boundaries, noise, car parking, nuisance, harassment), but others will involve conflicts between relatives, former friends, landlords and tenants, or with organizations.

Figures for rates of referred cases getting to mediation are much higher in the USA and Australia than they are in Britain. The traditional explanations for this have tended to be in terms either of the project mediators having less confidence in the process themselves, so that they do not 'sell' the idea as forcefully, or of the parties themselves being culturally different, less extrovert and less prepared to face their antagonists in a direct meeting. These explanations may have a little weight, but one important fact points to an alternative reason. This is the fact that when diversion referrals from justice agencies are omitted from the American and Australian statistics, the rate of getting to a meeting of the parties is substantially lower – usually between 10 and 20 per cent, as against the 50–80 per cent typical overall. It seems, therefore, that the main difference is not a matter of culture or experience but of the type of mediation involved – M1(under pressure to settle) or M2 (community-based referrals).

While most of the community-based schemes in each of the countries started with a formal model of mediation (many, for instance, obtained initial training from the Institute for Mediation and Conflict Resolution (IMCR) in New York, which is justice system based and represents the M1 model) and although they still hold to the ideal of a round-the-table meeting, in practice they have had to adapt to a large proportion of referred cases not being amenable to such a formal process. Either one of the parties is unwilling to be involved, so that the project must work with one party only (providing information and advice, educating them in negotiation techniques), or the project is able to communicate with both parties but they are not keen to meet together formally. In the latter case, the mediator's role again becomes one of stimulating the mind-set and skills that will enable the parties to negotiate directly or coping with informal meetings that occur impromptu (e.g. over the garden fence).

The emphasis inevitably in this kind of work is on relationships rather than settlement, because parties, one of which is often under no external pressure to come to any agreement, will be prepared to contemplate this only when they feel convinced that the other party is willing to be reasonable and prepared to make an effort to 'get on'. It follows that the mediation style will not emphasize process, with stages working towards agreement, but empowerment, or inculcating skills and knowledge for the parties themselves to work through conflict more constructively. This is the M2 model, in which mediation is not the process but, if everything eventually turns out well, the end-point – the enshrining of progress in a practical agreement. In many cases even this end-point may be unnecessary, because with improvement in relationships or increase in tolerance the practical issues become unimportant or disappear, being only a symptom of the underlying interpersonal problem. In other cases the presenting problem may actually be insoluble – e.g. partitions between apartments that are not sufficiently sound-proof to allow residents to lead ordinarily noisy lives. The task for the mediation project becomes one of working towards a mutually agreed definition of the problem, some minor behavioural adjustments to lower tension, and leaving it to the parties to co-operate (perhaps with other neighbours) on taking up the issue of adequate sound insulation with the owners of the block.

In Britain, the first community mediation project to be started, Newham Conflict and Change Project, London, in 1984, with strong grassroots origins (see Marshall and Walpole 1985; Miller 1986; Marshall 1988), soon reacted to the discrepancy they encountered between the American M1 model of mediation and their actual practice by formulating a model that stresses reconciliation, and community development through education in conflict-handling skills, along the lines of M2 (see Gosling 1989). They find the greatest similarity in the United States in the San Francisco Community Boards, which also stress these wider roles. Not only is this dialectic between practice and theory affecting what projects are doing in Britain, and the development of grounded definitions of the conflict resolution process, but also theory is developing towards more sophisticated differentiation of processes within ADR (e.g. Matthews 1988), the differences between which may be greater and more important than the original contrast between ADR and law.

NOTES

1 For instance
  1 mediator's opening statement (setting the ground-rules)
  2 uninterrupted time for each person to tell their story
  3 the exchange (questions, responses, debate)
  4 building the agreement (defining issues, brainstorming ideas, refining suggestions)

5 writing and signing the agreement
6 mediator's closing statement (review of accomplishments, compliments to each party, arrangements for follow-up).

(Based on Beer *et al.* 1982)

2 FIRM is a registered charity, a network of individuals, organizations and projects involved in, or interested in promoting, more constructive ways of dealing with conflict – without violence or unseemly aggression, and with minimal bitterness. FIRM provides an advice and information service on the use of mediation, setting up new schemes, procedures, training and so on. It organizes seminars, conferences and training workshops regionally and nationally. It publishes a quarterly magazine *Mediation*, which has an international circulation, and a more frequent newsletter. Both cover events in this country and abroad.

FIRM's basic aim is to promote wider knowledge and understanding of constructive methods of coping with our own conflicts, to further the establishment of practical mediation schemes in a multitude of social contexts, and to formulate and work for high standards of practice. (For more information on FIRM see FIRM 1988; 1989.)

FIRM's address is Forum for Initiatives in Reparation and Mediation, 19 London End, Beaconsfield, Bucks HP9 2HN.

7 Negotiation and mediation

From inelegant haggling[1] to sleeping giant[2]

Karl J. Mackie

We have known for some time several important truths or truisms about the role of negotiating as a technique in dispute resolution. First, it seems by far the most common dispute resolution technique in most, if not all, sectors of social relations[3]. This should be an unsurprising point to make in the context of a functioning social community, particularly one based largely around exchange activities of various kinds. It helps explain the plethora of instructional manuals on the topic, largely geared to the business world. However, most such manuals rightly observe in their introductions that we are in fact negotiating a great deal of the time in human encounters although we may refer to it by other labels – influencing, persuasion, argument, putting our point of view across, sorting things out, being diplomatic, and so on.

> Negotiating is a basic means of getting what you want from others. It is back-and-forth communication designed to reach an agreement when you and the other side have some interests that are shared and others that are opposed.
>
> (Fisher and Ury 1982: xi)

Of more direct interest in the context of this work is the relationship between negotiation and other forms of dispute resolution, particularly legal action. First, we know that many negotiations are conducted in ways which, deliberately or otherwise, do not necessarily take account of the legal rules or pressures available to the parties (Macaulay 1963; H. Beale and Dugdale 1975; Weekes *et al.* 1975). In these cases the parties value the agreement or relationship more highly than they do the values embodied in relevant legal rules. (An institutionalized version of this process occurs in the commercial world where arbitration agreements can seek to exclude or control legal intervention: Ferguson 1980.) Second, even in those disputes where the parties' relationship is such that a failure of negotiation has led them to enter the adversarial system of litigation, *nevertheless* most such cases still end up by settling through negotiation before the forum of adjudication is reached. Studies in the United States and the UK repeatedly demonstrate that *over 90 per cent* of civil actions end up as out-of-court settlements. (Negotiating as a technique in criminal justice is less readily apparent, but may be observed at street-enforcement level, and in the context of plea bargaining practices – see Baldwin and McConville 1977.)

Indeed, the system might collapse if settlement was not the typical outcome:

> In practice it is recognised universally that the functioning of the system of Civil Justice depends on the propensity of most cases to settle. Were it otherwise, the burden on the system, and the resulting delays, would become intolerable. It is perhaps for this reason, and notwithstanding the importance of settlements, that the formal procedures laid down in the Rules of the Supreme Court and the County Court Rules focus hardly at all on specific measures aimed at achieving settlement. Involving itself directly in the settlement process would defeat the need of the system to minimise its workload.
>
> (Lord Chancellor's Department 1987: 135, 51)

While the courts have turned a blind eye to the details of settlement negotiations (R. Williams 1989), it is equally true that academics have turned their attention to negotiation as a process only relatively recently, as part of the new 'legal realist' movement in legal education (Gold *et al.* 1989) of which ADR is an important strand. A review and critique of some of this recent work follows on pp. 76–87.

Nor is negotiation important to lawyers only in the context of litigation. Lawyers spend a fair amount of their time in areas such as contractual and commercial transactions, more typical perhaps of normal commercial negotiations, where they are engaged in a form of 'rule-making' or 'private legislation' creation (see Eisenberg 1976) or in negotiation about rights arising from previous private rule-making – the difference between negotiating to agree a contract and negotiating over the application or interpretation of a contract.[4] A strong element of negotiating activity is likely in other areas of legal practice such as family disputes, planning applications, and so on. (One of the outcomes of limited academic interest is that there does not appear to be much evidence of how much negotiation occurs, how it is distributed between different sectors of legal practice, and what differences occur in approach or techniques in different sectors.)

Between the two 'extremes' of negotiation – negotiation as part of the flow of common social relationships and negotiation in the shadow of the law (the most dramatic form of which is settlement 'on the steps of the court') – lie a range of negotiating situations whose character is therefore still surprisingly unresearched. Part of the difficulty for anyone attempting to survey or analyse this field, is that the characters speak different languages and have different nuances even when they use similar terminology. And as any skilled negotiator knows, the outcome of a negotiation is heavily dependent on the ability to 'read' interests and the signals conveyed by such nuances.

The most common theoretical debate in the field has turned around the rather simplistic conceptualization of negotiators as 'co-operative' or 'competitive'. Again, however, these terms have been used by different authors with different emphases. The problems created by this are outlined in more detail on pp. 81–82. Rather than add another chapter to this confusion, therefore, I have opted for the form of reviewing three recent important texts in this area in the hope that this will assist in the creation of a more precise and shared language system and analysis. The three texts are Gerald Williams's *Legal Negotiation and Settlement* (1983), Hazel Genn's *Hard Bargaining* (1987) and Roger Fisher and William Ury's *Getting to Yes* (1982). The main thrust of my review rests on the claim that we need to distinguish *levels* of analysis in reviewing the role of negotiating techniques – whether in terms of negotiator *style*; *strategies* and *tactics*; the negotiator *process*; or the *social context* of negotiation.

The ADR movement has also led to renewed interest in the range of third-party techniques which can be used directly to assist parties to reach their own agreement, including for example judicial settlement conferences or expert opinion. The domain of '*assisted*' or '*structured*' *negotiation* or settlement is of great interest in ADR because the method retains the value of a *consensual* settlement (therefore offering what is often a more satisfying, sophisticated and stable settlement than a 'win–lose' trial verdict) while smoothing the path towards such settlement by means of third-party intervention. Of the techniques proposed, the main category of third-party intervention is mediation, although such mediation can take a number of forms, for example voluntary or court-ordered. Sometimes the term 'conciliation' is also used. The difference normally drawn between the terms – in one case, the third party seeks to encourage the parties to reach their own agreement (conciliation), in the other case the third party makes positive recommendations for settlement (mediation) – is often a little contrived and difficult to distinguish in practice. An added difficulty is that the terms are in some countries or forums reversed in terms of their meaning. It is a distinction that is worth bearing in mind therefore but not crucial to sustain for the purposes of this chapter. The second section of the chapter therefore considers mediation as a process, and how it relates to negotiation skills and techniques.

LEGAL NEGOTIATION AND SETTLEMENT

The starting-point for an interest in negotiating techniques is not only the frequency with which settlements are reached outside litigation, but also the often unstated assumption that negotiating skills and techniques make a difference to the outcomes (i.e. as opposed to power or informational imbalance *per se* between the parties, including power arising from predictability of legal judgment on the facts.) Professor Gerald Williams's study in the United States began with a simple exercise of giving parties identical information and observing the disparity in outcomes reached. Williams gave twenty pairs of practising attorneys a personal injury case file and asked them to negotiate a settlement. The settlements reached (by fourteen pairs who reached a signed agreement) ranged from $15,000 to $95,000 with the others ranged randomly in between, suggesting support for the case that individual differences in negotiating skills do make a difference to outcomes. (As Williams points out, of course, the question of negotiating *effectiveness* may need to be judged by more criteria than the mere numerical figures achieved, e.g. the costs of the negotiation, the ethics of the negotiators, etc.)

The major part of the study is an attempt to classify attorney orientations to negotiation, and to assess their effectiveness. Williams used a number of research methods, principally asking attorneys to rate other attorneys in their real-life negotiations according to a list of characteristics or personal traits, as well as in terms of their effectiveness. Statistical analysis of the results indicated the presence of two basic types of legal negotiators, the *co-operative* and the *competitive*. The majority of attorneys were rated as 'co-operatives' (65 per cent), with 24 per cent rated as 'competitives'. (The remainder could not be categorized in terms of any particular style.)

Of interest is Williams's finding that either type could be rated as effective. Successful negotiating, in other words, is not associated particularly with one orientation, but can be demonstrated in either mode. However, it appeared to be significantly harder to be an effective competitive as a much smaller proportion of competitives in Williams's sample were rated as effective. (A quarter of competitives compared to over one-half of co-operatives.)

What distinguished the effective negotiator from the ineffective? Amongst the important qualities of the *effective co-operatives* were their desire to get a fair settlement, avoid litigation and at the same time maximize settlement for the client. The *ineffective co-operatives*, on the other hand, lacked perceptiveness and were not convincing, realistic or rational. *Effective competitives* were tough in negotiations, and sought to maximize settlement for the client (and their fee) *and* outdo or outmanoeuvre their opponent. They treated negotiating as a game to win by getting the better of the other side. *Ineffective competitives*, however, were described as irritating, headstrong, unreasonable, arrogant and obstructive, lacking the perceptiveness and realism of the effective competitiveness – 'The problem of the ineffective/competitive is relatively easy to define: he is obnoxious' (G. Williams 1983: 39).

> In contrast to the friendly, trustworthy approach of the co-operative/effectives, effective/competitives are seen as dominating, competitive, forceful, tough, arrogant, and uncooperative. They make high opening demands, they use threats, they are willing to stretch the facts in favour of their clients' positions, they stick to their positions, and they are parsimonious with information about the case. . . . rather than seeking an outcome that is 'fair' to both sides, they want to outdo the other side; to score a clear victory.
>
> (G. Williams 1983: 24)

The key qualities which effective competitives and effective co-operatives *shared* were that both were seen as experienced (hence confident), ethical and trustworthy (despite the competitive's tough gamesmanship), observed professional customs, were in general realistic, rational and analytical, were fully prepared on facts and law, were legally astute, self-controlled, perceptive and skilled at reading their opponent's cues. Also both were rated creative, versatile and adaptable – effective competitives are apparently tough but not obstinate. Linked to these qualities, a significant feature was that *both were good trial lawyers* who could deliver if negotiations failed. However, as one might predict, effective competitives took cases through to trial more often than effective co-operatives (33 per cent, compared to 16 per cent). Less expected was that ineffective competitives *settled more often* than ineffective co-operatives, who had the highest trial rate of all (an extraordinary 64 per cent compared to the 33 per cent of ineffective competitives). Williams speculates that this may relate to competitives resorting more to bluffing and having to cave in before trial (being unprepared), while the ineffective co-operatives probably recognized their own bumbling ineptness in negotiation, and felt that they owed it to their client to take a case to trial (although they were also less effective as trial lawyers).

The study is a major landmark in studies of legal negotiations, both for its strong empirical base, and for its capacity to deal with the complexities of 'effectiveness' in negotiation and the relations between negotiating styles, settlement and litigation. The findings are a caution against the idea that there may be one 'good' style. The two orientations identified have their advantages and disadvantages, particularly if not handled effectively, and even then the effective tough negotiator may have to live with a lower settlement rate. More lawyers, however (if one can generalize from a single US-based study), are co-operative in orientation, and more co-operatives are 'effective' (as rated by their peers). Williams's work is a pointer to some of the qualities which will enhance effectiveness, whichever style might suit one's personal inclinations. It also suggests that a major saving in trial time could be made if one were to improve the negotiating skills of ineffective negotiators.

Williams's work, however, is most clearly centred on *personal qualities* as perceived by other attorneys. It has less to say on the substantive tactics and strategies within a negotiation (although there is a clear assumption that there is a correlation between personal style and preferred tactics, e.g. high opening positions). There is also limited study of the *structural factors* which underlie legal negotiations, which may determine questions of what makes for 'good judgment' when one talks of 'legal astuteness' – questions of the interplay between legal rules, social power in its various forms, and solicitor–client relationships. Aspects of these dimensions are developed in an important British study of negotiations in the context of litigation.

HARD BARGAINING

Hazel Genn's (1987) study (based mainly on interviews and a survey question-naire) provides an insight into settlement practice in the context of personal injury actions in the English legal system. Negotiation as a dispute resolution technique in this context can be measured against the fact that some 99 per cent of all personal injury claims are settled out of court (Harris *et al.* 1984). Settlement, however, is perhaps more common than any real negotiation – 63 per cent of those claiming for personal injury damages accept the first offer made to them by the other side. Settlement or negotiation, the significance of this area of civil dispute is that it is highly geared to the substantive and procedural legal rules and anticipated outcomes of negligence actions – negotiation operating in the 'shadow of the law' with its 'bargaining endowment' of procedural and substantive rules as bargaining counters to exploit or resist (Mnookin and Kornhauser 1979). 'It is the coercive, menacing character of the court process that is valued – it is the anvil against which the hammer of negotiations strikes; it is the second hand clapping' (Galanter 1984). 'Notwithstanding the pervasiveness of settlements, the touchstone of the parties is ultimately the hypothesized trial' (Genn 1987: 59).

The integral nature of the process echoes Williams's finding that effective negotiators are also good trial lawyers. Part of Genn's argument is a criticism of those solicitors who fail to take into account just how closely negotiations and litigation are integrated in this context (what Galanter has described as 'litigotiation'):

> negotiation and litigation are not alternatives, but part and parcel of the same process . . . those solicitors who regard litigation as a last resort may deprive their clients of the opportunity to settle claims advantageously.
>
> (Genn 1987: 50)

> The opportunities [to strengthen the plaintiff's bargaining position] are often forgone as a result of lack of case preparation, lack of time, and an orientation to claims management which stresses negotiation and settlement as an *alternative* to litigation, rather than as the *product* of preparing for litigation.
>
> (Genn 1987: 123)

At the same time, however (and perhaps somewhat at odds with the above position), Genn's study is a forceful critique of the view that settlements are achieved solely or predominantly on the basis of some anticipated or hypothesized trial outcome (and the 'economic' bargaining models associated with such views of dispute resolution). A number of factors conspire to inhibit and defeat plaintiffs and their advisers. The conceptual elasticity of the principles of the tort of negligence, so valuable to judicial flexibility, leads to an accumulation of uncertainties faced by a client – was there a duty of care? Was that duty breached by the defendant? Did the breach cause the injury? Was there contributory negligence? How much is the injury worth? Will I recover all my legal costs? This is compounded by the early reluctance of many plaintiffs to take legal action, thus delaying and lessening the likelihood of collection of reliable evidence, and by their subsequent worries over the costs and stress of such action. The uncertainty of the likely award level on the quantum of the claim for particular injuries and circumstances, and the rule of loser paying the other side's costs (unlike the US system), further intensify the pressure for settlement. On the other hand, insurance companies gain commercially from delaying payment, their employees and their advisers are thoroughly familiar with the procedural and legal aspects of personal injury actions (and they tend to retain more control over the case *vis-à-vis* their legal advisers than do plaintiffs), and they have the resources to withstand pressures for unsatisfactory settlements: '[T]he parties in personal injury litigation are, in most respects, utterly unequal, and this inequality affects every stage in the progress and settlement of claims' (Genn 1987: 12).

The system is a thorough example of Marc Galanter's often-quoted distinction between 'one-shotters' and 'repeat-players' in the courts. To add to the plaintiffs' difficulties, ordinary members of the public have (had) little assistance in identifying personal injury specialists amongst solicitors and are less likely to be able to evaluate the service they do receive than perhaps in other areas of law (Rosenthal 1974; Genn 1987: 39–40). As a result many end up with solicitors who, rather than offset the plaintiff's 'one-shotter' characteristics, are themselves 'one-shotters' (or more accurately 'occasional-shotters'). Those practitioners' unfamiliarity and unease with the system, together with problems of recovering their costs for much of the work involved, contribute to tendencies to support early settlement and to avoidance of litigation procedures or adequate evidence collection.

Genn's study is an important reminder that negotiations exist against a background of, and are permeated by, influences generated by *social structures* and *system structures* of various kinds. These structures embody and create both distinctive power allocations and inequitable effort–reward outcomes in the settlement process, despite the proximity of the process to adjudication. (Indeed the system often appears to inhibit negotiation completely – the earlier Oxford national survey of personal injuries found that 63 per cent of those making a claim accepted the first offer made by the insurance company: Harris *et al.* 1984.)

No negotiation professional has ever been unaware, of course, of the importance of power. In the real world no negotiation is ever an encounter of equals. Frequently, however, negotiating skills trainers emphasize the degree to which 'power' is manipulable – by a party altering strategy, developing alternatives to a negotiated agreement, readjusting his or her position in relation to certain power elements, or succeeding in readjusting *perceptions* of the power distribution in the other party's eyes. Genn points to the more successful efforts of the trade union solicitors in personal injury actions who are more specialist, more geared to litigation, and immune from private plaintiff costs worries, while 'much of the uncertainty, delay, and costs pressures which plague plaintiffs and weaken their resolve is deliberately manufactured or exacerbated by defendants' manipulation of legal and procedural rules' (Genn 1987: 167).

To the extent that a real and serious imbalance exists between parties, clearly there is room to question either the social validity of negotiation as a dispute resolution technique or to seek to offset some of the elements of inequity in the system. Thus Genn concludes her study by calling for improvement in the access of plaintiffs to specialized personal injury practitioners (a development now taking place); for speeding up the processing of personal injury claims, including an incentive for defendants to settle claims quickly; and 'for providing a means by which out of court settlements become more visible or subject to scrutiny' (Genn 1987: 169).

The study is less helpful on the detail of negotiating as a technique, partly because Genn concludes that the structural and situational factors are more significant although she admits the study does not lend itself to a measure of effectiveness (1987: 46). Nor was she allowed access to face-to-face negotiations for research observation other than in the case of one claims inspector. The major distinction discussed draws on Gerald Williams's classification of 'co-operative' and 'competitive' bargainers. Genn's research suggests that a common response by plaintiff solicitors to the problems of uncertainty, costs and their lack of expertise was to adopt a co-operative or 'reasonable' approach. Another group, found to be more common amongst specialist solicitors, were more combative or confrontational in approach. The distinction between the two is drawn in terms of readiness to start and press forward with proceedings and with the various stages of litigation. The co-operative solicitors were more ready to postpone the issue of proceedings and to stress the need to avoid antagonizing the other side.

> The first approach emphasizes the need for reasonable negotiation, and the desire to avoid antagonizing the defendant. The second . . . disparages the first approach and is consistent with the view that a relentless and apparently uncompromising push towards trial is the best way to stimulate early realistic offers from insurance companies.
>
> (Genn 1987: 40)

Although she could not measure the effectiveness of the different negotiating philosophies, she clearly sympathizes with those solicitors who emphasized that, given the structural factors involved, the confrontational approach is likely to be more effective and give more leverage to the plaintiff. Many solicitors are in fact reluctant to issue proceedings until the possibilities for settlement are exhausted. The Oxford survey of personal injury settlements found that proceedings were issued in only 40 per cent of settled claims.

Unfortunately the lack of observational evidence in the study precludes it from enriching our knowledge of negotiating on three important counts. First, we cannot be certain as to how closely differences of *philosophy* over negotiation are actually translated into *action*, given the limitations of the research methods adopted. Second, the study cannot develop the model posited by Williams that *both* competitive and co-operative orientations can be effective or ineffective, depending on how they are played. Williams's work would in fact lead one to presume that both effective co-operatives and effective competitives would be better at predicting outcomes and more capable of going to trial and winning *if necessary* to pursue a successful outcome. Third, the two authors use the terms with different emphases. Genn focuses on the question of the degree of persistence with litigation, while Williams articulates a number of dimensions more closely related to 'gamesmanship' (and indeed found that 'ineffective co-operatives' had the highest trial rate).

In other words the differences between the two orientations are perhaps more subtle and more skill-based in negotiating theory than Genn allows for. Indeed a number of the quotes from solicitors cited by Genn on the qualities needed for success refer to the importance of 'negotiating skills' even in the context of a confrontational orientation (1987: 54–8) or reflect a sense of Williams's dif-ferentiation between style and effectiveness, for example – 'Thorough in taking instructions. On the ball. *On the offensive (though not offensive!)*. Keeping up the

pressure' (Genn 1987: 56, Case 193, my italics). Equally, and somewhat surprisingly, as many as 43 per cent of personal injury *specialists* agreed with a
questionnaire statement that 'The best approach to personal injury work is to be
reasonable towards everybody' (1987: 44, 59 per cent of non-specialists agreed
with this statement).

Genn does not go on to differentiate the styles of insurance company claims
inspectors, but tends to categorize them in general terms as relatively combative
in approach (in the sense of working to purely commercial cost-saving objectives
for their employer) while giving an impression on the surface of exhibiting a
co-operative approach. Again however the quotations cited cover a spectrum of
negotiating orientation, including competitive:

> When the law's against you, bang away at the facts. When the facts are against
> you, bang away at the law. And when they're both against you, bang away at
> the table.
>
> (Genn 1987: 59)

The quotations cited in relation to her finding that claims inspectors tend to react
with some vehemence to 'aggressive' plaintiff solicitor approaches, are more
indicative of frustration with rigidity (Willaims's ineffective competitive) than
with the factor of litigation persistence which could in theory be combined with
a 'co-operative' approach (see Genn 1987: 47–8, refusal to negotiate or give
details of special damages). Also at odds with a finding of a competitive approach
are inspectors' claims that they are largely not responsible for delays in
processing claims (a claim of which Genn is sceptical, 1987: 100). Nor do they
often use the potentially major weapon of payments into court, which could
increase substantially the worries of a plaintiff on costs, the major worry for most
plaintiffs (1987: 111–13).

Genn's real interests, however, lie in the structural factors underlying this
negotiating arena rather than in the techniques of negotiation as such. Thus her
work starts from, and concentrates on, a different *level* of analysis than that taken
by many other writers on legal negotiations. She offers in this sense an excellent
critique of any school of legal negotiations which places lawyers' actions outside
of their social context. But the work is also essentially a critique of the litigation
system, given the nexus between the nature of personal injury litigation and
negotiation and settlement practices. The inefficiency and injustice of the litigation system has the consequences of a more hazardous negotiating environment, likely to deter the weaker party. The exercise of effective negotiating skills
has always been influenced profoundly by the alternatives available.

GETTING TO YES

Roger Fisher and William Ury's book (1982) has become something of a best-
seller, and has been incorporated widely into legal skills teaching programmes.
Like the other two texts already described, their starting-point in the consideration of negotiating techniques deals with the difference between co-operative and

competitive bargaining, although they use the terminology of 'soft' and 'hard' negotiating orientations.

> The soft negotiator wants to avoid personal conflict and so makes concessions readily in order to reach agreement. He wants an amicable resolution: yet he often ends up exploited and feeling bitter. The hard negotiator sees any situation as a contest of wills in which the side that takes the more extreme positions and holds out longer fares better. He wants to win; yet he often ends up producing an equally hard response which exhausts him and his resources and harms his relationship with the other side. Other standard negotiating strategies fall between hard and soft, but each involves an attempted trade-off between getting what you want and getting along with people.
>
> (Fisher and Ury 1982: xii)

However, *Getting to Yes* concentrates on a 'third way' in a negotiator's approach to getting disputes resolved. That third way is described as *principled* negotiating, which they argue is a more effective way of approaching all disputes. (The approach is also sometimes described as 'problem-solving' negotiation.) Its essence is to be 'hard on the merits, soft on the people' without tricks or posturing. 'Unlike almost all other strategies, if the other side learns this one, it does not become more difficult to use; it becomes easier' (Fisher and Ury 1982: xiii).

Principled negotiating allows the parties to avoid the dangers inherent in the hard and soft approaches to negotiating. Fisher and Ury describe the last two merely as two extreme variants of 'positional bargaining'. The parties decide on which outcomes they will claim and then haggle over these outcomes, gradually shifting positions until sufficient compromise is made to allow agreement. The problem with this method is that the parties may become more and more locked into their claims as they argue, failing to explore other options or the real interests which underpin their desire for an agreement. The soft negotiator approaches this process in a more trusting manner, seeking to appear reasonable and to induce reasonableness by making offers and giving concessions. The hard negotiator sticks rigidly to his or her stated desired outcomes, not moving at all or moving very little and only in response to concessions. In neither case is a wise settlement necessarily reached, nor is the negotiation efficient (particularly hard–hard modes), and in the case of hard–hard or hard–soft bargaining unlikely to maintain or improve the parties' relationship.[5] Multi-party negotiating problems are heightened by a positional bargaining mode.

Principled bargaining on the other hand is said to bring different rules into the game, providing a different process of negotiating. The four key elements of this approach are outlined below.

1 *Separate the people from the problem*

In most negotiations, parties have interests in both the substance of the problem and the relationship around it (or to follow it). The human side of negotiating, in other words, is ever-present. Since problems involve emotional issues for the parties, positional bargaining can intensify such aspects and divert the parties from focusing on the problem before them. Principled bargaining suggests that one approaches negotiation with a readiness to deal separately with the merits of the issues and the question of the human element. Difficult areas of emotion can be dealt with directly rather than through the problem in the form of resisting or granting concessions, for example by making explicit the need to separate personality issues from the problem; by using psychological techniques of good communication and empathy; respecting their right to see things differently, etc. (In fact, Fisher and Ury recommend giving as much weight to developing a good relationship as to attacking the problem, 1982: 55–7; 'Be hard on the problem, soft on the people'.)

2 *Focus on interests, not positions*
Underlying interests can be obscured when a party seeks to concentrate on a position, for example price of the goods for delivery. Principled negotiating builds on the tactic of asking 'Why?' and 'Why not?' to elicit the real interests and needs of the parties which may be quite different from the stated position in positional bargaining (e.g. the negotiating business's cash-flow requirements may be more important to them in a particular negotiation than the price obtainable). Interests are usually more multiple than positions, and can be compatible or shared as well as conflicting. Interests admit of more options for settlement. Working on a compromise based on positional bargaining may leave the parties' real interests unmet. Part of the skill of negotiating is to make the other party see the legitimacy of your interests, while on your part acknowledging the legitimacy of theirs.

3 *Generate a variety of possibilities before deciding what to do* (i.e. *invent options for mutual gain*)
Principled bargaining suggests a need to take time out to brainstorm possible options for settlement, to avoid premature judgment or thinking blinkered by attention only to one's own aims. Digging in to positions narrows one's vision to the detriment often of both sides. The skills in this area are the ability to think creatively about both sides' interests, and to make a decision easy for the other side in the negotiation.

4 *Insist on objective criteria*
Where interests remain opposed, a fairer method of resolution is to seek to agree some objective standard rather than rely on the more inefficient and potentially damaging approach of insisting on one's own position or suggested standard. The authors suggest the remedy is to use various objective criteria – trade standards, outside experts, custom, law, as guides and means to disarm a position-inclined opponent. 'Objective' criteria in Fisher and Ury's terminology include giving each other equal opportunities through chance, e.g. drawing lots to decide. Objective criteria can be used in relation either to the substance of the negotiation (what is the market value?), or to the procedure (as in the classic case of children arguing over who gets what slice of cake – the solution is one cuts, the other chooses), or in choosing between objective standards (what would an outsider say was the

fairest?). The use of an outsider gives an opportunity to manage negotiation in many different forms – as a neutral adviser or expert, as a conciliator or mediator, as an arbitrator, as a monitor of an agreement.

In answer to some of the common criticisms of the problem-solving approach, Fisher and Ury have three basic recommendations. First, *'What if their negotiator is more powerful?'* They suggest working on the development from an early stage of your Best Alternative To a Negotiated Agreement (BATNA). Working out what you will do if no agreement is reached not only gives you a better sense of what agreement can offer as against alternatives, but also is likely to increase your confidence in negotiating, and provides a more effective and flexible trip wire than the standard 'bottom line' strategy.

Second, *'What if they won't play?'* If another side refuses to engage in discussion of interests, options and criteria but persists in positional bargaining, three strategies are recommended. First, persist with principled negotiating as they may be won over. Second, use a technique called 'negotiating jujitsu'. Do not push back when they attack, but sidestep the attack and deflect it against the problem – tackle their statements of position by searching for the interests behind them and treating the statement as one option rather than coming back with one's own position; invite criticisms and advice and build on their criticisms by exploring what they see wrong with your view, or by seeking their advice on what to do – rather than resisting it; recast attacks on you as attacks on the problem rather than become defensive. Two key tools to use in this are questions and silence. 'Statements generate resistance; questions generate answers' (Fisher and Ury 1982: 117). Silence generates discomfort and readiness to answer or follow up.

Third, *try a third party trained in the techniques of principled negotiating.* Fisher and Ury especially recommend the 'one-text' mediation procedure. A mediator can more easily separate the people from the problem and talk of interests and options. The mediator develops a list of all the expressed interests and criteria to satisfy the parties, shows each the list and asks them to criticize it, and to suggest further improvements. The mediator then comes up with a rough draft to meet the points set out. After further comments on the draft, the mediator comes back with another draft and seeks their views, and so on until he or she can say this is the best text of agreement I can produce, based on precedents, standards, etc. Now there is only one decision to make – yes or no and one can make yes conditional on the other side saying yes.

'What if they use dirty tricks?' There are various manipulative tactics that negotiators can use, which one can classify as illegitimate on the grounds that they fail a reciprocity test – they are designed for use by one side only. 'Tricky bargaining tactics are in effect one-sided proposals about negotiating *procedure*, about the negotiating game that the parties are going to play' (Fisher and Ury 1982: 135). They are countered in three stages – recognizing them (which reduces their intended effect), making them explicit (which may cause the other party to cease employing them) and if necessary using principled negotiating tactics to negotiate over procedure just as one would over substantive issues

emphasizing the intention to negotiate on the merits, looking for objective criteria such as fairness to determine tactics, and in the last resort opting for one's BATNA but leaving them the opportunity to offer a better deal.

Fisher and Ury provide a persuasive argument of the advantages of the principled method against the extremes of hard and soft bargaining. Their work has promoted a healthy sense of equitable and assertive approaches to bargaining, and laid new emphasis on creativity and inventiveness in bargaining. Life has perhaps more shades of grey, however, including in relation to negotiating on the merits, than they are prepared to acknowledge. One can compare the account of negotiating in the work of two other Harvard scholars, Lax and Sebenius (1986). They point to the fact that every negotiation contains a contradiction – that parties can 'create value' by a recognition of what they have to gain jointly from agreement, while also most negotiating situations allow a party to 'claim value' against the other party. This is the '*negotiator's dilemma*' – even if successful in 'expanding the pie' for mutual benefit, there remains the question of how to cut it to divide the spoils. Such a process is likely to be sustained in a number of guises – via Williams's effective competitives and co-operatives, Genn's tough litigation specialists or pretend-co-operative insurance claims assessors.

One can consider the issues more specifically in the world of personal injury claims already described. How does one apply a principled negotiating approach to such situations (where Genn implies the need for 'hard' bargaining)? Clearly the situation contains the shared interests outlined by Fisher and Ury – the parties both want to save costs and avoid 'unnecessary' legal action. The solution would appear simple in the Fisher and Ury chart, yet as Genn has outlined the situation is full of pressures which imbalance the situation and make the *evaluation and articulation of interests* problematic. And the common abstract interest of saving costs has a quite different specific valuation for the insurance company, a trade union, and an individual plaintiff. To the extent that there are therefore no effective objective criteria, the parties are thrown back on their desire to achieve a settlement which satisfies them rather than which meets common interests. To the extent that the parties remain apart on what will satisfy them, they are left with the requirement to 'develop your BATNA'. But the BATNA in this case is normally and most obviously the litigation option, i.e. prepare thoroughly for trial. And if this approach or an existing negotiating orientation suggests a return to interest bargaining, how again are interests to be evaluated? The 'objective criteria' in the case are most fully represented by a trial hearing, yet it is precisely the uncertainties of trial which make claims negotiating so inefficient and inelegant in form, and which interact with other factors to weight the dice against the plaintiff achieving a wise outcome.

Finally, we can turn to the 'create options for mutual gain' route. But these take us back to the starting-point of saving unnecessary costs and conflict. In personal injury claims at least, the real alternative option would appear to be through a 'systems' route, namely to devise a 'simpler' test of objective criteria. One route to this would be reform of the civil justice system of personal injury litigation to allow for a more simple calculation of liability and likely damages (assuming a 'fault' system remains). Another would be to look to the varied options for alternative dispute resolution outlined in this handbook which could speed up the process of dispute – agreements to adopt third-party assistance by way of arbitration, expert opinion, inquisitorial procedures, rapid processing procedures for particular types of claim, a mini-trial. *In each case, however, one does not avoid the 'claiming value' process, whether such claims be made through the medium of negotiation or the medium of persuasion and advocacy.*[6]

What one can hope for, however, is that such techniques will provide simpler and more effective mechanisms to allow parties to look to improve the efficiency or effectiveness of their negotiating process, or which provide a degree of independence to assist with avoidance of destructive positional confrontations or confrontations guided merely by the distant and uncertain prospect of adjudication. Let us therefore consider one version of how this might be achieved by the example of a mainstream ADR technique which develops negotiation beyond 'inelegant haggling'.

MEDIATION

Mediation, intervention by a third party to assist disputing parties to reach a settlement, has been described as the 'sleeping giant' in ADR (Henry and Lieberman 1985). Although only one of a number of variants on third-party intervention, mediation is the ADR technique *par excellence*, at the core of attempts to awaken interest in methods other than adjudication. Through a process of mediation parties can be helped to shape their own agreements and sustain a relationship (or, as in agreements over division of marital property, separate a relationship) without the polarization or loss of control which adversarial adjudication may induce. One of the strengths of mediation is its flexibility and applicability to a range of types of disputes, from the 'good offices' intervention by a neutral country in international disputes to the formalized mediation option available in industrial relations disputes. It has a considerable history (Moore 1986: 19–24; Stein 1984) and has flourished again with ADR developments since the 1960s, particularly in the neighbourhood justice (Tomasic and Feeley 1982) and family sectors (Parkinson 1983), and more recently in planning and environment, and business disputes (Henry and Lieberman 1985; Coulson 1987).

The most obvious alternative to mediation (other than adjudication) would be one of the many forms of 'fact-finding' intervention, for example expert opinion, ombudsmen, summary jury (mock) trial. Such techniques, however, arguably represent *hybrids* of mediation-adjudication, methods of influencing negotiators or disputing parties to move their positions by appeals to external standards ('objective criteria') a technique which represents *one* of the tools of skilled mediation or one of the functions of adjudication. Techniques concerned with grievance-handling or 'maladministration' such as ombudsmen can also be drawn conceptually as hybrid forms of mediation-adjudication, but linked less to formal negotiation than to means of assisting with the enforcement of 'service standards' in an organization or sector. The rules of the particular process will determine how closely it approximates to mediation or adjudication in form. They are all versions of 'assisted negotiation' or 'structured settlement' techniques.

There is sometimes an overlap or confusion with the term *conciliation* – usually defined as a less proactive form of intervention where the third party aids the disputants to reach their own agreement rather than seeking, as in mediation, to suggest actively the terms of a possible agreement. (However, in some countries and contexts, e.g. international law, this distinction between the terms may be reversed.) For the purposes of this chapter, the subtlety of this distinction need not be explored other than as a way of illustrating that the process of mediation may take a number of forms.[7] Attempts to refine the rules of mediation in this way are, however, probably less than helpful unless one is dealing with disputants who are very sophisticated in their use of third parties, or where there are community interests in setting standards for intervention. One of the strengths of mediation is its flexibility, the opportunity it gives to the mediator to play a number of roles to achieve a successful outcome, so that one can sometimes 'be tempted to say that it is all process and no structure' compared to the rule-guided process of legal decision-making (Fuller 1971: 305).

When is a mediator useful?

Mediation can be an important technique to consider as an option whenever there are parties in dispute who *might* be able to reach an effective agreement with outside intervention, where otherwise they could not reach such an agreement or could only reach it at the expense of unnecessary cost to themselves or to others. Situations where this might happen are as follows.

1 The parties have stopped (or never started) communicating to each other.
2 The parties cannot communicate skilfully (e.g. inexperienced negotiators) or easily (e.g. a lack of trust of each other; commitment to stated public positions).
3 The parties cannot themselves find a solution to meet their respective positions in the negotiation or dispute.
4 The parties feel they may lose face by changing their previous demands.
5 The parties do not know how to negotiate or the structures to allow a form of negotiation are not in place.
6 An impasse or delay in negotiations will have damaging effects on the parties, on their relations with other parties, or on the community.
7 Mediation will be more effective/efficient even if the parties could negotiate with some likelihood of success.
8 A private, (usually) voluntary and non-binding procedure is preferable to a procedure which does not have all or some of these characteristics.
9 There is an imbalance of power between the parties which can be effectively counterbalanced by use of an intermediary.

10 There is a need to influence the settlement terms in accordance with some external standards and the parties need to be made more aware of these than they might otherwise be.

(In the last two cases the role of mediation is of course shading into the sphere of adjudication. One of the debates about mediation is the extent to which mediators should be guided by concerns other than what will obtain agreement between the parties[8] – see Goldberg *et al.* 1985: 108–23).

How does mediation work?

The short answer given by many practitioners in mediation would be: by whatever it is necessary to do (within the bounds of ethical conduct) to bring the parties to an agreement. Mediators perform a variety of functions in the process of mediation, but the central element is to take the parties out of an impasse or deadlock in their discussions or relationship and forward into constructive agreement. It is perhaps best conceived of as an extension of negotiation, and many of its skills and requirements can be compared, for example, to principled negotiating as outlined by Fisher and Ury (see my analysis, pp. 82–86, and Goldberg *et al.* 1985: 93–4). The mediator helps the parties separate the people from the problem, can explore and explain interests more neutrally, can invent options for mutual gain, can more ably represent and raise objective criteria (see the suggested 'one-text' procedure outlined in Fisher and Ury 1982: 118–22, a process of shuttling between the parties with a single document which attempts to reflect their joint interests, until refined to acceptability – see also Gibson's techniques in Chapter 11).

The mediator can achieve this in a number of forms of intervention – by chairing a joint meeting of the parties, by sitting in on negotiations as a neutral facilitator (as in the mini-trial described by Applebey in Chapter 3), by caucusing with the parties and shuttling back-and-forwards between them, or a combination of methods. Raiffa (1982) suggests mediators can assist negotiators in the following respects.

1 *By establishing a constructive ambience for negotiation,* e.g. acting as neutral chairman or smoothing out interpersonal conflicts, translating demands into acceptable language.
2 *By collecting and judiciously communicating selected confidential material.* The negotiator's dilemma referred to earlier, of not only needing agreement but also wanting the best terms for such agreement, can be utilized by the mediator who can determine from discussion with each party whether there is a zone of agreement.
3 *By helping parties to clarify their values and to derive responsible claims,* e.g. by stressing to each party the implications of failure to agree.
4 *By deflating unreasonable claims and loosening commitments,* e.g. by minimizing excessive posturing put on for the benefit of the other party, by preparing parties for the need to concede.

5 *By seeking joint gains*, e.g. by being more creative in solution-finding or encouraging the parties to find new options.
6 *By keeping negotiations going*, e.g. by holding the channels of communication open until there is a more auspicious external environment or more appropriate stage for agreement.
7 *By articulating the rationale for agreement*, e.g. by promoting the reasons for acceptance.

(Compare Moore's suggested list of mediator roles (1986: 18) – opener of communication channels; legitimizer of parties' involvement; process facilitator; trainer; resource expander; problem explorer; agent of reality; scapegoat; leader.)
    The skills of the mediator can therefore take many forms:

1 developing relationships
2 problem-solving (for/with the parties)
3 communication (finding the right words to persuade or justify acceptance; showing a readiness to listen; articulating a party's viewpoint)
4 meetings management (as chairman or intervenor or facilitator)
5 persuasion and education (convincing parties of the need to move positions, values, relationships, perceptions, assumptions, judgments)
6 'public' relations (accepting the role of scapegoat for the parties to sell the agreement to their constituents or others).

Stulberg lists the following personal qualities for inclusion: 'capable of appreciating the dynamics of the environment in which the dispute is occurring, intelligent, effective listener, articulate, patient, non-judgmental, flexible, forceful and persuasive, imaginative, resourceful, a person of professional standing or reputation, reliable, capable of gaining access to necessary resources, non-defensive, person of integrity, humble, objective, and neutral with regard to the outcome' (Goldberg *et al.* 1985: 96). (Question for readers: what are the qualities of an adjudicator and where do they overlap or differ from Stulberg's list and the other lists above?)

Advantages of mediation over adjudication

The advantages of mediation over adjudication follow those articulated in general for the ADR movement – the participation of the parties in deciding processes and outcomes, the creativity and flexibility available in deciding terms of agreement, the mutually satisfactory outcomes available – as set against the inherently win–lose, adversarial, rule-based judgments of adjudicative processes. Many further dimensions can be explored in articulating this comparison. For example Tomasic (1982), in a helpful review of the assumptions behind support for mediation in the context of the American Neighbourhood Justice Centres movement, lists *eighteen* assumptions or hypotheses that can be traced in the statements of supporters of mediation. Although he sees only some of these as primarily linked to a comparison with adjudication, in fact one can say that virtually all are.

1 mediation deals with the *roots of problems*
2 mediation improves disputants' *communicative capacities* (educational role)
3 mediators act as '*friends*', not 'strangers', to the parties
4 mediation is *non-coercive*
5 mediation is *voluntaristic* (allows parties to solve problems themselves)
6 mediation centres provide *easier access to the legal system*
7 *disputants prefer it* to courts
8 there is such a thing as a *sense of 'community'* influencing the dynamics of disputes, and . . .
9 unlike judges, mediators '*represent' the community* and share its values (this statement may be less applicable to areas outside neighbourhood justice, but might hold true of some, e.g. some business or labour relations contexts)
10 mediation *reduces tension* in the community
11 mediators are *not professionalized* and do not require long periods of training
12 mediation centres are *non-bureaucratic*, i.e. flexible and responsive
13 mediation is able to deal with a *wide range of disputes*
14 mediation is *speedier*
15 mediation is *less costly*
16 mediation is *fairer*
17 mediation *can reduce court congestion and delay*
18 mediation is *more effective in preventing recidivism*, i.e. produces more stable outcomes.

Virtually all of these can find some parallel in arguments for mediation in other spheres than Neighbourhood Justice Centres. But are these benefits automatic? Given my earlier analysis of the complexity of judging 'effectiveness' in direct negotiations, it should come as no surprise that the added complication of third-party intervention does not in turn provide any automatic or magic solutions. Tomasic's review of the evidence and literature on these assumptions in the context of Neighbourhood Justice Centres suggests that all of them are, in varying degrees, problematic; based often on simplistic views of mediation, or on a 'leap of faith' justified by oversimplified comparisons with other societies. The Neighbourhood Justice Centres movement in particular owes much to the comparisons with dispute resolution studies of other social systems, but such comparisons ignored the fact that mediation in these societies was linked closely to community norms and social life, and drew its strength from a background of other forms of social coercion and control (Merry 1982). They also took too little account of the fact of the disintegration of such norms in modern technological, mass societies.

Tomasic therefore concludes that the necessary reforms to achieve some of the claimed benefits of mediation need to be located in reform of the *legal system* (as the developed dispute resolution form of modern society), the preferred approach amongst European reformers in the field of community justice. Mediation, he suggests, needs to be considered in the light of a more sophisticated, and restrained, analysis and in more specific, localized social contexts – note, for example, its common use in the labour–employer community, or in the context of marital breakdown. However, this analysis begs the question; an equally critical approach can be taken to *assumptions underlying adjudication* as a vehicle for dispute resolution; the debate about the appropriateness of dispute resolution mechanisms cannot be based on whether the assumptions underlying them may be problematic but *when is a particular procedure more appropriate and more effective, and under what conditions*? What is the *optimal* approach to such conflicts? How do we choose on practical grounds, balancing the normal variables of efficacy and efficiency? *If* mediation does have apparent advantages over adjudication, what other factors need to be incorporated for such benefits to be realized? How does one determine when adjudication is more appropriate? Usually adjudication is favoured where (1) there is a need to apply external rules to the parties' case in order to comply with community or other external rule standards or justice; and/or (2) there is an imbalance of power between the parties such that third-party assistance in any other form will be overborne by the effects of the power imbalance. Some of the major critiques of mediation and ADR have focused on the failure of these to take sufficient account of such factors (Fiss 1984) although such criticisms often compare ADR with an idealized rather than actual portrayal of adjudication.

Mediation in practice

Given that mediation has theoretical advantages over adjudication, we are left with a number of practical questions to guide evaluation of the development of mediation. First, in what areas is mediation (or a form of mediation) not used at present where there would be considerable advantages in adopting it? Second, in what areas is mediation used, but its use could be made more widespread or more effective, or more efficient? Third, is there a role for court-annexed mediation? Linked to this last question is a subsidiary point applicable to all contexts where mediation can be used – when, if ever, should mediation be compulsory rather than voluntary?

Other chapters in this handbook consider contexts where mediation is currently used: see, for example, Applebey (Chapter 3), Walker (Chapter 10), ACAS (Chapter 8), Gibson (Chapter 11), Palmer (Chapter 15), Newton (Chapter 16) and Marshall (Chapter 6). Mediation in more than an *ad-hoc* sense is being used in some form in family and labour relations disputes, and to a degree in community disputes. Given its claimed advantages, however, mediation is not as widely used as one might expect. In particular, there is a surprising absence of use in the fields of commercial disputes (where arbitration remains the preferred option, failing negotiation or avoidance mechanisms – but see Mackie (1989: ch. 11) on Australia, and Henry and Lieberman (1985) on the United States), and in court procedures (where arbitration again dominates, in small claims, or pre-trial hearings with an emphasis on technical matters of litigation procedure rather than on bringing the parties closer). Similar findings of under-utilization in the USA have led to suggestions that mediation is a 'solution in search of a problem'.

However, there are clear signs that the growth of the ADR movement in the USA may be stimulating more widespread use of mediation. In the commercial arena, the 'flagship' of ADR, the mini-trial (Mackie 1989: ch. 11; Henry and Lieberman 1985; Applebey in this volume, pp. 34–5) has provided a focus for interest and activity in ADR which has moved further towards mediation and private commercial mediation services, and there is growing use of and judicial interest in court-annexed schemes through, for example, experiments with the Multi-Door Courthouse concept (Goldberg *et al.* 1985). The extent to which momentum can be sustained and the assessment of the value of these developments are still open questions.

However, a key factor in the developments is a re-education of the legal profession and legal educators. Undoubtedly a major stumbling block in the limited progress of mediation as a dispute resolution technique, has been the 'standard philosophical map' of lawyers (Riskin 1982). This framework has limited the ability of the profession to work with techniques other than the standard win–lose, adversarial, rule-based (and hence 'backward'-looking), and 'quantum'-based (complex client concerns and interests become translated into the simple currency of estimates of 'damages') systems of litigation, even where, as in personal injury work, the system is so obviously creaking at the seams. Since lawyers play a central role as third parties in disputes, their standards for processing disputes are important determinants of the models in use. Clients, for whom disputing is not a regular occurrence, are hardly going to be the source of new dispute resolution methods. The problem of a need for a more effective mechanism may be there but the solution resisted because of lawyers' dominance in dispute resolution products, working on a design base of traditional and limited character. As we have seen, this restricted horizon has been true even of the study of negotiation despite its common use. There is likely to be even greater effort necessary to raise appreciation of the opportunities for mediation initiatives.

Riskin sees the answer in reforming legal education so that lawyers' horizons may be widened. In addition, however, one can speculate that mediation is unlikely to be capable of major advance until appropriate institutional forms are found for channelling disputes before neutrals. For a system of third-party intervention to work, there must be a pool of third parties who can develop the trust of the disputants, and mechanisms (e.g. contract clauses) for calling on them without loss of face or of positional strength. A lawyer acting for a client is not lightly going to admit the value of a third party in negotiating an agreement with the other side's lawyer. Thus there are structural obstacles too to the development of mediation. However, its advantages and value are clear, and subject now to a considerable amount of experimentation in the United States (and see Palmer in Chapter 15 on China). Given a degree of leadership, vision and action, therefore, it is not inconceivable that the 'sleeping giant' may be wakened to fill the yawning gap between inelegant haggling and win–lose adjudication.

NOTES

1 This phrase is used by Genn (1987) in a somewhat dismissive judgment of lawyer–insurance company face-to-face negotiations in personal injury claims.
2 Henry and Lieberman (1985) describe mediation as a 'sleeping giant' in terms of its potential for contribution to dispute resolution developments.
3 How it compares with dispute *avoidance* strategies might be a more difficult calculation.
4 One can find a formal distinction in American labour relations practices between 'interest' (new) and 'rights' (existing agreement) arbitration along the same lines. In this author's experience, one of the most common forms of negotiation in commercial deals is the 'renegotiation' where one party finds itself unable to fulfil part of a contract. Again, there is little or no research on this specific area and how it relates to litigation.
5 These three factors – Is the negotiation efficient? Does it improve or at least not damage the relationship? Does it produce a wise agreement if agreement is possible? – are cited by the authors as fair criteria for judging a negotiating method (Fisher and Ury 1982: 4). 'A wise agreement can be defined as one which meets the legitimate interests of each side to the extent possible, resolves conflicting interests fairly, is durable, and takes community interests into account.'
6 The field of disaster litigation, for example, has begun to create an impetus for new forms of agreement to resolve the complexities of individual claims and costs factors. Similarly widespread industrial diseases such as deafness or asbestosis or pneumoconiosis also lend themselves to approaches which avoid individual litigation. Henry and Lieberman (1985) point also to US insurers and injury victims finding common interest in settlements which take the form of small, periodical payments over the large capital sum route. But this route, like the others, also has potential for 'claiming value' – How are the amounts to be calculated and agreed? For what period? With what protection for price/earnings-inflation factors? What are the implications of recovery? All of these bring the parties back to some process of haggling or use of outside intervention to assist or provide a decision.
7 This distinction is, unusually, operationalized in terms of the ACAS UK industrial relations role, conciliators being drawn from the ranks of ACAS staff, mediators being drawn from a panel of independents – see Chapter 8 by ACAS.
8 Such concerns may include, for example, how far a mediator should exert pressure on parties to reach a settlement favoured by the mediator; or how far third-party interests sould be taken into account in the search for an acceptable agreement, for example, if there might be consequent damage to a thirty party or the public interest if agreement takes a particular form.

Part II
Disputes in social context

Introduction

Practitioners in industrial relations dispute resolution tend to react with bemusement when they come across the 'new wave' enthusiasm for ADR. Processes of conciliation and arbitration, often in statutory form, can be traced back to the early years of the century or even earlier in many countries' systems of industrial relations (e.g. Mackie 1987 on Australia). There is a significant degree of institutionalization therefore present in this field, reflected in this handbook in terms of the only institutional contribution amongst the chapters. ACAS is a statutory body with a number of significant strands of responsibility and a shopping bag of dispute resolution methods: individual conciliation (in the context of legal claims), conciliation, mediation and arbitration in collective disputes, an advisory role, and (a recent acquisition) a quality of working life research unit. The ACAS chapter explains the background, constitution, methods and outcomes of this third-party role.

The historical significance of ADR in this field, alongside the successful institutionalization of a third-party role, raises wider issues of some importance to the development and theory of ADR – why has ADR been so prominent in this field in comparison with other fields? Why has conciliation developed as the preferred vehicle of intervention while in commercial disputes arbitration has emerged as the preferred model? The answers to such questions not only are of intrinsic historic interest, but also would help clarify the inter-relationship of methods and social context in promoting ADR as a wider social mechanism.

John Birds and Cosmo Graham (Chapter 9) chart the development of dispute resolution in one of the increasingly important industrial sectors: financial services. The advance of dispute resolution in this field has been through 'hybrid' mechanisms, hybrid in the sense of inserting public law grievance mechanisms in the context of private industry. Thus the favoured method adopted in insurance, banking, building societies and recently the unit trust industry and pension schemes has been the model of the ombudsman, although the authors point to important differences between the various structures and methods evolved. However, the common theme is a preference for a more activist, inquisitorial or mediatory role than that of adjudication. The limited publicity for the Personal Insurance Arbitration Service, however, makes difficult a ready comparison between dispute resolution approaches. The evolution of hybrid forms is also apparent in their account of the 'self-regulatory' complaints systems set up under the umbrella of the Securities and Investment Board as an outcome of the Financial Services Act 1986. An issue common to both developments is the question of the extent to which such complaints systems serve the purpose of remedying individual grievances, or the purpose of quality, or systems, control. The authors find a common tendency to favour the former rather than intrude too far into industrial mechanisms and standards. In this sector, there is an intriguing array of processes, despite the rationale of a common approach intended by the Act. While the authors suggest that future rationalization is called for, perhaps this diversity may also admit of useful research comparisons at a later date once the systems have bedded down.

Janet Walker (Chapter 10), one of the project leaders in the Lord Chancellor's Department's sponsored research into family conciliation, sets the results of their findings within the context of an analysis of dispute resolution, emphasizing, however, the unique characteristics and institutional relationships within the family dispute area, for example, the dominant ideology of conciliation within this field, the blurring of the boundaries between adjudication and conciliation options, the primacy of third-party (child) considerations in many cases. This dispute sector has perhaps witnessed the most explicit recent debate in the UK on the benefits of ADR. Perhaps sadly for the idealists, but less surprisingly for practitioners, the Newcastle research suggested that it may not be possible to meet at one and the same time objectives of cost-saving and quality, and that quality of dispute resolution may itself raise in turn a number of complex ideological and practical issues, on questions such as who owns the process of conciliation and how it links to other values and actors in family dispute resolution.

Dr Tony Gibson (Chapter 11) provides a stimulating and creative essay on the theme of 'common ground', both literal and metaphorical. His practical techniques in the field of community disputes and planning developments have won wide acclaim. Their value, to use Fisher and Ury language from negotiating theory, lies in the devising of a technique which can take people out of 'positions' and into an open exploration of 'interests'. Also, that this can be achieved by, and is rooted in, the simple use of working models which separate individuals from an idea, and which allow those who are less articulate to have an equal 'say' to the experts or the verbally fluent who would otherwise tend to dominate. Gibson's approach is also significant in that, unlike many of the other contexts described in this book, it applies to *communities* rather than to disputes between individuals or a few parties.

Finally Richard Thomas (Chapter 12) considers strategies for consumer protection and consumer complaints mechanisms, ranging from the small claims system, through the arguments for reform from its failure to provide 'access to justice' to the main alternative schemes since developed, arbitration and ombudsmen. Statistics on the coverage of the various agencies for consumer complaints are set out. He concludes with an assessment of the strengths and weaknesses of 'private' dispute resolution, and develops a set of criteria by which to judge the effectiveness of a dispute resolution system. It is an appropriate point to remind us of the interplay between context and procedure in dispute resolution.

8 Industrial relations disputes: the ACAS role

Advisory, Conciliation and Arbitration Service

HISTORY

A voluntary conciliation and arbitration service was first established by government in Britain in 1896. During the Second World War this service was augmented by the provision of free advice on industrial relations and personnel matters to employers and unions. In 1960 these functions became known as the Industrial Relations Service, renamed the Conciliation and Arbitration Service (CAS) in 1972 when the duty to conciliate in complaints of unfair dismissal under the jurisdiction of industrial tribunals was added. Although since their inception collective conciliation, arbitration and the advisory services had been provided from a government department, a number of commentators in the late 1960s and early 1970s came to a view that this was making it increasingly difficult for such services to operate effectively. In response to these criticisms in September 1974 the then Secretary of State for Employment established the CAS on an administrative basis as a separate service at arm's length from government. Renamed the Advisory, Conciliation, and Arbitration Service, ACAS was established as a statutory body on 1 January 1976 by Section 1 of the Employment Protection Act 1975.

Terms of reference

It is charged with the general duty of the improvement of industrial relations with particular reference to collective bargaining. ACAS was not given, nor does it seek, any statutory power to compel either the use of its service or adherence to agreements reached by the parties under its auspices; organizations and individuals using its services do so voluntarily. The corner-stone of the new service was its independence from government. The Act lays down that 'the Service shall not be subject to directions of any kind from any Minister of the Crown as to the manner in which it is to exercise any of its functions under any enactment'.

Funding

The Service continues to be funded by government through a grant-in-aid from the Department of Employment and is required to present accounts annually in such form as the Secretary of State may direct.

Constitution

ACAS was set up as an independent body in September 1974 and given statutory form by the Employment Protection Act 1975. Under that Act, the Service was charged with the general duty of improving industrial relations. It provides conciliation and arranges for arbitration in industrial disputes and advises both sides of industry on industrial relations matters.

ACAS is directed by a council appointed by the Secretary of State for Employment. Previously in addition to the full-time chairman, the council has consisted of nine part-time members, of whom three have been appointed to represent employers and three to represent workers, after consultation with appropriate organizations. The other three are independent. The Secretary of State has now decided to broaden the council by appointing two additional members to represent employers and workers respectively.

Staffing

Although independent, ACAS is a Crown body and its staff have the status of civil servants. In 1988 it employed 618 staff, the majority of whom work from the seven regional offices in England and from the national offices for Scotland and Wales. The Head Office in London, amongst its other duties, provides collective conciliation services in national or other major industrial disputes.

Function

The Service is empowered to undertake a range of activities. It may inquire into any industrial relations matter, provide advice on industrial relations and the development of effective personnel policies, and issue codes of practice containing practical guidance on the improvement of industrial relations. It may offer or respond to requests for help in resolving industrial disputes through collective conciliation, or through providing facilities for arbitration, mediation or committees of investigation. It can also offer conciliation in disputes over statutory employment rights between individual employees and their employers.

Advisory services

The independence and impartiality of the Service makes it acceptable to both sides of industry. It can encourage through its advisory work a joint approach to resolving a wide range of employment problems which may avoid or mitigate industrial conflict. There were 320,000 requests for information on employment matters, 7,925 advisory meetings and 1,002 longer-term in-depth involvements with companies and unions in 1988. Close links are maintained with the conciliation arms of the Service. Work on longer-term problems can be undertaken by the Advisory Service either immediately a dispute is settled, or as a means of resolving an underlying cause of dispute.

In-depth exercises may consider more than one dispute, discipline procedures occurring most frequently (38.3 per cent) followed by grievance procedures (31.7 per cent), rights of individual employees (25.6 per cent) and payment systems (21.7 per cent).

Work Research Unit

The Work Research Unit (WRU), which became part of ACAS in 1985, focuses on the human aspect of work. It gives advice on employee involvement, job design, stress, work patterns, payment systems to match new work structures, management of change and other topics affecting the quality of working life. The WRU completed seventeen in-depth assignments and made 297 advisory visits in 1988. The most common subjects arising in in-depth WRU exercises are employee involvement (19.6 per cent), management of change (19.5 per cent), and organizational strategy (13.9 per cent).

DISPUTE RESOLUTION

Collective and individual

Collective and individual dispute resolution are two distinct areas of ACAS activity with separate histories. Collective dispute resolution in its modern form traces its history to the Conciliation Act 1896 and the Industrial Courts Act 1919. Three main methods are used: collective conciliation, arbitration and mediation. Individual dispute resolution traces its history to the Industrial Relations Act 1971 where individuals were given the right to complain to an industrial tribunal if they felt that they had been unfairly dismissed.

Collective conciliation

Collective conciliation has been a widely accepted feature of British industrial relations for almost a century. The 1896 and 1919 Acts made provision for the appropriate minister to take steps to bring about a settlement of trade disputes through conciliation or other means. Current legislative provision is made by Section 2 of the Employment Act 1975, which empowers ACAS to offer assistance where a trade dispute 'exists or is apprehended', to offer its assistance by way of conciliation or other means with a view to bringing about a settlement.

Matters which can be the subject of a trade dispute are those covered by the very broad definitions contained in Section 29(1) of the Trade Union and Labour Relations Act 1974.

Definitions

ACAS follows the International Labour Organization in defining conciliation as

> the practice by which the services of a neutral third party are used in a dispute as a means of helping the disputing parties to reduce the extent of their differences and to arrive at an amicable settlement or agreed solution. It is a process of orderly or rational discussion under the guidance of the conciliator.
> (International Labour Office 1983)

In practical terms ACAS views conciliation as assisted collective bargaining. Its essential characteristics are that its use is voluntary and that agreements reached in conciliation are the responsibility of the disputing parties. Consistent with this view of conciliation, ACAS seeks to uphold the authority of the negotiating procedures established by employers and trade unions for the avoidance and settlement of disputes. Collective conciliation is normally appropriate only when the parties have exhausted their own procedures without resolving the dispute or when they agree that other overriding considerations apply.

Sources of conciliation requests

Requests for conciliation come from either trade unions or employers. The number of joint requests has risen steadily over the years from 24 per cent at the time ACAS was established to over 50 per cent at the present time (see Table 8.1).

Table 8.1 Completed conciliation cases analysed by source of request*

| | 1988 | | 1987 | |
	No	%	No	%
Union	335	31.6	336	31.9
Employer	109	10.3	127	11.1
Joint	575	54.3	608	53.0
ACAS	40	3.8	46	4.0
Total	1,059	100	1,147	100

Note: * The figures exclude conciliation on individual complaints.

Subjects of conciliation

As can be seen from Table 8.2, rather more than half of all collective disputes referred to ACAS are about pay and terms of conditions, with trade union recognition and dismissal and discipline accounting for the bulk of the remainder. These proportions have stayed broadly constant over the years.

Table 8.2 Completed conciliation cases analysed by cause of dispute*

	1988		1987	
	No	%	No	%
Pay and terms and conditions of employment	594	56.0	652	56.9
Recognition	165	15.6	140	12.2
Changes in working practices	42	4.0	43	3.8
Other trade union matters	37	3.5	60	5.2
Redundancy	35	3.3	52	4.5
Dismissal and discipline	148	14.0	147	12.8
Others	38	3.6	53	4.6
Total	1,059	100	1,147	100

Note: * The figures exclude conciliation on individual complaints.

Numbers

Although the numbers of collective conciliation cases has declined from 1976 onwards (Figure 8.1), since the establishment of ACAS as an independent agency it continues at a much higher level than was previously handled by a direct departmental conciliation service. Moreover since its inception, ACAS has consistently been involved in more disputes than there were stoppages. This supports the view that ACAS has established its acceptability on both sides of industry and is therefore often in a position to secure a settlement before industrial action has begun. In about 90 per cent of cases the request for conciliation comes before industrial action.

Running alongside

Collective conciliators spend a proportion of their time in maintaining private and informal contact with parties in dispute without becoming involved in any formal public sense in conciliation. A record of these activities has been kept only since July 1982. In 1988 there were 524 such informal and private contacts. In this way the Service maintains contact with the parties in virtually all lengthy stoppages and in other important disputes and can be of some assistance as a

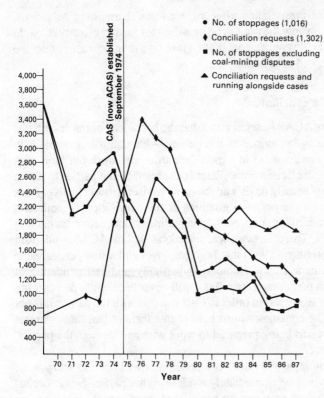

Figure 8.1 Work stoppages and conciliation requests 1970–87

private channel of communication or a sounding board for ideas to assist the parties in the resolution of their differences.

Recruitment and training of conciliators

Collective conciliators are most commonly recruited from experienced ACAS staff. The usual pattern is for the new conciliator to have some years' experience on advisory work and before that experience in doing individual conciliation although the latter is not invariably the case. The foundation of the training is a basic collective conciliation course designed and run by ACAS itself. The aim of the course is to give participants a basic understanding of the conciliation process and to enable them to have some low-risk practice so that they start to develop judgement and a sense of timing and become more self confident about handling the conciliation process. The course involves a mixture of case studies and role-playing on CCTV. There are twelve participants on each course so that during the role-playing exercise each participant can in turn have experience as a union representative, as a management representative and as a conciliator. The role-playing is analysed by the tutors so that the participants see how their behaviour and style of presentation affects the parties' bargaining behaviour, suggestions are made on how they might be modified for greater effectiveness. In the twelve months after the course, conciliators take on a range of cases under the tutelage of an experienced conciliator.

Personal qualities of a conciliator

In training conciliators ACAS bears in mind that the behaviour of the conciliator can affect the bargaining behaviour of the parties. Although the conciliator in theory establishes an environment in which the parties can work out their own settlement, in practice an effective conciliator is expected by the parties to play a more active role – most usually devil's advocate or adviser. How effectively this can be done depends on the personal qualities of the conciliator. Conciliators must be patient, quick thinking, understand the realities of collective bargaining and be verbally acute. There is evidence, anecdotal within ACAS, and from independent research (Hiltrop 1987) that both employer and union parties value above all in a conciliator trustworthiness, impartiality and independence; it should be clear to each party that a conciliator will never knowingly do anything to harm their interests. However, in order to establish this with the parties it is not sufficient to say so. The conciliator must behave in a manner that demonstrates these qualities. This means being prepared to work with and through the parties, which will take patience.

In order not to harm a party's interests a conciliator will need to know what they are and this may not be immediately evident. What parties bring to conciliation are positions which may or may not uniquely represent the interests that they hope to enhance or defend. The conciliator must establish quickly the interests that lie behind the positions; sometimes a party will have a hidden agenda which they will seek to conceal from the other side and are reluctant to reveal to the conciliator unless he or she has their complete confidence, sometimes a party will become so emotionally committed to a position it will lose sight in changing circumstances of the interests that that position was meant to serve. To recover the underlying interest, including where appropriate its historic origins, requires the conciliator to think quickly and to be aware of the nature and realities of collective bargaining.

To maintain independence and impartiality, and above all to obtain the trust of the parties, while still able to play an effective devil's advocate or adviser, requires presentational skills of the highest order and this takes verbal acuteness.

All of these qualities must be retained under pressure. It follows that collective conciliation is not an activity that either appeals to everyone or for which everyone, however effective they may be in other areas, is suited.

Mechanics of conciliation

Conciliation is voluntary, non-directive and confidential: no one has to go; having gone, no one has to stay. ACAS will not divulge, confirm or deny any part of the proceedings beyond saying that discussions are taking place. There are no formalities in setting up a meeting. A telephone call to the nearest ACAS office will put the contending parties in touch with the conciliator. Meetings are set up usually within days and occasionally within hours.

While involved in the conciliation, parties may find themselves at various times in three types of meetings – joint, separate and caucus (sometimes known as private) meetings. The choice of the appropriate type of meeting at the right time is as much art as science and it is possible only to sketch out some of the considerations a conciliator would have in mind.

Joint meeting

In a joint meeting the parties come together in the same room under the chairmanship of the conciliator. A conciliator has to bear in mind that the number of cases where both parties accept enthusiastically a need for conciliation is relatively low. The fact that the matter has come to conciliation at all may mean that the normal bargaining relationship between the parties is no longer functioning as well as it might. Although the conciliation process itself may help to restore that relationship this will usually take some time. A conciliator who holds a joint meeting too early runs the risk that the parties will continue to rehearse their differences in a highly partisan way, which far from progressing the issue can make matters worse. Joint meetings can, however, be useful in ratifying final agreements or conversely in clarifying ambiguity at the point of breakdown.

Separate meeting

In separate meetings the parties are in different rooms within the same building. All contact is through the conciliator. This is where most of the business gets done: through detailed questioning the positions of the parties can be explored and possible solutions examined. The reaction of the other party can be discovered through the conciliator without commitment or loss of face. The parties may if they wish make any point in separate session in confidence to the conciliator. However, the conciliator will need to be given sufficient latitude to explain each side's position to the other if progress is to be made.

Caucus meeting

In a 'caucus' meeting the lead negotiators from both sides are invited into a private session with the conciliator. These are used when the parties are close to agreement but a precise form of words has to be drafted to reflect a verbal consensus. At the other end of the scale they are often used close to the point of breakdown where the conciliator will want to confirm that the negotiators are fully aware that breakdown is imminent and of the consequences that might follow. A third use of the caucus is where discussions become technical and are best left to experts on both sides with an ACAS conciliator in the chair.

Success rates

There are two separate measures by which ACAS judges the success of its collective conciliation efforts. The first consists of regular monitoring of the outcomes of conciliation references.

Table 8.3 Completed conciliation cases*

	1988	1987
Conciliation resulting in a settlement or progress towards a settlement	876	955
Conciliation unsuccessful	183	192
Total	1,059	1,147

Note: * The figures exclude conciliation on individual complaints.

As can be seen from Table 8.3 the success rate stands at just over 80 per cent. Although successful cases are analysed into a number of categories for ACAS internal purposes, in broad terms success is defined as either a settlement under ACAS auspices or significant progress such that any industrial action is lifted, previously deadlock negotiations can be resumed or the gap is sufficiently narrowed to enable the parties to proceed to arbitration.

The other less quantitative measure of the success of the conciliation process is the attitude of those employers and trade unions who have gone through it. In a 1985 independent study 91 per cent of management respondents and 95 per cent of trade union respondents indicated that they would use ACAS conciliation again for a similar dispute (Hiltrop 1987).

Arbitration

Section 3(1) of the Employment Protection Act 1975 empowers the Advisory, Conciliation and Arbitration Service to refer a dispute to arbitration, at the request of one or more of the parties and with the consent of all the parties to the dispute. Before referring a matter to arbitration, however, Section 3(2) requires the Service first of all to consider the likelihood of it being settled by conciliation, and second, where agreed procedures exist, requires those procedures to have been used and to have failed to result in a settlement. These provisions underline the view held by ACAS and by employers and trade unions that arbitration is the valuable instrument of last resort. When other methods have failed arbitration is seen as a civilized and peaceful method of resolving differences between the two sides of industry.

Definitions

The essential difference between conciliation and arbitration is that conciliation is a process in which an independent third party helps the parties to a dispute to reach a settlement. The conciliator has no mandate to impose a settlement on the parties, but acts as a catalyst in the attempt to reach agreement. Arbitration, on the other hand, can perhaps best be described as the determination or settlement of an issue, on which the parties have failed to agree, by an independent third party. In seeking arbitration the parties have given authority to the third party to impose a settlement. The arbitrator, or occasionally the Board of Arbitration, appointed by ACAS *determines* the issue.

Most arbitrations are undertaken by a single arbitrator who decides the case. There are circumstances, however, usually involving major national issues, for example over pay for a significant country-wide group, where the parties request or it might be more appropriate to appoint a Board of Arbitration. A Board would normally consist of an independent chairman appointed by ACAS and two side members representing both sides of industry though not directly connected with either party to the dispute. A breakdown of the different types of arbitration and mediation arranged by ACAS, and the range of issues considered, is given in Table 8.4 (see pp. 111–12 on mediation).

Table 8.4 Issues and cases referred to arbitration and mediation

	1988		1987	
Issues	*No*	*%*	*No*	*%*
Annual pay	35	25	25	17
Other pay and conditions of employment	24	18	32	22
Dismissal and discipline	54	39	61	42
Others	25	18	27	19
Total	138	100	145	100
Cases	*1988*		*1987*	
Single arbitrator	123		122	
Board of arbitration	4		10	
Single mediator	8		12	
Board of mediation	1		—	
Central Arbitration Committee	2		1	
Total	138		145	

Although an ACAS-appointed arbitrator imposes a settlement of the issue on the parties they are under no legal obligation to honour the award. Section 3(5) of the 1975 Act specifically excludes ACAS arbitration from the Arbitration Act

1950. However, ACAS will not agree to refer a matter to arbitration unless both sides have committed themselves in advance to accept and implement the arbitrator's award. ACAS arbitration awards are therefore binding in honour and have invariably been implemented.

Arbitrators

The success of arbitration depends on the goodwill and common sense of the participants and the skills and wisdom of the arbitrator. What makes a good arbitrator? Who are these impartial, independent third parties? What qualifications do they have? What is their background? Arbitrators are not members of the ACAS staff. They are appointed by ACAS to a panel or list from which they are assigned to cases by the ACAS secretariat. In the late 1970s when arbitrations peaked at just over 400 in one year to the late 1980s level of around 150 a year, the number of arbitrators on the ACAS list fell from about 100 to just over 60 in 1989. The total number of cases referred to arbitration and mediation since 1970 is illustrated in Figure 8.2.

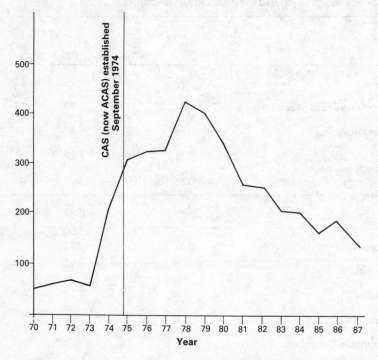

Figure 8.2 References to arbitration and mediation 1970–87

Potential arbitrators come to the notice of ACAS in one of three main ways. Some are recommended by existing arbitrators, some make personal application and other suitably qualified individuals are recommended by ACAS regional directors who have come into contact with them in the course of their work. ACAS is looking for individuals who

1 have a high standing in a relevant discipline such as labour law, labour economics or industrial relations
2 are thoroughly knowledgeable about the practicalities of industrial relations
3 are, and will be seen to be, completely impartial and independent
4 have sufficient presence, self-assurance and other social skills to be able to conduct a hearing with authority, gain the confidence of the parties, and leave each side feeling that it has had the opportunity to set out its case
5 are able to grasp the essential points of often complex and difficult problems quickly, balance conflicting submissions, and weigh the more salient considerations carefully in reaching an award.

Some first-hand experience of industry or commerce is also desirable but acceptability to both parties as independent and impartial persons is in practice a more important consideration in assigning cases. Academics who are qualified in industrial relations, labour law or a similar discipline and have the other qualities mentioned earlier are usually acceptable to both parties and can meet the demands of the job. Many also have some industrial or commercial experience either before going into the academic field or through research or consultancy work.

Mediation

ACAS is empowered under Section 2 of the Employment Protection Act 1975 to appoint a mediator or Board of Mediation to make recommendations to facilitate a settlement. Mediation can be defined as a method of settling differences whereby an independent person makes formal recommendations on how the dispute could be resolved. Mediation is a flexible process which is often more suitable for issues which need a fair degree of positive intervention. It is not generally regarded as an appropriate medium for the resolution of straightforward distributive conflicts, for example an annual pay claim where it might just be another stage in the negotiating process. On the other hand it can be more suitable than arbitration when issues are particularly complex and interdependent, for example a major reorganization of jobs or grades or work patterns. Boards of Mediation are very rare.

Unlike arbitrators, mediators do not impose solutions – they offer a solution by making recommendations which may be accepted by the parties or at least are likely to form the basis for further negotiations. In the way that the mediator makes formal recommendations, he or she goes further than the conciliator, who moves between the parties in an attempt to assist them to reach their own settlement, without making formal recommendations in any sense.

Mediation differs from arbitration in another important respect in that the parties are not given a binding *decision*. The mediator will offer recommendations, which the parties are expected to treat seriously and to act upon and which are intended to assist the resolution of the problem. The precise manner in which the dispute is eventually concluded remains, however, firmly in the hands of the parties and they therefore retain control of the outcome. Throughout recent history the number of cases referred for mediation has run at no more than 10 per cent of the cases referred for arbitration.

A further recent development in this area of industrial relations is the use of what can perhaps best be described as mediation/arbitration which is particularly well suited to complex, multifaceted disputes in which the parties request arbitration-type assistance but want to retain the discretion to be able to resolve voluntarily some or all of the constituent parts of a wider problem. The independent person appointed may hold several meetings to clarify the parties' views on all the problem areas and arbitrate on the residual items of difference on which agreement cannot be reached with the help of the mediator.

The process of arbitration

Although forms of compulsory arbitration were introduced in Britain during both World Wars, the voluntary principle prevails and there are now no statutory requirements for any industrial relations disputes to be referred for arbitration. Normally the decision to provide for arbitration will have been taken by employers and unions before any dispute has arisen when they are negotiating their procedure agreement. Rather more agreements providing for arbitration exist in the public sector than the private sector. In some areas of the public sector, agreements provide that arbitration may be invoked at the instigation of one party although in practice most arbitrations arise from a joint request.

The parties have the choice of a single arbitrator a Board of Arbitration or the Central Arbitration Committee (see p. 114). By far the most popular method is the use of a single arbitrator. Single arbitration tends to be less complicated and can usually be arranged within a couple of weeks; the award is usually available within a further week or so. Where a speedy decision is paramount, parties will almost invariably opt for a hearing by an arbitrator sitting on his or her own. Where the issue is confined to one plant or company, a single arbitrator is also usually preferred.

Boards are committees of three people. Usually the independent chairman has the power of umpire in the absence of unanimity and it can be argued that it would have been speedier and simpler to refer the issue to a single arbitrator in the first place. Boards tend to be used in important issues, for example a national industry-wide pay claim or cases of unusual complexity. One advantage of boards is that the burden of responsibility in reaching a decision is spread.

The hearing

Prior to the hearing the terms of reference will have been agreed, possibly with the help of a conciliator. The parties will have been asked to submit written statements of case to the arbitrator and to exchange them. The arbitrator is thus armed with background information and details of the claim and offer. At the hearing, often on ACAS premises, the parties will be invited to develop their cases orally and to raise points on the other side's submission through the chair. After the parties have completed their submissions, the arbitrator puts appropriate questions to each side in turn. The extent of the arbitrator's questioning will depend on the complexity of the case and the extent to which the parties themselves have gone into detail of their case. After confirming that the parties are satisfied that they have said all they want to say the arbitrator will close the hearing. Occasionally there is an additional stage – the arbitrator may decide that a visit to the workplace would be useful to enable him or her to understand more fully the nature of the problem, perhaps a particular work process or working conditions. Such site visits may take place before or after the hearing itself.

The award

The arbitrator rarely if ever announces the decision immediately. Normally time is needed to digest the facts and arguments, to weigh the evidence and prepare the report. The report will usually contain a little of the background to the dispute, a summary of the main submissions by both sides, the considerations taken into account and the award itself. Whether awards should be reasoned has provoked much debate over the years. Eminent industrial relations practitioners past and present have taken the view that arbitrators should give reasons on the grounds that otherwise parties have no knowledge of the criteria used by the arbitrator in considering the merits of the case and reaching a conclusion. Others, equally eminent, have said that to give reasons for the award will, in general, run the risk of the reasons themselves being open to challenge and may result in prolonging the dispute and possibly exacerbate the differences by transferring the area of controversy from the main issue to the reasons given for the award. ACAS encourages its panel of arbitrators to set down in their reports the considerations they have taken into account in reaching a decision – no more.

Splitting the difference

A criticism often levelled is that arbitrators simply 'split the difference'. However, they rarely do so in a fashion which is equidistant from the position of the two parties. Arbitrators do not hesitate to decide wholly in favour of one party or the other if, for example, a 'claim' is unfavourable or an 'offer' derisory. However, in seeking an acceptable solution to the problem, and an award which both parties can live with, it is inevitable that an award is a compromise. It is precisely for the reason that the parties have themselves been unable to compromise that they have handed the problem to a third party. An arbitrator has to find a solution which reflects the parties' arguments, the pressures upon them and, very often, the thoughts of the constituents they represent. This is very much a balancing exercise for which the expression 'splitting the difference' is a total misrepresentation of the practice.

Other ACAS activities in arbitration

Apart from disputes which are referred to arbitration by ACAS under Section 3 of the Employment Protection Act 1975, the Service is involved in the activities of some standing arbitration bodies in the public sector. It is responsible for providing the secretariat to the Police Arbitration Tribunal and the Railway Staff National Tribunal.

Committees of inquiry

ACAS is also empowered to institute, at its own initiative, an inquiry into any aspect of industrial relations. This has traditionally taken the form of the appointment of an *ad-hoc* committee, of three independent people, which has been asked to investigate the industrial relations within a particular industry or the background and conduct of a specific dispute between an employer and a trade union. The proceedings are concluded by the publication of a report containing the committee's findings and its advice to the parties. ACAS has arranged only a few formal inquiries since its inception and its present policy is to tailor the shape and form of this type of assistance to the precise needs of the parties. An example of this was the appointment in 1986 of an independent panel to guide and advise the parties involved in the schoolteachers' dispute.

The Central Arbitration Committee

The Central Arbitration Committee (CAC) was established on 1 February 1976 as the successor to the Industrial Arbitration Board and, before that, the Industrial Court. It is an independent statutory body with a permanent chairman, Professor Sir John Wood, and staff. Over the years it has dealt with those matters within industrial relations which were more appropriate to resolution by arbitration than by a judicial process, such as disputes arising under the Fair Wages Resolution 1946, now rescinded. The present workload comprises the determination of disclosure of information claims under Sections 19–21 of the Employment Protection Act 1975, and voluntary arbitrations, the latter often arising from procedure agreements which provide for a reference to the CAC as the final stage.

ALTERNATIVE DISPUTE RESOLUTION – INDIVIDUAL CONCILIATION

ACAS handles some 44,000 disputes annually between individuals and employers in matters where statutory employment rights exist. In these the individual has a statutory right to present a claim to an industrial tribunal where he/she considers that he/she has cause to complain about the infringement of rights, including among others:

1 unfair dismissal
2 equal pay

3 sex discrimination
4 racial discrimination
5 written statement of reasons for dismissal
6 unlawful deductions from wages.

A good proportion of these disputes is resolved before reaching a tribunal hearing by conciliation provided for in statute and carried out by conciliation officers (COTs) of the Advisory, Conciliation and Arbitration Service. The parties in these disputes often see conciliation as a preferable alternative to the tribunal hearing as a means of resolving their differences.

History and legislative basis

The idea of using conciliation as a means of settling individual rights issues originated from the Donovan Commission Report of 1968. The report visualized that the chairmen of industrial tribunals would hold informal meetings with the parties to attempt to resolve the issue by amicable settlement, failing which, the matter would be resolved by a tribunal hearing. However, the Industrial Relations Act 1971, which introduced the first unfair dismissal provisions, did not implement the report's proposals. Instead it made provision for the appointment of conciliation officers of the Department of Employment who would be independent of the tribunal system. In 1974 the role of conciliation was transferred to ACAS.

Success rates in individual conciliation

The first complete year in which ACAS provided conciliation in tribunal claims of unfair dismissal was 1975: 29,100 new cases were received in that year. Of those completed in the year 31 per cent were settled in conciliation, 26 per cent were withdrawn for various reasons, leaving 41 per cent to be determined by an industrial tribunal.

During 1976, ACAS acquired the statutory duty to provide conciliation in a further ten individual rights jurisdictions under provisions of the Equal Pay Act 1970, the Sex Discrimination Act 1975, the Employment Act 1975 and the Race Relations Act 1976.

By the end of 1977, these new rights, together with an increasing number of unfair dismissal cases, resulted in ACAS receiving 43,899 cases (an increase of 79 per cent over 1975). In that year 33 per cent of cases were settled, 26 per cent were withdrawn and 41 per cent proceeded to a tribunal hearing. Not all conciliation is carried out in cases where a formal complaint has been made to an industrial tribunal (IT1 cases). ACAS also has a duty to conciliate in circumstances where no formal complaint has been made but could be (non-IT1 cases).

Since 1977 the numbers of cases received from both these sources has, apart from the odd fluctuations, remained reasonably stable, though the proportion of non-IT1 cases has increased during this time (see Table 8.5). In 1988, 44,443 cases were received. The number of jurisdictions in which ACAS provides conciliation has risen by a further twelve to a total of twenty-three. The overall settlement rate has risen from 33 per cent in 1977 to 61 per cent in 1988 (see Table 8.6).

Table 8.5 Cases received by ACAS for individual conciliation

Year	IT1 cases	Non-IT1 cases	Total
1976	41,178	752	41,930
1977	41,511	2,388	43,899
1978	41,642	3,071	44,713
1979	39,779	3,627	43,406
1980	37,799	8,648	46,447
1981	41,602	5,438	46,447
1982	40,864	6,132	46,996
1983	36,841	6,102	42,943
1984	36,030	6,693	42,723
1985	34,113	8,774	42,887
1986	38,606	12,825	51,431
1987	27,549	13,254	40,803
1988	28,237	16,206	44,443

Table 8.6 Individual conciliation: clearance rates 1985–88

	1985	1986	1987	1988
Completed cases	39,797	49,414	40,912	44,024
settled	48%	51%	56%	61%
withdrawn	25%	23%	20%	19%
to IT1	27%	26%	24%	20%

Discounting the non-IT1 cases the settlement rate still rose by about 9 per cent over this period and the percentage of cases proceeding to a tribunal hearing dropped from 43 per cent to 32 per cent.

Reasons for success

ACAS believes that a significant reason for the success of its individual conciliation role lies in the degree to which ACAS has come to be accepted as an independent impartial third party with no axe to grind. This independence stems from the statutory independence of ACAS as a body which, although financed from government sources, is independent in its operational matters, and operates under a council responsible for the general conduct of the Service. The Employment Protection Act 1975 specifically prohibits ministers from instructing ACAS as to how it should carry out its functions. Also, the COT performs no duties on behalf of the industrial tribunal. Any information given to a conciliation officer in connection with conciliation is not admissible in evidence before an industrial tribunal without the consent of the person who communicated it. This confidentiality in discussions is extremely important since it enables the parties to be completely open in talking to the COT, who in turn will ascertain what is confidential and what can be discussed freely with the other party.

Settlements reached under the auspices of the COT are legally binding and, once entered into, can deprive the individual of the right to pursue the complaint to an industrial tribunal. Any agreement reached either before a complaint has been made to a tribunal or after proceedings have been commenced will be effective to block an employee's right to claim if a COT has acted in accordance with the statutory duty.

Cost also plays a part in directing the minds of the parties towards a voluntary settlement. Complex cases can often lead to legal representation for either or both parties and a long-drawn-out case can involve an employer in the additional cost of staff time or other resources. Because conciliation is provided by ACAS, without charge, as a statutory duty it can mean a considerable saving in time and cost; since the outcome in many cases is an agreed settlement, both parties can feel that an equitable settlement has been achieved. A tribunal decision creates a winner and a loser.

Although the number of cases dealt with annually and the number of jurisdictions which provide for conciliation has increased greatly since ACAS first undertook the role of conciliator in individual rights cases, the way in which the COT carries out his or her duties has remained the same.

The conciliation role in more detail

Within the overall duty of seeking to promote a settlement of a complaint without the need for it to be determined by an industrial tribunal, the conciliation officer has first to explore the possibility (in dismissal cases) of re-employment. If, for whatever reason, an employer or individual decides that this is not practicable, the COT explores the possibility of reaching a settlement by some other means, usually for a sum of money. Should there be a possibility that the issue could be resolved through the employer's existing grievance or other procedures, then the COT will encourage the parties to process the dispute through those procedures before attempting further conciliation. The same procedure applies in cases in which a complaint could be presented to an industrial tribunal but the parties wish to reach a voluntary settlement instead.

During separate discussions with the individual and the employer, the COT will explain his/her role in the conciliation process, stressing that he/she is not a representative of either party. The conciliation officer will try to establish the facts and clarify the points of view of the parties, and will also provide whatever information or guidance on the legislation, case-law precedents or tribunal procedures as is necessary to help the parties become aware of the options open to them and which will assist them in taking informed decisions on the issues confronting them. At no time will the COT voice an opinion as to the merits of the case or create the impression that the officer is taking sides, or has the role of an arbitrator. Whatever course of action the parties choose to take is the decision of the parties themselves.

Discussions with the COT may encourage either or both parties to seek a conciliated settlement, or it could strengthen the conviction of either or both parties to prefer the case to go forward to a tribunal hearing. The complainant may decide to withdraw the complaint altogether and although COTs do not seek to persuade complainants to withdraw, they would be failing in their duty if the attention of the parties was not drawn to the necessary qualifying conditions, case-law, the possible strengths or weaknesses of the case and the possible risks of costs being awarded if the tribunal decided either party had acted in a frivolous, vexatious or unreasonable manner.

Should the parties decide to pursue the dispute to an industrial tribunal, or if it is clear to the COT that there is no prospect of conciliation, conciliation is withdrawn. Nevertheless the COT remains available to the parties for information or to recommence conciliation should they wish.

If the parties are willing to accept conciliation, the COT will assist them to reach a mutually agreeable settlement. As stated earlier, the COT will not suggest or impose a particular form of settlement but will help the parties to record it formally. The COT will confirm that they are fully aware of the implications, that they understand the terms of the agreement and that, once reached, the agreement is legally binding.

If settlement is reached and the terms recorded, each party keeps a copy of the signed agreement and in cases where a complaint has been presented to a tribunal, a copy is sent to the tribunal for promulgation in the form of a tribunal decision.

CONCLUSION

From the earliest days of ACAS it was the non-statutory part of its dispute resolution service – keeping the fate of the parties in their own hands, the ease and informality with which it could be used, and the view of the Service that it was not an interpreter or in any other way an instrument of government pay policy – that enabled it to establish itself so quickly in the turbulent industrial relations scene of the time. These elements of the ACAS approach at its foundation remain just as relevant today: the use of its services must be voluntary, free of charge to whomever requires them and clearly seen to be provided in an independent and impartial manner and at arm's length from government. These are the corner-stones of the ACAS reputation which have enabled it to enjoy its present high standing with the industrial relations community which it serves.

SELECT BIBLIOGRAPHY

Arbitration

Bassett, P. (1986) *Strike Free: New Industrial Relations in Britain*, London: Macmillan. Section on pendulum arbitration: pp. 109–16.

Burrows, G. (1986) *'No-Strike' Agreements and Pendulum Arbitration*, London: Institute of Personnel Management.

Concannon, H.M.G. (1986) 'The practice of voluntary arbitration in British industrial relations: a study focused on the method of single arbitration organised by the Advisory, Conciliation and Arbitration Service', Ph.D. thesis, Department of Business and Management Studies, University of Salford.

Donovan Report (1968) *Royal Commission on Trade Unions and Employers' Associations 1965–68*, London: HMSO, Cmd 3623.

Gladstone, A. (1984) *Voluntary Arbitration of Interest Disputes: A Practical Guide*, Geneva: International Labour Office.

Hepple, B.A. (1987) 'Labour courts: some comparative perspectives', working papers no. 6, Faculty of Laws, University College, London.

Hunter, L.C. (1983) 'Arbitration', in D. Robinson and K. Maynew (eds) *Pay Policies for the Future*, Oxford: Oxford University Press.

Institute of Directors (1984) *Settling Disputes Peacefully*, Position Paper, London: Institute of Directors.

International Labour Office (1983) *Conciliation and Arbitration Procedures in Labour Disputes: A Comparative Study*, Geneva: International Labour Office.

Labour Relations Agency (1981) *Case Studies on Arbitration*, Belfast: Labour Relations Agency.

Lewis, R. (1988) 'Strike-free procedures: are they what they seem?' Warwick papers in industrial relations no. 20, Industrial Relations Research Unit, University of Warwick, Coventry.

Lockyer, J. (1979) *Industrial Arbitration in Great Britain: Everyman's Guide*, London: Institute of Personnel Management.

Meade, J.F. (1982) *Stagflation*, vol. 1, *Wage-fixing*, London: Allen & Unwin, ch. 8, 'Not-quite-compulsory arbitration'.

Mortimer, J. (1982) 'Arbitration, the public interest and labour relations', in Lord Wedderburn of Charlton and W.T. Murphy (eds) *Labour Law and the Community: Perspectives for the 1980s*, London: Institute of Advanced Legal Studies.

Rideout, R.W. (1982) 'Arbitration and public interest: regulated arbitration', in Lord Wedderburn of Charlton and W.T. Murphy (eds) *Labour Law and the Community: Perspectives for the 1980s*, London: Institute of Advanced Legal Studies.

Advisory

Armstrong, E. and Lucas, R. (1985) *Improving Industrial Relations: The Advisory Role of ACAS*, London: Croom Helm.

Collective conciliation

Hiltrop, J.M. (1987) 'Hiltrop Report: survey of ACAS collective conciliation', unpublished paper, University of Bradford.

Individual conciliation

Graham, C. and Lewis, N. (1985) *The Role of ACAS Conciliation in Equal Pay and Sex Discrimination Cases*, London: Equal Opportunities Commission.
Kumar, V. (1986) *Industrial Tribunal Applicants under the Race Relations Act 1976: A Research Report by the Commission for Racial Equality*, London: CRE.
O'Brien, N. and Kibling, T. (1988) *Settling Industrial Tribunal Claims*, series of articles produced by the unit since May 1988, London: Legal Action.

9 Alternative dispute resolution: financial services

John Birds and Cosmo Graham

INTRODUCTION

The financial services industry has become increasingly important to the economic life of the United Kingdom, at both a macro-economic and an individual level. In the past decade the industry has been undergoing revolutionary changes, not least in the regulatory systems that have been developed (Page 1987; Moran 1988). Moran has argued that the new regulatory systems created by the Financial Services Act 1986, usually described as 'self-regulatory', are hybrids, being neither pure market nor bureaucratic-administrative regulation. In effect, public powers and duties are delegated to private interests to fulfil, subject to certain conditions and monitoring imposed by government. An integral part of any regulatory system will be mechanisms for dispute resolution; those that have grown up in the financial services industry, and are the subject of this chapter, show the same hybrid character. In particular, public sector devices, such as ombudsmen, have been imported into the private sphere in a prime example of what Poggi (1978) has referred to as the 'compenetration' of the public and private spheres which characterizes modern society. One of the most interesting theoretical issues is under what social conditions such transference is raised as a possibility and the conditions under which such a transfer will be successful.

The need for alternative institutions to the formal legal system for solving consumer disputes is apparent if the growth of bureaucratic power is considered. By this we mean the increasing development of large organizations, public and private, who administer programmes on the basis of rules, often self-developed, within the context of a complex division of labour aimed at increasing their efficiency. The individual in dispute with such organizations is no longer faced with someone in a roughly equivalent position. As Galanter (1974) has put it, the individual is the 'one-shotter' and the organization the 'repeat-player': this gives the organization certain structural advantages in dealing with disputes within the formal legal system.

In British public administration the most well-known device to have been developed, in order to counteract his problem, was the ombudsman. A similar problem existed in the private sector because, prior to the 1970s, there were few devices designed specially for consumers in dispute with large private organizations. By and large, they were expected to use the ordinary court system. Dissatisfaction with this state of affairs crystallized after the Consumer Council report *Justice Out of Reach* (1970), which examined the work of the county courts and found that, far from being used by individual consumers, they were used mainly by companies as a means of debt collection. The report argued that what was needed was a specialist small claims court, although it recognized one possible alternative was a special tribunal for consumer complaints (1970: 27–8). Although this option was not favoured, the Consumer Council thought much could be borrowed from the tribunal procedure for their proposed small claims courts.

In the end, only a small claims *procedure* within the county court system was created. Although this marked an advance, doubts have been cast on its effectiveness (Applebey 1979; National Consumer Council (NCC) 1979; Whelan 1987) and some changes are to be made following the Civil Justice Review (Lord Chancellor's Department 1986; 1988). The other major development in the private sector has been the growth of arbitration schemes sponsored by the Office of Fair Trading (OFT) under Section 124 of the Fair Trading Act 1973. It is difficult to make any judgement about their performance, due to a lack of information, but it seems that only three schemes are performing at all satisfactorily (OFT 1981; Thomas 1988: 208–9).

These brief remarks indicate that, by the mid-1980s, there were definite doubts about the functioning and effectiveness of the existing consumer protection schemes. By contrast, the ombudsmen system had established itself as a mechanism for consumer redress in the public sector, albeit not without some reservations. Before going on to look at the importation of public sector techniques into the private sector, we need to set out criteria for assessing the performance of complaints mechanisms.

Assessing the effectiveness of complaints mechanisms

We have discussed this issue at great length elsewhere (Birds and Graham 1988: 315–17) and so will just set out our views schematically. First, complaints mechanisms are about more than just the resolution of individual complaints. Although important, they have another positive role: that of *quality control*, the raising of standards and performance. Second, any complaints mechanism must have an *independent* element; a complainant, when using internal procedures, should be able to have recourse to someone who was not involved in taking the original decision. This does not mean the independent element acts in isolation from the body (or bodies) it supervises; liaison and communication is both necessary and helpful. The third criterion is *openness*; it must be possible to assess the performance of the independent bodies. Ideally a watchdog body should scrutinize the performance of the complaints mechanism, e.g. the Select Committee for the Parliamentary Commissioner for Administration. If the bodies are not statutory their terms of reference should be freely available, they should publish an Annual Report and it should be possible to read their decisions in individual cases. The fourth criterion is *accessibility*. Consumers must be aware of the existence of a means of redress and the procedures must be reasonably easy to use. Finally, the procedures must be *fair and effective*; not only must the complainant be given a fair hearing but also the institution must, in some way, be able to redress the inequality in power between the complainant and the institution he or she is complaining against. The body must be able to obtain information, and have effective remedies.

THE OMBUDSMEN

The idea of an Insurance Ombudsman goes back to 1973 when it formed part of the Consumers' Association's submission to the Scott Committee (1973) on linked life assurance. The committee rejected the idea for insurance (1973: paras 237–9) but it was endorsed in a note of reservation by Eirlys Roberts. The Office of Fair Trading put pressure on the industry to reform its complaints procedures and there were criticisms of the insurance industry's supervisory and complaints mechanisms from other sources. The industry appears to have been divided on the issue of complaints (Morrison 1981) and in the end five major companies created the Insurance Ombudsman Bureau (IOB) in 1981. Even after its formation the British Insurance Association made no formal recommendation to its members, pro or con. Another response was the formation of the Personal Insurance Arbitration Service (PIAS), which we deal with on p. 130. It might be hypothesized that the formation of the IOB was an attempt to head off further government controls on the industry. For example, the statutory reform of certain aspects of insurance law, recommended by the Law Commission (1980), could be seen in this light. The only evidence, however, is a speech by the General Manager of General Accident some years before the formation of the IOB (*The Times* 7 March 1974), an editorial in the *Chartered Insurance Institute Journal* (December 1981) and the fact that the founding companies took care to consult the consumer bodies, unlike PIAS (*Financial Times* 13 November 1981).

The reasonableness of this hypothesis can be tested by comparing the experience of the banks and the building societies. The starting-point for both was a report by the National Consumer Council (1983) which recommended that an ombudsman be established for both bank and building society customers and that the IOB should be taken as a model. It has been reported that although the banks were considering one for some time (*Financial Times* 10 May 1984) pressure mounted after the NCC report and, indeed, the Banking Ombudsman has acknowledged that the threat of legislation was *one* factor behind the creation of the Office of the Banking Ombudsman (OBO) (Morris 1987: 133).

In contrast, the Building Societies Association (BSA) rejected the idea out of hand (BSA 1983: 12) and this position was accepted up to publication of the Building Societies Bill. However, the NCC continued to press for the introduction of an ombudsman, as did the Building Societies Members' Association. At least two Conservative back-bench MPs were enlisted to the cause and, at the committee stage, the government gave an assurance that a scheme would be introduced: this was duly done in the House of Lords. As we shall see, the scheme (enshrined in Building Societies Act 1986 Schedule 12) is less flexible than the other two, provides the Building Societies Ombudsman with greater powers and gives the Building Societies Commission oversight functions (Schedule 13).

From this brief, and necessarily fragmentary, sketch of the origins of the ombudsmen schemes, it appears that the motivation behind these institutions has been primarily defensive. Therefore we should expect that individual dispute resolution will be uppermost in the ombudsmen's minds and that quality control and the raising of standards will come second. We now proceed to examine the functioning of the schemes.

Independence and openness

All these ombudsmen take the legal form of a company limited by guarantee. The board of directors consists of senior management of the participating companies, elected in the usual way at the company's annual general meeting. Oversight of the scheme is *not* the responsibility of the board but is vested in a council. So the relationship between the board and the council, set out in the Articles of Association, is critical. For the IOB not more than three council members are to be appointed by the board, subject to the approval of the council, which is not to be unreasonably withheld. No more than nine are to be appointed or re-appointed by the council, subject to board approval, which is not to be unreasonably withheld. The council is to use its best endeavours to ensure that at least four appointees are representative of the public and consumer interest (Article 60). The OBO is slightly different. The board appoints the chair, subject to the approval of the council, and the council, excluding the chair, is made up of an even number of members, being not more than eight, nor less than four. The council, subject to the board's approval, appoints half its members and the board, subject to the council's approval, appoints the other half. The council will use its best endeavours to ensure its appointees are representative of the public or consumer interest (Article 70). The Building Societies Ombudsman Bureau (BSOB) is different again. All members of the council are appointed by the board, of whom no more than four are to be 'independent' and no more than three to be building society members. The directors appoint all members but independent members are appointed only after consultation with the council. The directors are to use all reasonable endeavours to ensure independent members are representative of public and consumer interests (BSOB 1987: Clauses 1, 5).

The various councils appoint the ombudsmen, subject to the boards' approval. The terms of reference of the Insurance Ombudsman are determined by the council, subject to the board's approval (Art 65). For the Banking Ombudsman, the board determines the terms of reference and may amend them. The council is to monitor the terms of reference and may recommend amendments to the board (Arts 24, 76). For the Building Society Ombudsman, the minimum requirements are laid down by statute and any scheme must be approved by the Building

Societies Commission (Building Societies Act 1986 Sec 83 (8)). Subject to these statutory provisions the council monitors the functioning of the scheme, takes all reasonable steps to ensure its satisfactory operation and recommends amendments to the directors (BSOB 1987: Clause 10). Given its powers, the Building Societies Commission would undoubtedly be consulted on any proposed amendments. The role of the commission can be illustrated in the recent debate over the jurisdiction of the BSOB. There was some doubt over whether pre-completion complaints, that is complaints relating to matters which occurred before the completion of a mortgage or investment, were within the jurisdiction. The ombudsman, with the backing of the council, wanted the terms of reference clarified to ensure that such complaints were included but the Building Societies Association would not agree. The commission was asked to exercise its powers to amend the 1986 Act but declined to do so for the time being.

The Board of the OBO appears to have the greatest formal powers. However, not too much should be made of the formal differences, because in all the schemes critical powers in relation to budgets and terms of reference are vested in the boards. The relationship between the board and the council is therefore crucial. Yet, only in regard to the BSOB is independent scrutiny of any changes in the terms of reference of the scheme built into the procedure through the role of the Building Societies Commission.

This was a matter which caused great concern to the Jack Committee (1989), who recommended that the Banking Ombudsman scheme should be put on a statutory basis, the responsibility for granting recognition of the scheme to rest with the Bank of England who would also have responsibility for approving the ombudsman's terms of reference, appointing the independent members of the council and approving the appointment of the ombudsman. In its response the Council of the Banking Ombudsman (1989) opposed a statutory scheme, arguing that the need for sanctions was vital, the banks were more willing to co-operate with a non-statutory scheme, and it was more flexible. They recommended instead that one seat on the board be allocated to a representative from the Bank of England.

As regards openness, all the schemes publish an annual report. Neither the IOB nor the OBO engages in systematic reporting of their cases, similar to the PCA (the BSOB has not established its practice yet). The IOB annual reports do discuss individual cases and the Insurance Ombudsman's summary advice has been published, but it seems the IOB lacks the resources to anonymize the cases and publish them (IOB 1983: 29; 1984: 4). However, it has made the point that its decisions are not secret, simply the names of the parties, and it has made previous decisions available to interested parties (IOB 1984: iv). The Banking Ombudsman has decided not to publish decisions so far partly because he has not broken any new legal ground: 'I have merely applied existing authorities to the facts of particular cases' (OBO 1986–7: para 12). He is keeping the question of publication under review.

This practice is, we think, unfortunate. Publication allows outsiders to assess, to some extent, how the scheme is working and such input can be potentially valuable. For individual complainants, lack of access to the reports does put them at a disadvantage in comparison to those who are aware of previous decisions. The Insurance Ombudsman has complained that his past pronouncements are being cited and argued over as if they were precedents in the law courts (although it is not clear whether this refers only to statements in the annual reports) (IOB 1985: 3; 1986: 1).

Accessibility

There are signs, as regards banks and building societies, that they have been reluctant to publicize the existing complaints mechanism. For example forty building societies failed to respond to the BSOB's request to display publicity material in their branches and, as of June 1988, no society had accepted the council's suggestion that information about the BSOB should be on the back of customer statements (BSOB 1987–8). General public awareness of these schemes seems low; research done by MORI for the OBO indicated that

> About 18 per cent of the public (21 per cent of bank customers) claimed to know that the banks had an independent ombudsman . . . this was a slightly lower percentage than for people claiming to know about the existence of the Insurance Ombudsman and a slightly higher proportion than for the Building Society Ombudsman.
>
> (OBO 1987–8: 21)

This seems equally to be a problem as regards internal complaints procedures about which there is little publicly available information. It has been reported that each bank has a system for reviewing complaints at regional and head office level (OBO 1985–6: 2), whereas procedures within building societies and insurance companies seem more varied. (Interestingly the OBO's terms of reference require its members to inform complainants of the existence of the ombudsman if deadlock in a dispute is reached, similar to the rules of the self-regulatory organizations created under the Financial Services Act 1986 but, apparently, unlike the IOB and BSOB.) The Jack Committee (1989: para. 15.33) felt it should be a matter of best banking practice to establish clear internal procedures and to inform customers how they worked and of the existence of the relevant ombudsman.

One of the other problems for accessibility is limits on the jurisdiction of an ombudsman. This has been a constant problem for the Commission for Local Administration and Parliamentary Commissioner for Administration (see Birkinshaw 1985: 131–5; Lewis *et al.* 1987: 25–32; Harlow and Rawlings 1984: 204, 214). The experience of the IOB so far indicates that it is also a problem in the financial services field. Inquiries about companies which were not members of the scheme constituted 70.9 per cent of all enquiries in the first year and have now been reduced to 32.7 per cent of all enquiries (see Table 9.1). Inquiries about member companies which are outside the scheme's terms of reference for ombudsman investigations have averaged approximately 20 per cent over the last five years (Table 9.2). There is little information on which of the jurisdictional limits in the terms of reference cause the most problems.

This is also a problem for the OBO. In the first nine months of operation 13.8 per cent of the complaints received were outside the terms of reference, as regards subject matter, while in the first two years of operation this number averaged roughly 25 per cent. The NCC (1987: 16–17) has recommended that the terms of reference be widened and there have recently been some changes, in particular the ombudsman is now allowed to consider the issue of mal-administration in decisions about lending or security. In comparison to both the IOB and the OBO the scheme for the Building Societies Ombudsman covers a wide range of subjects with less exclusions (see Building Societies Act Schedule 12). In the first year of operation, excluding the vexed question of pre-completion complaints, only 8.2 per cent of complaints were outside the jurisdiction of the BSOB.

Table 9.1 IOB enquiries and non-member companies

Year	Enquiries	Enquiries v. non-members	
			(%)
1981	1,517	1,076	70.9
1982	2,504	1,272	50.8
1983	3,279	1,637	49.9
1984	3,477	1,372	39.5
1985	4,728	1,674	35.4
1986	5,873	1,922	32.7
1987	7,433	2,470	33.2
1988	8,176	2,541	31.1

Source: IOB Annual Reports.

Table 9.2 Enquiries outside terms of reference

Year	Enquiries v. members	Outside jurisdiction/general	
			(%)
1981	441	144	32.7
1982	1,232	296	24.0
1983	1,642	318	19.4
1984	2,105	440	20.9
1985	3,054	533	17.5
1986	3,951	790	20.0
1987	4,963	758	15.3
1988	5,635	640	11.4

Source: IOB Annual Reports.

Procedures and outcomes

This represents a major departure from the traditional ideas of adversarial, oral court hearings in front of a mainly passive tribunal. Ombudsmen procedures are generally written, the ombudsman takes a more active role in investigating the facts of a case and settlements between the parties are more actively encouraged (for details of the procedures see OBO no date: 3–4; IOB 1982: 30–1; BSOB 1987: 17–22). It appears that the common way of proceeding is to make decisions solely on the basis of written evidence and submissions (although exceptionally the parties may be allowed to present their case orally).

In order to conduct a satisfactory investigation an ombudsman must be able to obtain information. In an analogous field, the lack of power to obtain information was one of the great weaknesses of nationalized industry consumer councils (see Prosser 1986: 159–60). Of the three, only the Building Society Ombudsman may require that information is furnished; the Insurance Ombudsman and the Banking Ombudsman can only request information and report non-compliance to the Council (IOB 1982: 32; OBO no date: para 5; BSOB 1987: Clause 25 (C)). The NCC (1987: para 19.5) has criticized this limitation as regards the Banking Ombudsman and suggested there should be a power to require production of documents; the Jack Committee (1989) also recommended that this power be available. The council has agreed that this would be a desirable extension of the powers.

Table 9.3 Case outcomes

Year	Enquiries	Withdrawals		Settlements		Adjudications	
			(%)		(%)		(%)
1981	441	96	21.8	59	13.4	39	8.8
1982	1,232	221	17.9	298	24.2	179	14.5
1983	1,642	117	7.3	475	28.9	284	17.3
1984	2,105	79	3.8	494	23.5	465	22.1
1985	3,054	NK		NK		629	20.6
1986	3,951	144	3.6	559	14.1	1,003	25.4
1987	4,963	297	6.0	983	19.8	1,426	28.7
1988	5,635	331	5.9	901	16.0	1,354	24.2

Source: IOB Annual Reports.
Note: Excluded are cases pending, outcomes unknown and where summary advice was given by the ombudsman.

For outcomes, and success rates of applicants, the major source of information derives from the IOB. Roughly one in four applicants have some success on applying to the ombudsman, with the percentage dropping to one in five if the case goes to adjudication (see Tables 9.3 and 9.4). By comparison, success rates for applicants reaching the stage of a Formal Recommendation at the Banking Ombudsman are much lower. These figures are, of course, too crude a basis for judging performance. First, the complaints the Insurance Ombudsman receives have already been filtered by the companies' own internal complaints mechanism. Second, the Banking Ombudsman argues (OBO 1986–7: 5) that a high proportion of the complaints which proceed to Formal Recommendation are those where his Informal Assessment has been unfavourable to the complainant and that those factors weigh in deciding the formal recommendation. So it may be possible that informal grievance resolution provides the most effective solution. In this context, it should be noted that the IOB has *never* made a formal award.

Table 9.4 IOB adjudications

	Cases adjudicated: company decision			
Year	Confirmed		Revised	
		(%)		(%)
1981	30	76.9	9	23.1
1982	141	78.8	38	21.2
1983	232	81.7	52	18.3
1984	386	83.0	79	17.0
1985	486	77.3	143	22.7
1986	785	78.3	218	21.7
1987	1,122	78.7	304	21.3
1988	1,080	79.8	274	20.2

Source: IOB Annual Reports.

One point worth noting in passing is that all these ombudsmen have experienced a substantial number of complainants who have dropped out of the process through not replying to letters. It is difficult to know what to make of this; the possibilities range from the dispute having been settled to the complainants' satisfaction to this being a demonstration of dissatisfaction with the process.

The final point in relation to procedures is the question of quality control, of the ability of the ombudsman to raise standards in the relevant industry. All of them are required to have regard to good principles of commercial practice in their areas and this could provide an opportunity for them to develop further general principles. The Insurance Ombudsman, however, has been reluctant to develop this aspect of his work, emphasizing repeatedly that he is not bound by precedent. Nevertheless, in the 1987 Report he did claim that various sets of principles have emerged and are regularly published in the annual report. The Council of the Banking Ombudsman seem to take a somewhat different view. They agree (OBO 1986–7; 21) that the ombudsman should act to raise standards but point out that the phrase 'good banking practice' has a recognized legal meaning and that it is this meaning that should be applied in judging complaints. Wider issues they are prepared to take up in their own reports. The Jack Committee (1989: ch. 16) recommended that all the banks should promulgate a Code of Banking Practice which should be formally presented to the ombudsmen as impartial guidance on best banking practice. The ombudsmen should also offer guidance in their annual reports on the extent to which, in their opinion, banks are complying with the Code.

Mention should also be made of the 'test case' provision in the Banking Ombudsman's terms of reference. Under this procedure, if a bank considers that a complaint involves an issue which may have important consequences for the business of the bank or a new and important point of law, the complaint can be withdrawn from the scheme and, after the bank's undertaking to pay the complainant's costs, brought to court. The Jack Committee (1989: para 15.14) recommended that banks should be allowed to exercise this power only with the agreement of the ombudsman. The BSOB scheme allows the participating building societies to request the ombudsman to state a case on any question of law for the High Court.

PIAS and Lloyds

Mention should now be made of these schemes. PIAS is a documents-only arbitration scheme which is, in its terms, less advantageous to the consumer. For example the decision of the arbitrator is binding on the customer, unlike the IOB. Furthermore, the arbitrator is confined to examining the 'letter of the law' and is not allowed to take into account principles of good insurance practice. No statistical information is kept on the workings of this scheme by the Chartered Institute of Arbitrators. We have dealt elsewhere (Birds and Graham 1988: 323–4) with Lloyds' existing practices and, from early 1989, Lloyds will be a member of the IOB. It will be interesting to see to what extent this affects the caseload of the IOB and the implications of an increased caseload for its working practices.

COMPLAINTS PROCEDURES UNDER THE FINANCIAL SERVICES ACT

The background to the development of complaints procedures here is the reform of the regulation of the City (see Page 1987; Moran 1988; Gower 1988). The outcome was the Financial Services Act 1986 under which certain regulatory powers are delegated from the Secretary of State to the Securities and Investments Board (SIB) and recognized self-regulatory organizations (SROs). (We have not examined recognized professional bodies or investment exchanges.) This delegation is subject to certain conditions, one of which is that SIB and SROs have provision for the *independent* investigation of complaints (Financial Services Act 1986 Schedule 7 para 4 (2)) against themselves and their members.

Originally SIB planned to institute an ombudsman scheme which would cover *all* the SROs and membership would have been compulsory (for details see SIB 1986). However, this plan was dropped because SIB (1987: Section 22 para 8) felt that the Act did not give it powers to make such proposals. The Financial Services Act 1986 does require that the rules of SROs offer equivalent protection to those of SIB (Schedule 2 para 3) and SIB expects approved schemes to be broadly similar to its proposed ombudsman arrangements. Nevertheless, there appear to be some interesting differences between the various schemes.

SIB's own rules require that firms subject to its jurisdiction should keep records of complaints, and action taken, and ensure that internal investigations within the firm are undertaken by someone not concerned with the original decision and who is a person of such experience, competence and seniority as to be able to investigate the complaint adequately (Conduct of Business Rules 2.10, 16.16). If a complaint is not settled at this level the complainant can have recourse to the independent investigator. It is also possible to have recourse to SIB's independent investigator when dissatisfied with an SRO's complaints mechanism. If the person complained against is a member of an ombudsman scheme approved by SIB, and subject to a reference under that scheme, the matter will not be referred to the independent investigator.

The most prestigious SRO is The Securities Association (TSA), formed by merging the Stock Exchange and the International Securities Regulatory Organization. The rules specify (Conduct of Business Rules, ch. IV, paras 1190.01–1190.05) that a firm shall have a written complaints procedure and that, unless settled at once, the complaint shall be investigated fully by an officer or employee of the firm of appropriate seniority who was not involved in the matter giving rise to the complaint. Individual firms are also under a duty to co-operate with the investigation of complaints by the TSA's Complaints Bureau and Complaints Commissioner.

Standing above the member firms are a Complaints Bureau and an Arbitration Scheme. The operation of the Complaints Bureau will be subject to the scrutiny of a Complaints Commissioner, who will report annually to the TSA on the performance of his/her functions. The Complaints Bureau will investigate complaints and may refer them back to the firm for settlement, attempt conciliation or decide that the merits of the complaint warrant no further action. If no settlement is reached, two types of arbitration are available. The first, for claims under £25,000, by private customers and expert investors, will usually be done on the basis of the papers and written statements, although the arbitrator has the discretion to order an oral hearing. The second, for claims above £25,000, and including disputes with market professionals and other firms, will be closer to court proceedings but with a streamlined procedure and provisions for expert advisors and a panel of arbitrators.

The Investment Management Regulatory Organization (IMRO) has a slightly different arrangement and has been joined in this by FIMBRA (Financial Intermediaries, Managers and Brokers Regulatory Association). Member firms are required to have a written complaints procedure, to submit a quarterly summary of all complaints to IMRO and to keep records of action taken on complaints. The internal procedure requires, for non-trivial complaints, that they are considered by personnel of appropriate seniority who were not involved in the matter, or, where this is not possible, an equivalent person (IMRO Rules ch. 7). For complaints not resolved at this level IMRO have proposed a Referee (who is supposed to be akin to an ombudsman – IMRO 1987: para 35). The Referee's first object will be to act as a conciliator, if this fails the Referee can offer his or her services to act as an adjudicator. The procedure of the Referee as adjudicator is left up to the discretion of the Referee and it seems envisaged that oral hearings will be allowed but legal representation will be exceptional. Also, conciliation and adjudication are kept as very separate procedures. For example the general rule is that the conciliator, if unsuccessful, will not adjudicate a case, another Referee will be used.

The rules of the Life Assurance and Unit Trust Regulatory Organization (LAUTRO) on the handling of complaints by member firms are similar to IMRO's (LAUTRO Rules part IX) and they will also be asking for regular summaries of complaints and their resolution times. If not resolved at this level, then the complaint can be passed to LAUTRO to investigate. The independent element is provided by either the IMRO Referee or the new Unit Trust Ombudsman who is to work alongside the Insurance Ombudsman within the IOB using the same administrative facilities. However, at the time of writing, fewer than 60 of Britain's estimated 170 unit trust management companies have so far joined this scheme. An interesting aspect of this is that LAUTRO has proposed joint sifting of complaints with the IOB. Those showing evidence of serious, deliberate or consistent breach of the rules will be dealt with by LAUTRO's enforcement staff, the others by the IOB (LAUTRO 1987: para 85). It is not clear what happens with firms which do not belong to either the IOB or the IMRO scheme. The implication is that either other arrangements may be approved (Rule 9.1 (3)) or that the disciplinary machinery will be invoked (LAUTRO 1987: para 83).

Whereas IMRO and FIMBRA share an ombudsman-type scheme, the arrangements envisaged for the Association of Futures Brokers and Dealers (AFBD) combine professional discipline and consumer complaints within the same procedure. All complaints, written or oral, may be made the subject of an investigation and, once the investigation is completed, the AFBD may take no further action, make recommendations or give advice by way of conciliation or refer the matter to a Business Conduct Committee, comprised of five appointees and with a QC as chair. The committee will deal with disciplinary as well as consumer complaints. The hearings may be either written or oral and the dissatisfied complainant has a right of further reference to SIB, as is the case with the other SROs.

CONCLUSIONS

Given the novelty of these institutions, our conclusions are only provisional. First, individual grievance handling seems to be the primary rationale, with the issue of raising standards very much taking second place. The Jack Committee's observations in relation to the Banking Ombudsman are equally applicable to the IOB and BSOB. Although the Financial Services Act 1986 procedures and institutions are seemingly better equipped to deal with raising standards, this again seems to have taken a back seat. Second, in the 'free-standing' schemes although much effort has been expended in ensuring the final tier of the complaints mechanism is independent, the sponsoring industry, in the shape of the board of directors or equivalent, still retains important powers. In the absence of independent external scrutiny, like the Building Societies Commission, this raises difficulties for the perceived independence of the schemes. Third, while the differences between financial markets/instruments are increasingly breaking down, illustrated by the decision of the Abbey National Building Society to become a public company and to seek recognition as a bank, each area has its own complaints mechanisms. The Banking Ombudsman, for example, is debarred from dealing with complaints which fall within the jurisdiction of SIB and the SROs. The member banks are authorized by IMRO, their stockbroking subsidiaries with TSA and most insurance broking subsidiaries are directly authorized by SIB, although some are members of FIMBRA (OBO 1987–8: 16). Although there are some similarities between the institutions, there are also important differences, which affect a consumer's ability to obtain redress. The result has been described as a 'mare's nest' by the Council of the Banking Ombudsman and a 'bugger's muddle' by the first Unit Trust Ombudsman, who resigned after only five weeks. The SIB has also recognized that complaints procedures under the Financial Services Act 1986 need reform but it is difficult to see how SIB will be able to do this if the principle that SRO rules must offer equivalent protection to SIB's rules is relaxed. In the long run some rationalization of these arrangements is surely desirable.

Acknowledgements

We are grateful to the National Westminster Bank and the University of Sheffield Research Fund for financial support for this project as well as the co-operation of everyone who took the time to answer our queries. Patrick Birkinshaw and Norman Lewis have given us some very helpful advice in writing this paper.

10 Family conciliation: from research to practice

Janet Walker

THE DEVELOPMENT OF FAMILY CONCILIATION IN ENGLAND AND WALES

Conciliation as an alternative dispute resolution process in separation and divorce is relatively new, particularly in this country. The last fifteen years have witnessed a burgeoning interest in alternative dispute resolution in general, reflecting a movement away from the use of adversarial legal processes except as a 'last resort', towards more participative processes designed to contain and reduce conflict. Conciliation is best known as the preferred way to settle industrial disputes,[1] but in recent years its use in settling family and community disputes has increased. Sander (1984) has pointed out that family disputes have a number of special characteristics which must be taken account of if conciliation is to be effective:

1 In family disputes there are usually continuing and interdependent relationships. It is therefore important that the dispute settlement process should facilitate constructive relationships for the future.
2 Additionally, family disputes usually involve emotional, personal relationships, and feelings can mask the true nature of the dispute. In Sander's view, it is important that disputants should be able to express these feelings if they are not to feel dissatisfied with the outcome.
3 Family disputes, particularly in relation to marital break-up, frequently involve other family members, notably children, who are not usually included directly in the dispute resolution process, but whose interests may be considered paramount, thus requiring them to be protected in some way.

Such characteristics seem to have rendered a simple transfer of the industrial bargaining model to family disputes somewhat problematic and Sander refers to Fuller's observation that the interventions in such disputes should be person oriented rather than act oriented. Family conciliation, in contrast to industrial conciliation, has consequently developed as a number of disparate activities.

Families spend much of their time settling disputes which arise in everyday living, and most are competent in the practice of 'private ordering'. This competence often continues even when the family is experiencing the stress of breaking up so that only a minority of disputes need to be settled in the public domain, or outside the family. It is argued that the law is a blunt instrument for dealing with such disputes and that conciliation is far better suited to the sensitive, emotional issues surrounding these family matters. Macdougall (1984: 3) suggested that negotiation is an 'effective, relatively inexpensive procedure for the just resolution of family disputes' judged against four criteria for assessing methods of conflict resolution: their effectiveness in ending the dispute; the cost of the process; the justice of the process and the outcome; and the promotion of social goals.

The claim that conciliation is the dispute resolution mechanism which best meets these criteria has been based on a largely unchallenged assumption that it is a better way to resolve matrimonial disputes than that traditionally promoted by an adversarial legal process. Concern about the rapidly rising divorce rate during the 1970s and the possible detrimental effects on children of bitter and hostile court battles made an alternative dispute resolution process – which offered the chance to reduce bitterness between separating spouses, encouraging them to take responsibility as parents for making decisions about the future and thus to settle their disputes civilly – look extremely attractive. In addition to these benefits aimed at improving the quality of life for families during and after divorce, conciliation claimed also to reduce the costs associated with legal battles, particularly in relation to children's issues, which place a heavy burden on the state legal aid bill. By contrast the 'traditional adversarial' system of civil justice was said to escalate rather than diminish conflict between separating spouses, and in so doing incur large costs in court time, legal fees, and in the preparation of welfare reports by probation services already overstretched, with civil work placed as their lowest priority by the Home Office (1984).

Historically family conciliation services have been more concerned essentially with benefits for personal welfare but have been forced to emphasize the possible financial savings in order to impress government and funding bodies. Without a bottomless state purse for the provision of legal and welfare services the introduction of new procedures often requires that financial benefits will accrue elsewhere in order to provide the necessary resources. However, cost saving aims are not accorded high priority by conciliators, nor by the judiciary and court officials (Ogus *et al.* 1987; Lord Chancellor's Department 1989b) but are seen as secondary benefits from the central focus which is to improve the process and outcome of separation and divorce for families in both the short and the long term.

Family conciliation gained popularity in the UK following the publication in 1974 of the Report of the Finer Committee on One-Parent Families. This report envisaged the development of conciliation within a newly structured, unified family court, and described it as

> assisting the parties to deal with the consequences of the established break-down of their marriage . . . by reaching agreements or giving consents or reducing the area of conflict upon custody, support, access to and education of

the children, financial provision, the disposition of the matrimonial home, lawyers' fees and every other matter arising from the breakdown which calls for a decision on future arrangements.

(Finer 1974: 183, 185)

The recommendations for changes in court structure and services were not taken up by government, leaving innovations in family conciliation to the legal and social welfare practitioners most closely associated with separating and divorcing families. Thus at the present time family conciliation may be offered by services independent of the court and statutory agencies – so-called 'independent services', or by the probation service acting as the statutory welfare service provided to divorce courts – so-called 'court based or in-court services'. The term 'mediation' has also been used as a direct substitute for conciliation, and frequently the terms are used interchangeably. These variations, together with the unfortunate similarity of the term 'reconciliation', have given rise to a number of confusions about what conciliation aims to do and about the most appropriate methods of intervention.

The varied benefits attributed to conciliation (Parkinson 1983; 1986) and the lack of central co-ordination in the development of family conciliation services has promoted the growth of a range of services with different priorities and different practice styles. The popular classification of 'in-court' and 'out-of-court, services is deceptively over simple (Walker 1987). There has been considerable cross-fertilization, and while court-based services are, in the main, provided by the probation service, conciliation may take place as an integral part of the legal process *within* the court, or at a separate time and venue, or as a mixture of the two. Although independent services operate away from court premises and outside the legal system, some are closely linked to local probation services providing an interesting backcloth more usually associated with the authority of the court. Most, however, operate from a community base sometimes in premises used by other voluntary welfare agencies.

THE EFFECTIVENESS OF CONCILIATION IN FAMILY DISPUTES

Despite the many claims made for conciliation there had been little systematic research until the mid-1980s. The studies undertaken mainly monitored the work of one local service (see e.g. G. Davis and Roberts 1988) and few attempted a comparative dimension.

Assessing the costs of conciliation has been recognized as difficult and most research has not included a remit to study costs. Effectiveness has usually been assessed by the 'settlement rate' – the number of agreements reached as a result of conciliation. Judged simply on this criterion conciliation appears to be respectably successful with agreement on some issues being achieved in well over half of the cases in every study recorded (Walker 1989).

Pressure on the government to extend and to finance conciliation services led to the establishment of an Inter-Departmental Committee on Conciliation (ICC) in 1982 to review the current arrangements and consider how far they should be developed. The research was disappointingly limited, as were the conclusions reached. Recommending that 'there is a role for conciliation', the ICC suggested that 'conciliation is best provided as an adjunct to the court system' (Home Office 1983: paras 5.25 and 5.26). Recognizing the limitations of this research, the report urged that a further study should be undertaken before policy decisions were made.

The Conciliation Project Unit

It was as a direct consequence that the Conciliation Project Unit was established in 1985 at the University of Newcastle upon Tyne. The terms of reference were

1 to collect information from all in-court and out-of-court conciliation schemes in England and Wales about their organization, staffing, funding and procedures, and on the basis of this to produce a classification of different types of scheme
2 to assess and to compare the costs of different types of conciliation schemes, having regard to the cost of operating schemes, the effect on legal aid costs and lawyers' fees, and the cost of processing divorce cases through the courts
3 to assess the effectiveness of the different types of conciliation, with particular reference to the nature and durability of agreements reached, reduction of conflict, the satisfaction and well-being of parties, and the professional skills and training of successful conciliators
4 to act as a clearing house for new ideas about conciliation developed in other countries.

(Lord Chancellor's Department 1989b)

and thereby aid the Lord Chancellor to decide whether or not a national conciliation service should be established, and if so, how such a service might best be organized and funded (Lord Chancellor's Department 1989b).

The first part of the remit involved a nation-wide survey of conciliation and divorce processes. This enabled us to develop a classification of conciliation services, using the notion of authority as a key factor (Ogus *et al.* 1987; Walker and Wray 1987). Six independent services and ten divorce courts served by court-based services were selected for in-depth study. These services reflected different theoretical bases and practice styles and were spread geographically to take account of urban–rural, north–south, and socio-economic characteristics.

We considered it important to compare conciliation services not only with each other, but also with other dispute resolution processes, notably welfare investigation and adjudication. We selected two divorce courts in areas where conciliation was not available, but the dominance of the conciliation ideology had influenced the legal and welfare practitioners to such an extent that their conciliatory approach meant that these courts could act only as comparators not controls in the strict methodological sense (Lord Chancellor's Department 1989b: ch. 9).

During an eighteen-month fieldwork period we collected a wealth of data about 1,392 families, all of whom were in dispute about the arrangements for the children consequent on separation or divorce. The focus was on obtaining accurate data about costs – financial (both direct and indirect), emotional and societal, and effectiveness – assessing the process and the outcomes on a number of dimensions. We recognized that conciliation was viewed as serving a variety of aims and providing a range of benefits. The conciliation services in our study offered substantially different modes of intervention, and hence the number, duration, and context of conciliation appointments varied considerably. Thus the process under investigation could involve combinations of negotiation, bargaining, counselling or therapy.

The analysis of costs drew on the methodology of economics and econometrics, notably regression analysis, while the identification and evaluation of the dimensions of effectiveness required us to employ a range of quantitative and qualitative methods from social research, particularly as we wanted to extend the measurement of effectiveness beyond 'settlement-rate' and broad notions of consumer satisfaction (Lord Chancellor's Department 1989b: chs 13–19).

The findings of the Conciliation Project Unit (CPU) study both challenge some of the claims made for conciliation as a 'better' way to resolve matrimonial disputes, and raise a number of thorny and complex issues about the current practice of family conciliation. In summary, we found that rather than reducing or saving costs, conciliation adds to the cost of resolving disputes for those cases involved in a legal process, and that independent conciliation appears to be more costly than court-based conciliation (Lord Chancellor's Department 1989b: chs 11–12). Since most disputes are settled out-of-court anyway it is impossible to substantiate claims that successful conciliation automatically reduces litigation costs. Rather than providing an *alternative* to the legal process, conciliation is frequently another step within it, particularly as most couples instruct solicitors who may well attempt to negotiate settlements themselves before referring clients to a conciliation service. Even if we were to assume that successful conciliation would avoid all litigation, it is nevertheless inevitable that there are costs involved. On the effectiveness side, although the settlement rate was impressively high in most services, our research found that conciliation did not necessarily *resolve* the dispute, and as one issue was settled, others seemed to emerge. At the end of our study many couples were still in disagreement about a range of issues despite 'settlements' in conciliation. Furthermore, conciliation was not particularly successful in improving communication between angry or hostile parents, nor was it able to increase significantly the well-being of these disputants. Judged against the first two of Macdougall's criteria, then, conciliation is not unquestionably successful as an alternative dispute resolution mechanism, although it seems to be at least *as* effective as the more traditional processes. Factors external to all dispute resolution processes such as the passage of time, economic stability, relationships with relatives, the emotional consequences of divorce, were important influences on post-divorce adjustment and the resolution or continuation of disputes.

Our evidence led us to a conclusion contrary to that reached by the ICC. We concluded that independent services were the most successful in achieving the varying aims of conciliation, perhaps because they dealt with a wide range of issues, were more likely to offer counselling and advice-giving in the process, thus providing a more comprehensive alternative to the adversarial process, unencumbered by the authority of the court and the pressures on disputants to reach *speedy* settlements. We determined a number of factors which appear to inhibit the effectiveness of conciliation as it is currently practised, and pointed to a number of issues which cannot be ignored in discussions about the future of family conciliation. We believe that the questions facing family conciliation are not unique to England and Wales but rather are universal to the development of alternative dispute resolution mechanisms.

FROM RESEARCH TO PRACTICE

Private ordering or judicial determination?

This question goes to the heart of the debate about the role of law in the lives of separating families, and raises issues about due process and natural justice. Divorce still requires a legal process, but with a move away from examining and proving 'fault', the court pays more attention to ancillary matters, in particular the paramountcy of the best interests of children, and therefore to the post-divorce arrangements for their care and control. Under present legislation arrangements for the custody, care and control of children, including access to the 'absent' parent, must satisfy a judge.[2] In the majority of cases, parents manage to make satisfactory arrangements and so the court acts mainly as a 'rubber stamp' on decisions reached through private ordering.

Conciliation is another form of private ordering for those parents who are in dispute about arrangements for the children which they cannot resolve by themselves. Conciliation recognizes that parents should accept joint responsibility for the consequences of their divorce, and that they know best what will be in their children's interests. Agreements reached in conciliation are subject to the same judicial scrutiny, and as such need to comply with some implicit set of standards about the most appropriate child-care arrangements following divorce. The standards include the provision of a 'stable' home for the child, ensuring adequate physical and emotional care, and the right of the child to be able to continue a relationship with both parents. Conciliators may well adopt a semi-judicial role when arrangements are being negotiated, aware of what will satisfy a judge. Conciliators are faced with the potential conflict of maintaining a neutral position, promoting client self-determination, while at the same time guiding parents towards legally and socially acceptable settlements which may be contrary to those which parents may wish to propose. Conciliators interviewed in the CPU study were acutely conscious of *their* responsibility to ensure children's best interests against a set of *legal* expectations. For a parent who believes he or she has valid reasons for denying access to the other parent, conciliation may be no more than a forum for applying pressure to 'give in', while conciliators may interpret any resistance as an artefact of the hostility between the parents. Reaching agreement in conciliation did not inevitably obviate a judicial request for a welfare investigation at a Section 41 appointment (Lord Chancellor's Department 1989b: ch. 14). G. Davis (1987: 308) has argued that 'the elevation of child welfare on divorce to the status of public issue, calling for a judicial imprimateur in each case' is both a distraction and an irrelevance. There is no legal means for checking on how far parents comply with court orders except in extreme cases where a matrimonial supervision order is made. Even then, sanctions for non-compliance are virtually non-existent. If conciliators truly believe that parents will be more inclined to ensure that arrangements work if they agree them freely, then directed outcomes in conciliation may be no more satisfactory than judicial decisions imposed by the court. The dilemma for conciliators is compounded by their professional expertise in child welfare, a prerequisite for practice in the UK, and their anxiety about the impact on children of some parenting arrangements, for example shared physical custody. In this respect conciliation in separation and divorce is substantially different from industrial conciliation where the conciliators are unlikely to be expert in the subject matter of the issue in dispute and do not have a vested interest in the outcome. Rather they are expert in negotiation and bargaining skills. This places family conciliation in a wholly different category and challenges the claim that it is *private* ordering.

Is conciliation the 'best' way to resolve disputes?

The concern that the legal process of adjudication may escalate conflict between disputing parents has encouraged the view that conciliation is a superior form of dispute resolution and that any other mechanism is undesirable. The failure to settle disputes in conciliation may imply negative criticism of one or both disputants as unreasonable, and at worst, as bad parents. Such a view denies the valid function of the role of law, as a 'higher authority' to impose settlements. It may be unrealistic to expect all couples to be able to be rational and civilized at a time of intense emotional upheaval. Interviews with parents demonstrate clearly that the passage of time and eventual readjustment to new family and personal circumstances are key factors in reducing conflict between divorced spouses and yet decisions about children need to be made as quickly as possible following family break-up if detrimental consequences are to be minimized. It would seem important to recognize that legal processes can have an important part to play in resolving disputes between couples unwilling and unable to negotiate, particularly when the pain of divorce is at its most intense.

The CPU study revealed that legal procedures for dealing with family disputes have become increasingly conciliatory, and it was not uncommon for welfare investigations to become fused with conciliatory aims and methods. In these circumstances the objectives of conciliation, which are said to provide an *alternative* dispute mechanism, become confused with the objectives of assessment, investigation, and adjudication. Clients experience not only bewilderment about what is being attempted, but also dissatisfaction and disappointment (Lord Chancellor's Department 1989b: ch. 17). It is appropriate to consider the view that if conciliation is an alternative to the legal process then it is not legitimate for it to be fused into a legal process rendering both less effective than they could be. Furthermore, such blurring of boundaries may, as Roberts (1986) has warned, result in the absence of the procedural safeguards which normally attend formal adjudication. Notions of privilege and confidentiality are also thrown into question since they are deemed to apply to conciliation, but not to the legal process of welfare investigation. Macdougall's criterion of the justice of the process and the outcome is seriously challenged, then, if conciliation is viewed as superior, and as such dominates other processes. Indeed, the belief in its superiority may be such that couples are virtually *required* to attempt conciliation before being allowed to proceed to adjudication. Pressure to settle through conciliation was much in evidence in the CPU study, and one conciliator admitted using a sort of 'blackmail' to get clients to use conciliation. G. Davis (1988: 114) expressed concern about the aggrandisement of conciliation which 'could lead to adjudication becoming so much a last resort that it is stigmatised as the refuge of the obsessive and the intransigent'. Not only is it problematic to view one dispute mechanism as always better than another, but also such a judgement questions the validity of private ordering which must surely rest on notions of free choice.

Is there an ideal post-divorce family?

It would seem, then, that the ideal divorcing and post-divorce family is one which is capable of responsible decision-making without recourse to legal processes, which produces arrangements that conform to a set of norms, deviance from which is rarely sanctioned. There is a dearth of knowledge about the theoretical, ideological and personal values which underpin conciliation practice. An emphasis on shared parenting may fly in the face of other family patterns and more traditional child-care roles. Again conciliation can be accused of assuming 'middle-class' notions of family life, a view which may seriously neglect gender and cultural issues. Is it significant that the clientele of independent services tends to come from the higher socio-economic groups, and to be predominantly, if not exclusively, white?

Unlike conciliators in industrial disputes, family conciliators have experience of the *context* in which the dispute has arisen. Many may even have personal experience of divorce, either as a marital partner or as a child. Such experiences must be expected to influence the conciliator's 'world-view' of family life and some interviewed in the CPU study admitted having certain prejudices against particular types of clients. The possibility of remaining neutral becomes increasingly difficult to maintain. Not only may the process become unbalanced, but also the problem of preferred or socially acceptable outcomes may predominate.

Another interesting dimension to the evaluation of the effectiveness of conciliation is its apparent success in achieving *reconciliation*. The aim of supporting marriages which have a chance of survival is established in the objectives of the Divorce Reform Act 1969, and has been publicly approved for a long time. Both the Denning Committee (1947) and the Morton Committee in 1956[3] argued that the state should have an interest in supporting family life in recognizing that the increase in divorce is a serious social issue. Although conciliators have struggled to differentiate between reconciliation and conciliation as quite separate processes, Parkinson (1986: 67) lists the 'concern to stem the rising tide of divorce' as one of six factors for the rapid growth of conciliation since 1975, and perhaps it is not surprising that services have been somewhat proud of their reconciliation rates! Such overlap in processes and outcomes was one of the factors which led us to recommend a broad-based agency capable of offering both reconciliation and conciliation as well as giving advice, counselling and other help to separating families. On Macdougall's criteria, conciliation would be seen as effective in promoting social goals, but this again must be evaluated in the context of the belief in private ordering.

Who owns conciliation?

Conciliators have put considerable emphasis on the distinctive characteristics of conciliation, and therefore its validity as a novel intervention. Territorial issues amongst those professionals closest to separating families have fuelled debates about which professionals in which settings should have the monopoly on conciliation practice. Some probation officers view conciliation as a natural extension of their statutory divorce welfare activities, and a few refuse to accept the need for a clear distinction in the roles (Wilkinson 1981; Shepherd and Howard 1985). Our research has confirmed the problems associated with the fusion of activities, and indeed we have recommended that probation officers, by virtue of their role and authority within the courts, should not undertake conciliation as part of their statutory duties (Lord Chancellor's Department 1989b: ch. 20). The National Family Conciliation Council has sought to limit the practice of conciliation to social work professionals, but in other jurisdictions, lawyers and accountants have been encouraged to become conciliators.[4] The issue must be whether or not experts in family dynamics and child care must conciliate family disputes or whether the emphasis should be on skilled negotiators regardless of their professional background. It may be important to minimize professional divisions, concentrating instead on the amalgamation of knowledge and skills from a range of disciplines. This is particularly relevant to the conciliation of *all* issues consequent on divorce. Hitherto, family conciliation has been restricted to tackling child-related issues, in the belief that lawyers must retain control of the settlement of finance and property disputes. The CPU research challenges this artificial division of family disputes, since families frequently are in dispute about a range of issues, money worries often dominate the conflict between parents, and not all couples seek legal advice, preferring instead to use conciliation as an *alternative*. One of the CPU recommendations is that conciliation should be comprehensive as it is in most other countries.

Who are the clients?

At first glance it appears obvious that the divorcing couple are the clients. However, this clarity blurs a little when we consider the varying aims of conciliation and the range of benefits attributed to it. If conciliation aims to protect the best interests of children, then are children the real clients, albeit somewhat removed from the process? Even this varies since some services include children as a matter of policy, some court-based services *require* children above a certain age to attend, most focus on the children's needs but do not include them in the process. Other services involve whole families – this has led to the accusation that family therapy rather than conciliation is being offered. The CPU research has been criticized for neglecting the child's point of view. We were thwarted in our plan to ask children about their experience of conciliation since so few were actually directly involved in the process. Where children were included parents were equally divided in their views about the helpfulness of their involvement. Some professionals have advocated that only if the post-divorce arrangements are satisfactory from the *children's* perspective should conciliation be considered effective. This is a difficult issue, however, particularly as most children would prefer their parents to remain together. A recent study by Garwood (1989) found that children who had been to conciliation were generally positive about the experience and reported improved access arrangements and increased understanding and communication within the family.

To some extent lawyers and the judiciary could be considered as clients. In the court-based services the actual structure and process of conciliation is determined in large measure *by the court*. The needs of the court to administer cases efficiently and expediently according to criteria unrelated to conciliation, can give the impression that the *court* is the client who uses a service in order to improve the efficiency of the administration of justice, in other words to restrict costly, lengthy judicial hearings.

Most referrals to the independent services come through solicitors. An interesting paradox for these services is that in order to gain status and authority they have sought support and guidance from senior members of the judiciary and lawyers. Without this the conciliation movement would not have survived in a society where there is no well-established tradition of self-help-seeking in the personal social services, and no private fee-for-service sector. An arrangement with the Law Society has enabled conciliators to charge a small fee as an extension to the legal aid provision for dealing with ancillary disputes, the fee being recognized as payment for a short report to the solicitors recording the outcome of conciliation. To some extent lawyers become clients of the service, sending their clients to settle disputes, who then return to the lawyers for the conduct of the legal proceedings.

Family members other than the divorcing couple and their children may have a vested interest in the settlement of the disputes. Most conciliation services do not involve grandparents, new partners, and others even when their roles in the family may be central to the dispute and its resolution. The present view that accepts the parents as representing the family may need to be reconsidered if conciliation is to be effective on a number of levels dealing with a wider range of issues, particularly if the benefits are expected to be long term.

FAMILY CONCILIATION – THE WAY FORWARD

Research studies have pointed the way to a reconsideration of the status and practice of family conciliation. So far, conciliation has been grafted on to an existing legal structure and incorporated into a set of adjudicative and investigative procedures. It does not constitute a distinct alternative as a dispute resolution mechanism. Dingwall and Eekelaar (1988) in their wider vision of divorce conciliation have pointed to the difficulties of fusing notions of cost-saving, welfare paternalism, and self-reliant dispute resolution in a movement for reform. They express disappointment that research has shown that five years after divorce, there is little difference in compliance between conciliated and adjudicated settlements (Pearson and Thoennes 1988). Since family conciliation has aimed to go beyond 'reaching agreements' the need to distinguish between legal and conciliation processes becomes essential.

The legal system aims to provide just and fair settlements based on evidence and facts, and does not necessarily seek to resolve conflict nor to effect any other welfare benefits. Conciliation, on the other hand, gives the parties to the dispute the power to reach their own settlements, and in so doing encourages the reduction of conflict and the improvement of communication, promoting increased interpersonal skills for the negotiation of any future disputes. These processes are significantly and fundamentally different. Ideally disputants should have access to justice as well as sufficient information to *choose* which dispute resolution mechanism best suits their needs.

Family conciliation in its rapid development has concentrated on the disputes which emerge in separation and divorce. Conciliation of disputes in intact families has hardly begun. Vroom *et al.* (1981: 10–11) have argued that conciliation can be useful at *all* stages of the family life cycle. In their view family conciliation is 'an ideal whose time has come', but so far has been restricted in its application.

NOTES

1 The Advisory, Conciliation and Arbitration Service (ACAS) began operation in 1974 and was established as a statutory body by the Employment Protection Act 1975. See Chapter 8 in this handbook and *The ACAS Role in Conciliation, Arbitration and Mediation* (1979), London: HMSO.

2 The Divorce Reform Act 1969 came into force in 1971, and is now embodied in the Matrimonial Causes Act 1973. No decree absolute of divorce or nullity, or decree of judicial separation, can be granted unless the court has made one of the orders in relation to the welfare of children specified in section 41 of that Act. Only the custodial parent is obliged to attend the section 41 Appointment.

3 A Royal Commission on Marriage and Divorce (Morton) was appointed in 1951 after a Bill to allow divorce after seven years' separation had received a second hearing in the House of Commons.

4 The National Family Conciliation Council was formally inaugurated in March 1983. Its aim is to promote good professional practice by co-ordinating independent conciliation services in England and Wales.

11 Articulating the power of 'us plus them'

Community conflict, compromise and consensus[1]

Tony Gibson

INTRODUCTION

As a youngster I read Ignazio Silone's *The Seeds Beneath the Snow*, and was gripped by its message that even in times of tyranny and deprivation, when the political and social landscape seems barren, life lurks beneath the surface. Deep down, people have within themselves the capacity and the need to think and act independently, to resist the pressures to accept and conform, to create their own future together because they have found they could rely on each other.

Not long after, I struggled, with my schoolboy French, through *Le Trahison des Clercs*, which brought home to me the underlying problem: those in our society who are good at talking and writing, who have the specialist knowledge and the professional training – the experts, the intelligentsia – may make sense to each other, but they seldom reach home to the rest of society. They are on a different wavelength, they talk a different language. Yet they assume that their specialist knowledge, and their capacity to put it into words of their choosing, entitle them to think that they know best.

Often they mean well but are unable to understand the feelings and the priorities and the intuitions of ordinary people. So they have gone their own way building the tower blocks and the top-heavy social and political systems which imprison us.

People have been deprived of the initiative, denied the opportunity to work together and gradually to come to rely upon each other, to gain confidence in each other and to achieve results for which they can share the credit. The evidence of this kind of deprivation is that even in relatively well-built housing estates there is a high incidence of depression, alcoholism, drug abuse and vandalism. People keep themselves to themselves for fear of each other.

My concern is to find ways in which the seeds of life beneath the snow can be helped to germinate and to grow. But I believe this can be done only when there is an effective alliance between the professionals – local government officers, civil servants, workers in specialist agencies – and the residents in each locality. Fundamentally there is a common cause, there could be common ground, but it needs a common language to articulate that hidden strength.

This common language is the language of shared experience. In what follows

I shall describe two ways of making it manifest. Both are concerned with the common ground that we all recognize and value: the neighbourhood, which in many countries of the western world is under threat.

To me a neighbourhood has a double lock. It is not just a patch on a map; it is also a collection of people, black and white, male and female, old and young, all sorts – every living soul who lives and works in that area. And no one else. To those who belong to the neighbourhood there is also the feeling that it belongs to them. It's 'our neighbourhood', which we have helped to make what it is, a congenial place in which old and young can feel at home.

The idea of 'our' neighbourhood, which we belong to and which belongs to us, is not dead yet. It showed up two generations ago during the wartime air raids when people took mutual aid for granted, and found by and large that in time of crisis they could rely on each other. More recently the same staying-power was shown in the support groups, often led by women, during the British miners' strike. This strength has local roots. People within reach of each other can get wise to each other, can come to depend on each other; what they achieve is there under their noses, and they can take and share the credit. This experience begins to restore self-confidence and to move people from indifference to commitment. It is a political as well as a social force.

THE LIGHTMOOR PROJECT

My work for the Neighbourhood Initiatives Foundation brings me into touch with many neighbourhood projects which are taking shape in different parts of this country, and abroad. In some I have already been quite deeply involved. One in particular, the Lightmoor project, which won the award for the outstanding community enterprise of 1987 from the Prince of Wales on behalf of *The Times*/Royal Institute of British Architects scheme, is a prime example of the shared experience which bridges the communication gap. Two years later Prince Charles came to see how we had progressed and was so absorbed that he overstayed his schedule. Afterwards I had a letter saying he was 'enormously impressed with what had been achieved so far and was particularly struck by the strong sense of community which binds the project together'. It is a very small project, fourteen homes and workplaces on a building site of about eight acres, with another fifteen acres of rough countryside to manage. It was developed from scratch by a handful of pioneer-minded people, some with jobs, some unemployed, and over the past few years they have been building their own homes, workplaces, the access road, the drainage system, the village green – a new neighbourhood to their own design but in active consultation with the professionals in local government and in the Town and Country Planning Association. The consultation process has been reversed: instead of the 'experts' working out what they think might fit the needs of the people, and then getting their approval, it is the people themselves who work things out, but use the experts for information and advice 'on tap but not on top'.

For the residents themselves, the shared experience of shaping a new neighbourhood creates a bond between everyone concerned, irrespective of age and
background, because we have shared in the rigours of decision-making, which
more often than not has been hammered out at the bottom of the trench together,
digging the drains, or coming up to the surface for a cuppa. We have held
innumerable meetings, of the Community Association and the Council of
Management (which includes representatives from the local authorities as well as
the residents), but their success and incisiveness has more often than not
depended on the preliminary double-digging, the turning over of the soil of
discussion, which went on, informally, as we got on with the job in hand.
Communication, the exchange of ideas and experience, came naturally. It has not
depended primarily on formal meetings where the talkers always win. Lightmoor
has shown that a hybrid approach, a mixture of skills, and in some cases no
technical skills at all, and a mixture of livelihoods or prospective livelihoods, and
a mixture of ages and social backgrounds – can become a *compound* with
properties of its own: interdependence, basic concern for each other, a capacity
to deal constructively with local authorities and a determination not to be
defeated by bureaucratic setbacks.

The compound is as different from its individual constituents as flour and
water are from bread. The working relationship is the yeast which makes the
dough rise. There is not much point in talking about it, devising verbal concepts,
labelling it in words. The means to understand it are there already in the
'language' of shared experience.

It can prove a very forceful language, challenging the conventional
distinctions between 'leaders' and 'rank-and-file'.

Neighbourhood leadership is counter-productive if it depends simply on
making speeches or manipulating committees. It's not so much leaders as
'moving spirits' which are needed: the yeast that creates the ferment, and loses
its own identity once the new compound forms.

The key feature of this new compound is *commitment*. People who have had a
share in creating a neighbourhood will want to maintain and safeguard it. This
applies just as much to the professionals who have been in support as to the
residents who have taken the strain. Both sides can share in the credit. But such
a combined operation can survive only when its components really understand
each other and can look far enough ahead to see the wood for the trees.

COMMUNICATION PROBLEMS

Lightmoor is only one of many varieties of community-led neighbourhood
development which are taking place, largely because the top-heavy 'mega-
schemes' favoured by central government and the big commercial developers are
fouling themselves up. It still takes a great deal of staying-power, on the part both
of the residents and of their professional supporters, to survive what Prince
Charles has called 'the cat's cradle of red tape which chokes this country from
end to end'. Residents or prospective residents need to know exactly what is on

offer – land, buildings, the possibilities for creating livelihood, planning constraints, costs, terms and timetable on which money can be obtained, the accessibility of expert advice, the opportunities to reinforce skills and experience by further training. They cannot be expected to commit themselves to a mishmash of if's and when's and maybe's. So the outsiders – the professionals – have somehow to provide precise answers, and present them intelligibly without pre-empting the choices which the insiders will make, and thus denying them effective 'ownership' of the projects they must sustain and safeguard. Without this clarity and precision, all the energy and drive are dissipated.

The outsiders need to understand their own special role. This isn't always as easy at first as one might think, because professionals are so used to knowing best and acting accordingly.

The insiders themselves will also need to develop their own capacities to make decisions together without the fluent talkers driving everyone else up the wall and out of the door. They need to see things whole without losing sight of relevant detail, to define policies, decide priorities and distribute responsibilities.

So, after all, we do need to define and systematize. It isn't enough to have a working relationship, and leave it at that. The relationship, if it is a good one, provides the motive power, the 'group dynamic', and this can involve and commit both 'Us and Them'. But creating this joint commitment is only half the battle. To win it and to make such a combined operation succeed, the power that is generated must be effectively applied. Not diffused but articulated, brought precisely to bear on needs and priorities and the resources to deal with them.

How can this precision be achieved through a 'language of shared experience' which does not primarily consist of words? Let me begin by setting out what tends to happen when human beings talk to each other before they know each other well and words are all that they can rely on. It's what I call the Problems of the Talking-Shop.

Normally a consultation brings various people together, face to face, to talk things through. Those who are good at talking tend to dominate (even though they may sometimes wish otherwise) simply because the others are not so fluent and find it difficult to get a word in edgeways. So their knowledge, experience and intuitive understanding get left out of consideration.

'Face to face' can be a problem. Some people like to put themselves across, as well as putting across a piece of information or a point of view. Others are less keen. They don't want to seem pushy. Or they are afraid that if what they say fails to catch on, they'll be left looking silly, in a minority of one.

Merely to be identified with a particular proposal can be a disadvantage. So and So has a reputation which rubs off on what he or she is saying – 'Here we go again' – and the message becomes distorted by what we know, good or bad, about the track record and the motivation of the messenger.

The physical conditions in which the talk takes place may impose fresh limitations. The layout of the meeting probably gives physical prominence to the 'officers of the committee' or the 'visiting experts', who are grouped together on one side of the table, or at the head of it.

The mere formality of the occasion may be off-putting. There is an agenda, decided beforehand for the best of reasons – to make sure that we stick to the point and tackle one thing at a time. But that may not be the best way to get people teasing out a problem, or exploring a range of options, at least to begin with. They may prefer to get a bird's-eye view of the whole situation, and then spiral down to a particular point of decision. But such 'brainstorming' works only when there's plenty of time and everyone concerned is used to saying succinctly whatever comes into their heads.

The point of bringing together people with different ideas and experience is to be able to go further together than any individuals could manage on their own. This means being able to reconsider, to have second or third thoughts, to respond to other people's ideas as well. *You cannot think unless you change your mind –* it's biologically impossible! But dare you re-think under the noses of everyone else, without the risk of appearing inconsistent, and losing face?

Finally, there's the question of confidence – not merely self-confidence, or confidence in a particular individual who happens to be holding forth, but confidence as a group in our ability to establish some common ground, and to get somewhere in spite of our differences. If the very first thing we identify together is the area of our major disagreement, and everyone begins by stating their strong feelings on that subject, the heat is on, and the atmosphere that builds up won't help anyone to see things clearly.

EDUCATION FOR NEIGHBOURHOOD CHANGE

So this brings me to my second example, the decision-making materials and techniques which have been developed over some twenty years of experiment at Nottingham University and in factories, schools and housing estates.[2]

The Education for Neighbourhood Change packs and manuals which embody this approach make it possible for people to *show* what they mean, not just talk about it. They consist of materials which can be seen and manipulated by many people working together, in groups that may range from half a dozen to upwards of a hundred or more. There are now over forty different decision-making and information packs in use by residents' groups and local authorities in the United Kingdom, and their own national versions have been developed by government-sponsored organizations in the Netherlands, Germany and Australia. (The ideas have even had an occasional application to the transactions between academics at faculty level!)

Although there are many different packs, devised to meet all sorts of decision-making situations – in industry, community enterprises, building design, land-scaping, budgeting, committee-mongering – the underlying principles are much the same (although not as apparent to us in the early days as they are now).

The starting-point is the use of a fixed 'ground' – which everyone can recognize and accept. This might be a 3D layout which represents a neigh-bourhood, or a housing estate, or a street, or a building, or even one room such as the kitchen within it. Or it might be a chart, split into different areas to show

NOW/SOON/LATER; or WE DO IT ALONE/WE DO IT WITH OUTSIDE HELP/PASS THE BUCK (there's another agency which can do the lot for us). The 3D layout or the 2D chart is something which everyone present can easily recognize and accept. If it is a model of the neighbourhood (made by local residents with a kit provided in the pack), it represents the place as it is, warts and all. If it is the NOW/SOON/LATER chart, that too is an indication of priority (immediacy not necessarily importance) which everybody can understand.

On the table space surrounding this 'ground' (a model or a chart) go moveable items, cardboard cutouts which indicate a range of possibilities to be explored by placing them on the layout or the chart, and perhaps rearranging them in the light of further consideration. The cutouts provided in the pack are all those that we could think of when we put the pack together, but there are also blanks which allow the users of the pack to add new possibilities of their own, if they see fit. So this is the second basis for general agreement: we all accept that the cutouts represent all the possibilities that anyone has been able to think of so far. Taken together, the fixed 'ground' and the moveables on it, are the tools which everyone shares and owns.

Everyone can begin to use them, together, at once. People are free to put any of the cutouts anywhere, and having put them down, those cutouts lose their connection with their users. They are there as propositions in their own right, no longer directly associated with the persons who put them there.

The process is deliberately 'bitty' (in the computer programmer's sense of 'bits') at first. We are initially concerned with many small considerations, which do not yet add up. No pattern is imposed to start with. But since all the cutouts are moveable, they can be rearranged, reconsidered, sorted afresh until they begin to form a pattern which makes sense.

In this process no one has to commit themselves until they wish to. Putting a cutout down, or subsequently moving it to what might seem a better position, or removing it and replacing it by something else, is an exploratory move, which can be reconsidered later in the light of second or third thoughts, one's own or someone else's.

At every stage everyone can see things whole – take a bird's-eye view, see the *Gestalt*. And observing how one thing relates to another, how relationships transform a particular situation, it is equally possible to home in on a particular area and adjust a particular detail. Detail and context are always in view. And as the possibilities are reconsidered, sorted and sifted, the grain begins to be more apparent, and the chaff gets rejected by general agreement. So even as the process develops there is likely to be good reason for further common agreement. We can see what we all agree is marginal, or unimportant, and should be rejected. We can also see some areas of conflict where the placing of one cutout contradicts another, and other areas in which there is no conflict, where we can presume a measure of agreement. We can recognize this situation with its negative and its positive elements, for what it is. Our common acceptance of those matters on which there is no dispute provides the confidence and the staying-power to cope with the controversial issues.

One of the most popular and effective of the packs is *Planning for Real*, in which a 3D neighbourhood layout enables people to sort out what needs to be done in order to improve the surroundings they know only too well. On a scale of about 1:200, your own front door is about half the height of your little fingernail, but it is immediately identifiable, and locating familiar landmarks is what attracts people around the model in the first place. The model is made up of many smaller sections so as to be easily portable; and it is so large – 12 or 15 ft across, or in one celebrated case 24 ft long by 6 ft across – that it takes up all the space that in a conventional meeting hall is divided between a 'platform party' and the 'audience'. The situation more closely resembles a jumble-sale, with everyone – officials, politicians, residents – milling round it, viewing it from different angles, conferring with their next-door neighbours with scarcely a look at each other's faces because they are concentrating their attention on the model itself, and the possibilities it begins to reveal. This change in the conventional eyelines is important. In a traditional, confrontational situation, people look at each other – become angry or bored or dominated or bemused or infatuated. Around the model the eyelines converge on the subject matter itself, the 'common ground' which it represents.

The cutouts are arranged beside the model, for people to pick and choose amongst them as they see fit. Labels saying 'preserve' or 'rehabilitate' or 'demolish', representations of allotments, play areas, chemist's shops, livestock sheds, police foot patrols, advice centres: every option anyone can think of. People are free, individually, to put whatever they choose wherever it seems best to them on the model. So in a matter of minutes the model gets covered with these cutouts. Then when everyone has had the chance to do all they want, there can be a stock-taking: 'Do we really want sixteen Adventure Playgrounds on one housing estate? If not, how many, and where?' So different groups can form, according to differing interests, and begin the process of sifting and re-sorting the cutouts on the model, together.

This is a serious but also a sociable process. It can be fun. As one old lady told me 'It's better than Bingo!' And even when major conflicts loom, they can be contained. One of the early Planning for Reals took place in a red-light area in the centre of Sheffield. Residents, councillors and local government officers used the model to sort out their ideas together, then split up into groups on housing, transport, care and so on and made good progress. In the housing group it gradually emerged that some of the old void houses were being used by prostitutes. Neither the housing officials nor the police were aware, but of course the residents were able to tell them precisely. So they concerted their efforts in order to get the houses quickly reoccupied when there was a flitting. In the transport group there was general agreement about several of the problems of parking space and traffic dangers to children. But then the discussions, which were taking place week by week in different people's homes, began to concentrate on the issue of the kerb-crawlers. On the whole the older generation in the group wanted to solve everything by moving on the prostitutes – sweep them all under someone else's carpet! Others were more concerned to go to the roots of the problem: unemployment, care, split families.

On one evening feelings grew so hot that one person went outside and kicked in the car headlights of another member of the group. . . . And both parties went on attending the group meetings, and talking to each other. When I asked a local councillor about it he said 'Well, we're like a family, you have quarrels, but that's not the end of everything'. It was still possible for the dialogue to continue, in words now, because there was already a basis of shared experience, built up throughout the Planning for Real operation, on which everyone could rest.

A housewife described this shared experience in the use of another pack, *Building Design and Conversion*, in which a table-top model is used in order to work out the internal layout of a house. A small group drawn from several different members of a prospective Housing Co-operative, with very little previous experience of each other, came together on one evening and manipulated cutouts which represented the kitchen sink, stove, store cupboard, windows, doors, party walls, household furniture, within the space outlined by the 'shell' of the notional house. This is how she described their experience:

> We saw what we were doing. You could translate words into actions . . . there was a definite affinity growing up, just as two people who live together can start off a sentence and you know the rest of it . . . we got on to common ground quicker, because with words everybody's words are the same: but the imagination may be different . . . in the mind everybody can be seeing a different thing and maybe not come to that consensus, stick out for their thing, because they could not see in their mind what was making it impossible . . . but where you have got the model . . . you looked at the thing and said 'let's try this'. So we tried it, if it was wrong we changed it . . . then other objections were raised – so 'all right let's try it again another way', and this is where we came to a consensus. . . .
>
> It was like speaking your thoughts . . . you visualized each other's thoughts, you project your thoughts into vision . . . we got to a state in the end where we didn't need to speak.

In the early days 3D seemed the obvious and natural medium for communication. Everyone could understand something that they could relate to their everyday surroundings. But later I was asked by many different neighbourhood groups to produce materials which would help them to deal with more abstract problems – deciding on the rules to adopt for a co-operative, working out the priorities involved in getting a neighbourhood scheme off the ground or planning a budget. So 2D took its place in the canon. And, rather unexpectedly, it released a new dimension to the decision-making process. Instead of cutouts representing the physical changes that might be made on a layout, there are cards, which can signify anything: 'Matters arising', which need to be arranged on an agenda: alternative versions of rules to be embodied in a constitution; responsibilities to be assigned; costs which have to be distributed.

All these are items which everyone can identify, and anyone can provisionally allocate. The 'ground' chart can represent periods of time, areas of responsibility, degrees of importance, cost centres and levels of decision-making. People gather round in order to sort out the cards which represent the possibilities under consideration, and place them as they please. But the added advantage over the 3D layouts and the option cutouts is that on the underside of each 'suggestion' card there is the word 'disagree'. Everyone is selecting cards and placing them face up in the areas of their choice, and then moving round the display area to see where others have put their cards. If anyone thinks that a card is wrongly placed, they can, quite unobtrusively, turn it face down. So once again everybody has a bird's-eye view of the whole situation. Within a few minutes it's possible to see all the placings on which there is no dispute – because the cards remain face up; at the same time it's possible to identify the areas of possible conflict – where the card has been turned over to show disagreement. This is all still common ground: we can all see where we must be prepared to argue things out.

Dealing with items on which there is disagreement becomes easier because there can be a high degree of anonymity. No one takes particular notice of who it was who placed a card face up, or who subsequently turned it face down. So those who do not wish to expose their views too soon can sit back, and let others unfold the arguments pro and con. Sometimes, as an observer knowing what to watch out for, I have seen people who took the initiative in putting forward a pro-position, or countering it, wait until they see how the discussion goes, and then chime in on one side or the other without ever revealing that it was they who started the whole thing off.

Once the disagreement cards have been identified they can in turn be priori-tized. Do we need to decide this NOW/SOON/LATER? And having worked that one out, what do we need to decide effectively? Is it an EASY decision, that can be done by vote on the facts already available? Or is MORE INFORMATION NEEDED? Or is the issue too hot to handle at this very moment? Does it NEED FURTHER CONSIDERATION? Or would we be better advised to LEAVE IT TO A TECHNICAL EXPERT?

Recently a group of residents on one stigmatized estate came together and set about reversing the long descent into apathy and bloody-mindedness. They spent months in turning over the possibilities, but they got their act together only when they decided to have a 'brainstorming' meeting, with the cards and the NOW/SOON/LATER chart. They had a preliminary meeting in order to list their main objectives. Then they began to break these down into scores of red cards, each with two or three words describing a particular activity, service, investigation, procurement or problem which would sooner or later have to be tackled. As other residents trickled in everyone set out to sort out the cards between them.

The first stage was to separate the cards which someone (not necessarily everyone) thought worth considering, leaving behind those which, on reflection, nobody thought worth bothering about. Then from the selected pile the cards were redistributed on to the three sections labelled NOW, SOON and LATER. From time to time, while this was happening, people were thinking of new items to put on fresh cards and place according to their notions of immediacy.

Very soon, upwards of a hundred cards had been laid out and scrutinized; the 'disagree' cards began to be debated, one by one, beginning with those in the

NOW section. Some were moved to another level of priority, others were re-worded or amalgamated, in order to reach a more acceptable consensus, or perhaps dropped right out. This reduced the number to just over sixty.

The next stage was to rearrange the cards at each priority level according to the agency most likely to be able to cope. So there were now vertical sections labelled 'Council', 'Charities', and 'Do it Ourselves'. Finally a new set of blank cards, yellow, was used to indicate the different kinds of training that might be required. Wherever a red card might imply a training requirement, a yellow card was made out and placed ahead of it on the priorities chart.

The residents' group and two 'outside' professionals remained intensely absorbed for well over two hours, and at the end of the session had sorted every card out to their satisfaction. One said 'I came to the session knowing what I wanted, but not able to find the words. Now it's all done!' Another: 'We could never have done all this in time in any other way'. They were finding out what countless other field applications of the packs had demonstrated: the whole process of decision-making by *showing what you mean* takes a fraction of the time that normally is spent on talking it out in a series of traditional meetings. And yet none of this appears to inhibit the talk. Quite early on in the research that went into the use of the packs in schools, the Scottish Education Department's Inspectorate decided to set up a series of promotions for the packs – as tools in *language* development. The word had come back from schools where the packs were in use that quite unexpectedly, those traditionally thought of as 'passengers' – non-achievers, who seldom had anything to say for themselves – suddenly came out of their shells and began to contribute their ideas and their experience. Much more recently, south of the Border, we heard of children who were literally truanting to school from home, where they were supposed to be on the sick list, on the days when the packs were in use.

When it is possible to exchange ideas and experience, on a level footing with other people without feeling at a disadvantage in face of their verbal fluency, quite suddenly the words themselves begin to flow. The frustration, and the 'aggro' it provokes, begin to diminish. The climate becomes more conclusive to exploring possibilities, seeking out new ways of tackling the problem, discovering solutions that had previously been overlooked.

So this is an empirical process, starting out without too many preconceptions and working together to narrow down the possibilities, establish what can be immediately agreed on, what needs fresh thinking, what are the relative strengths of agreement or disagreement when it comes to the point. In all these respects it is quite close to everyday life. We do not usually begin by classifying everything we see. We take in a situation as a whole, pick up various impressions about it, consider and reconsider, narrow things down to the bare essentials, and so gradually make up our minds. We could do this with varying success, as individuals, and attempt to convince others that we know best. But this is not usually the best way of carrying conviction. It is only when we can share with others the process of sorting out, and narrowing down, and reaching a conclusion together, that we are able to develop, through the process itself, the kind of mutual confidence and respect which are needed to make us want to safeguard whatever decisions are finally reached.

CONCLUSION

What I have described are two kinds of working models. The first is a project such as the Lightmoor Project, which brings people together in a shared activity, through which they begin to work out their own relationships, define their own goals, generate their motive power. What they do, together, can be seen by others, and understood in a way that mere words cannot convey. *Seeing is believing*, and others, who are less pioneer-minded, less highly motivated, can grasp the idea and catch the enthusiasm.

An ounce of practice is worth a ton of talk. It is something there to see and feel; and understanding comes, gradually, through the interaction of those involved.

It is this process which is reproduced in the Education for Neighbourhood Change decision-making packs.

In both cases the most important thing to be shared is experience, through working together in a situation which is supportive, not threatening. Suddenly people find they can talk to each other as children do in the playground, or as husbands and wives do over supper at the end of the day: not as strangers or antagonists but as old acquaintances. Mutual confidence rests on the many small achievements which have been made together. These create the staying-power to survive disappointments, contain conflict, protect the common accord.

This is the unifying motive-power on which social, political and economic progress depend.

NOTES

1 An earlier version of this chapter appeared under the title 'Come Riconquistare L'iniziativa locale' in *Volonta* (1989) 1(2).

2 The Education for Neighbourhood Change publications and price list can be had, together with information on the training and consultancy services provided, from the Neighbourhood Initiatives Foundation, Chapel House, 7 Gravel Leasowe, Lightmoor, Telford TF4 3QL.

   The original research was done at the University of London Goldsmiths' College and at Nottingham University, in the late 1960s and early 1970s, first in upwards of 200 schools over a wide age and ability range from 9 year olds to 18 year olds, and from IQs of 135 to below 70. Later, with backing from the Department of the Environment, and a study of action groups in industry and the community commissioned by the Rowntree Memorial Trust, the basic principles were applied to decision-making at adult level, within communities, and between residents and professionals in local authorities and central government, and more recently between shop-floor and management in industry.

12 Consumer protection: strategies for dispute resolution

Richard Thomas

> For this is not the liberty which we can hope; that no grievance ever should arise in the commonwealth, that let no man in this world expect; but when complaints are freely heard, deeply considered, and speedily reformed, then is the utmost bound of civil liberty that wise men look for.
>
> (Milton: *Aeropagitica*)

This chapter is *not* an attempt at a considered assessment of the extent to which complaints are 'freely heard, deeply considered and speedily reformed' under the various schemes that have been set up, within and outside the court system, for the resolution of consumer disputes. Instead, I shall

1 indicate how the courts handle (or do not handle) consumer disputes
2 outline proposals for reform
3 describe the main schemes which have been set up outside the court system
4 attempt a general assessment of the strengths and weaknesses of 'private' dispute resolution.

CONSUMER REDRESS

I start with some necessary context. It is manifestly in the interests of consumers that there should be effective and accessible means for resolving disputes and enforcing rights. This rests on two main planks. First, the possibility of recourse to such means for resolving a dispute strengthens the consumer's hand at the complaint/negotiation stage; second, such means may have to be used in order to establish and/or enforce substantive rights.

I do not need to elaborate the difficulties faced by individual consumers who need or wish to vindicate or defend their rights by formal action. Most (but not all) consumer claims are 'small claims'. Where the injury, loss or damage is relatively small the conventional approaches to litigation are inappropriate. The nature of the problem was recognized as long ago as 1913 by Roscoe Pound (Pound 1913) and was first fully articulated in this country by the Molony Committee on Consumer Protection (Molony 1962: paras 394, 403, 409 and 482). The economics of small claims dictate that, if they are to be resolved at all, it must normally be without the benefit of legal services – whether obtained privately or provided at public expense. The unrepresented litigant, engaged in legal action as a 'once-in-a-lifetime' experience, is therefore the classic 'one-shotter', often engaged in battle against a 'repeat-player' who will be more powerful, more experienced at litigation, less susceptible to delays, and more likely to have the benefit of legal advice and representation (Galanter 1974).

Once it is recognized that individuals and consumers will usually be unrepresented, the economic and other features of the 'small claims problem' become apparent. The psychological and cultural barriers associated with the conventional courts assume major significance. It can be intimidating – even for the most confident – to pursue a dispute, on a 'do-it-yourself' basis, through a court which is largely accustomed to dealing with professional representatives. It is only gradually being appreciated that 'Many small claims, debt and housing cases are in effect conducted on a basis of inequality between the parties. . . . Unrepresented litigants are unlikely to know what to do or to get on and do it' (Lord Chancellor's Department 1988: para 349).

In 1970 the (original) Consumer Council published *Justice Out of Reach*, which exploded the myth that county courts operated as small claims courts. As that report made clear, the county court – far from being the little man's court – was the place where the little man gets taken to court. From 1972, as a direct response to that report, the small claims procedures were introduced and since then have been successively reviewed and reformed (Applebey 1978; NCC 1979; Thomas 1982).

SMALL CLAIMS IN THE COUNTY COURTS

The present small claims procedure in England and Wales deals with disputed claims up to £500 (not just consumer disputes), involving some 45,000 hearings a year. Its main distinguishing features are

1 it is applicable to almost all kinds of disputed claims, including those where the consumer is the defendant
2 hearings are intended to be informal, and the registrar may conduct the proceedings in whatever manner he or she thinks best to achieve a just result
3 the winner cannot normally recover the costs of representation from the loser.

These provisions are intended to keep costs to a minimum by encouraging cases to be handled personally. The overall purpose is to provide an accessible, quick, cheap and informal means of deciding disputed claims which involve comparatively small sums of money.

A full description of the small claims procedure, and a summary of the findings of the 1986 factual study, are set out in the *Report of the Review Body on Civil Justice* (Lord Chancellor's Department 1988: ch. 8). (Fuller materials are to be found in the Small Claims Consultation Paper and the Factual Study itself (Lord Chancellor's Department 1986). The Civil Justice Review concluded that, although for most people the litigation process is likely to be seen as complex, strange and unpredictable, the small claims procedure emerges as substantially sound in that it is able to produce results, without major delay and cost, which satisfy a large number of those who use it. It is workable in that it produces these results by a process which many litigants are able to operate without undue difficulty. However, litigants may be prejudiced by a lack of uniform procedure and by considerable inconsistencies of approach around the country.

The Civil Justice Review's proposals for reform in this area have been widely welcomed. The Courts and Legal Services Act 1990 paves the way for their introduction. The proposed reforms include

1 an increased jurisdiction to £1,000
2 proposals to sharpen the identity of the system as a 'small claims court' within the county court
3 a self-contained set of small claims rules
4 an overhaul of forms and explanatory materials – to make them easy to understand and simple to use
5 a single substantive hearing wherever possible
6 proposals to require registrars to adopt an 'interventionist' approach and to give reasons for decisions
7 a presumption in favour of lay representation
8 better links between courts and advice centres.

ACCESS TO JUSTICE: ALTERNATIVE DISPUTE RESOLUTION

The Civil Justice Review's final report included a chapter on 'Access to justice' which opened with the declaration that 'Ease of access for the public is an important test of the effectiveness of the civil justice system'.

The county court small claims system emerged from the Civil Justice Review with a reasonably clean bill of health and has provided pointers for reforming many other parts of our civil justice system (Thomas 1990). Certainly most of the litigants who actually used the small claims procedure seemed broadly satisfied with the procedure; indeed 81 per cent said that they would be very or quite likely to use it again should the need arise.

By improving ease of use, the reform proposals should also improve ease of access. But it is more difficult to evaluate the system from the viewpoint of the *non-users*. The Civil Justice Review's attempt to probe the circumstances of a small sample of 'potential litigants' was somewhat inconclusive. There remains repeated concern – particularly from those closest to consumers in dispute – that many genuine cases never reach the courts. This, in turn, reflects fear (real or imagined) about costs and also considerable antipathy and ignorance amongst many private individuals towards the courts. (A 1978 survey showed that 55 per cent of respondents believed that county courts dealt with shop-lifting offences, compared with 19 per cent who thought that they dealt with complaints about faulty goods – NCC 1979.)

The National Consumer Council's recent study of the English legal system – *Ordinary Justice* – concluded that 'the greatest disappointment is that cases are rarely brought by consumers' (NCC 1989). The NCC calculated that the grand total of consumer disputes handled by the small claims system is about 12,500 per annum. This compares with over 600,000 consumer complaints received by local authorities and advice centres (Office of Fair Trading 1988). It also compares with an Office of Fair Trading survey which indicated that some 30 million consumer problems are encountered each year.

About 12 million of these problems related to categories where the average price was over £100 – furniture, household appliances, cars, car servicing, building work and holidays. Although the survey shows that those who complained and persevered were most likely to receive satisfaction, some 4.5 million problems remained unresolved after the consumer had taken some form of action to secure redress (Office of Fair Trading 1986).

Of course, many – perhaps most – of these problems may have been unjustified on the facts and/or the law. And I am certainly not suggesting that over 4 million cases are awaiting some form of dispute resolution. The fact remains that the survey revealed that less than 2 per cent of the consumers who took some form of further action threatened court action. And not a single person in the survey (almost 5,000 respondents) actually took court action.

Concern about the high levels of non-use of the courts has influenced a number of initiatives to set up 'alternative' methods for the resolution of consumer disputes.

PRIVATE SMALL CLAIMS COURTS

The Voluntary Arbitration Schemes in London and Manchester were essentially private small claims courts providing an arbitration service. They broke new ground by attempting to combine oral hearings with fast, cheap, informal and interventionist procedures. In particular the administrators of the schemes helped litigants to prepare their cases. The schemes received support from charitable foundations, local authorities, the legal profession and academic institutions. Their procedures were widely publicized. Actual cases were broadcast on radio and television in order to inform the public of their existence. By the time of their demise (in 1979–80) both schemes were swamped with cases that they could hardly handle. Both schemes foundered because of their inability to secure any long-term financial support for their operations. But they undoubtedly served useful functions by demonstrating the demand for quick, cheap and simple machinery, by showing what could be done with a pioneering spirit and initiative, and (above all) by serving as a laboratory in which new approaches to decision-making could be adopted.

The schemes were widely acclaimed but they also demonstrated some weaknesses of this form of private justice. The Manchester scheme had to adopt rigid geographical boundaries to limit its jurisdiction. The voluntary nature of both schemes demanded an amenable defendant who would consent to having the dispute resolved by arbitration. Above all, their dependence upon insecure sources of funding extinguished any thoughts of a comprehensive alternative to the court system.

ARBITRATION UNDER CODES OF PRACTICE

A sectoral approach is probably inevitable if the financial resources for private justice are to come from the business community. This has been the pattern with the various conciliation and arbitration schemes which the Office of Fair Trading (OFT) has encouraged, with the commercial ombudsmen, and with the complaints schemes run by professional bodies.

Under section 124 of the Fair Trading Act 1973, the Director General of Fair Trading has a duty to encourage trade associations to prepare codes of practice. So far twenty-four such codes have been negotiated by the Director General under these provisions. As Table 12.1 shows, many of these codes include conciliation and arbitration facilities. The usual framework under each code is that the consumer is advised to pursue his or her complaint in the first instance with the trader concerned; failing satisfaction, contact with a local advice agency is recommended. The third stage is to involve the trade association, which will attempt to conciliate. Finally, most of the codes offer independent arbitration as an alternative to recourse to the courts.

Table 12.1 Redress facilities available under OFT-approved codes of practice

Code	Conciliation (by trade association, unless otherwise indicated)	Arbitration (through Chartered Institute of Arbitrators, unless otherwise indicated)	Other facilities
Domestic laundry and dry cleaning	Yes	No	Independent fabric testing centres
Tour operators	Yes	Yes	—
Domestic electrical appliance servicing	Yes	Yes	—
Selling, siting and letting of holiday caravans	Yes	Yes	—
Photographic industry	Yes	Yes	—
Shopping at home	Yes (independent Code Administrator)	Yes (independent Code Administrator)	—
Domestic electrical appliance servicing by electricity boards	Yes (by electricity consultative councils)	Yes	—
Footwear	No	No	Footwear testing centre

Table 12.1 continued

Finance houses	Yes	Yes	—
Glass and glazing	Yes	Yes	—
Motor industry	Yes	Yes (arbitration set up by trade associations)	Institute of Automotive Assessors
Motorcycles	Yes	Yes (arbitration set up by trade associations)	Institute of Automotive Assessors
Mail order publishers/ direct mail	Yes	No	Mail Order Publishers Authority
Catalogue mail order	Yes	Yes	—
Funeral directors	Yes	Yes	—
Shoe repairs	Yes	No	—
Furniture	Yes	Yes	—
Post Office	Yes (with PO Users National Council)	Yes	—
Selling and servicing of radio and television, etc.	Yes	No	—
Vehicle body repairs	Yes	Yes (motor industry arbitration scheme)	Institute of Automotive Assessors
Mechanical breakdown insurance	Yes	Yes	—

Goods and services covered by arbitration schemes include cars, holidays, servicing of household electrical appliances, double glazing, photography, catalogue mail order, furniture, funerals, holiday caravans and consumer credit. Under these codes, the trader accepts an obligation to submit to arbitration if the consumer pursues that option.

The consumer must pay a registration fee, based on a sliding scale, which is refundable in the event of success. There is normally no further cost or risk to the consumer. The arbitration is normally conducted by a member of the Chartered Institute of Arbitrators. The arbitrator normally proceeds on a documents-only basis, although there is power to call for further information from either party. In addition, independent technical experts can be appointed and, if need be, asked to examine the subject-matter of the dispute. The arbitrator's award is binding on both parties.

In 1981 the OFT published a report – *Redress Procedures under Codes of Practice* (OFT 1980; 1981) – which set out its conclusions following a review of the conciliation and arbitration stages. That report renewed support for the schemes, but recognized that various improvements were necessary. Eleven main conclusions were reached, most of which have now been implemented following negotiations with the trade associations and the Chartered Institute of Arbitrators.

Perhaps the most important specific conclusions were that arbitration should normally be on a documents-only basis, that arbitrators should always give reasons for their decisions, that time targets should be adopted and that, ideally, a standard arbitration scheme should be adopted. It was also recognized that increased publicity and closer monitoring were required. The OFT's 1984 booklet – *I'm Going to Take it Further*, of which over a quarter of a million copies have been distributed – has served to publicize these schemes and to give consumers guidance as to whether to go to court or seek arbitration.

As Table 12.2 indicates, use of the schemes varies considerably. The great majority of arbitrations have concerned package holidays, where 1,764 cases were referred to arbitration over the four years 1983–6 inclusive. Disputes involving cars (mainly where the trader is a member of the Motor Agents Association) are the next most numerous. By contrast the remaining arbitration schemes have been hardly used at all – for example only three disputes involving furniture were referred to arbitration over the same period, only one involving the servicing of household electrical appliances and none at all appear to have been referred concerning photographic equipment, funerals, vehicle body repairs or motor cycles.

Table 12.2 Consumer conciliation and arbitration cases handled by selected schemes and results 1983–86

	ABTA	GGF	MAA	MRA	NARF
Number of cases conciliated by trade association	42,253	N/k	2,759	1	3,063
Number of cases referred to arbitration	1,764	106	159	0	3
Claims upheld by arbitration	1,362	46	19	0	1
Claims wholly rejected by arbitration	340	23	57	0	2
Claims split/compromise agreed	[62]	28	71	0	0

Notes:
ABTA = Association of British Travel Agents
GGF = Glass and Glazing Federation
MAA = Motor Agents Association
MRA = Motor-Cycle Retailers Association
NARF = National Association of Retail Furnishers

PRIVATE OMBUDSMEN

Insurance Ombudsman Bureau

A different sectoral approach, again dependent upon business funding, has been adopted in the world of insurance and financial services. The Insurance Ombudsman Bureau (IOB) was set up by a number of leading insurance companies in 1981. The IOB has been established as an independent organization with its own constitution. It is financed by member companies who are represented on a Board, but it is the IOB Council which has the general responsibility (without involvement in individual cases) of employing the ombudsman and ensuring that he remains impartial and effectively fulfils his duties. The nine-strong council has seven members representing public and consumer interests and two representatives of member companies.

The general objects of the IOB are to deal with complaints, disputes and claims concerning policies taken out by or for private individuals with companies who are members of the IOB. The member companies of the IOB account for over 80 per cent of the domestic insurance market. The membership of almost 200 companies has recently been joined by all Lloyds underwriters. The ombudsman is empowered to act as counsellor, conciliator, adjudicator or arbitrator in regard to cases submitted to him. Policy-holders can put their disputes to the ombudsman if and when they have failed to get satisfaction from the chief executive of the company. The ombudsman, who is solely responsible for his decisions, proceeds on the basis of the full company files and any papers submitted by the policy-holder, together with any personal interviews and meetings he feels necessary and the advice of expert consultants. There is no charge to policy-holders.

Three features are particularly worth highlighting. The ombudsman's decisions are binding upon member companies up to £100,000 – but not on policy-holders. In other words, policy-holders are not required to abandon their legal rights, can reject the ombudsman's decisions and pursue the claim through the courts. Second, the ombudsman may have regard to 'general principles of good insurance practice', as well as to the contract terms and applicable rules of law. Third, the publication of a full annual report, drawing attention to the ombudsman's work and to points of particular interest, attracts regular press coverage and impacts upon the procedures and policies of insurance companies.

Annual reports reveal that cases passed to the ombudsman over the four-year period 1983–6 as follows:

Cases passed to ombudsman	4,051
Company decision revised	492
Company decision confirmed	1,889
Cases outstanding, withdrawn, resolved by summary advice, and so on.	1,670

By 1988, the cases received by the ombudsman had increased to 1,528 in a single year. In addition, large numbers of cases are resolved by the companies after the ombudsman's staff have referred the case to them and the IOB receives substantial numbers of enquiries which are outside its terms of reference (for example relating to non-member companies).

Private Insurance Arbitration Scheme

A small minority of insurance companies have chosen not to join the IOB scheme but have instead set up the Private Insurance Arbitration Scheme (PIAS). This scheme has been set up in conjunction with the Chartered Institute of Arbitrators. The scheme is simpler than that offered by the IOB. There is no separate organization, as such. Instead, a policy-holder in dispute with a member of the PIAS scheme may seek to have that dispute resolved by an arbitrator appointed by the Chartered Institute. Both parties must first agree to be bound by the decision of the arbitrator. The policy-holder must therefore abandon the right to pursue any legal remedies through the courts. Since there is no organization, the scheme cannot be as active as the IOB in promoting its own services and nor can it follow the example of the IOB in terms of producing annual reports and seeking to improve consumer satisfaction with insurance.

Banking Ombudsman Scheme

The Banking Ombudsman Scheme, dealing with complaints arising after 1 January 1986, directly followed a recommendation of the report on *Banking Services and the Consumer* produced by the National Consumer Council (1983). All the major clearing banks are members. It is closely modelled on the IOB Scheme.

The Fourth Annual Report of the Banking Ombudsman Scheme (covering 1988–89) indicates that over 7,000 complaints had been handled since its inception in January 1986 up to September 1989. Since the scheme started it has been strengthened in various ways, directly responding to criticisms voiced in some quarters (Morris 1987; National Consumer Council 1987; Jack Committee 1989). The Banking Ombudsman's jurisdiction has been increased to £100,000. He may deal with cases of maladministration, there is power to require production of documents or other information from banks, and the membership of the independent council has been strengthened.

The report of the Review Committee on Banking Services Law (Jack Committee 1989) gave this scheme a strong endorsement, but recommended that it should be placed on a statutory footing. This has, however, been resisted by the scheme's council, which is fearful that this would in fact have the effect that awards could not be made mandatory on banks.

Building Societies Ombudsman

A variant of the ombudsman theme, where awards are ultimately non-mandatory, is to be found with the Building Societies Ombudsman, who started work on 1 July 1987. This scheme is statute-based in that Part IX of the Building Societies Act 1986 requires the setting up of such a scheme; this scheme, involving all building societies, has been duly recognized by the Building Societies Commission. The Building Societies Ombudsman is empowered to deal with claims involving breach of legal rights, unfair treatment or maladministration. The compensation limit is £100,000 and there is power to require production of relevant documents and information. The building society is required to comply with a decision of the ombudsman *unless* (and this is unique) it undertakes to give such publicity as directed by the ombudsman for its reasons for not doing so.

Other ombudsmen schemes

Following the success of the original three ombudsmen, a plethora of schemes have been set up, announced or (in some cases) rather vaguely promised. Some have been 'voluntary', others statutory. Under the Financial Services Act 1986, the Securities and Investments Board (SIB) is required to set up a complaints scheme for aggrieved investors. The Act does not, however, give the SIB the power, comparable to that incorporated into the Building Societies Act, to require investment businesses to subscribe to a common ombudsman scheme. Individual self-regulatory organizations have each produced separate schemes.

Alongside these initiatives, a Unit Trust Ombudsman was set up, but subsequently absorbed into the insurance scheme. A Corporate Estate Agency Ombudsman has been established. Newspaper editors have each undertaken to appoint an ombudsman. A timeshare company has said it will appoint its own ombudsman. And the Courts and Legal Services Act 1990 seeks to establish a Legal Services Ombudsman *and* a Conveyancing Ombudsman.

PROFESSIONAL BODIES

Hybrid schemes for dealing with complaints – essentially 'self-regulation' within a statutory framework – have been organized by many professional bodies. They are normally concerned with discipline, rather than redress, however. Examples are the schemes covering surveyors, architects, accountants, and the medical professions. Changes have recently been introduced for solicitors, following criticism of the Law Society's former direct role (National Consumer Council 1985). A new Solicitors' Complaints Bureau was set up in 1986 by the Law Society as an independent body to investigate complaints against solicitors. Its Investigation Committee has a majority of lay members. The Bureau is primarily concerned with the investigation of alleged breaches of the rules of professional conduct and can itself deal with lesser offences, while reporting serious cases to the Solicitors Disciplinary Tribunal. In addition, however, under the Administration of Justice Act 1986, the Bureau can deal with complaints of 'shoddy work' – work which is sub-standard while not amounting to negligence. In such cases solicitors can be ordered to reduce their bill, rectify any mistakes or take any other necessary action. Compensation as such cannot, however, be ordered. Negligence claims (if they cannot be resolved by a solicitor on the 'Negligence Panel' or otherwise) must be pursued through the courts or through the Arbitration Scheme which was set up by the Law Society in 1986 in conjunction with the Chartered Institute of Arbitrators.

The Lord Chancellor's Green Paper on the legal profession expressed some continuing criticism of the new arrangements. The Solicitors' Complaints Bureau was described as 'not yet' successful at achieving public confidence (Lord Chancellor's Department 1989a). The proposal that a Legal Services Ombudsman should oversee all complaints against providers of legal services (including barristers) was carried into the Courts and Legal Services Act. The

Lord Chancellor has also announced an intention to give the Solicitors' Complaints Bureau direct powers to award compensation for negligence in less substantial cases.

The self-regulatory system of advertising control has no statutory authority, but operates alongside statutory controls (for example in the Trade Descriptions Act 1968) and has now been underpinned by the Control of Misleading Advertising Regulations 1987, which will enable the Director General of Fair Trading to refer complaints to that system and require him, in exercising his powers, to have regard to the 'desirability of encouraging the control, by self-regulatory bodies, of advertisements'. Under the self-regulatory system, the Committee of Advertising Practice (drawn from the advertising and publishing industries) is responsible for drawing up, revising and administering the British Code of Advertising Practice. It also deals with complaints from competitors. Separately the Advertising Standards Authority (ASA) oversees the operation of the entire system and deals with all complaints from members of the public. The ASA has an independent chairman and a majority of council members who are independent of the advertising industry. The scheme is financed by a 0.1 per cent levy on the gross cost of all relevant advertisements (press, posters and cinema). The ASA publishes an annual report and monthly Case Reports, giving a digest of important decisions. Over the four-year period 1983–6 the ASA received 30,409 complaints, of which 7,581 required investigation (Advertising Standards Authority 1983–6).

ASSESSMENT

I turn now to a brief assessment – in general terms – of the relative strengths and weaknesses of privately organized systems for resolving consumer disputes.

There are undoubtedly positive aspects. First and foremost, the existence of an alternative means of pursuing a complaint and – if necessary – securing the resolution of a dispute provides the consumer with additional choice, especially where a documents-only approach is preferred. Indeed, if the conventional redress procedures are inaccessible or unattractive – or, at least, appear to be so – then the 'alternative' scheme may in reality be the only one. Few consumers will be happy at the idea of taking an insurance company, a bank or a solicitor to court. Likewise, if the claim is above the current small claims limit of £500, arbitration under a code of practice or recourse to an ombudsman are likely to be the only options which are relatively risk-free and designed for litigants-in-person.

Moreover the driving force of self-regulation which lies behind the private schemes should mean that there will be a commitment to make the schemes work. Trade associations and other commercial bodies sponsoring the schemes ought to be able to put pressures on recalcitrant traders which no court could or would impose. There should be a positive attitude towards publicizing the schemes and securing an approachable image. Some schemes also offer the consumer more than is available through the courts. For example the Insurance Ombudsman can go beyond the rather draconian provisions of insurance law – such as the rules on non-disclosure of material facts – and can take good insurance practice, including the Statements of Insurance Practice of the Association of British Insurers, into account. Moreover, complainants who are successful under a private scheme have a far better prospect of actually obtaining their awards. It can be notoriously difficult to enforce a court judgment. But it will be rare for a trader who has voluntarily submitted to the jurisdiction of an arbitration – whether organized commercially or independently – to fail to meet an award.

The next strength of private schemes which can be identified is their scope for innovation. The ordinary courts are often charged with being resistant to change. (In this characteristic the courts are perhaps little different from all suppliers of services which enjoy an effective monopoly.) The creation of a new scheme provides the opportunity to find a design which is genuinely suitable for the needs of the specific users of the scheme. Likewise, a new scheme is able consciously to promote an approachable image, can adopt an 'interventionist' style of fact-finding and is free to pursue informal, simple and flexible means of reaching decisions.

The specialist jurisdiction can be seen as a further strength, avoiding the need for the litigant to obtain expert evidence. Those involved in the processing of complaints and disputes may themselves have specialist knowledge or the sponsors of the scheme may be able to provide that knowledge. There are also substantial advantages in the ability to tailor the procedures for the particular type of dispute.

An important benefit of private schemes which is not shared by the courts is that they are far better placed to observe and systematically draw attention to trends and practices revealed by individual disputes. Regular or occasional reports may be published to highlight particular problems affecting the relevant sector, and making appropriate proposals. The scope for this sort of approach to be effective is obviously greater where the scheme has some separate existence and enjoys a sufficient degree of independence.

There are, finally, wider public interest benefits which can be associated with private alternatives to the ordinary courts. Choice entails competition and this may be more broadly beneficial. If consumers are, or were to be, sufficiently attracted to alternative schemes, that ought to have the effect of stimulating improvements in the court system itself, and providing working examples of features which might be incorporated.

THE WEAKNESSES

Private alternatives to state-provided machinery of justice have been subjected to a number of criticisms. Even some of the advantages may not in fact necessarily be unique to the alternative schemes. For example, there is no reason *in principle* why only privately organized schemes should possess attributes such as innovation and informality or procedural features such as an interventionist style of decision-making. Indeed, the county court small claims procedures are going some way on all these aspects. Some of the advantages may in fact be two-edged.

There is at least a risk that, rather than a beneficial choice of available machinery, the consumer may end up confused and bewildered by a multiplicity of different schemes.

A similar double-edged 'advantage' may be the competitive effect upon the official court system. There is a danger of the opposite result. In other words, the time and energy which is needed to establish and improve private schemes may well divert attention away from the more urgent and pressing tasks of reforming the county courts and other parts of the official court system. This point was explicitly recognized by the Royal Commission on Legal Services in Scotland:

> We certainly do not want to discourage arbitration. . . . We firmly believe, however, that the civil courts are, and should remain, the principal means for resolving civil disputes. We are anxious lest undue resort to remedies outwith the court may lead to the needed reform of court procedures being delayed and neglected. The aim should be to develop in the civil courts themselves those same qualities of cheapness, speed and informality.
>
> (Hughes Committee 1980: para 14.6)

More specific drawbacks of private schemes relate to their limited jurisdiction, their dependence upon private sponsorship, and the degree of actual and apparent independence.

The jurisdiction of private schemes may have to be limited in terms of both geography and subject-matter. Private schemes could never replicate the geographical coverage of the ordinary civil courts which are reasonably accessible to the entire population. The 'independent' small claims courts – in London and Manchester – had to limit their caseload to claimants residing within defined geographical limits. The arbitration and ombudsmen schemes do not have any geographical barriers but the problem of physical coverage imposes constraints on the style of service which can be provided. This is one reason why code arbitration has to be on a 'documents-only' basis (OFT 1981: para 2.2).

Of greater significance, in terms of limited jurisdiction, is the fact that private schemes obviously do not extend to disputes which involve non-participating traders. These schemes are of no value or relevance where a consumer is in dispute with a trader who does not belong to the relevant trade association or who does not otherwise come under the ambit of a private scheme. It is a trite comment to point out that it will tend to be the more reputable traders – with higher standards, fewer complaints, and more positive attitudes towards complaints – who will be covered by the schemes. The 'rogues' are left outside. This may leave the participating traders at a competitive disadvantage. More pertinently consumers in dispute with the less reputable traders who are not willing to adopt this form of self-regulation do not have the option of using a private scheme. This must seriously reduce the effectiveness of such a scheme. In 1985/6, 62,703 formal complaints concerning furniture and floor coverings were notified to the Office of Fair Trading. That year, although it is true that many disputes were resolved by conciliation, only three arbitrations were held under the code of practice for the furniture industry.

The dependence of private schemes upon non-public sources of funding may pose problems, although it is increasingly clear that the court system is far from immune from resource starvation. At least, however, the state accepts a continuing obligation to fund the court system. By contrast, the private small claims courts were not able to maintain their funding and (despite much voluntary activity) were forced into closure. Schemes which are funded from commercial sources may be rather more prosperous, but even here there cannot be long-term guarantees about the availability of funding. There would obviously be considerable pressures on the commercial sources to maintain funding (not least self-interest), but it is by no means beyond the realms of possibility that funding for a scheme could cease or be substantially reduced at fairly short notice. There may also be an unfortunate (but inevitable) link between funding and the outcome of cases. It has not yet happened in this country, but it may need only one or two businesses to express disgruntlement at a decision, or a series of decisions, for the entire edifice of a scheme to be placed in jeopardy.

Less tangibly reluctance to produce adequate resources may result in half-hearted promotion of the schemes. This is not a criticism which can be levelled at the ombudsmen schemes or the Solicitors' Complaints Bureau, all of which have actively pursued a high-profile strategy. But, with the exception of the schemes for package holidays and cars, public knowledge about the various arbitration schemes seems low, as reflected by the very low levels of use.

The problem of resources seems to lie behind a low profile. The OFT's 1981 report noted, in relation to the scope for increased publicity about these schemes that

The trade associations were apprehensive that if this information (about the outcome of arbitration cases) was made available, the number of applications for arbitration would increase, sometimes in cases for which arbitration was not really appropriate. One major association was particularly hostile to this recommendation, not wishing to repeat the experience of earlier publicity on arbitration. . . . Another voiced a similar concern, saying that a dramatic increase in cases might result in a 'commercially unacceptable risk' to manufacturers in terms of additional administrative costs. This association added that the matter of publicity is 'unquestionably a delicate area'.

(OFT 1981: para 10.3)

Despite this, the OFT concluded that publicity should be increased. As mentioned, a booklet has been published (OFT 1984) but it has not yet proved possible to publish the intended digest of arbitration decisions.

A final criticism which is often directed at private redress schemes is that their independence can easily be called into question. It is said that the financial relationship means that the schemes can never claim absolute independence. There clearly cannot be the same degree of independence from the parties which courts can manifestly offer. The lack of 'absolute' independence may not matter. Perhaps more important is the point that – whatever arrangements are made to maximize the degree of independence – such schemes may not be *seen* or understood to be independent. The efficacy of any system of justice must rely heavily upon its reputation. It would be a serious handicap for any system to carry – however inaccurately – a reputation of non-independence. This concern must be especially acute with some recent schemes set up or promised by traditional businesses. There are fundamental problems which go directly to the structure of schemes of private justice. It is imperative that confidence in a scheme should not in any way be shaken by virtue of excessive identification with the business interests which provide the finance.

Fortunately for the most part the business community has largely recognized the importance of independence and impartiality and the need to avoid conflicts of interests; hence the use of arbitrators appointed by the Chartered Institute and the presence of independent members on the governing bodies of most of the separately constituted schemes. The main ombudsmen, too, have been quick to proclaim and demonstrate their independence.

It must be hoped that the complainants – actual and potential – also appreciate the independence of these arrangements and, especially those who are unsuccessful, do not harbour any suspicions about the scheme because of its links with the 'sponsoring' industry.

CONCLUSION

This chapter has been limited to the pursuit of redress of individual consumers. I have not dealt with class or group actions (Scottish Consumer Council 1982; Australian Law Reform Commission 1988). Or with so-called public interest litigation where the state or public-interest groups might pursue redress on behalf of consumers. Nor have I dealt here with the use of legal sanctions – criminal and administrative – to deter businesses from causing harm or loss to consumers, or to punish certain forms of wrong-doing.

I have, however, attempted to describe and review various formal mechanisms – 'public' and 'private' – for consumer dispute resolution. I conclude by suggesting that any effective system of dispute resolution must be able to satisfy as many as possible of the following criteria:

1 it must enjoy the confidence of both complainants and those complained against
2 it must be accessible, easy to initiate and easy to use
3 it must be speedy
4 it must involve minimum expense to the parties and to the 'sponsors' of the scheme
5 it must be procedurally fair and achieve just results
6 it must be actually and visibly impartial and independent
7 it must be adequately resourced and financially secure.

Part III
ADR: some international experience

Introduction

Ideas for the development and appraisal of dispute resolution mechanisms can be stimulated by reviewing the nature of the mechanisms used in different social sectors, albeit that one could never expect to 'translate' an institution or mechanism in its exact form to a new context. This is also true of comparative studies at a national level. However, the provisos academics are fond of making about the uniqueness of social and cultural context, should not be stretched too far. Many of the legal systems around the world, the common law a prime example, owe their origins to just such attempts at direct 'translation'. Similarly our use of the 'ombudsman' is an outgrowth from another country's language and dispute resolution mechanism (Sweden). And much of the ADR movement owes its roots to developments in the United States. Finally, there are sectors of dispute, such as international politics or international business disputes, which are intrinsically global or international in character, which in turn impacts on the design of commercial arbitration or other dispute resolution systems. In this part of the handbook, we examine some examples of developments in Europe, North America, Australia and China, not in an attempt at comprehensiveness, but in an attempt to give a flavour of the influence of national situation on dispute resolution efforts.

Dorothee Eidmann and Konstanze Plett (Chapter 13) continue the theme set out by Richard Thomas in Chapter 12 with a review of the operation of the 'Schiedsstellen' in West Germany, organizations associated with trades and the professions for the handling of consumer complaints. They set their discussion in the context of a recognition of the novelty of the 'consumer' as an emergent form of social status. As well as outlining the origins, methods and fields of application of these consumer dispute boards, they explore the use of Schiedsstellen to narrow the definition of disputes solely to price–product exchange relationships, and dispute resolution mediated in terms of 'technical expert' analysis of defects in products or services. In this respect they argue that the boards represent a unique form of development 'logic' within ADR, and an alternative logic to the norms of legal intervention (thus perhaps explaining the ambivalent response of the legal profession and the courts to these developments).

One of the notable areas of ADR growth in recent years has been the attempts to manage international commercial disputes in order to avoid business deals becoming entangled in inappropriate local legal systems (see R.E. Wight's Chapter 5). Bonita Thompson (Chapter 14) provides a case study of one of the institutionalized expressions of this development, the international commercial arbitration centre. Such centres have a dual purpose of providing a means for businesses to resolve disputes without frontiers, while bringing in valuable business custom to the economy of the neutral venue. Thompson describes vividly the politics, processes and pressures in the formation of the British Columbia International Commercial Arbitration Centre. While she rightly points to the uniqueness of this process within a national context, this perhaps underplays the extent to which her story is recognizable to those who have observed these developments in process in a number of countries. In particular, the fact that in the beginning the arrival of customers in these dispute resolution 'boutiques' can be agonizingly slow, encouraging centres to take on other kinds of dispute resolution business to sustain their existence.

Michael Palmer (Chapter 15) reminds us of the major impact culture can have as we move further from nations which share our historical experience. His review of Chinese mediation practice and its pervasive role in Chinese society is an important reminder of a point raised in the first chapter of this book: namely that much of ADR is not new so much as 'back-to-basics'. That at other times and in other countries, particularly in Asia, the attempted emphasis was on harmony and not on dispute, of giving support to the other party rather than claiming from them. Conflict was a sign of failure, and so litigation runs counter to this important cultural consciousness and ideology. The massacre of citizens in Tiananmen Square in 1989 is a reminder, however, that a philosophy of harmony has its limits. Palmer also suggests that the development of Chinese society may create increasing tension over the appropriateness of the mediation approach (particularly in a coercive form) for some kinds of dispute where legal rule-based approaches may have more attraction.

Finally, David Newton (Chapter 16) describes the development of interest in commercial ADR in Australia, culminating in the establishment of the Australian Commercial Disputes Centre of which he is Secretary-General. He outlines the range of techniques and approaches adopted by the Centre to achieve credibility and to implement ADR. The outcomes, he suggests, are indicative of the success of the Centre in meeting a business need not met by traditional adjudicative approaches.

13 Non-judicial dispute processing in West Germany

The *Schiedsstellen* contribution to the resolution of social conflicts and their interaction with the official legal system[1]

Dorothee Eidmann and Konstanze Plett

During the last two decades, in all highly industrialized western countries, one can identify the emergence of new boards and activities for out-of-court resolution of conflicts which were previously brought to the courts or regulated informally by the parties themselves (whether or not the parties first consulted advisory or mediatory organizations or experts). These boards exist in a wide variety of forms and often their status may be considered experimental or temporary. Despite the diversity between national developments, the common denominator may be adduced to the fact that they provide bargaining facilities for conflicts which should not (or no longer) be submitted to highly differentiated court-proceedings, the latter having historically achieved the most elaborated form of securing social consensus. Nor can the conflicts in question be resolved by everyday and 'common-sense' oriented strategies. These activities document an effort to resolve new or newly recognized social conflicts, which may no longer be ignored, and at the same time, the redefinition of societal means for resolving them. Looked at more closely, there is at least one class/type of these new boards in all countries, which seems to have gained stability and thus may represent a new type of intermediary institution: namely the boards for consumer–business conflicts. (Tentative international surveys are provided by Denti and Vigoriti 1983; Blankenburg and Taniguchi 1987; for the USA see Gottwald 1981; Abel 1982a; for West Germany see Blankenburg *et al.* 1980; 1982; Morasch 1984.)

This chapter will present initial results of ongoing research which was originally undertaken to explain the emergence of these new boards, in an attempt to answer the question concerning the conditions and extent to which legal systems are (or are not) able to integrate social interests (subsystems) and the conflicts arising and thereby provide a legal solution.[2] Hence the interaction of these new out-of-court boards with the official legal system has to be analysed (cf. Gessner and Plett forthcoming). From another point of view, it was hypothesized that these new boards document a push to new societal ways of conflict resolution, which differentiate themselves from the court-logic for the restitution of social consensus, so that the patterns of conflict resolution by these boards have to be studied in detail (cf. Eidmann 1988, 1989). Starting with an overview of these new intermediary institutions in West Germany, their construction, their fundamental ideas and their action fields, we shall then turn to the logic implied in and behind their construction and indicate how this thinking is put into practice, that is, what patterns of conflict resolution they have developed. Finally we shall consider the interaction of these new boards with the official legal system giving special regard to their legal basis and their treatment by different actors in the legal field.

THE EMERGENCE OF NON-JUDICIAL CONCILIATION BOARDS, THEIR ACTION-FIELDS AND ESSENTIAL CONCEPTS

The emergence of the new boards should be seen against the background of the historical formation of a new social figure: 'the consumer'. During the past century this – rarely explored – 'social type' has been differentiated (and isolated) from other recognized communities (family, labour, citizenship) and introduced to the public scene, thanks to the collective achievements of consumers' organizations and their political and juristical assistants (Ruffat 1987; Nader and Shugart 1980; von Hippel 1986).

Until the early 1960s 'the consumer', whose social amorphousness impairs nearly any type of joint action, was not really a problem for the market and/or business. Business, trade and even professions knew very well how to manipulate or to bamboozle consumers, meeting their claims with a flat refusal or making them feel deviant: 'You are the first person to complain' (Nader and Shugart 1980: 67). This situation has changed fundamentally. To cut a long story short, the consumer has been promoted to a champion of legitimate interests and rights. New principles of the 'public weal' are expressly formulated with respect to this emergent social figure. These are mostly designed to improve the 'market power' of consumers and a reformulation of the exchange relations between them and the providers of goods or services. These relationships, primarily formulated in terms of service/goods and prices exchange relationship, are to be raised on to a new level of rationality, promising consumers the effective reclamation of this rationality for themselves. In the case of defects and damages, losses are no longer to be borne by the consumer. In short: the consumer's money is at stake.[3]

With the reformulation and extension of consumers' recognized rights and claims, the basis for new social conflicts was laid, and ways of settlement had to be found. In this regard, it was accepted in all the different countries that conflicts (concentrated essentially on the potential redress for either defective or inadequate goods/services) should not be submitted to the normal civil procedure. Besides the well-known pragmatic and economic reasons (courts' overload, costs of civil procedure, etc.) this consideration suggests that the nature of consumers' conflicts is not perceived as requiring the differentiated logic of professionalized (or court) legal intervention.

In West Germany special boards, called *Schiedsstellen* or *Schlichtungsstellen* (conciliation boards) had been established even before judicial and government representatives raised the question of alternatives to cope with the notorious overload of the courts, though they welcomed them as suitable in this respect.

Table 13.1 Types of Schiedsstellen in West Germany by responsible associations and their dissemination[a]

Schiedsstellen	Responsible associations				Dissemination[b]
	Trade/commercial/ professional associations only	Trade etc. associations + consumer organizations	Trade associations + industrial agency[c] + public agency + consumer organizations	Professional associations + public agencies[d]	
Car repair			+		*
Used car dealing			(+)		*
Dry cleaning	(+)	+			*
Electrical repair	(+)	(+)			=
Shoe repair	(+)	+			=
Landlord–tenant	+	(+)			=
Trade (general)	+	(+)			=
Commerce (general)	+	(+)			*
Building trade	+				*
Medical care	(+)			(+)	=
Architects	+				*
Lawyers	+				=

Notes:

a + dominant type; (+) locally varying type

b * country-wide; = only single boards in some states or cities

c 'industrial agency' occur in the car business: DAT (organization of self-employed car engineers)

d 'public agencies' are in car repair: TÜV (technical survey institution for vehicles of any kind); in medical care: public and private insurers or physicians

These boards are always established by trade, business and/or professional associations who thus indicate that they themselves are taking permanent care and remedial measures by providing new institutions and procedures, promising to balance out the interests of consumers and providers of goods and services. Sometimes this new idea is emphasized through institutionalized collaboration with consumers' organizations (see Table 13.1).

Table 13.1 shows that only a small section of business or professional associations have established these boards, namely those of small (or medium size) enterprises (car repair, used car dealing, dry cleaning, etc.), the building trade and – in unusual company – those of the freelance academic professions: architects, lawyers and physicians. Despite all the assumed differences between market-oriented business and the 'classical' professions (physicians, lawyers), their affinity rests upon the fact that all these enterprises and professions are highly specialized, mostly indispensable for everyday life and – above all – are self-employed, that is they act within the range of occupational and professional standards operating on their own responsibility and within the control of their associations. As a whole, the establishment of the new boards could be seen as a venture of highly specialized, self-employed occupational groups, or their associations to cope with customers' claims. The boards of the chambers of trade/commerce act as a kind of reservoir for consumers' quarrels with a variety of occupational groups and enterprises who, for whatever reasons, are not motivated to leap on the band-wagon and establish such boards on a more occupation-specific level.[4] Only the establishment of boards for landlord–tenant conflicts may not be subsumed to this pattern.[5]

It is possible to make an informed guess on the motives for establishing bodies of this nature. These motives are not altruistic but follow the logic of necessity and rationality in highly specialized business/professional organizations which are increasingly obliged, for the sake of their own interests, to promote and secure their markets in order to take care of the social demands formulated by the welfare state and consumers' organizations (progress, prosperity, improvement of consumption). To the consumer they promise quality and a guarantee of goods and services, thus extending the consumer–business relationship from single purchase transaction to a lasting care and guarantee.

Obviously – and they do not deny it – the associations were reacting to the growth of public criticism of fraud, botched work and an increasing lack of generosity and fairness towards consumer complaints (Demant *et al.* 1984). The growth of complaints or (especially in case of allegation of medical malpractice) civil lawsuits forced the associations to undertake a search for conflict resolution and/or to negotiate with consumers' organizations for co-operative problem-solving. The problem was to find a solution not only assuring the consumers or clients that their claims would be met but also attractive enough for trade/professions to submit to the *Schiedsstellen*-procedure, knowing that the latter may close their ears to consumers' complaints and that the associations' coercive power is extremely restricted. In other words, it was intended to protect business and professions against 'unreasonable' claims (Int. E1, E2, M1, J6)[6] and harmful, potentially ruinous publicity (always a possibility of court procedures even in cases of final acquittal) and to reassure the consumers that they may trust in strict examination, if the work has been done according to professional standards. In sum it was expected to calm down public resentment against business/ professions by strengthening intra-professional control. Besides, most of these associations had practical experiences in successful informal mediation between the opponents from case to case (Int. M1, M2, J3, J5, J6) and it seemed promising to extend these informal attempts to a formalized procedure, thereby allowing a multiplicity of cases to be handled according to the same rules by a special staff. In addition, these practical intentions also promise the achievement of an added benifit of restoring the damaged image of trade, commerce and the professions. It was also rumoured that, by accepting this responsibility themselves, the associations might prevent the state taking action in response to consumerism (Falckenstein 1977: 170). We can assume that a whole bundle of motives must have coincided, to put this new attitude into operation.

From a macro-theoretical viewpoint these trade, business and professional associations have replaced the traditional model of one-sided means of collective action by a new model 'where it is in the interest of an organised group to strive for a "categoric" good which is at least partially identical with a "collective" (or public) good' (Streeck and Schmitter 1985: 17). In this sense these new boards may be classed within the phenomenon of 'private interest government', as defined by these authors. (For a similar view see Macaulay 1986; Ramsay 1987.) Now it seems more accurate to interpret their establishment as an effort to introduce a new type of formal conflict resolution by relatively autonomous occupational/professional groups or their associations.[7] This raises the question of the dispute patterns accordingly developed.

THE *SCHIEDSSTELLEN* MODEL OF CONFLICT RESOLUTION AND DAY-TO-DAY PRACTICE

Concerning the working of these new boards one group of socio-legal scholars sees them as an obstacle to the development of consumer rights and emphasizes their less than optimal allocation of 'justice' as measurable by their procedural provisions. This view has been strongly put forward by Abel (1982b); in West Germany it is stressed especially by legal scholars (Reich 1982; Micklitz 1983). Another view sees them as providing a pragmatic solution to the consumer problem where other channels, especially the courts, have failed, and approves that these new boards bring 'a little more justice' for consumers (Blankenburg 1980; Demant *et al.* 1984). We shall argue that both views which consider the boards only as gradual, positive or negative 'deviates' from the legal system and its procedures, fail to appreciate the particular construction logic and its implied special *Schiedsstellen*-logic. We shall try to analyse the specific *Schiedsstellen* contribution to modes of social conflict resolution, which will not restrict itself just to external and formal measures. Or, to put it into jargon, we shall try to promote substantial comprehension of their 'alternative' action logic.

In order to fulfil their self-defined tasks of meeting consumers' rights by providing intraprofessional 'after-sales' control, sometimes 'under the gentle wings of consumers' organisations' (Int. E2) who act as 'honest brokers', they developed their own action frame and rules for handling the conflicts by a special staff. In principle the *Schiedsstellen* – and this holds true for all the different types – commit themselves to specialized scientific expertise relevant to the subject matter in dispute and restitution of consensus so that court proceedings should be superfluous. In fact the court alternative remains open; procedures are completely voluntary.[8] (Even the obligation of association members to submit to the *Schiedsstellen* procedure must not be overestimated, since the associations have no coercive power to sanction deviant members.) The options are in favour of customers and clients. Each case is investigated; there are only rudimentary procedural 'hurdles' as to periods of limitation or minimum values; fees are minimal or non-existent.[9]

The guiding principle is to find competent and acceptable solutions, obviously on the tacit assumption that specialized scientific expertise on the subject matter of conflicts would be a solid basis for agreement. Referring to the *Schiedsstellen* provisions for conflict resolution and available results on their day-to-day practice we want to sketch how this thinking is put into practice. Starting from the *Schiedsstellen* for car repair, dry cleaning and the building trade, their specific contribution to conflict resolution will be exemplified, and it will be briefly explained why the identical action frame will vary depending on the type of conflict in dispute.

The *Schiedsstellen* always check if the services/goods were delivered in conformity with the current standards of 'ordinary care' or 'due diligence' and if the price was 'reasonable and fair'. But these principles which are also central as general clauses for handling comparable disputes before the courts (cf. Civil Code: sections 157, 242, BGB), are specifically interpreted by the *Schiedsstellen*, who restrict them to their purely scientific, technical and book-keeping significance. They systematically investigate if the workshop/trade has correctly recognized objective deficiencies or properties of the objects to be treated – for example of unroadworthy cars, warped doors, damp walls, characteristics of building ground and materials, malfunction of heating systems, dirty textiles – and treated/repaired them according to the exigencies of products, materials, their components and probable interactions of these factors, dictated by technical norms and corresponding know-how of 'competent' treatment. Prices and values of products and services are highly standardized and pre-calculated. In case of failure redress is calculated from prices paid for goods/services and reduction of value through wrong treatment.[10] Put succinctly, the boards offer to ensure parity – if not identity – between services/goods and prices, presupposing that such a parity is attainable. Consumers are not usually technical experts and for them mechanical or technical defects, and their persistence after repair, are a social problem, limiting consumers' freedom, their budgets, and, perhaps, damaging their emotional links towards the objects under dispute; for all that their complaints 'to get a reasonable return for what has been paid for' (CD 1)[11] mainly indicate their suspicion of being duped. The *Schiedsstellen* ultimately exclude mere allegations of fraud but guarantee to clear up possible mistakes and breakdowns and to balance out the services/goods and prices relation to an 'equal proportion'. This is their specific rationality and was the central motive for the establishment of the new boards. Therefore this is the kind of 'justice' they will supply.

This basic attitude – if not exactly ideology – is obvious from their founding statutes, application forms and public relations activities. More importantly this principle has obviously achieved intrinsic motivating power:

> Fraud? That's not our job, that's a matter for the courts. Our concern is to investigate if the workshop has done its task. That's a matter of sober facts. . . . We'll find out . . . and if the workshop has failed, it has to pay.
>
> (Int. E2)

This guiding principle is self-perpetuating through staff-recruitment, procedural provisions and the norms guiding discussions and final recommendations for agreements. If we allow that it may not be a matter of course to produce the desired parity between prices and goods/services, we must discover how the staff, procedural and normative provisions of the boards will make it possible for this to be achieved.

Staff

The most prominent actor in the *Schiedsstelle* is the expert in the special field, followed – depending on their varying procedural models (see Table 13.2) – by trained employees. These experts work mostly as self-employed engineers, doctors, etc. and often have experience as experts within court proceedings. Sometimes they are employed by one or the other founding associations, for example as representatives of consumers' organizations or public agencies involved (cf. Table 13.1) or they are designated as 'honorable' and (though for other reasons) elected representatives of the business associations.

Even legally trained members of the staff are similarly and by job definition principally concerned to check if the work has been done according to current standards of technical knowledge and corresponding standards of care, or if the goods have the qualities promised (Int. J6). Within the *Schiedsstellen* framework of action, which expressly commits them to find solutions other than legal ones, their role is designed to conduct negotiations and thereby influence proceedings mainly in tactical ways.

Specific knowledge and expertise for members of the trained staff is purveyed and promoted in regular workshops arranged by the associations and organizations involved (car repair, dry cleaning, building trade). Here, again, experts of the special fields give lectures on technical developments and product innovation (Int. M1, M2, E2, J5). Strictly in conformity with this emphasis on expert opinion and the reduction of legal knowledge merely to the back-up prudent business, the relevant procedural provisions are oriented towards the avoidance of unnecessary confrontations with the legal order.

Table 13.2 Schiedsstellen by procedural model

Procedural model	Types of Schiedsstellen
I Expert opinion	*Schiedsstellen* for
• Complaints are investigated by experts and trained staff	• dry cleaning
	• shoe repair
• No hearings	• trade/commerce general
• Result: expert evidence about matters of fact including suggestions for redress	• medical care
	• lawyers
• Not binding for either party	• architects
II Expert opinion + conciliation	*Schiedsstellen* for
• *Phase 1* Complaints handled by experts or trained staff	• dry cleaning (exception)
	• trade/commerce general
• Result: expert opinion, parties arrange themselves or go to court	• landlord–tenant problems
	• electrical repair
• *Phase 2* Hearings before the board's commissions with lawyer as chair	• car repair
	• used car dealing
• Result: expert opinion or settlement	• medical care
• Not binding for either party	•
III Quasi-professionalized conciliation	*Schiedsstellen* for
• Each case is heard by the commission (lawyer as chair)	• architects
	• medical care
• Expert evidence only if necessary	• lawyers
• Result 1: parties' agreement or commission's decision, not binding for either party	
• Result 2: legally binding agreement	• Building trade
• Result 3: legally authorized decision	• No *Schiedsstelle*

Procedural provisions

According to the *Schiedsstellen* formal provisions (see Table 13.2), their procedures vary from conflict settlement by means of sole expert opinion (type I) through additional facilities to reach agreements within hearings (type II) to 'quasi-professionalized' or 'quasi-juridical' conflict resolution with a judge or lawyer in the chair (type III).

The procedural provisions merely specify the staff, periods of limitations, fees and other formal conditions as to the parties who may call in the *Schiedsstelle*, etc. Regularly they reject cases already filed at court, exclude publicity from their proceedings and refuse a new call or hearing. But there are no provisions to direct the conducting of the procedure, or naming criteria for the (re)construction of 'truth' or evidence of parties' chances for objections or defence, that is those elements constituting the rationality of court proceedings. This confirms that it was far from the *Schiedsstellen*'s programme to offer a more or less reduced duplicate of court proceedings. For the same reason we may not easily read what dispute patterns they will develop from their procedural provisions, but have to study their actual proceedings to find out how the *Schiedsstellen* (re)construct the facts under dispute for working out agreements or accepted decisions.

According to the first type, the complaints, as written on the application forms, are investigated by experts and trained staff under consideration of pure facts which may be proved by documents (order and material forms, invoices, spare parts lists, etc., and available documents of treatment and work by the firms), or handing in the defective product or parts of it. The application forms are simple; it mostly suffices to explain the defect perceived in the goods/services. According to the principle 'we'll find out' the requirement to offer formal evidence is kept to a minimum. Each case is thoroughly examined to find out the technical reasons for the defects and/or the extent to which the firm may be responsible for the defect. This can be measured according to the state of the products, their perceived defects and the scientific probability/plausibility as to how treatment/work may have caused the defects:

> we have instruments we need, an excellent magnifier, a measuring tape, and we have a 'lie detector', working with ultraviolet light, we have water to prove the fastness of colours, and special tests for chemical defects, and we have, what we can't present you at the table, experience, basic knowledge and, of course, a little knowledge of human nature.
>
> (E2, public session of the *Schiedsstelle*, held once a year for public relations)

Thus the *Schiedsstellen* of this type reconstruct 'evidence' by quasi-experimental scientific probability. According to this approach the social reasons which may account for under-achievement of the individual firm are totally unimportant as well as the personal value of the damage to the complainant. Workshops/professions may not argue that an apprentice has done the work or that it was a 'blue Monday'. Nor may customers insist on 'perfect' treatment if technical knowledge does not yet allow for it. They have no entitlement to reclaim redress for all the social costs and consequences the defect actually had for practical rearrangements to be met because of the defects (for example costs for taxis, loss of 'living standard', invested hours for self-knitted pullovers, and so on). This is mostly excluded from consideration. Thus conflicts are transformed to their purely quantitative aspects of an exchange logic guided by technical norms and pre-calculated price standards:

> The consumer complains about the shrinking of her pullover after dry cleaning. . . . Our investigation has shown that the cleaner has either failed to reduce the water supply to the cleaning detergents or of the pullover's moisture content itself. The cleaner should pay compensation according to the pullover's value.
>
> (Expert opinion submitted to a consumer)

> We concern ourselves with the information on the application forms: when bought, what was the price. Here we have to trust the honesty of the customers, then we have our tables and conclude, such a pullover has a life expectancy of three years and then we can calculate its actual value.
>
> (E2, public session)

As a rule expert opinions are submitted to the parties who then may find a solution or go to the courts. In a minority of cases parties actually use expert opinions for further negotiations as to the modalities of redress (cash, a new dress, credit notes, etc.). In those cases the *Schiedsstellen* work as a sort of 'transmission shaft' to restitute the capacities for social consensus on the basis of technical expertise.

During the last few years we observe an increased trend towards expanding the procedural provisions into the second type ('expert opinion + conciliation'), providing for personal hearings by commissions with an extended staff and a lawyer as chair. But as may be seen from Table 13.3, these provisions are in practice reduced to the first type, since the overwhelming majority of cases are dealt with in the first phase, delivering a written 'expert opinion' to the parties, who then may take their own actions to arrange themselves:

> The car owner claims for redress of careless repair. . . . Our investigations have shown that the firm is not responsible for the breakdown of the motor shortly after first repair. Instead we found an unhappy coincidence between the repaired defect and an emerging new defect. Though we know today that both defects are indicated by similar symptoms this knowledge was not published at that time. . . . There is no reasonable ground for redress. . . . Although the parties may come to an accommodation for other reasons.

Even if the second phase of this type is entered, the pattern does not change fundamentally. As may be tentatively suggested from our first results, hearings are used to get more knowledge of technical facts, especially in cases where the documents and parties' comments do not yet allow the *Schiedsstelle* to suggest proposals for agreement according to their intrinsic habit of quasi-experimental scientific reconstruction of probable and plausible connections between treatment and perceived disfunctions of the matters under dispute. Whereas the legally trained members of the commission during these hearings tend to

Table 13.3 Practice of the Schiedsstellen: per cent of cases handled[1]

Schiedsstelle	Car repair[a] (1982)	Used car dealer[b] (1980)	Dry cleaning[c] (1980)	Commerce general[c] (1982)	Trade general[c] (1982)	Building trade[d] (1985)	Medical care[e] (1985)	Architects (1987)	Lawyers
Number of yearly complaints	12,000	4,600	5,600	21,000	25,000	unknown	4,000	unknown	unknown
Number of yearly cases per board[2]	150	100	150	unknown	120	15	60–300	15	unknown
Per cent of cases handled according to procedural model (see Table 13.2)									
Model I:			100						
Model II:									
Phase 1:	60	35	—	84	90	—	75		
Phase 2:	12	2	—	16	10	—	unknown		
Model III:									
If the case, almost 100 per cent of cases are handled during hearings.									

Sources: [a] Hanel 1985; [b] Seeling 1984; [c] Demant et al. 1984; [d] Plett 1989; [e] Eberhardt 1988.

Notes:
1 Boards of shoe repair, repair of electrical goods, landlord–tenant problems are ignored here. Columns do not add to 100% because of rejections and pending cases.
2 The boards generally work within the regional competence of associations, nearly corresponding to the state boundaries.

reconstruct the social (or 'contractual') genesis of conflicts in terms of legal relevance, that is credibility and truthworthiness of the parties' stories about the genesis of conflicts, these attempts are sooner or later interrupted by the experts:

(In the course of hearings the workshop argued that the customer wanted to save costs in a first repair of brakes, obviously tending to explain the necessity of a second repair shortly after the first one.)

J: (lawyer in chair) What do you mean, they tried to save costs?

W: (workshop) We phoned them that the brakes were blocked and asked if we should renew them or just make them workable.

E: (expert, car engineer, to W) But you can't leave that to a layman to decide on.

W: On order, on order.

E: That's your business.

J: (to the complainant) OK, they phoned you and asked.

P: (complainant, Mrs Bush) No, unless they talked to my husband, but I'm sure they didn't.

J: So we should ask Mr Bush, please call him in (Mr Bush cares for the couple's baby in the lobby during the hearings).

E: (to the chairman) But Mr Fisher, technically that is totally irrelevant, that doesn't matter at all. He has overhauled the brakes, they functioned or seemed to, and if they really worked, they can't be blocked again after 7,000 km. That is out of question, just impossible.

J: Yes, OK, accepted.

Within the *Schiedsstellen* hearings the aforementioned possibilities for parties to achieve social consensus on the basis of expert opinions are further reduced while simultaneously there is promoted the *Schiedsstellen* idea that 'experts will do it' and conflicts will be resolved by establishing a parity between services/goods and prices. Especially if one or the other party is not willing to accept the *Schiedsstellen* reconstruction of evidence in terms of technical plausibility, conflicts are ultimately reduced to the skeleton of bare facts, measurable and quantifiable in terms of technical requirements and corresponding prices.

Let us now turn to the discussions between experts, the legal chairman and the representative of the consumer organization (himself a car engineer) to find a solution for the already cited conflict over car repair. In the mean time, the parties were waiting in the lobby. This may demonstrate how the *Schiedsstellen* idea becomes manifest during hearings: the legal staff merely produce arguments in support of the experts' findings while considerations of possible redress for the consumers' further social costs stemming from the defect are 'forgotten' in the course of discussions:

J: (to the experts and C, representative of consumer organization) I have to ask you – that's out of my competence now – but I have to ask the question precisely, was the first repair in due order and the second also? If not, it is out of question that Mrs Bush has a claim for redress for both accounts she paid. . . .

E: OK, but we have to examine to what extent she profits from replaced parts, we have to deduct it.

C: In my view, we should make an example. I would award her the full amount of both accounts, all the quarrels Mrs Bush finally had, she can't bill them.

J: No, that's impossible.

C: OK, but now they had to do without the car, and rented another one . . .

J: Yes, they could reclaim these costs.

C: I think we agree, that both repairs were not in due order.
(Commission members study again all the accounts and material forms and discuss the items.)

J: (trying to find an end) Let us ask that way, what would have been the price for Mrs Bush if the work – now after the third repair [which was finally successful, D.E.] – would have been done properly in the first place.
(Commission members study again their documents.)

E: She, she would had to pay the amount of the second invoice.

J: That means she has about DM 1,300 . . .

E: That means she would have paid DM 895 . . .

J: So we have to say that she has paid about DM 1,300 more than necessary.

E: She has, she had to pay DM 895, for this price she could have due repair. . . . If we examine exactly we have to calculate somewhat more accurately, eh, there are some parts she has use of though repair was not successful, for an agreement proposal we may stop here, but if we have to decide, we must calculate more exactly . . .

To sum up, the agreement proposal of the commission was not accepted by the firm, and the commission calculated, item for item, the 'fair return' for Mrs Bush on the basis of the hypothetically found 'fair price' for 'due repair' and deducted this value, including those for useful spare parts, from the actual accounts for useless repairs.

Returning to the traditional socio-legal concept of 'conciliation', dispute settlement is primarily oriented at the restitution of each party's social esteem and both parties' consent to 'indigenous' moral values thus restituting the disturbed social relationship between them (Falke and Gessner 1982; Nothdurft and Spranz-Vogasy 1986). Our case studies alternatively suggest that the modern type of conciliation presents itself as an effort to restitute social consensus by totally amoral technical norms and corresponding price standards. These are out of the consumers' disposition and reaffirmed as a must for the firms – obviously on tacit presumption that these highly abstract technical and economic norms will directly promote social consensus. This literally 'technocratic' approach to the resolution of social conflicts, suggesting that these norms *per se* have a compulsory quality, seems to be nourished by a corresponding state of social consciousness. This is all the more the case then when written expert opinions mostly suffice for parties' rearrangements. As our data show, the boards for car repair and dry cleaning are highly 'efficient', since over 80 per cent of their recommendations are met by the firms. Thus the *Schiedsstellen*, especially in cases of conflicts about highly standardized technical products and services (electrical goods, cars, textiles, etc.), may restrict themselves to procurement and supply of expert opinions so that from a purely external point of view their actions mostly resemble those of bureaucratic administrations.

Let us finally consider type III (see Table 13.2), mostly reserved for conflicts with the building trade, freelance (e.g. architects) and 'classical' professions (e.g. lawyers and, though exceptionally, physicians). At least the external characteristics in boards of this type would tentatively fit the ideal type of 'professionalized' juridical action, implying a highly experienced judge or lawyer as chair, who by 'seismographically' exploring the genesis of conflicts in each case thus constructs and works out new social problems, which are then legally transformed.[12] However, the *Schiedsstellen* approach to conflict resolution keeps in line with the other types, in so far as reconstruction of 'evidence' follows the logic of quasi-experimental or scientific plausibility by experts of the special field. Moreover, conflicts are not transformed legally but kept below the normative provisions of the legal programme, thus preventing any sort of legal precedent for handling the next case. Nevertheless, conflict resolution within these types of boards is highly individualized and leaves much room for differentiated solutions with regard to the special case. Under closer scrutiny of the types of conflicts, it may be hypothesized that in the long run this type will remain the exception or – in the final result – will tend in yet another direction.

In the case of the building trade, we observe that the court alternative seems to be more attractive especially for private builders (Plett 1989). Besides other reasons (costs – legal insurance schemes do not pay out for the *Schiedsstellen* procedures), we have to consider that all these boards are primarily oriented to balancing out costs and losses in terms of scientific and technical standards. This presupposes, to a considerable extent, parties' willingness to discuss matters under dispute in terms of what is technically/scientifically possible and disposable mainly from the perspective of the firms/professions involved. If we consider that a private building mostly implies a biographical 'project' for the future of its owners, not to speak of the financial value of these highly esteemed profit objects, it is quite obvious that private builders will not easily submit to a procedure mainly intending to balance out the services/goods and prices relationship according to the *Schiedsstellen* idea. As indicated by interviews with two private builders, they prefer the more reliant formal evidence provided by the judicial machine to protect themselves against business fraud and incompetence. Moreover, they will not waive their claims for redress of all the additional social costs they have to bear nor accept the reduction of the personal and aesthetical value of their building project. Thus these boards will fail to attract laymen's confidence and preserve themselves to insiders of the building trade whose most important interest is to keep business and workshops working.[13]

Whereas the *Schiedsstellen* for workshops, trade, commerce and the building trade may reconstruct the subject matter of conflicts in terms of what is technically possible and measurable and corresponding prices, and may (more or less successfully) convince the customers that their own ideas are of secondary importance, the action field of physicians clearly follows another logic. Human beings and their organisms just do not act like machines and their possible reactions to treatment are not the same way pre-calculable as is the case with technical goods and services. Consequently accusations of medical malpractice may not be reconstructed only in terms of a doctor's mastery of medical machines or of knowledge of scientifically/statistically known side-effects of drugs and their components. Even less may the possible losses for patients be calculated in terms of 'investment' for treatment and care. Diametrically opposite to the underlying idea of the other boards, the *Schiedsstellen* for medical care are forced to reconstruct the case with special consideration of the individual psycho-social and biological peculiarities of the patient. Only if they thoroughly investigate both sides of the conflict's genesis, may they reconstruct whether in this particular case the doctor has failed, or if the case under dispute may be a typical example of doctors' experimental treatment under conditions where medical knowledge dos not yet have answers (cf. the history of medical discovery of AIDS). Therefore the traditional model of juridical predominance in settling these conflicts within court procedures will tentatively work towards further standardization and in this sense de-professionalization of doctors, who, under the thumb of judicial control, may restrict their venturesome medical experimentalization (cf. 'liability for medical malpractice').[14] Therefore these types of boards could – in the long run – be a step to 're-professionalization' of doctors. To this extent 'malpractice' will be discussed in terms of medical knowledge and experience and medical experts will intensify intraprofessional discussion, ruthlessly clarifying if, in this particular case, the doctor has failed or if the case in dispute must be interpreted as new experience of medical knowledge with regard to the still incalculable reactions of human organisms. For good reasons at least some lawyers prefer the *Schiedsstellen* procedure before going to court and some courts presuppose a *Schiedsstellen* procedure before accepting a claim. They approve that the medical profession has developed its own highly differentiated rules and norms, which may not easily be controlled by the legal profession, the latter having only rough criteria for medical practice (e.g. negligence). There seems to be some evidence that within these boards the quality of medical expertise has been improved in comparison to medical expert witness within court proceedings (Eberhardt 1988).

Stock of norms

As already stated, the *Schiedsstellen* have developed their own rules and norms. As shown, they have developed only rudimentary provisions for 'procedures', giving much room to substantiative norms and measures, which are not preformulated but allow for greater flexibility. In practice these measures are predominantly oriented at scientific and technical knowledge and corresponding price standards. As our research suggests, the *Schiedsstellen* simply reverse the ideal-typic legal or court-logic of conflict resolution. Within the legal action frame norms and measures for conflict settlement are stipulated, reinterpreted and validated by the legal profession according to legal knowledge experience; expert evidence from other fields is gathered from case to case if necessary, thus providing precedence of legal norms as against scientific and technical norms within the social construction of 'justice'. The *Schiedsstellen* action frame provides the exact converse of this judicial model – logic. Conflicts are reconstructed immediately in terms of technical and scientific knowledge by experts of the special fields without a second transformation into legal concepts. Instead the legal members of the staff are referred back to tactical aid and legal 'expertise' (e.g. they may refer to maximum redress allowed by the courts within comparable law suits). Within the *Schiedsstellen* action logic legal rules are contingent but not constitutive for the restitution of social consensus.

Thus we may conclude that the Schiedsstellen seem to be new pioneers, pushing ahead and bringing to social consciousness the victory of a scientific and (with regard to conflicts with workshops, trade, commerce) technocratic ordering of the social fabric, tentatively ruling out the world of legal norms and its striving for universality, or – at least – predominance of juridical transformation of conflicts.

Coming back to the historical emergence of 'the consumer', we may speculate that these new boards will develop this concept in a further direction. Again, we have to distinguish between the boards for workshops, trade, commerce and those for the 'classical' professions (esp. physicians). Where conflicts arise over highly standardized technical goods and services (cars, textiles, building materials, etc.), our case studies suggest that the *Schiedsstellen* exclude the social dimension of conflicts and restrict themselves to standardized compilation of technical details and corresponding prices. In so far as conflicts are reconstructed as technical defects and stripped of their social dimension, these boards will objectively represent a further step to technocratic patterns of conflict elimination, thus ultimately reducing 'the consumer' to an exchange logic guided by technical norms and economic price standards. This raises the further – culturally interesting – question, whether such an instrumentalization of conflicts may not be appreciated as reasonable, because of its ability to promote a social consciousness of fatalistic treatment of technical defects and mistakes thereby cooling-off overestimation of these products. Obviously the situation for patients (and lawyers' clients) is totally different. Illness (or punishment) in fact disturb the psycho-social integrity of patients and clients and these stigma are not easily compensatable in terms of 'hard currency'. Just for this reason the *Schiedsstellen* for physicians and lawyers may not restrict themselves to providing 'cash' for mistakes and failures. On the contrary, their 'effectiveness' must be seen against the background of the extent to which they will actually promote intraprofessional discussion and thus (indirectly) restore the obviously disturbed trust and confidence of laymen in their practice.

For the time being we may conclude that the *Schiedsstellen* present a challenge to social conflict resolution with regard to their capacity to promote new forms of social consciousness for handling conflicts and, simultaneously, with regard to the emerging necessity for rearrangements between the 'experts' for legally institutionalized conflict resolution (the legal profession) and experts/professions from other fields.

THE INTERACTION BETWEEN THE *SCHIEDSSTELLEN* AND THE OFFICIAL LEGAL SYSTEM

Out-of-court dispute processing – as provided by the *Schiedsstellen* – and court procedure reflect a continuous tension between private autonomy and the state. On the one hand, we have in West Germany the monopoly of the state to adjudicate (i.e. to confirm legal rights), on the other hand, there is the principle of leaving it up to private persons and institutions to regulate their affairs in substantive as well as in procedural aspects (freedom of contract).

We have seen that the *Schiedsstellen* as described above have been erected, and are supported, by associations of the private economy or service sector. No governmental body is directly involved. Nevertheless, the establishment of the *Schiedsstellen* was highly welcomed by the administration of justice as well as by legal writers. This was mainly for two reasons. The first one was related to the push which the consumer movement experienced in the late 1960s and early 1970s all over the western world. It was expected that any additional dispute-processing institution might promote consumers' access to justice and thus provide consumers with opportunities to exercise their newly acknowledged rights. The establishment of *Schiedsstellen* was expressly encouraged by the federal government for this reason.[15] The second reason was related to the increase in court caseloads as observed from the early 1960s onwards: it was hoped that out-of-court dispute settlement opportunities might help to relieve some of the demand on the courts. This was explicitly uttered in the context of the emerging ADR movement in the USA, which came to Europe first through the exchange of socio-legal scholars (cf. Blankenburg *et al.* 1980; *et al.* 1982). These originally separate reasons were fused in the late 1970s and early 1980s when government officials discovered that they could possibly 'kill two birds with one stone',[16] that is pacify consumers' and judges' demands without increasing the expenses for the judiciary.[17]

What makes dealing with *Schiedsstellen* difficult for legally trained professionals and simultaneously creates much ambivalence is their novelty with respect to the set of legal forms for out-of-court dispute processing provided by the official legal system. Obviously the *Schiedsstellen* 'borrowed' from the existing types of legally accepted forms for out-of-court conflict settlement, tempting courts and the judicial administration to accept them for only formal measures. We shall first describe the kind of procedures which the legal system itself has to offer besides the courts of law, and then take a look at how this is related to the *Schiedsstellen*.

If private persons or institutions are not able to settle their disputes themselves, court proceedings seem, from a legalistic point of view, the ordinary way for finding a decision and enforcement of the result. When looking at the type of procedure provided for disputes by the official legal system which is employed for the types of disputes for which also *Schiedsstellen* are available, we find that there is some sort of 'competition' with courts of law in building construction, medical malpractice, and landlord–tenant cases. The general court caseloads comprise a considerable amount of these cases. In contrast we find very few cases related to car repair and used car dealing, and almost none in the areas of dry cleaning, radio and television or shoe repair.

The ultimate goal of either party to a dispute is the opponent's compliance with one's claim, unless they agree on a novation of their reciprocal obligations. Since taking the law into one's own hands is prohibited by law, one needs to involve the state machinery for enforcement. This regularly requires a final judgment or, to put it the other way around, court judgments are the principle precondition for commissioning a bailiff (or initiating other means of execution). Other entitlements for setting enforcement machinery into operation are in-court settlement, submission to execution of court judgement in a certified document by the obligated party, settlement before a so-called *Gütestelle* (acknowledged conciliation board), and arbitration judgment.

A *Gütestelle* is from its outset an institution facilitating dispute settlement and being given the competence to approve the settlement to be enforced. This competence follows the acknowledgement of the *Gütestelle* by the ministry of justice of that state where the board is located. The preconditions for such an acknowledgement are not regulated. The ministries simply ensure that the procedure is fair and does not deprive a disputant of any legal rights. From the sample of *Schiedsstellen* dealt with in this chapter, only the building construction boards have been acknowledged in this way.[18]

Arbitration is the oldest form of out-of-court dispute processing. It is even older than the present form of civil procedure in West Germany, although the latter is in its structure more than a hundred years old. The basic rules of arbitration have been incorporated into the Code of Civil Procedure when it was issued in 1877. Arbitration is the only legally recognized way of excluding courts of law, that is to choose a private procedure instead of court procedure and private judges instead of official judges. The preconditions and minimum standards for arbitration as set out in the last part of the Code of Civil Procedure require that if and when the parties to a dispute prefer arbitration to litigation, they have to agree on the procedure in a written contract, and some indispensable standards are observed as to the parties' right to be heard and the right to be represented by a lawyer before the arbitration court. The arbitrators are paid by the parties, unless they work on an honorary basis.[19] They are recognized by the legal order as 'real' judges, that is performing the same function as the judges at courts of law, namely adjudicating in a legally binding way. That means that judgments by courts of arbitration can be enforced like those of law courts. There is only a limited number of reasons to involve an official court once a court of arbitration has been involved.

The original model of arbitration procedure provides that the parties determine the arbitrators in their arbitration agreement. If they do not, the law rules that each party calls one arbitrator; usually then the two arbitrators call a third one. However, many commercial associations offer a standing court of arbitration. In that case parties may determine such an institution as 'their' arbitration court. The free choice of arbitrators is then restricted to persons affiliated with the standing arbitration court, although mostly the parties may still choose 'their' arbitrators from a list.

Arbitration jurisdiction is also found within organizations, that is social institutions or associations, with the task of deciding on matters concerning the organizations' relations with their members.[20] Arbitration is mainly used for commercial disputes. From the sample for which *Schiedsstellen* are available, only building construction (including architects) employs the arbitration method of dispute processing.

Another form of legally sanctioned means, involving a third party in a dispute, is the so-called *Schiedsgutachter*, who is usually an expert on the subject matter. This legal institution goes back to medieval Roman law and means that disputants can commission a person to decide on the facts in dispute. It is necessary that the parties agree on such a person and submit to what that person will determine. If legal writers use Latin terms, they call the *Schiedsgutachter* 'arbiter' in order to distinguish him or her from the arbitrator.[21] The typical legal distinction made between an arbiter and an arbitrator is that the latter can finally adjudicate while the former is restricted to giving an expert opinion. Typically an arbiter is prevented from deciding on legal matters, whereas an arbitrator may do exactly the same as a court. In practice, however, this cannot be clearly distinguished because sometimes merely clarifying the subject matter actually means that one decides on a dispute also in its legal aspect. The consequence is that arbitration judgments can be enforced like court judgments, whereas arbiter decisions if not obeyed voluntarily have to undergo court procedure prior to any enforcement attempts. In turn this is used as a distinctive criterion if the interpretation of a parties' agreement on their dispute processing procedure is later called into question by either one. If the agreement clearly rules out official court proceedings, then their intention is interpreted as arbitration; if the agreement is not definite in this respect, it hints at intended arbiter proceedings. The legal consequence of arbiter procedure is that if either party files a lawsuit later the court is bound to the fact-findings: they can be overruled only if the expert opinion stating the facts is 'obviously wrongful'.

Any alternative to the official court system mentioned so far presupposes a mutual agreement between the parties to a dispute: either to a formal arbitration process that replaces the court procedure, or to an arbiter who decides on those facts the parties want him to decide on. Also the employment of a *Gütestelle* requires an agreement: if one party disagrees, the *Gütestelle* cannot take action. Beyond these legal forms parties to a dispute may naturally call in a mediator to facilitate a settlement between them, but again only if they do so jointly. Then there is no restriction, because anyone may oblige himself in a contract (as long as this is within the limits of civil law). If mediation fails there is no legal consequence: no restriction of going to court, and no continuing effect in possible future court proceedings.[22] This is the legal distinction between arbiter procedure and mediation.

If we now return to the rules as provided in the standing orders of the *Schiedsstellen* (regulating composition of staff and way to proceed), we find that they are a combination of pre-existing legal forms. They are based in part on the image of arbitration courts, in part on voluntary mediation/conciliation procedure. This becomes important because the *Schiedsstellen* do not act in some sort of 'outer space' in the law. However, contact between the *Schiedsstellen* and the official legal system does take place. If lawyers and courts are questioned on the legal consequences of concrete *Schiedsstellen* proceedings, they have to take a stand on it. Therefore they have to develop an opinion as to how the *Schiedsstellen* fit or do not fit into the legal system.

Lawyers

The legal profession (practising lawyers) initially appeared somewhat reluctant towards these new institutions. This became obvious when they withdrew from original participation in setting up *Schiedsstellen* (Plett 1989).

The lawyers' associations rather insist that dispute resolution without court involvement, that is prior to filing a lawsuit, is their original business: they claim themselves to be an alternative to court (Hahndorf 1983). Of course it may be considered some sort of 'bureaucratic overkill' if lawyers should involve *Schiedsstellen* in case they cannot reach a settlement with their client's opponent. The alternative to lawyers' failure to settle disputes is court proceedings or the arbitration court, not *Schiedsstellen* procedure. On the other hand, where a dispute concerns only a technical matter and contains no legal problem, *Schiedsstellen* are welcomed also by lawyers because the *Schiedsstellen* relieve lawyers from dealing with questions outside their professional knowledge and skills. This is true for car repair and dry cleaning disputes, for instance.

As to the remaining – more complex – conflicts for which *Schiedsstellen* are available (building construction and medical care), it is obvious that there arises some competition between free-practising lawyers and the *Schiedsstellen*. It could be read 'between the lines' of early utterances of lawyers regarding the emergence of all these new institutions that they feared competition which they had not to deal with previously. But in the mean time, outside this quasi-official position taken, some lawyers did participate in proceedings before the medical care and building construction boards (Eberhardt 1988; Plett 1989). However, in view of the *Schiedsstellen* logic as established above, it is not surprising that lawyers are rarely found in *Schiedsstellen* proceedings of the other types (Gottwald 1987): where only an expert opinion is available, there is little space for a lawyer's performance, whose original task is to supervise the procedure and to see that rules of evidence are observed. Altogether, the lawyers' attitude towards the *Schiedsstellen* is still ambivalent. Thus it remains an open question in which direction the lawyers as a profession will tend in the future.[23]

Courts

The view of the courts concerning *Schiedsstellen* becomes evident through their judgments in *Schiedsstellen* lawsuits. If we thus look at single court decisions, we may find a somewhat contradictory tendency. Lower courts that had been involved in ongoing disputes already handled by a conciliation board have decided that they cannot revoke the board's statements of the facts. Subsumption of the *Schiedsstellen* procedure under the arbiter procedure was the easiest way of getting rid of those cases. Any other decision would have required more careful argumentation. These few cases, with one exception, were terminated without redress to a court of appeal. But also in the exceptional case, the court of appeal approved the decision of the court of first instance.[24] (It has to be admitted that the substance of the judgment was correct although the argumentation is not convincing.) Following this decision all major commentators quoted this judgment for the justification of conciliation boards and their procedures.

It was only when the *Verbraucherschutzverein* (a consumer protection organization) filed a suit against the car trade association claiming that their general contract terms were not in conformity with the law, that there was more careful scrutiny of non-judicial dispute resolution. These general terms of contract had made the conciliation procedure obligatory for consumers. The court held that the procedure for consumers is only on a voluntary basis and that free trade associations are prevented from making *Schiedsstellen* obligatory unless the providers of goods and services themselves make an individual agreement with their customers.[25] (But this just does not happen in highly specialized and standardized businesses.) The respective contract clause used by the car trade was not in accordance with the Unfair Contract Terms Act (AGBG), especially because the procedural provisions of the car repair *Schiedsstellen* require that the *Schiedsstellen* fact-finding is binding in a subsequent lawsuit. In the court's opinion, this might trigger the impression that filing a lawsuit after the *Schiedsstellen* procedure was excluded, though it is not, and therefore the clause was deceptive. However, it was upheld that the procedure is an arbiter procedure if the procedural provisions determine that the *Schiedsstellen* fact-finding is binding also in a subsequent lawsuit.

The courts involved in this suit on the general contract terms were considering an issue different from single consumer–business disputes and were provided with different and better arguments by the plaintiff, the Verbraucherschutzverein. But nevertheless, they abstained from making a decision on the procedure itself. They gave no opinion on whether certain procedural standards have to be observed, and if so, which ones. Therefore, it is still undecided if *Schiedsstellen* procedures of types I and II (see Table 13.2) in general may legally be considered as arbiter procedures, or if they are simple conciliation boards with no effect whatsoever on a subsequent lawsuit.

In sum, we cannot disregard that some boards do not only solve disputes but also raise some when they get into contact with the official legal system. Beyond the question of their legal qualification as described here, some legal writers call into question whether or not the boards are really neutral with respect to disputants, and whether or not indispensable procedural standards (like the right to be heard and the right to be represented) are observed (see Plett and Eidmann 1987). But this in turn is related to the question whether or not there ought to be specific legal preconditions for *Schiedsstellen*. Legal debate on the conciliation boards is difficult and far from definite, because legal writers often represent competing interests with the consequence that they come to different conclusions. Thus one has to find out to what and whose interest they are close. Another problem is that there is little probability of trying a case up to the federal court because the amount at stake in consumer disputes is generally too insignificant for getting there. At least there has been no test case to date.

In our opinion it depends on whether the *Schiedsstellen* themselves want legal sanctions. If they consider themselves disconnected from the official legal system, they are free to regulate the procedure however they want to. If, however, they want to have their activities acknowledged by the official legal system, then they should obey minimum procedural standards. For example the building construction boards wanted to be acknowledged as *Gütestellen*, and thus they had to, and do, observe minimum standards.

It is too early to make a prognosis for the future of the *Schiedsstellen*. We see three possibilities. The first (and least possible) is that they will die out. The second one is that there will be a test case sooner or later, and that would be a first step in the direction of a take-over by the official legal system (cf. Gessner and Plett forthcoming). The third possibility is that the *Schiedsstellen* will consolidate and the official legal system as above all represented by the courts, will acknowledge them as they are. If this comes about, it would mean a self-constraint by the courts: they would abandon their original and monopolized task of deciding disputes according to the law and on the basis of facts established in their own procedure.

NOTES

1 Our thanks to Deidre Leahy (ZERP) for revising the English version and to Karl Mackie (University of Nottingham) for comments on an earlier version of this chapter.
2 Research is funded by the DFG (Deutsche Forschungsgemeinschaft) and done, together with Volkmar Gessner, at the ZERP (Zentrum für Europäische Rechtspolitik), Bremen.
3 In a sense this social formation of the consumer, sometimes postulated as a new 'historical subject' (Gartner and Riessman 1974; Ruffat 1987), implies a little irony of history: what has once been the basis of Marx's critique – namely the model of a rationally functioning capitalistic economy without any fraud, which the proletariat should overcome for the sake of human emancipation – seems to have gained empirical reality. In this way it has lost the proletariat but won 'the consumer' as its affirmative opponent.
4 It seems appropriate here to add a remark on the organization of the West German economy. All self-employed suppliers of goods and services as well as the self-employed professions are organized in so-called chambers (professional

associations). We have chambers of commerce, trade, physicians and lawyers. Their establishment is regulated by federal and/or state laws, providing a relative autonomy for trade/professions to regulate their own professional affairs and simultaneously committing them to the official legal order. Where chambers exist, membership is obligatory. Their main authority lies in the control of entrance to the respective trade or profession through elaboration of training standards, and control of members' conduct, as well as exercising disciplinary power. These chambers are the founders of the boards for physicians, architects, lawyers and trade or commerce in general. Besides, traders and professionals may organize themselves voluntarily in free associations, which are primarily oriented towards the promotion of their members' particular interests resulting from division of labour and economic processes. These free associations are – sometimes together with consumers' organizations – responsible for the establishment of the boards for car repair, used car dealing, dry cleaning and the building trade, though the chambers of trade or commerce are always more or less directly involved.

5 Although it may be taken into consideration that private owners increasingly delegate their problems with tenants to special interest organizations who in turn have established these boards (sometimes together with tenant organizations or with lawyers specializing in landlord–tenant problems).

6 Results from our interviews with E (= experts), M (= trained employees), J (= lawyers) of the different boards (1 = car repair; 2 = dry cleaning; 3 = building trade; 4 = medical care; 5 = architects; 6 = chambers of trade).

7 In so far we question the concept of 'informal justice' that occupied socio-legal discussions for such a long period (cf. Abel 1982a).

8 See p. 197 as to the attempt (which finally failed) in the car repair trade to make the *Schiedsstellen* procedure obligatory.

9 Important exceptions are the boards for building trade, whose fees are calculated as to the time invested by the board members. One hour costs about DM 300. Median values of fees are DM 22.000 (Plett 1989). Equally the boards of architects charge considerable fees.

10 Hardly different is the situation with the sale of goods or used cars, where it is examined, if the goods have the promised properties.

11 CD . . . refers to *Schiedsstellen* documents gathered by the *Stiftung Warentest*.

12 This in the strict sense is the meaning of 'professionalized' juridicial actions (Oevermann 1979; Caesar-Wolf 1985).

13 According to our experience customers inform themselves very well before calling in the *Schiedsstelle*.

14 Such a development is suspected by physicians in the USA.

15 Cf. Erster Bericht der Bundesregierung zur Verbraucherpolitik (First Report of the Federal Government on Consumer Policy), 18 October 1971, BT-Drs. VI/2724; Zweiter Bericht . . . (Second Report . . .), 20 October 1975; BT-Drs. 7/4181.

16 The date of this fusion can for West Germany quite correctly be determined by an international conference organized by the Federal Ministry of Justice and held at Stolberg in September 1981. The conference is documented in Blankenburg *et al.* 1982.

17 The relatively continuous increase of the judiciary in the first twenty-five years of the existence of the FRG had come to a temporary end with the first oil crisis in the mid-1970s. From then onwards, because of the increased court caseload the demand could no longer be met by an according increase in the number of judges, so that the search for alternatives began.

18 In the cities of Hamburg, Bremen and Lübeck, we have so-called public legal advice and conciliatory offices which are such recognized conciliation boards. But they rarely function as conciliators (Falke *et al.* 1983). Usually the disputants go there only for getting settlements certified. Therefore they have not been considered in this

article. Another type of conciliation institution we have refrained from dealing with here is even older: the so-called *Schiedsmann,* who works on the community level. His or her task is to mediate in minor criminal or civil disputes. Despite some attempts to revitalize this institution in our context, it is rarely addressed at all by disputants (Jansen 1987).

19 Arbitration is a rather expensive procedure because the arbitrators have to be paid according to the amount in dispute by the parties. The fees for the arbitrators are much higher than those for the courts of law. It pays only for cases where the parties want a private process (there are no public hearings in arbitration whereas the public hearing is one feature of the law courts), or for cases with millions of D-Mark at stake.

20 The establishment of such an inner-organizational arbitration court has even been made obligatory for political parties in the Act on political parties (*Parteiengesetz*).

21 As far as we understand English and the Anglo-Saxon context, both would be named 'arbitrators' and both procedures 'arbitration'. However, there is a difference if a third party called in in a dispute is entitled to act like a court and to adjudicate the matter, or if the third party is entitled just to decide without the full consequences of adjudication. So the English language may be less differentiated in this respect than reality requires.

22 But prudent parties see that the use of such voluntary 'procedure' does not take more time than the statutory rules of limitation allow for.

23 In this context also the external conditions for lawyers' actions (fees, etc.) will play a role for lawyers' engagement.

24 LG [district court] Nürnberg-Fürth, *Neue Juristische Wochenschrift* 1975: 972.

25 BGH [federal court], 14 July 1987, *Verbraucher und Recht* 2 (1987): 336ff.

14 Building an arbitration and mediation centre from international foundations to domestic rooftops

A case study of the British Columbia International Commercial Arbitration Centre

Bonita J. Thompson, Q.C.

INTRODUCTION

The stages of development and the business goals of an international commercial arbitration centre are unique in each circumstance and are a product of the social, economic, legal and political conditions of a particular geographic location as well as the imagination and creative insight of particular individuals spearheading the endeavour. Accordingly the experience or case study described here may differ markedly from the experience of other centres.

This chapter will demonstrate, however, some of the common problems and issues faced by individuals and organizations which endeavour to establish a solid and credible centre which attracts international businessmen, counsel and arbitrators for the resolution of international commercial disputes. It will also illustrate how it was necessary to expand the role of the contemplated centre to embrace the domestic market and to offer other forms of alternative dispute resolution services – all a result of a greater appreciation by the organizers of the long developmental period required to attract and sustain international commercial dispute resolution business.

It is probably useful at this point to clarify my use of the phrase 'international commercial arbitration centre'. In the international commercial arbitration community today the term is used in two ways. Most commonly and historically it has been used to describe a locale or city in which international commercial arbitration frequently takes place. Often this has occurred as a result of the availability of highly skilled arbitrators in that location, as a result of that location being a financial or commercial centre or as a result of the perceived neutrality of the location. These arbitrations need not have been under the auspices of a particular organization and probably took place in a variety of unrelated physical premises throughout the locale.

In the 1980s there has been a proliferation of arbitral organizations around the world which have established actual centres or physical premises out of which they have promoted and conducted international commercial arbitrations. In many instances these organizations have called their place of business 'centre' and have marketed their organizations under that title. It is this latter sense in which I shall be describing a case study on the establishment of an international commercial arbitration centre and, more particularly, the British Columbia International Commercial Arbitration Centre.

It is probably useful to understand my personal role in this development. In the spring of 1985 I was a member of the Attorney-General's Civil Law Branch. The Attorney-General appointed me as his representative to a Task Force on International Commercial Arbitration. Subsequently when a decision was made to establish a centre he instructed me to take all the necessary steps to ensure the opening of the Centre. Given only eight months within which to accomplish this task I used the resources of government as much as possible. A month before the Centre was opened, responsibility for the Centre was handed completely to the ICA Foundation of British Columbia (BC) which appointed me the Centre's first Executive Director just prior to its opening.

'No man's land'

To truly appreciate the monumental task before the organizers of the BC Centre it is important to understand certain of the social, economic, legal and political conditions existing in Canada and in the Province of British Columbia which had delayed or inhibited the development of arbitration and other methods of alternative dispute resolution in the commercial sector in Canada.

In the commercial community there has been no history of resort to non-judicial methods of resolving disputes in the community generally or in particular sectors of that community. Unlike the long-established commercial centres of Europe, Canadian business people had not found the need to develop their own mechanisms to resolve business disputes. The Canadian legal system was young and fairly well financed and there were – until the 1980s – sufficient public resources available to ensure speedy access to a publicly funded system of justice. In addition our judiciary in Canada has always been highly respected in the business community.

As a result of this level of comfort with the Canadian legal system, there was no legislative infrastructure demanded by the business community to support other methods of dispute resolution. All of the Canadian provinces, who have competence to legislate in this area, had enacted in the late nineteenth century an Arbitration Act based upon the English Arbitration Act 1889. With a very few exceptions in a few of the provinces, no amendments were made to that legislation over the next 100 years, notwithstanding a series of very significant amendments made to the English legislation over the same period of time.

As a result, in a very short period of time, all the Canadian provinces had arbitration legislation which did not reflect the needs of current commercial practice and further which reflected a judicial and legislative philosophy prevalent in nineteenth-century England – that arbitrators needed to be strictly supervised by the courts. Under these conditions, Canadian business people proceeded into the arbitration arena at their peril – knowing that they may have to bear not only the costs of an arbitration but also a myriad of court applications in respect of that arbitration.

The federal government of Canada during this last 100 years had no arbitration legislation in place to govern its own commercial activities and indeed had a government policy prohibiting arbitration of disputes. In respect of those matters where the federal government had competency to legislate, such as maritime matters, there was also no arbitration legislation available. The legislative inadequacies of the Canadian legal system certainly inhibited the conduct of domestic and international arbitrations but there was an even greater obstacle to the development of international arbitrations: the problem of award enforcement.

In 1958 the international business community addressed this problem when the *UN Convention on the Recognition and Enforcement of Foreign Arbitral Awards* provided a mechanism to enable arbitral awards to be easily enforced from one country to another. All of Canada's trading partners became members of that Convention over the years. But Canada did not. Citing lack of provincial support for treaty accession and an apathetic commercial community, the Canadian government refused to take steps to accede to the Convention. As a result, Canadian business people were severely restricted in their options for addressing dispute resolution in their contracts. Without Canadian accession to the Convention, Canadian business people could not assure their trading counterparts that an award made in another state could be easily enforced in Canada. Without Canadian accession to the Convention, Canadian business people could seldom negotiate an arbitration site in Canada. This was because many of Canada's trading partners had made the 'reciprocity' reservation when they acceded to the Convention, that is to say, they said they would enforce a foreign arbitral award in their state, only if it was made in a reciprocating state – another state which was also a party to the Convention. Accordingly an arbitral award made in Canada could not be easily enforced under the 1958 Convention in the states of most of our trading partners. Because of all these unsatisfactory conditions, until the summer of 1986, Canada was quite properly characterized as 'no man's land' for arbitration (Chiasson 1986).

The winds of change

The winds of change, preceding the events of the spring and summer of 1986, were generated by the galvanizing of political will in Canada. Since the early 1980s legal academics and business organizations had increased pressure on the federal government to become party to the 1958 Convention thus responding to the needs of business people to reduce the risks associated with conducting international business. Justice officials had also begun to take a closer look at methods of alternative dispute resolution in an effort to find solutions to a growing crisis in the judicial system causing increased cost and delay to litigants.

In British Columbia in January 1985, Attorney-General Brian Smith, QC, on the recommendation of Dean Peter Burns, QC, of the University of British Columbia Faculty of Law, established a Task Force on International Commercial Arbitration to study the United Nations Commission on International Trade Law (UNCITRAL) Model Arbitration Law for possible enactment. In the summer of

1985 the Uniform Law Conference of Canada, a conference of senior representatives of provincial and federal governments developing and promoting uniform legislation across Canada, prepared draft legislation for implementation of the 1958 UN Convention and strongly suggested its adoption by Canada.

The spark

From the spark of an idea exchanged between Sir Michael Kerr, President of the London Court of International Arbitration, and his long-time friend Attorney-General Brian Smith, QC, in the summer of 1985, Canada took a giant leap in nine months into the modern practices of international commercial dealings.

The commitment

In September 1985 Attorney-General Brian Smith enthusiastically recommended to his Cabinet colleagues in the Province of British Columbia that an International Commercial Arbitration Centre should be established in the City of Vancouver to service fast-growing Pacific Rim trading relationships. The Provincial Cabinet – already committed to assisting the establishment of Vancouver as an international commercial and financial centre – agreed to take all the necessary steps to create a 'hospitable legal environment' for the development of such a Centre and to provide start-up funding for it of $1.5 million (Canadian) for a period of three to five years.

The original Cabinet submission contemplated a rather modest infrastructure. The Centre would be run by a non-profit society and would have an executive director and secretary. These two staff would have small offices in the commercial centre of Vancouver. The submission contemplated a close working relationship with the University of British Columbia Faculty of Law – the Dean and faculty members of which had supported the proposal – with administrative and research support being provided through the Faculty to the Centre.

Such a Centre was perceived as a very viable operation because Vancouver was seen to be geographically convenient and culturally suitable for international commercial arbitrations.

1 Vancouver was centrally located on the Pacific Rim and had excellent international air links and first-class restaurants and accommodation.
2 English, the predominant language in international commercial agreements, was the principal language used in British Columbia. If translation needs arose, however, Vancouver had a wide range of nationalities from which support could be drawn.
3 Vancouver was a neutral location – a particularly relevant factor where disputants were the government of a developing country and a multinational corporation.

4 Finally, Canadians had reputations as mediators and peace-makers in an international context.

With the intent to make necessary legislative changes, British Columbia was also seen to have an appropriate legal environment for international commercial arbitrations.

1 The law of British Columbia was based upon the English common law system, which had traditionally enjoyed the confidence of the international trading community. The British Columbia International Commercial Arbitration Centre could also draw upon the expertise of civil law jurists from other provinces of Canada whenever necessary.
2 Vancouver, British Columbia, had local legal expertise in the law of the Pacific Rim nations and in international commercial arbitrations. In addition, the Faculty of Law at the University of British Columbia, situated in Vancouver, had pioneered in Canada the teaching of and research in law of the Asia–Pacific regions and had formal exchange agreements or established contacts with universities in the Pacific Rim.

The submission contemplated the provision of arbitration services in an international commercial context only.

Most projects of this size are preceded by the inevitable marketing and feasibility study. In this case, the timetable of the initiative – scheduled to be opened when British Columbia hosted the 1986 World Exposition on Transportation and Communication – did not permit such analysis. There was limited consultation – albeit with very informed parties. But the vision was essentially a personal one, strongly supported at a political level at a point in British Columbia's history which could not have been better timed had it been planned for many years.

The Attorney-General tested his idea in September 1985 at a series of meetings of the Chartered Institute of Arbitrators throughout the Pacific Rim. It was well received. He formally announced the project in a Canadian context in Quebec City in October 1985 at the first International Commercial Arbitration Conference held in Canada. This Conference, hosted by the Faculty of Law, Laval University, highlighted the legislative weaknesses in Canada in this area and certainly provided additional momentum to the significant steps which took place in Canada over the next few months.[1]

In November 1985 the Attorney-General gave me the 'green light' to open the British Columbia International Commercial Arbitration Centre on 2 May 1986, a date which he indicated should also be the occasion of an International Commercial Arbitration Conference to help to publicize the Centre's opening.

ESTABLISHING AN HOSPITABLE LEGAL ENVIRONMENT

The UN Convention

Our most pressing and urgent problem was to convince the Government of Canada that it was absolutely essential to the establishment of the Centre to have Canada become a party to the 1958 Convention. Since 1958 the overtures of academics, commercial organizations and business associations had fallen largely on deaf ears at the federal government level. In Canada only the federal government has the constitutional power to accede to a treaty or convention although the provinces and territories must also implement the terms of any treaty into their own legislative bases when the subject matter is within their competence. The federal government had made it a practice never to accede to a treaty or convention without the provinces and territories first having enacted the necessary implementing legislation for such a treaty or convention.

In early December 1985 it became clear that the federal government was strongly supporting the initiative of the British Columbia government and the will to accede to the Convention was present. At this point our biggest enemies were time (just six months) and the competing interests of provincial legislative programmes which would be required to enact the necessary implementing legislation. In order to show BC's commitment, I was asked to prepare implementing legislation for this Convention for introduction by the BC Attorney-General in December 1985.[2] Much of the preparatory work for this legislation had been done the previous summer by the Uniform Law Conference of Canada although BC recommended – and other provinces except Saskatchewan subsequently agreed – that the 'reciprocity' reservation should not be taken. It was the BC view that if Canada wanted to develop international commercial arbitration it should be sending an 'open for business' message to the world. Taking the 'reciprocity reservation' seemed to be unnaturally limiting and counter-productive.

Armed with only provincial government commitments to implement the Convention (whereas in the past the federal government has required implementing legislation to be in place), the federal government passed the necessary legislation to accede to the Convention on late Friday 9 May 1986 – just in time for the opening of the British Columbia Centre on Monday 12 May 1986. Needless to say this action required an enormous amount of orchestrated effort and a high degree of co-operation between the two levels of government – not an everyday occurrence in the Canadian context. On 11 August 1986 – ninety days after Canada deposited documents of accession in New York – Canada became the seventieth state to become a party to the Convention.

Arbitration legislation

International

The second pressing legislative matter for BC was to introduce new legislation governing international commercial arbitration. Happily this was a matter more easily dealt with as the BC Task Force on International Commercial Arbitration had been working very hard during the fall of 1985 in anticipation of the new Centre. With a few minor changes and additions the Task Force recommended the implementation of the United Nations Commission on International Trade Law (UNCITRAL) Model Arbitration Law adopted by the UN General Assembly on 21 June 1985. This legislation, which reflected an international consensus of sixty-one countries and international organizations, embodied two strongly held principles necessary to attract international commercial arbitration – a minimal degree of judicial intervention and a significant degree of party autonomy. BC had the opportunity to market itself as the first jurisdiction in the world to introduce this new legislation into its law. The Task Force consulted with Gerold Herrmann, Senior Legal Advisor of UNCITRAL, and principal draftsman of the Model Law. Our initial inclination was to redraft the Model Law into BC drafting style and format. Mr Herrmann persuaded us, however, that BC would be a much more attractive site if the Model Law language was left intact and only necessary modifications made to it. He convinced us that foreign parties coming to BC would be comforted by the familiar legislative language. Our new International Commercial Arbitration Act reflects these decisions.[3] The few changes and additions which were made were considered necessary for two main reasons. First, to make BC a more appealing legislative environment than any other jurisdiction which might subsequently adopt the UNCITRAL Model Law, and second, to try to ensure that our judiciary understood the major policy implications of the new legislation in order to encourage them not to inhibit the development of this new international business. (For a complete discussion of the International Commercial Arbitration Act see Herrmann 1987: 65–76.)

The work of the BC Task Force subsequently became the basis of the deliberations of the Uniform Law Conference of Canada meeting from January to March 1986; most of the modifications recommended by BC were incorporated into the Uniform Law Conference legislation recommended to the rest of the provinces. The federal government and all the provinces and territories of Canada have now passed international commercial arbitration legislation based on the Model Arbitration Law.

There is another matter well worth mentioning in the context of this Act and once again it is purely a marketing consideration. Legislation governing the legal profession in BC would likely have prohibited foreign counsel from representing their clients in an arbitration in BC without being licensed to practise law. The Attorney-General consulted with the Law Society of BC and advised them that he wished to exempt foreign counsel from such a requirement. Subsequently a regulation-making power was incorporated into the statute with the acquiescence of the Law Society and the exempting regulation was passed in July 1986.[4]

Domestic

During the course of preparing the international legislation there was a lobby by members of several arbitrators' associations in BC to have BC domestic arbitration legislation amended to enable domestic commercial arbitration business to develop as well. We were convinced that it was essential to the healthy development of international arbitration business to ensure a strong arbitration business domestically. We became convinced that if we could encourage the development of a strong domestic commercial arbitration business that we could, in a very short time, have the skilled arbitrators we needed for international arbitrations. The need for this domestic business became even clearer after the Centre opened and we realized very quickly that international business was not likely to fill the Centre for some ten to fifteen years,[5] not three to five years as originally anticipated. Accordingly domestic business became identified as the source of much needed cash flow during our formative years.

The domestic Commercial Arbitration Act was introduced one week after the international legislation in April 1986. It was introduced at the same time in order to reinforce a message to our judiciary that the international legislation was substantially different from our domestic legislation. The domestic legislation was based on recommendations of a 1981 report of the Law Reform Commission of BC. The new legislation addressed many of the difficult issues raised by the outdated Arbitration Act. Its most important changes were to repeal the difficult 'stated case' application, to remove a right of appeal for an error of fact on the face of the record and to give a very limited right of appeal for an error of law on the face of the record (for a discussion of the legislative changes see Thompson 1987a). It contemplated a greater degree of judicial supervision than the international legislation and contains many of the principles of the English Arbitration Act 1979. There was an opportunity for arbitrators' associations to make comments and suggestions before introduction of the legislation. This consultation was considered very useful to ensure not only the workability of the legislation but also the support of the local arbitration community for the new Centre.

There has been some considerable discussion in other Canadian provinces about whether or not there should be a different arbitration regime for domestic and international matters (Institute of Law Research and Reform 1987). My own view, shared by many others, is that it would be preferable to have one regime. The federal government has taken that view and the UNCITRAL Model Arbitration Law which it adopted applies to both domestic and international matters. In BC however we had only six months to make legislative changes. We had recommendations for new domestic legislation and we had the Model Arbitration Law: it was decided to enact two regimes. I believe that the introduction of these two regimes at the same time will help to ensure that the judiciary will take a 'hands off' approach to international arbitration because it has been given a clear signal by the legislature to treat the two regimes very differently. To date, the judiciary has had few occasions to consider our new legislation but the first indications are very positive. Recently Madame Justice Proudfoot of the Supreme Court of British Columbia stated:

Finally, the most compelling reason why the court should not intervene is simply the legislation sets up a mechanism to expediently and inexpensively resolve these types of disputes which occur from time to time. This process should be allowed to continue.

If the courts are to become involved by way of granting leave each time an award is made and a party is not happy, the objectives and intentions of the legislation will never be fulfilled.

Everyone talks today of mechanisms for 'alternative dispute resolution'; here is just such a mechanism; that scheme should be allowed to flourish.[6]

Immigration and employment legislation

Although I did not address this issue until about a year after assuming responsibilities as Executive Director of the Centre, I think it is important to mention this issue now as it was part of the issue of making Canada an hospitable legal environment. We wanted to make sure it was as easy as possible for visiting foreign parties, their counsel and arbitrators to enter BC (Canada actually) to conduct their cases. Any difficulties in this area could be a complete obstacle to our efforts as we expected that in many cases parties coming to BC would have no connection with Canada and would be coming here only because of convenience and British Columbia's legislative environment. Representations were made to federal officials in charge of these matters and within a remarkably short period of time we were advised that the matter had been reviewed and changes in policy implemented to minimize any immigration and employment requirements. As a result of all these efforts, the Attorney-General of British Columbia was able to announce that an hospitable legal environment was in place for the opening of the Centre on 12 May 1986.

THE NON-PROFIT SOCIETY

In order to facilitate the financial support of the Centre by the provincial government, it was determined very early on that it should be a non-profit society incorporated under provincial legislation. At the same time, however, it became crucial to ensure that the Centre could assure its potential clients that it was a completely neutral body and that the government had no managerial interest in its operations. This could prove to be a very important issue if the government were ever involved directly or indirectly in a dispute referred to arbitration under the rules of the BC Centre.

The ICA Foundation of BC was incorporated in April 1986 just prior to the Centre's opening. The Board of Trustees has nine to fifteen members – a majority of whom must represent the business community. This was, once again, a marketing strategy. We wanted to send a clear signal to the business community that the Centre was designed to meet their needs and was not to be run by lawyers. The balance of the Trustees are from the legal and arbitration communities. There are five fixed, representational positions on the board. One is the Attorney-General, two are from the University of British Columbia Law Faculty and two are from the Vancouver Board of Trade. This is an acknowledgement of the role of these parties in the early stages of development of the Centre. Three members of the current Board are also members of three arbitrators' associations in BC. The role of the Board of Trustees is to guide future developments of the Centre but probably more importantly to take an active and ongoing role in the marketing of the Centre.

The Centre initially retained two full-time staff members – myself as Executive Director and my Executive Assistant. With the addition of new programmes it has been necessary to introduce another staff position for the administration of those programmes. In my view, to do a proper marketing job it is necessary to have additional staff but our limited financial resources have not made that possible. Other centres have had directors on a half-time basis only. I'm sure it must be very difficult to market a new centre with only part-time staff – indeed an almost impossible task.

It might be useful to mention at this point the Centre's relationship with other arbitrators' associations – this is, I believe, an important issue to be dealt with in any institutional setting. I made the decision very early on that although it was very important to co-operate with and be supportive of arbitrators' associations I wanted the Centre to be in the position of complete neutrality. I didn't want the Centre to be tied to any group. This would give the Centre the opportunity to choose neutrals from anywhere in the community whether they belonged to an organization or not. This has given the Centre the real advantage of choosing only the best arbitrators in the community – our credibility depends upon our ability to make excellent appointments and we take this task most seriously. This has been a delicate 'political' issue however, as one of the groups in particular – with limited resources and no office – wished to use our facilities as a mailing address. To date I have resisted that pressure and believe my decision has been right.

In addition I have been encouraging these associations to concentrate their energies in educating and re-educating their members. This will give the Centre the human resources it needs to administer its programmes and will alleviate the need of the Centre to move into the education field – a move which would require considerably more staff and greater cost.

Our approach on the issue of relationship with arbitrators' associations has not been typical. Other arbitration centres have been created to meet the needs and demands of arbitrators, often of a particular organization. The establishment of those centres has been a tool to help market the skills of a particular group of arbitrators. This is an obvious boost to the centre. It provides a group of users who will immediately support the centre and provide cash flow. It also provides the centre with a financial backer – the association itself. Strong financial support is essential in the initial stages.

Advisory Committees

The first Board of Trustees also recognized the problem that the BC Centre would have breaking into a very well established market-place concentrated in the North Atlantic and Europe. It was decided to establish an International Advisory Committee which would serve as a resource for the Centre in any problems or issues arising in its formative years. Being associated with the well-known names in the international arbitration community would also help to establish the credibility of the Centre and these individuals would perform a useful marketing function for the Centre. The members of our International Advisory Committee are Chief Justice Nathan Nemetz, Chief Justice of BC, Sir Michael Kerr, President, London Court of International Arbitration, Sigvard Jarvin, former Secretary-General of the ICC Court of Arbitration, Michael Hoellering, General Counsel of the American Arbitration Association, Gerold Herrmann, Senior Legal Advisor of UNCITRAL in Vienna, and Attorney-General Brian Smith as Chairman. These people have been very supportive and have provided advice and information.

In order to increase the involvement of the business and legal communities in the affairs of the Centre, I recommended industry advisory committees to my Board. It has never ceased to amaze me how enthusiastic busy business people can be. We have established several advisory committees and all the members have approached their roles with great energy and without compensation. The tasks of the advisory committees are essentially threefold:

1 to identify the commercial needs of a particular industry in the field of commercial arbitration and mediation
2 to advise the Centre on the best methods to market to a particular industry
3 to carry out a personal education or awareness programme to colleagues in a particular industry.

This concept has worked exceedingly well. The following Advisory Committees have been established: Maritime Arbitration, Pacific Rim Marketing, Insurance, Construction and ADR for Personal Injury Claims. Leading members of the commercial community, legal community and senior court judges are members of these voluntary committees.

By way of illustration to show how useful these committees can be let's look at the Maritime Arbitration Advisory Committee. This Committee quickly identified the need for skilled maritime arbitrators to develop this area. Three months after formation, the Committee members incorporated the Vancouver Maritime Arbitrators Association (VMAA), which now has over sixty-five members. The Association adopted a set of Maritime Rules and the Centre prepared a set of special administrative procedures to accommodate these Rules. There have been a significant number of Vancouver arbitration clauses inserted in contracts to date, as a result of the members' advocating its use. On 26 and 27 May 1988, the VMAA and the Centre co-hosted an International Maritime Arbitration Conference – the first to be held in Canada. It was staged to 'piggyback' the ICCA (International Congress of Commercial Arbitration) meeting in Tokyo 1–5 June 1988.

Each of these committees has its own approach and agenda and I have been very happy with them. The key is to find open-minded and enthusiastic people who have a sense of commercial community betterment. It is also crucial to keep the amount of time required to act on these committees as limited as possible. Finally it is important to keep a tight rein on the agenda to ensure that the committee continues to focus on its real responsibility – the promotion of the Centre and its services – and not on some other goal.

THE CENTRE PREMISES

This was certainly a most challenging part of my work in the short few months before opening the Centre. I had never been to another arbitration centre and I was not authorized to carry out any on-site research. Accordingly I did the best I could. I phoned several Centres and had them describe their facilities and asked them to send copies of drawings by fax where possible. One of my advisers was to be in New York, London and Paris and I sent him along with a measuring tape.

It quickly became apparent that if we were to send out any strong message to the international business community about our long-term commitment we had to establish a physical presence which reflected the fact. A simple office, contemplated in the original Cabinet submission, was quickly abandoned in favour of a fully self-contained facility with all the amenities required to provide complete arbitration services in one location. Indeed, designing the Centre in this manner gave us another opportunity to market our Centre by offering a product no other Centre could supply. This approach has been criticized by some European arbitrators who have traditionally resorted to hotel rooms for arbitration and who believe we are emphasizing a superficial aspect. On the other hand our efforts have been praised by lawyers, arbitrators and business people who have had their fill of dingy smoke-filled rooms and inadequate communication systems and administrative support.

The Centre was situated in the heart of Vancouver's commercial and financial community in a new building housing many companies and organizations involved in international business. We decided that an obscure location would inhibit early developments. Indeed, our location has encouraged a great deal of 'drop-in' business and interest and has allowed our business neighbours to support the Centre actively by promoting it to their own customers and clients.

From design of the space, completing the renovations, manufacturing the furniture, purchasing the equipment and printing stationery – a period of ten weeks went by – and the Centre was opened. The opening of the premises was celebrated with an International Commercial Arbitration Conference co-hosted by the Ministry of Attorney-General and the University of British Columbia Faculty of Law. Professor R. Paterson and I co-chaired the Conference attended by 140 arbitrators and lawyers from countries in Europe, North America and the Pacific Rim. It was a wonderful way to introduce the Centre to the international arbitration community. Subsequently the papers of the Conference were published as *UNCITRAL Arbitration Model in Canada* (Paterson and Thompson 1987). The book also contains an analysis of the International Rules of Procedure of the Centre. The book has a motif based on the Centre's logo and will be a useful tool to market British Columbia in the international arbitration community.

THE CENTRE'S SERVICES

The functions of the Centre can be broken down into four areas:

1 information and advice
2 appointment of qualified and skilled neutrals
3 development of rules and procedures
4 provision of physical facilities and administrative services.

When the Centre first opened, these functions were focused only on the needs of the international business community and on arbitration. Within a period of only a few months, the focus was expanded to include the domestic business community and other ADR processes. This expansion was a result of the realization that the Centre could not become self-sufficient on international commercial arbitration in the near future. This is a result not only of the time it takes to penetrate a very well established market, but also of the nature of the business we are trying to attract. If our model arbitration clause is inserted in a large international contract today, a dispute may never arise or if it does and is not resolved by negotiation, it may not arrive on our desk for as long as five to seven years.

Information and advice

Information and advice was one function for which there was a crying need in Canada. Canadian lawyers and business people lacked information about arbitration and other ADR processes, and about arbitral information available in the world, the services they perform, rules they use and fees they charge. They also lacked basic information about how to access arbitration and how to proceed with an arbitration if a dispute arose. Accordingly our first step was to collect information about all the arbitral institutions and to keep it on-site for clients. We also developed a compact but fairly complete commercial arbitration library with basic texts and reporting services. Much of my time as Executive Director has been spent fielding inquiries, providing information and giving advice. We have been filling a real void in Canada by providing this service. We provide it without charge and see it as part of our ongoing promotion of ADR generally.

Appointment of qualified and skilled neutrals

Our second function is to provide a pool of qualified and skilled persons as neutrals, that is arbitrators and mediators. This has been a very important function and although the demands for this service are just beginning we must be prepared for any inquiry at any time. The Board of Trustees established a Credentials

Committee, which prepared a list of criteria for placing an individual in our international or domestic pool. Recruitment is an ongoing issue. We received many unsolicited applications which required careful screening. We have also solicited applications from individuals with whom members of our Board are familiar. Our pools are not published. That list is a source of revenue potential for the Centre. We are able to save parties a great deal of time by pre-screening individuals who are competent and skilled. We decided that if parties wished us to assist them with appointing an arbitrator that we would give the parties the opportunity to comment. Instead of making an immediate appointment on request (or under our Rules), we use the list method. A list of names and biographical sketches are supplied to each party. Within a set period of time, each party has the opportunity to veto and prioritize the names on the list. This approach supports the concept of parties being in control, as much as possible, of their own arbitral procedure.

Before we recommend any name we take into account any qualifications required by the parties, the nature and substance of the dispute and the nationalities of the parties. Under our Rules of Procedure and legislation each arbitrator must be completely independent and impartial. Before appointment, a proposed arbitrator must sign a statement verifying his independence and impartiality.

In the event that we do not have suitable individuals to be recommended in a particular case, I am able to solicit assistance from administrators of other arbitral centres or organizations with whom I have cultivated a co-operative working relationship. Several of these relationships have been reduced to writing but most are as a result of an informed but very effective network among individuals managing arbitral institutions. I am of the opinion that these relationships are very important to the long term success of an institution like ours.

Development of rules and procedures

The development of rules and procedures for arbitration, our third function, took a significant amount of time in the first six to eight months of the Centre's opening. Two things are absolutely essential to a successful arbitration – a skilled arbitrator and effective rules of procedure. Accordingly we prepared two sets of Rules – one for international arbitrations and one for domestic.[7] We felt this was necessary because we had two legislative regimes and because parties involved in domestic and international arbitrations had different needs.[8]

A major decision was made which does deserve mention here is our decision *not* to provide 'supervised' arbitral procedure. We became aware of a considerable amount of criticism of the ICC Court of Arbitration's Procedures even before we opened the Centre. The criticism was of excessive cost and delay. Briefly the ICC process contemplates ongoing supervision of the arbitration by a member of the Secretariat of the Court in Paris – no matter where the arbitration is sited. The advantage of this degree of supervision is a very high percentage of awards which are *not* overturned by national courts. This is particularly helpful in arbitrations involving unsophisticated parties or parties from the Third World. But the disadvantages are substantial delay and cost.

We opted for 'administered' arbitrations. Our Centre would provide assistance to the parties and arbitrators whenever, and to the extent, they wished. Our Rules and Procedures would also allow the parties to request the assistance of the Centre in several controversial issues to avoid the necessity of requesting judicial assistance. Administered arbitrations appeared to be the best approach given the criticisms we heard from lawyers and business people. For me, however, the jury is still out. It may be the best of all worlds for the users but it may not provide the degree of financial security required to sustain the Centre.

Provision of physical facilities and administrative services

The last function I mentioned is the provision of physical facilities and administrative support services. The BC Arbitration Centre occupies 3,800 sq. ft. on the sixth floor of the World Trade Centre of Canada Place in Vancouver. It is a fully contained, completely equipped and beautifully furnished facility for the conduct of commercial arbitrations – both domestic and international. The Centre has two fully sound-proof hearing rooms. The Skeena Room will accommodate up to eighteen people and the Nootka Room up to ten. The Skeena Room has a built-in sound system for transcribing as well as a completely equipped simultaneous translation booth. Both hearing rooms share modular tables for flexible seating arrangements and have temporary document and library storage.

The Centre has a growing commercial arbitration library with microfiche access to the library collections in the Vancouver Courthouse Library and the UBC Law Library. A completely secure locker facility permits counsel or parties to leave their papers and exhibits behind during lengthy adjournments. A fully equipped kitchen provides continuous coffee and tea service and catered meals can be arranged at short notice. There is a comfortable witness waiting-room with telephone and writing desk and access to a 70-foot outdoor balcony.

Arbitrators are given 24-hour access to a retiring-room with local and long-distance telephone, dictating equipment, desks, shelving space and sofas. Four counsel rooms are similarly equipped. Clerical support can be provided by the Centre. There are telex and telecopier machines for instant communication and the usual office support equipment for convenience of other parties. Secretarial support can be provided at short notice.

We are very proud of our Centre and have been advised that it is the most complete and best equipped centre in the world.

PROGRAMMES

Once our two sets of rules were published, along with our model arbitration clause, I moved on to develop some particular programmes: the ADR Programme for Personal Injury Claims and the Vancouver Board of Trade Centre Association

Commercial Dispute Resolution Service. These domestic programmes were designed to provide a more immediate cash flow. Programmes associated with a particular organization or industry gave us the advantage of another organization or industry publicizing our services for us while at the same time providing an innovative new membership service for its members. These types of programmes have proved to be very beneficial to future development of the Centre. Other centres have offered similar programmes and I am advised that in some cases the Centre has been able to elicit an annual retainer to provide such a programme.

The ADR Programme for Personal Injury Claims has been a very large project to get off the ground and has occupied about 50 per cent of my time over the last year. In BC we have a Crown corporation (ICBC) supplying mandatory automobile insurance coverage. ICBC was interested in a pilot project to refer cases to mediation or arbitration rather than to litigation. Excessive delay and escalating costs were forcing ICBC to explore new alternatives. To ensure an effective service and to garner support, we established an Advisory Committee with representatives from the judiciary, plaintiff and defence bars, and ICBC. We prepared procedures, set fees and printed information brochures. We held a number of information meetings to convince a reluctant bar of the advantages of the programme.

Our largest task was identifying skilled mediators. We decided to focus on mediation as opposed to arbitration as it was faster and cheaper. We drew from lawyers in the community who had been active in family law mediation, put them through a special training programme, screened them and identified several of them as members of our panel.

This programme, which has been in operation since 1 October 1987, has been very successful. Of the referrals to date about 25 per cent have been supported by plaintiff counsel. Our function is to talk the other side into participating and if there is agreement, to appoint a mediator and supervise all the necessary administrative details. At the time of this writing we have had sixty-four agreements to mediate. Out of those fifty-four have gone to a scheduled four-hour mediation and forty-one (76 per cent) have settled within that time. The range of settlements is $15–200,000 (Canadian).

We work very closely with our mediators and have periodic meetings to share information and advice. Mediators, counsel and parties have expressed great faith in the programme and we are very encouraged by its early successes.

Another specialized programme currently in the developmental stages is the World Trade Centres Association Commercial Dispute Resolution Service. This Association agreed in October 1987 to allow our Centre to establish a global dispute resolution service for its members. The service will begin for a period of two years in the Pacific Rim. The service based on common procedure will be administered by a network of arbitration centres located around the Pacific Rim and will be co-ordinated by our Centre initially. The hallmarks of the service will be speed and low cost.

FEES

Another very important issue appropriate for discussion at this point is the establishment of fees for the Centre. There are two main factors which guided my recommendations in this area. The first is that people should be paid for services they render. Arbitrators and mediators are devoting quality time to their task and should be adequately remunerated. Some organizations such as the American Arbitration Association take a different approach and have their arbitrators – at least in domestic matters – donate their time.

The second factor is that the market-place should be taken into account. In this respect, aside from programmes offered by the Centre, where neutrals' fees are included in a set programme fee,[9] we decided that the neutral should negotiate his or her own fee directly with the parties. The market-place has also had a say in the administrative fees the Centre is charging. In the international sphere, parties are accustomed to paying a fee based on a percentage of the value of the amount in dispute. Accordingly but mindful of the criticisms of high costs levelled against other centres, we followed suit but fixed a ceiling on our fees which is three to four times lower than the ceiling of fees for ICC.

In the domestic sphere, we do not have an existing market to which to refer. Our task is to create a demand for our service and there is extreme price resistance. Accordingly we established a fee for service schedule – with a range of very modest fees payable only if and when a particular service is requested. Our domestic fees are not based on the amount in dispute.

At the moment we do not have the experience to know if our decisions were right or our fees appropriate. Most of the business of the Centre, to date, is *ad-hoc* arbitrations using our facility where our Rules have not been incorporated into the agreement. None of the contracts incorporating our model arbitration clause have yet come to the Centre in an arbitration. If I can make an educated forecast, however, it is my view that our international fees are right and our domestic fees are too low. The nagging worry always is, however, can the Centre pay its own way? At the fee level currently used with the level of business currently in place, we do not expect the Centre to be self-sufficient for another four to five years. Part of this is caused by the decision to create a completely self-contained facility in prime real estate in Vancouver. In my view this decision was the right one even though it may give me sleepless nights worrying about cash flow. The lesson here I suppose is that it is essential that an institution like our Centre be given long-term financial support by a governmental body, private industry or an association. It cannot be expected to pay its own way in the short term.

It is possible of course to make decisions which keep annual operating costs to a minimum, for example part-time directors, limited physical facilities, shared office accommodation. All of these are possible and have been used by centres around the world. My sense is that a half-hearted effort is going to be met by a half-hearted response. In that event – why bother? The competition is tough enough as it is.

MARKETING

It was only after I was named Executive Director of the Centre that I began to contemplate the enormity of the marketing task before us. In the international context, we were competing with organizations such as the ICC, London Court of International Arbitration, American Arbitration Association – all in the business for 60–100 years. The Centres for this business were in London, New York, Paris, Geneva, Stockholm – not the Pacific Rim. 'Big name' arbitrators lived and worked in Europe – not the Pacific Rim. We had to find a way to break a habit, to make lawyers and business people realize there was another choice. Aside from our steps to make sure we had a completely hospitable legal and physical environment, our 'pitch' has concentrated on cost and convenience and has been levelled at what we believe is our best market-place – Americans doing business in the Pacific Rim. Why go to Europe? Why not come to Vancouver, a neutral location that is mutually convenient (or inconvenient) and which costs significantly less than other international cities.

Our task on the domestic side was much different: to create a demand for ADR services where none previously existed. In this area our marketing had to concentrate almost entirely on education – education of lawyers and business people. And it has been at times a formidable and frustrating task. Without any marketing experience of any kind but armed with a strong albeit relatively uninformed sense of what was needed, I plunged into marketing without any written plan of attack. Not (I might add) a good way to begin! My impression (rightly or wrongly) was that most of the arbitral organizations had taken a rather low-key, conservative approach to marketing. Much of it was characterized by rather dreary folders distributed at international meetings. I decided I wanted written materials produced which caught a reader's eye and which capitalized on the fabulous city in which we live. I also decided to produce a complete briefing book for lawyers or international businessmen. It contains our legislation, our Rules of Procedure, Administrative Services, Model Clause and Fee Schedule. It was designed to introduce our jurisdiction to potential users and to provide all the information necessary to make an informed decision about our Centre. No other centre has produced such briefing material. It was also prepared from high-quality materials and is intended to be part of a permanent reference library.

I also decided that as our physical location was very attractive – particularly for any lengthy arbitration proceedings – that we should utilize that beauty to our advantage. We produced a thirteen-minute video entitled *Common Ground*, which shows our Centre in Vancouver context. It has been a very useful marketing tool when I or other Centre supporters have been giving presentations across Canada and around the world. I have also sent copies to potential users of the Centre who want to know who and what we are. The video has been used by companies negotiating our clause into their contracts.

On the domestic side, our materials, produced of the same high quality, have been almost entirely educational: explaining what arbitration is, what its advantages are and how to involve it. There is a complementary video, quite different from the international, which shows a domestic commercial arbitration in the Centre.

On the international side, we focused first on the international arbitration community, trying to ensure that this small and well-defined group was aware of our existence. On the domestic side, we focused first on the legal community to try to defuse the hostility many lawyers had to arbitration and other ADR processes.

Our efforts to contact a widening circle of individuals and companies have been limited to date primarily by lack of human and financial resources. Unfortunately for us, the best method to market our innovative services is by person-to-person contact. I am convinced that an institution like ours must undertake and continue an aggressive marketing campaign. The Centres which have withered on the vine are those which have been unable to get their message to the business community. Our services are no different from any others. They must be sold. They do not sell themselves.

Our latest endeavour to try to maintain contact with the 8,000-name mailing list we have built up since our opening is a newsletter. I have been criticized in our community for failing to 'follow up' on initial contacts with potential users. Unfortunately that is not possible with two staff. Accordingly a newsletter seemed to be the answer. It allows us to keep our name before a user, reminding him or her we are still here; it allows us to publicize developments at the Centre (such as new programmes); it allows us to relate – to the extent possible – important cases which have used the Centre's services; it allows us to provide supporters of the Centre with information about developments elsewhere which might be very useful to them. Once again the newsletter is professionally published and thus rather expensive. But I am convinced it is worth it.

CONCLUSION

Do I have any useful insight for you? I suppose it is first to assure you that there is a very important role for institutional support in ADR. There must be some neutral infrastructure to bring the parties together with a minimum of rancour and to allow them to resolve their disputes efficiently and at reasonable cost under credible and reasonable procedures.

Second, make sure you have a market niche to satisfy or a very good sense of a new market niche you want to create. People will not come running just because you exist. They must come to realize that they need you. Develop a marketing plan.

Third, recognize the realities of the business. It takes a long time for work to come through the door, particularly at an international level. (It is much like setting up a wills practice.) Have a realistic sense of your operating costs and expected revenues and shore up the shortfall with some kind of *committed* financial support.

Fourth, retain and compensate skilled people to ensure that your services are properly managed and marketed.

Fifth, make sure that you have a pool of highly qualified neutrals. In my experience most people overrate their abilities; remember a poor appointment can cause irreparable harm to your programmes. Keep an eye out for the 'old boys' network'. It can unwittingly sabotage your operation.

And finally, don't be discouraged. It is a very exciting and rewarding area. It offers an incredible sense of personal satisfaction and wonderful possibilities for new services and challenges.

NOTES

1 On 15 January 1987, the Quebec National and International Commercial Arbitration Centre was officially opened in Quebec City with Professor Nabil Antaki of Laval University named as President.
2 Foreign Arbitral Awards Act, S.B.C. 1986, c. 74.
3 International Commercial Arbitration Act, S.B.C. 1986, c. 14.
4 *International Commercial Arbitration Regulation* (B.C. Reg. 168/86 deposited 18 July 1986).
5 This information was gained from administrators of other Centres after reviewing what few statistics are available on the business from those organizations during their formative years.
6 *Century 21 Vernon Lowe Realty Ltd* v. *Royal Lepage Real Estate Services Ltd. and The British Columbia Real Estate Association*, unreported decision, Supreme Court of BC, 22 October 1987.
7 See Rules for International Commercial Arbitration and Conciliation Proceedings in the British Columbia International Commercial Arbitration Centre; Rules for Domestic Commercial Arbitration Proceedings of the British Columbia International Commercial Arbitration Centre.
8 For an analysis of our Rules of Procedure for International Commercial Arbitration based substantially on the 1976 UNCITRAL Rules see, Thompson (1987b).
9 In our ADR Programme for Personal Injury Claims, we offer four hours of a professional mediator's time in the facilities of the Centre for a fee of $450 (Canadian) per party to the dispute.

15 Mediation in the People's Republic of China: some general observations

Michael J.E. Palmer

Following the fall from power of Mao Zedong's radical supporters in the late 1970s, the Chinese leadership embarked on a sustained programme of resurrecting and strengthening formal legal institutions. The Ministry of Justice, legal education, the people's courts, the people's procuracy, public notaries, the legal profession, codified law and other areas have all been revived during the past decade. These developments have been an important part of a sustained attempt to promote social stability, stimulate economic growth, control party power, regulate official conduct and so on. The post-Mao leadership has viewed law as an important mechanism for the elimination of many of the difficulties experienced during the turbulent period of the cultural revolution and the interregnum which followed (1966–76), and as a tool for combatting many traditional Chinese norms and values that are thought to be incompatible with the regime's programme of socialist modernization. In 1979 the Chairman of the Standing Committee of the National People's Congress emphasized that the 'evils' of both radical Maoist socialism and 'feudal' legacies

> easily give rise to autocracy, bureaucracy, 'special privilege' mentality and a patriarchal style of work, as well as petit-bourgeois individualism, liberalism and anarchism. Now in some areas and units people's enthusiasm and initiatives are still inhibited, while people's right of the person, and their democratic and other rights are sometimes under no reliable guarantee. All this shows that, to fully realize a socialist democracy, it is imperative to gradually improve the socialist legal system, so that our ... people will have a rule to go by in their actions, and the evil-doers will be restrained and punished for doing evil deeds. Therefore, the law enjoys popular support and all the Chinese people long for a sound legal system.
>
> (Peng Zhen 1987: 420)

In addition to this concern to develop formal legal institutions, however, the post-Mao leadership has consistently stressed the value of relatively informal modes of dispute settlement and sanctioning. One very important manifestation of this policy is that the bulk of civil disputes and minor criminal cases are handled by extra-judicial mediation committees (*tiaojie weiyuanhui*):

Some people say that mediation committees handle 80 per cent of all civil disputes, others say 90 per cent but, briefly stated, they handle the vast majority.

(Peng Zhen, quoted in Jiang Fuyan and Chen Cuiyin 1982: 12)

Moreover, mediation (*tiaojie*) is the preferred form of judicial process in civil actions. There are indications that courts are expected to mediate at least 80 per cent of all civil cases that come before them (Palmer 1989: 145).

The concern to avoid third-party adjudication and to rely instead on mediation as the principal mode of dispute resolution appears to be more pronounced than in many other 'developed' legal systems. Indeed, the Chinese claim that the rest of the world has much to learn from the experience of the People's Republic of China (PRC) of informal dispute settlement. This experience owes much to traditional Chinese preferences for extra-judicial conflict resolution and is an integral part of the current leadership's attempt to build a 'socialist legal system with Chinese characteristics'. One of the principal advantages claimed for socialist China's approach is that the ready availability of extra-judicial mediation organs has proved extremely useful in preventing minor disagreements from degenerating into complex civil disputes or serious violations of the criminal law. It is officially estimated that the timely intervention of mediators in disputes saved the lives of more than 60,000 persons in 1984.[1] Another important benefit which the PRC considers is brought by the emphasis on mediation in general and extra-judicial mediation in particular is the change in disputants' attitudes that it can achieve. Value change through consensual rather than coercive means is a central component in this strategy of social control.

The only way to settle questions of an ideological nature or controversial issues among the people is by the democratic method, the method of discussion, of criticism, of persuasion and education, and not by the method of coercion or repression.

(Mao Zedong 1977: 368)

Disputants are best reconciled and minor criminal offenders most satisfactorily corrected if they can be persuaded to look at their problems in a new light. They should exercise restraint, recognize their own failings, accept the criticisms and education given by mediators, and be prepared to control better their conduct in the future in order to ensure that similar difficulties do not reoccur. Underlying this approach is Mao Zedong's theory of contradictions, according to which social conflict may be divided into antagonistic and non-antagonistic forms. The former arise between the people and the enemies of the people, are inherently dangerous, and should be settled by coercive methods. The latter occur among the people, are less serious in nature and are best handled by the consensual methods of mediation.

As a result of the preference for avoiding third-party adjudication, conduct which in many other societies might be dealt with by the police and the courts is often handled in China by the local mediation committee. An example of this aspect of the Chinese approach was provided by a group of mediators interviewed recently by myself and others during a visit to metropolitan Shanghai.[2] In a dispute between two brothers over the ownership and control of a small private business that they were jointly operating, the younger sibling arranged for a gang of hooligans to intimidate his older brother into making concessions. However, in attempting to put an end to the resulting affray the brothers' father received knife wounds to his hand. The younger brother, realizing that matters had gone too far, rushed off to the local mediation committee and thereby ensured a timely intervention. The affray was terminated and in their subsequent efforts to reconcile the brothers the mediators were successful. Although the conduct of the younger brother in instigating the fight could have been characterized as a fairly serious criminal offence (punishable by several years' imprisonment under Articles 135 and 137 of the Criminal Law 1979) the mediators considered that his prompt action in summoning their assistance indicated an important shift in his thinking. He had realized the error of his ways and reformed his attitude. It was therefore unnecessary to involve the Public Security Bureau and the Criminal Law in the matter.

Mediation committees are crucially important mechanisms of social control and dispute resolution in both the countryside and the city. They are 'mass organizations' which, officially at least, operate under the guidance of the basic level people's courts and government and the leadership of the Communist party. In urban areas the committees are usually key elements in the local system of neighbourhood organization and comprise between three and eleven members who, typically, are elderly housewives or retired schoolteachers. In rural areas the committees are closely linked to local villagers' committees and although similar in size to their urban equivalents they are more likely to be composed of middle-aged men – the continuing importance of traditional Chinese patriarchal social values in the countryside means that women tend to make ineffective mediators. Reports in the Chinese legal press indicate that by 1985 over 939,000 mediation committees had been established in the PRC and more than 4,570,000 mediators had been elected to serve on these institutions (Palmer 1988: 221).

The structure and operations of local mediation committees have until very recently been governed by the Provisional General Rules for the Organization of People's Mediation Committees.[3] These were originally promulgated and put into effect in 1954. They were reissued in 1980 with slightly amended provisions which allowed for the development of mediation committees in the countryside – in the pre-cultural revolution period the committees were mainly confined to urban areas. In June 1989 the Provisional General Rules were replaced by the Organic Regulations of the People's Mediation Committees.[4] According to Article 6 of both the 1954 Provisional General Rules and the 1989 Organic Regulations the work of mediation committees in handling civil disputes and minor criminal offences must adhere to the following principles:

1 compliance with government policy and the law
2 gaining parties' consent and not imposing mediation

3 comprehending that mediation is not a compulsory procedure that must be carried out before a litigant commences an action in the courts.

In addition, mediation committee members are specifically barred under Article 7 of the 1954 Provisional General Rules and Article 12 of the 1989 Organic Regulations from taking bribes or practising favouritism, punishing the parties or taking them into custody or using force against them. Mediators are also required, by Article 8 of both the 1954 Provisional General Rules and the 1989 Organic Regulations, to conduct mediation in an amicable, reasoning and patient manner. They should also maintain a record of the case and, where appropriate, furnish the parties with a certificate of mediation (1954 Provisional General Rules Article 8; 1989 Organic Regulations Article 9).

Mediation committees in post-Mao China have been revived on a scale which far exceeds that which prevailed during the mid-1950s when the value of extra-judicial mediation work was also given great emphasis. At that stage in China's development there were only about 1 million mediators and 170,400 mediation committees in operation. During the cultural revolution and its aftermath, when a wide variety of important social institutions were attacked, mediation committees were abolished in many areas on the ground that their work promoted excessively harmonious relations between the classes. At other periods, such as the late 1950s and early 1960s, mediation committees have functioned in a highly politicized manner, using interpersonal disputes for purposes of political mobilization rather than conflict avoidance and resolution (Lubman 1967). In 1979, however, the formal system of class categories and the system of discrimination against bad class elements and their offspring was abolished. As a result, mediation committees are no longer required to treat disagreement as an example of class struggle but, rather, are now expected to encourage disputants to make mutual concessions and thereby to effect a reconciliation and achieve a settlement satisfactory to both parties. Indeed, one of the principal intended functions of mediation work in rural areas appears to be the elimination of the problem of *hongyanbing* or 'red-eye disease' – that is envy stemming from the development of disparities in wealth and status associated with the rapid expansion of market forces in the countryside. In line with this crucial shift in the meaning of mediation – from class struggle to class harmony – the efforts of mediation committees in resolving disputes are now viewed as an important complement to the work of more formal legal institutions such as the courts. In earlier and more radical periods of socialist rule the mediation committee was considered to be an ideologically more satisfactory alternative to formal legal institutions. In its post-Mao revived form, however, the mediation committee is intended to supplement the work of more formal legal institutions in a society faced with serious shortages of finance, of cadres trained in law, and so on. The official view now being promoted is that the good work of mediation committees enables the courts to devote their very limited time and resources to the more difficult cases which come before them.

Accordingly significant efforts are now being made to improve the quality of mediation work. Examples of problematic mediations are highlighted in the legal press in an attempt to ensure greater conformity with the rules governing people's mediation work (Palmer 1988: 241–3). Readers are advised that cases of rape, for example, should be treated as serious violations of the criminal law. Such cases should not be unlawfully mediated and resolved by compensation accompanied by a public apology in the form of a banquet as sometimes occurs. If mediation committees exceed the scope of their powers in this manner then the 'contradiction' between parties may degenerate into homicide. Lassitude, unnecessary interference in the lives of others, a tendency to sacrifice principles of policy in the attempts to achieve a successful mediation are other deficiencies currently noted in mediation committee work. Indeed, some commentators now criticize mediation as being far too 'wishy-washy' and stress that it must not be permitted to occupy an overly important position in future legal developments. In the light of these and other perceived shortcomings important efforts are being made to recruit better-educated mediators, to develop comprehensive networks of committees in large urban areas in order to facilitate dispute settlement, and to extend to mediators some kind of payment-by-results scheme through the application of the responsibility contract system to extra-judicial dispute settlement (see Palmer 1988: 275–7; 1989 Organic Regulations Articles 4, 7, 13, 14 and 15).

The Chinese preference for avoiding adjudication extends to the work of the people's courts. In many basic-level courts almost all the cases handled are civil actions and Article 6 of the Law of Civil Procedure (LCP) 1982 provides that 'in trying a civil case, the people's court should stress mediation. If mediation is ineffective then the court should pass judgment without delay.' It seems very clear from the Chinese legal press, however, that the second rule in Article 6 is not regularly adhered to and that prolonged mediation by the court and a distinct reluctance to pass to the formal adjudicatory stage appears to be a common practice, especially in divorce cases. In addition, it seems to be an important axiom of court work that the people's courts should always attempt to resolve disputes through persuasion and other techniques of mediation before accepting a case for trial. It is probably as a result of this approach that lawyers now spend an increasing amount of their time in '*lüshi tiaojie*' or lawyer's mediation, that is pre-trial negotiations from which the courts expect a successful resolution of matters so that proceedings will not actually commence in court. Lawyers, of course, tend to be more involved in economic (that is 'commercial') cases. In other types of disputes, however, the courts directly exert pre-trial pressure on the parties in order to avoid formal litigation, in many instances buttressing this pressure with help from the relatives and colleagues of the parties who attempt to dissuade the litigants from going to trial. In this connection it should be noted that Article 98 of the LCP 1982 stipulates, 'as far as possible court mediation should be done on the spot' and that Article 99 provides, 'in conducting mediation, the people's court if necessary may solicit assistance from the relevant individuals concerned. These units and individuals should, when requested, assist the people's court in conducting the mediation.' Thus, it is clear that there is a pronounced working and statutory emphasis on the courts to provide informal justice through mediation rather than formal justice through litigation and adjudication.

Of course, several of the considerations underlying the promotion of extra-judicial mediation also help to explain this emphasis on judical mediation. In particular, Mao's theory of contradictions and China's long pre-socialist tradition of settling disputes through *tiaojie* are important factors. In addition, however, it seems very likely that, especially in rural areas, there are significant political pressures on the courts to provide mediated rather than adjudicated decisions. The following extract from a recent report on court work provided by the PRC's Supreme Court highlights the problem:

> For historical reasons and especially because of the pernicious influence of the decade of turmoil [that is 1966–76] there are many cases involving contempt of court, 'replacing law by order', 'suppressing law with authority' and obstructing the lawful operations of the people's courts. Some people do this because they are ignorant of the law, while others are simply biased or wish to demonstrate their power, or are seeking personal gain by taking advantage of their authority. Within the economic sphere, some cadres have treated laws pragmatically, regarding legal rules as tools for protecting their own areas, instead of viewing laws as weapons with which to protect people's legitimate rights and interests. If a court's verdict benefits the interests of their own area they are happy and say that the court is a good court, but if the court decides that they should repay debts which are owed to persons in another community they are displeased and accuse the courts of 'operating in other people's favour'. In some circumstances they even obstruct the court from accepting a case or reaching a verdict or enforcing an order. . . . During the past two years more than eighty court cadres and bailiffs have been beaten up and injured when carrying out their tasks, and some have even died in the line of duty.
>
> (Zheng Tianxing 1986)

In such circumstances, a mediated compromise agreement – rather than a clear-cut adjudication – helps to fudge the issue, saves the continuing and important Chinese commodity of 'face' (*lianzi*) and avoids alienating seriously the losing party (who may be politically very influential at the local level).

The 1982 LCP not only contains a number of provisions dealing specifically with judical mediation but also lays down several rules which encourage procedural informalism. Article 104 provides that in trying civil cases 'the people's court should where necessary and possible conduct mobile court sessions on the spot. With the exception of major or complicated cases the people's court applies simple procedures (*jianyi chengxu*).' This emphasis on simplified procedures not only is found in the regular courts but also is a particularly important feature of the work of the *piachu fating* or dispatch tribunals (Palmer 1989: 157–9). These operate in both the countryside and the cities on a circuit basis and require only one judge rather than a normal bench of three judges or a judge and two people's assessors. The tribunals are expected to with the bulk of the disputes that mediation committees are unable to handle. It is important to bear in mind, therefore, that for many prospective litigants the effective choice is not between a 'proper trial' and judicial mediation but, rather, between the latter and a simplified procedure trial. It is perhaps not surprising, therefore, that most parties whose disputes are handled by the dispatch tribunals allow their cases to be mediated rather than handled by a simplified-procedure adjudication.

In recent years there have been some doubts raised in the Chinese legal press regarding the value of the emphasis on judicial mediation (Palmer 1989: 159–69). The scepticism is perhaps most noticeable with reference to Article 153 of the CCP 1982, which provides, 'in hearing an appeal, the people's court of the second instance may mediate between the parties concerned'. In economic disputes in particular it is thought that this provision is being misused by those who lose their case at the original trial in an adjudicated decision. They invariably appeal because they are confident that the case will be mediated by the appeal court and the terms of the final settlement therefore be less onerous than those of the original result. As a result, some commentators believe that appeal courts should, in otherwise clear-cut cases, 'reject the appeal and preserve the original decision' (*bohui shangsu, weichi yuanpan*). In less clear-cut circumstances mediation should be conducted only with the explicit approval of the respondent. Other commentators continue to maintain, however, that as Article 6 of the CCP 1982 states that the court should stress mediation so courts are obliged to emphasize mediation throughout, regardless of whether the proceedings are a first or an appeal hearing (see e.g. Sun Zhenming 1985: 29).

Another increasingly contentious area is divorce proceedings. According to Article 25 of the Marriage Law (ML) 1980 court mediation is mandatory in a defended divorce petition. The court's priority is to achieve a reconciliation. As a result of the continued influence of traditional patriarchal values, divorce is not looked upon favourably by the authorities – especially as the vast majority of petitioners are women. A court will therefore make strenuous efforts to achieve 'reconciliation'. If, however, it is not successful in these efforts then the court will either reject the application or proceed to mediation in the sense of getting the divorcing spouses amicably to agree on questions of custody, property and so on. If this conciliation fails then the court will, reluctantly, impose its own decision. In some cases this will mean a rejection of the divorce application. It should be added here that although it is not a mandatory requirement to go through extra-judicial mediation prior to the court hearings nevertheless in practice it seems very difficult for unhappy spouses to escape the pre-trial attentions of the local mediation committee (see Palmer 1988: 257–8). Moreover, the court will often attempt informal mediation prior to the trial. As a result, a divorcing couple may have to experience four or more rounds of mediation before their marriage is dissolved. The route to divorce is, of course, easier if the spouses are both agreed on the need to break their marriage tie – divorce by mutual consent does not require court approval (ML 1980 Article 24). However, even in these cases strenuous efforts will be made by both the marriage registration organs and the mediation committee to get the couple to patch up their troubled relationship.[5]

This emphasis on the sanctity of the marriage tie is further manifested in the fact that mediators may attempt reconciliation even after a divorce has been completed. Thus, during the recent interview with Shanghai mediators noted earlier one of the informant's proudest moments was her account of the restored marriage (*fuhun*) of a young divorced couple. As a result of the extraordinarily persistent efforts of local mediators a 'flighty' divorcee and her stubborn ex-husband had a change of heart and agreed to restore their marriage several years after divorce.[6] The husband had been awarded custody of their child by the divorce court and was persuaded that if he were to marry another woman there was every possibility that relations between his child and the stepmother would not be amicable. The ex-wife was convinced by the mediators that her boyfriend had no real intention of marrying her and that marriage to the former husband would be the best way to maintain strong ties with the child.

The other side of the coin in this approach to matrimonial disputes is the unhappiness that many wives are expected to endure. A recent survey of more than 500 runaway wives revealed that a major cause of their decision to leave home, and subsequently to 'commit bigamy' or 'lapse into promiscuity' or allow themselves to be 'sold' to other men, was a refusal by the court dealing with their divorce petition to accept that mediation had failed and to move to the adjudicatory stage in the proceedings. Their divorce applications were thereby effectively blocked (Zeng Fangwen 1987).

A further area in which the utility of judical mediation is being questioned is the PRC's new system for litigating administrative cases. Early in 1987 the Supreme People's Court directed basic-level people's courts to establish new chambers in order to handle administrative suits. This and subsequent related developments aim to make governmental and other administrative organs more accountable to the individual citizen, and represent a crucial development in a society in which bureaucratism and arbitrary rule are acknowledged to be special problems. Administrative litigation is, however, governed by the LCP 1982 – Article 3 stipulates that 'the provisions of this Law are applicable to administrative cases that by law are to be tried by the people's courts'. Accordingly judicial mediation has been used in settling administrative cases, and this gave rise to a vigorous debate between courts in different parts of China, with some judges supporting the policy laid down in the Law of Civil Procedure, and with others arguing against the suitability of mediation for dealing with administrative cases such as those involving, for example, police brutality (see Palmer 1989: 164–6). Several drafts of an administrative litigation law were prepared. The earlier versions permitted the use of mediation in administrative suits in order to handle questions of compensation, but the final draft unequivocally stipulates that 'the people's court shall not use the method of mediation in handling administrative cases'.[7]

More generally there is developing among many leading jurists a belief that the role of judicial mediation in civil cases should be systematically reduced. On the one hand, the 1986 General Principles of the Civil Law are seen as providing the courts with a new body of civil law norms and principles which will enable Chinese judges to dispense with mediation and, instead, to adjudicate cases in a firmly equitable manner.[8] On the other hand, there is a growing feeling that despite China's reliance on a system of codified law that owes much to the continental civil law tradition, there is a need to introduce a system of judicial precedent. This would give the courts an important law-making function, thereby enabling the law to adapt more readily to China's rapidly changing social and economic environment. However, the introduction of a system of case law is not really compatible with the long-standing stress on judicial mediation for the latter means, of course, that similar cases may be decided in a number of different ways. Moreover, mediated outcomes cannot throw into sharp relief the meanings and the boundaries of parties' rights and duties (see Palmer 1989: 168). A significant step in the direction of judicial precedent was taken in the spring of 1989 when plans were laid for the Chinese Minister of Justice to visit London in the summer of the same year in order to study the English approach to case law. The Beijing Massacre of 4 June and the politically hard-line policies that have been pursued in China since that tragic event have – for the moment at least – put an end to this and other plans that would have taken the People's Republic further along the road toward the establishment of a credible legal system. The Chinese leadership since 4 June 1989 seems to have only a very low regard for law, and has embarked upon a reign of terror in which law and legal institutions are blatantly manipulated in order to maintain in power men who see the courts as essentially coercive tools of the state and the party rather than as mechanisms for protecting and promoting the rights and interests of individual citizens.

CHINESE TERMS

bohui shangsu, weichi yuanpan　驳回上诉维持原判

fuhun　复婚

hongyanbing　红眼病

jianyi chengxu　简易程序

lianzi　胲子

lüshi tiaojie　律师调解

paichu fating　派出法庭

tiaojie　调解

tiaojie weiyuanhui　调解委员会

NOTES

1 'Yi Jiu Ba Si nian renmin tiaojie gongzuo tongji' (Statistics for people's mediation work in 1984), in Guo Xiang *et al.* (1986: 38).
2 First Anglo-Chinese Legal Colloquium (20 December 1987 to 6 January 1988): interview with mediators in Wusonglu Ward, Hongkou District, Shanghai, 30 December 1987.
3 For a Chinese-language version of the Provisional General Rules see Guo Xiang *et al.* (1986: 8–9); an English-language translation is provided in Cohen (1968: 124–5).
4 'Renmin Tiaojie Weiyuanhui Tiaoli' (The Organic Regulations of the People's Mediation Committees), *Fazhi Ribao* (Legal System Daily) 4 July 1989, 1,508: 2.
5 Marriage registrars are responsible not only for conducting the registration of marriages but also for the supervision and registration of divorces by mutual consent (Palmer 1987: 40).
6 The notion of 'restored marriage' is currently given great support in the Chinese legal press (see Palmer 1987: 53).
7 'Zhonghua Renmin Gongheguo Susongfa' (The Administrative Litigation Law of the People's Republic of China), 1989, Article 30, *Fazhi Ribao* (Legal System Daily) 11 April 1988, 1,436: 1.
8 See in English, *The Laws of the People's Republic of China 1983–1986*, compiled by the Legislative Affairs Commission of the Standing Committee of the National People's Congress of the People's Republic of China, Beijing: Foreign Languages Press, 1987: 225–49; in Chinese, *Zhongguo Falü Nianjian 1987* (Law Year Book of China 1987), Beijing: Falü Chubanshe (Law Publishing House), 1988: 68–75.

16 Alternative dispute resolution in Australia

David A. Newton

A DEFINITION

Alternative dispute resolution (ADR) is most generally understood as meaning dispute resolution by means other than court adjudication. The definition encompasses a wide range of court-oriented initiatives which are designed to facilitate a more effective administration of justice and help overcome delays which may occur through the normal court processes.

The definition also encompasses many processes which may be used independently of court action even though litigation may or may not have been commenced. These processes fall into two areas. One is the adjudicative type such as arbitration where the independent person makes a decision which binds the parties. The other area consists of the negotiation-based processes such as conciliation, mediation, independent expert appraisal and mini-trials.

There is an increasing tendency when referring to ADR to mean processes other than arbitration and such adjudicative processes. For instance the Alternative Dispute Resolution Association of Australia (ADRAA) adopted the following definition of ADR:

'Alternative dispute resolution' (ADR) means dispute resolution by processes:
(a) which encourage disputants to reach their own solution and
(b) in which the primary role of the third party neutral is to facilitate the disputants to do so.

THE ORIGINS OF MODERN ADR IN AUSTRALIA

In commercial disputes in Australia ADR was not widely practised before the creation of the Australian Commercial Disputes Centre Limited (ACDC). In fact the arbitration community had resisted its use despite calls by industry to provide conciliation.

ACDC was very much the idea of the former Chief Justice of the Supreme Court of New South Wales, Sir Laurence Street, who for many years had been concerned that many disputes could more efficiently be handled by means other than court adjudication. In 1985 the New South Wales Government decided to conduct a survey of business people in Sydney to see whether there was support for the creation of an ADR service provider for commercial disputes. In late 1985 the survey results showed that there was very strong demand by the business community for a new option to resolve business disputes particularly as arbitration in Australia had become more expensive than litigation and just as complex. Accordingly in January 1986 the Australian Commercial Disputes Centre Limited was incorporated as a company limited by guarantee. This means that the company is essentially non-profit in character. The staff of ACDC were in place by August 1986.

During its initial years ACDC is subsidized by the New South Wales, Western Australian and Queensland State Governments. However, ACDC is not established by legislation and is not part of the public service but is a totally independent company with its own Board of Directors. The Board mainly consists of leading Australian businessmen and lawyers. A Director from each Australian State is on the Board.

ACDC: FUNCTIONS

ACDC is the first and only body in Australia providing an overall ADR dispute resolution management consultancy for the commercial community. ACDC provides its services nation-wide across Australia and has offices and staff in Sydney, Brisbane and Perth.

ACDC provides a dispute management service to help companies and businesses resolve their commercial disputes quickly and inexpensively. The aim is to be able to maintain goodwill in business relationships that can often be destroyed through prolonged disputes. By ACDC methods parties are assisted by an independent third person to reach their own agreement, an agreement by which both parties are more likely to be able to happily continue their business relationship into the future. Also, ACDC processes are aimed at achieving a satisfactory and imaginative solution for both sides such as may not be able to be achieved through litigation or arbitration.

Experience overseas indicates that ADR processes, such as assisted negotiation, conciliation, independent expert appraisal and mediation are likely to be the most increasingly used methods of dispute resolution in the future. ACDC provides arbitration services but in almost all cases users of ACDC's services prefer mediation and other ADR processes because of their speed and cost-effectiveness.

ACDC focuses on commercial disputes but not on industrial relations disputes. ACDC also assists with international disputes as well as domestic disputes. The users of ACDC services are most likely to be companies, businesses, industry groups or government departments which are seeking to resolve a dispute of a commercial nature. Lawyers may also engage ACDC to help them resolve their clients' disputes. ACDC's services can be summarized as follows:

1 A staff facilitation service to meet with and persuade the other company or companies in dispute to seek settlement through ADR processes and to assist

them to agree on an appropriate dispute resolution procedure for their dispute.

2 A service to assist companies to resolve commercial disputes by identifying, training, suggesting and appointing external independent experts to assist companies to reach agreement. ACDC's legally qualified staff are also trained and experienced mediators.

3 Provision of neutral meeting facilities for dispute resolution conferences.

4 Training in negotiation and mediation skills.

5 Seminars on the latest developments in ADR processes.

6 Publication of a newsletter, *Resolution*, to explain ADR and ACDC's services.

7 General encouragement of the use of cost-effective and expeditious dispute resolution methods.

ACDC DISPUTE MANAGEMENT SERVICES

A company in dispute on contacting ACDC will be offered a no-obligation meeting at which ACDC staff facilitators will explain how ADR processes may be able to assist them. We shall offer to meet similarly with the other company or companies in dispute. We shall also meet with both or all parties together with their lawyers if they so wish.

At the initial meetings assistance will be given with what may be an appropriate way to resolve the dispute. ACDC will assist the parties to agree on such matters as who pays the costs, which procedure or combination of procedures will be used, the timetable for the dispute resolution, and whether or not there will be representation by lawyers.

Once the parties have agreed to a process to attempt to resolve their dispute, names and career résumés of several persons available to act as a conciliator, mediator, independent expert or arbitrator will be given by ACDC. Once the parties have agreed on one or more of the persons suggested, ACDC will then arrange a meeting between the independent third person and the parties in dispute. Only at that stage does ACDC issue an invoice for its services. If the parties do not agree to use ACDC then no charge applies except for any travel disbursements.

ACDC may also assist the independent third person by making suggestions for solving the dispute and has available material from around the world on imaginative new ways to resolve disputes. ACDC staff also monitor the progress of any dispute resolution to ensure that it is being conducted to the satisfaction of all parties.

Companies and businesses are involved in negotiations on a day-to-day basis in order to prevent and resolve disputes. ACDC's unique contribution to that fact of everyday business life is to help negotiations succeed when otherwise they would fail when attempted by the parties alone. ACDC contributes these important factors for the first time in Australia:

1 *ACDC can help create the desire in the other side to explore settlement possibilities without this appearing to be an expression of weakness to the client or to the other side* ACDC can help the parties come to trust each other sufficiently to negotiate in good faith and constructively.

2 *ACDC provides an expert neutral person to assist the two or more sides to come to an agreement* That person often plays the role of a conciliator or mediator or simply an independent chairman depending on the wishes of the parties. That person's role is to help the parties to reach their own agreement, and not to adjudicate (except where the parties especially want arbitration). ACDC provides mediators from different professions who have been trained by ACDC in mediation.

3 *ACDC provides a means to enable effective communication and mutual education to occur so that agreement can be reached* Even large and sophisticated companies become embroiled in disputes which they cannot resolve alone. ACDC often finds that the characteristic of these disputes is difficulty in communication because of the personalities involved, the number of parties involved, or misunderstanding between the parties. ACDC provides a central neutral co-ordinating focus to enable each party to communicate to the others and by doing so to educate the others as to the issues in dispute. Once this process is in train settlement almost always results.

4 *Suggestions of cost-effective techniques to make negotiations more likely to be successful* ACDC is constantly up-to-date with the latest developments in these techniques from around the world.

5 *Informality* Because ACDC's emphasis is negotiation and settlement, meetings most often are quite informal. The complex formalities which apply to litigation do not exist and control of the dispute negotiation rests with the company executives. The independent person is only there to help so that costs are kept to a minimum. Lawyers may or may not be used as the parties so wish. Rules of evidence usually do not apply. ACDC's approach is sometimes referred to as neutral assisted negotiation.

6 *Priority Focus* ACDC's involvement focuses the parties' attention on a dispute so that time priority is given to seeking resolution rather than just allowing it to continue.

7 *Flexibility* ACDC finds that parties often use a mixture of dispute resolution processes in any one case. This is because ADR processes generally allow for substantial flexibility. Hence, for example, it is possible for the parties to agree to attempt mediation and then if there are any outstanding issues to have those issues arbitrated by a person other than the mediator.

ACDC has also assisted companies to structure simplified and fast-tracking arbitrations not only in the presence of an arbitrator but also in the presence of a separate mediator. In other cases ACDC has suggested both a mediator and a separate independent technical expert who were both jointly appointed by the parties.

ACDC has its own Conciliation Rules and accompanying Procedural

Notes which offer a suggested means to resolve commercial disputes. If the parties wish to adopt those rules they are still free to amend them as they may wish so that they can effectively create their own flexible method of resolving the dispute.

Other procedural suggestions from around the world, particularly on mini-trials, are available from ACDC.

Not all companies and businesses have sophisticated negotiation skills. Even for these companies that do, negotiations often break down for a variety of reasons. This is where ACDC staff assist by arranging an independent third person to help both parties to negotiate more effectively. ACDC staff facilitators also assist sometimes by engaging in shuttle diplomacy between the parties until they are ready to negotiate face-to-face.

Australia until now has experienced only adversarial approaches by its institutions to commercial dispute resolution. Many societies overseas, particularly in Asia, have a much more consensual or conciliatory approach which strongly features conciliation or mediation rather than adjudication.

ACDC emphasizes dispute resolution processes which are based on negotiation principles. The role of the independent person is not to hand down a binding decision which the parties must accept but is to assist the parties to reach their own agreement by identifying common ground between the parties so that they can continue their business relationship into the future to their mutual satisfaction.

Under most of ACDC's processes the parties commence in the hope that agreement will be reached which will then be incorporated in a binding contract at the conclusion of negotiations.

Even if the processes are not totally successful to resolve the dispute many of the issues will have been clarified and agreed. Hence the cost of any subsequent litigation or arbitration will have been significantly reduced.

One $700,000 (Australian) dispute resolved through ACDC was resolved in eight weeks for a total cost to both parties of $5,000. A similar dispute between the same two parties went to arbitration and litigation and was resolved in eight months for an estimated cost of $250,000. Those eight months were taken up with procedural arguments and the issues in dispute were not even canvassed. Another dispute involving a claim of $400,000 was settled by shuttle mediation involving only six hours between the parties meeting face-to-face. The parties had tried unsuccessfully for two years to negotiate and had started court proceedings. The parties not only resolved that claim but other claims between them totalling a further $1 million.

It is acknowledged that ACDC's processes will not be suitable for all cases and that the more traditional methods such as litigation and arbitration may need to be used. Cases where the processes may not be suitable include the following:

1 situations where one of the parties is not acting in good faith during the conduct of the dispute – however, ACDC often helps parties see that in fact

the other party is acting in good faith and that there has been a misunderstanding

2 situations where one of the parties wishes to prolong the dispute and legal proceedings in the hope that the other party does not have the ability to continue the proceedings

3 situations where one of the parties is unable to pay out the claim and finds it cheaper to pay legal costs in the hope that the claim will not be pursued further

4 situations where one of the parties for whatever reason does not wish to explore the possibility of settlement; ACDC has no power to compel this to occur, but can play a very vital role in persuading a difficult party to explore settlement.

ACDC SUCCESS RECORD

Typically disputes are resolved in one or two days of mediation within eight weeks after the appointment of the mediator. ACDC so far has an almost 100 per cent success record in assisting the parties to reach agreement and to avoid litigation.

DEVELOPMENT ISSUES

Issues which have been significant in the development of ADR in Australia include the following.

1 *Unfamiliarity with ADR processes* ACDC has largely dealt with this by inviting overseas experts to Australia to lead courses, give presentations and meet with key influence leaders. ACDC conducts an active programme of seminars and explanatory sessions for companies and law firms. This programme has been very successful to establish credibility and to spread understanding. Sufficient enthusiasm for ADR has developed as a result of these endeavours in key areas including the legal profession and the judiciary for separate ADR initiatives to develop outside ACDC. These initiatives include LEADR (Lawyers Engaged in ADR) which was formed by lawyers to educate the profession in ADR.

2 *Reaction by the legal profession* The Law Council of Australia significantly adopted a policy in favour of ADR in 1989. As regards law firms an increasing number are including ADR as part of their practice in real and substantial terms. Some, especially those with strong arbitration practices, are finding it difficult to accept and adopt non-arbitral ADR methods. Generally law firms are commencing a significant practice of ADR much more than initially expected. Crucial to this has been a responsible approach by ACDC to present ADR as a practice opportunity for lawyers and to welcome and to encourage the role of lawyers in ADR. The Bar Association in Queensland has commenced its own mediation programme.

3 *Mediators* As in North America the supply of people interested to be mediators exceeds the demand for mediators. As most of ACDC's ADR cases are in the building and construction industry and as parties want appropriate industry experience in their mediators, many people without experience may not be considered by disputants as mediators despite their skills as mediators. There is much to be said for developing a core group of people to obtain substantial experience as mediators. ACDC staff are gaining an increasing reputation as competent mediators. It was necessary for ACDC to provide the first business dispute mediator training in Australia as until then no such training was available. This we did with assistance from overseas trainers.

4 *Rivalry* There is in Australia a traditional rivalry between Sydney and Melbourne. ACDC is Sydney based, while in Melbourne the Institute of Arbitrators, Australia, and its subsidiary, the Australian Centre for International Commercial Arbitration, have their headquarters. This inter-city rivalry has made it difficult for some to understand the very different roles and methods of operation between these bodies. ACDC emphasizes consensual ADR while the other bodies emphasize traditional arbitration which in Australia has many similarities with litigation in terms of procedure and cost. In fact ACDC and the other bodies have complementary roles. Also ACDC operates with professional dispute management experts on its staff.

5 *High-level support* A vital contribution has been made by state governments giving funding support, by key judicial figures and by leading business executives and lawyers as ACDC Board members. This has helped to give credibility to what is a remarkably different approach to traditional conflict resolution methods.

6 *International assistance* Also quite vital was establishment and development assistance from experienced international ADR experts. This includes areas such as mediator training, ADR process expertise, pricing for services, development expertise and management issues.

7 *General promotion of ADR* ACDC adopted a strategy which proved to be very successful at promoting ADR heavily to the corporate sector in the initial stages. This created an interest and tapped a high demand for an alternative to litigation. This in turn attracted the attention of law firms as their clients sought information from them. ACDC then undertook substantial work to educate law firms in ADR.

8 *Universities* Tertiary education institutions started teaching ADR courses especially in law schools in 1988. Bond University has established a Centre for Dispute Resolution to provide education and research in ADR. This has given further credibility to the processes.

9 *Reaction by the judiciary* The judiciary in Australia is concerned about the cost and delays often associated with litigation. Attention is now being given by some courts to introducing mediation into court procedures.

10 *Preferred ADR processes* Parties have preferred mediation, non-binding

expert appraisal or a combination of both. Mini-trials have not been used often. Binding expert appraisal as distinct from arbitration under arbitration legislation is becoming increasingly popular. ADR is being seen by the corporate world as alternative to arbitration as much as an alternative to litigation.

11 *Fragmentation of the market* In Australia other dispute resolution services are commencing. While this is commendable and a sign of healthy development it is questionable whether they will all be economically viable.

ACDC SUPPORTERS

ACDC has created a Declaration of Support:

> If a commercial dispute arises between ourselves and another party which has made a Declaration similar to this, we will, before resorting to full-scale litigation, explore whether the dispute can be resolved by negotiation or by means of mediation, conciliation or arbitration (alternative dispute resolution – ADR – techniques). If either party believes that the dispute is not suitable for negotiation or for ADR techniques or if attempts to settle the dispute by those means do not produce results satisfactory to the disputants, each party is free to pursue any means it chooses to resolve the dispute.
>
> I have no objection to this Declaration being made public by the Australian Commercial Disputes Centre Limited.

Over 330 Australian companies have so far signed the Declaration. Those companies include AMP Society, IBM Australia, Volvo Australia, Quantas Airways, Coca Cola (South Pacific), BHP, Transfield, and many other leading Australian companies. By signing the Declaration those companies have indicated their desire to resolve disputes wherever possible and practicable by non-adjudicative methods.

ACDC also has a similar Declaration of Professional Support which law firms, accountancy firms, industry associations and other professional firms are invited to sign. There is no fee associated with signing the Declarations nor is it necessary to sign the Declarations before using ACDC's services.

ACDC: INTERNATIONAL DISPUTE RESOLUTION SERVICES

ACDC has established working relationships with similar organizations outside Australia so that international disputes involving Australian companies can be managed co-operatively by ACDC and those organizations. ACDC is a foundation member of the Council of Asia Pacific Commercial Dispute Resolution Centers.

In co-operation with the American Arbitration Association ACDC has created the Australia–US Trade Dispute Service to help resolve disputes between Australian and US companies.

ACDC: INDEPENDENT RESOURCES

ACDC conducts mediator training courses led by leading US mediator trainers. People trained by ACDC as mediators and suggested by ACDC to the parties so far include former judges, engineers, architects, accountants, lawyers, computer specialists and shipping experts among others. Over 200 people have been trained as mediators. ACDC staff also perform the role of mediators.

ACDC will approach individuals in Australia or elsewhere who may have the necessary skills and expert knowledge to act as an independent third person to assist parties in dispute if they so wish. ACDC has also been approached by people from a vast range of professions and industries who have offered to act as independent third persons. These people include architects, engineers, lawyers, computer specialists, accountants, builders, insurance experts, manufacturers, shipping experts, surveyors and valuers among others.

ACDC STAFF

The distinctive aspect about ACDC's services is its staff facilitator role in bringing the parties together into an ADR process and supporting the process until its successful conclusion. ACDC has eight staff members (including five lawyers). ACDC dispute resolution staff are trained and experienced mediators.

CONFIDENTIALITY

Proceedings are strictly private and confidential to the extent allowed by law. Disclosure of any sensitive information may be protected by ACDC's simple standard form agreement providing for confidentiality and non-admissibility of the information in any subsequent court proceedings. Such provisions are also included in ACDC's Conciliation Rules.

ACDC'S RULES

ACDC's charges as of January 1990 are as follows (Australian dollars).

1 *Dispute resolution service fee per dispute:*

Amount in claim	Fee per party
$50,000 and under	$750
Over $50,000 to $100,000	$750 plus 3 per cent for each dollar claimed over $50,000
Over $100,000 to $1 million	$2,000 plus 0.333 per cent for each dollar claimed over $100,000
Over $1 million to $5 million	$5,000 plus 0.05 per cent for each dollar claimed over $1 million
Over $5 million	$7,000 plus 0.025 per cent for each dollar claimed over $5 million
Not readily quantifiable	Subject to determination in each case

This fee is payable only where both or all parties have agreed in writing to use ACDC. The fee is reduced where limited ACDC staff time is required. Any air fares, accommodation and living expenses are additional to the above fee and are to be reimbursed on production of receipts irrespective of whether any conciliation service fee is payable.

2 *Independent person's charges*

The fees of the independent third person are additional. The fees of such independent persons are between $750 and $2,500 per day or part thereof depending upon the person chosen plus any travelling expenses. The parties most often agree to split those charges in equal proportions and the amounts are generally cost effective.

3 *Other charges*

Payment of ACDC's dispute resolution service fee in full usually includes use of ACDC's meeting facilities for three days. Additional charges apply for transcription, photocopying, facsimile, access to trust account, telephone and other disbursements.

ACDC: SUGGESTED CONTRACT CLAUSES

ACDC suggests the insertion of clauses in contracts, invoices, conditions of sale, conditions of purchase and other documents to provide for ACDC's assistance with any future disputes. These clauses are as follows.

1 For use where negotiated settlement is sought with the help of an independent expert third person who does not have power to hand down a binding decision but whose role is to assist the parties to reach their own binding settlement agreement:

Any dispute, controversy or claim arising out of or relating to this contract or the breach, termination or invalidity thereof shall be referred to the Australian Commercial Disputes Centre Limited ('ACDC') for its assistance. Any meetings organised through ACDC shall be held in Sydney (or name any other place) or such other place as may be subsequently agreed by the parties.

2 For use where the parties instead require a binding decision handed down by an independent expert third person:

(a) Generally – local and international contracts:

Any dispute or difference whatsoever arising in connection with this contract shall be submitted to arbitration, administered by the Australian Commercial Disputes Centre Limited, conducted at Sydney (or name any other specified place). The arbitrator shall be a person agreed between the parties chosen from a panel suggested by ACDC and failing agreement shall be a person nominated by the Secretary General of ACDC.

Subject to the foregoing the arbitration shall be held in accordance with and subject to the laws of the State of New South Wales (or name any other specified jurisdiction).

(b) Special provision which may instead be used for international contracts: Any dispute, controversy or claim arising out of or relating to this contract, or the breach, termination or invalidity thereof, shall be settled by arbitration, administered by the Australian Commercial Disputes Centre Limited (which shall be the appointing authority), conducted at Sydney (or any other specified place) and held in accordance with the Arbitration Rules of the United Nations Commission on International Trade Law (UNCITRAL) in force at the date of this contract.

3 For use where the parties wish to attempt conciliation first and then arbitration should conciliation not resolve all issues in dispute:

Any dispute, controversy or claim arising out of or relating to this contract or the breach, termination or invalidity thereof shall first be the subject of conciliation, administered by the Australian Commercial Disputes Centre Limited ('ACDC') conducted and held in accordance with the Conciliation Rules of ACDC in force at the date of this contract. In the event that the dispute, controversy or claim has not been resolved within twenty-eight (28) days (or such other period as agreed to in writing between the parties hereto) after the appointment of the conciliator by the parties hereto the dispute, controversy or claim shall be submitted to arbitration, administered by ACDC. The arbitrator shall be agreed between the parties from a panel suggested by ACDC or failing agreement an arbitrator appointed by the Secretary General of ACDC. Subject to the foregoing arbitration shall be conducted and held in accordance with and subject to the laws of the State of New South Wales (or name any other jurisdiction). The arbitrator shall not be the same person as the conciliator. Any conciliation or arbitration meetings and proceedings shall be held in Sydney (or name any other specified place).

TYPICAL ACDC PROCEDURE

1 Enquiry received from one or all parties.
2 Explanation of how ACDC operates and of suitable dispute resolution processes is given to the enquirer preferably in person at the enquirer's office.
3 The consent of the non-enquiring party/ies, to use ACDC is obtained. This can be done in any one of these ways:
   3.1 The enquirer suggests to the non-enquiring party that ACDC staff meet with it to explain how ACDC operates and to explore a suitable dispute resolution process which ACDC will custom design for their dispute, or
   3.2 ACDC contacts the non-enquirer at the request of the enquirer, or
   3.3 ACDC meets with both parties together.
4 In the course of paragraph 3 ACDC is preparing the parties for a possible

attempt at dispute resolution through ACDC and custom designing a process for them. A clear and common understanding should be had by both or all parties.

5 No charge is made by ACDC until the parties agree to the process and to ACDC's involvement.

6 The parties sign ACDC's appointment agreement if they wish to proceed and return it to ACDC.

7 CVs of three suitable referees/mediators/experts are sent to all parties together with our invoice.

8 The agreement of all parties to appoint one of these referees/mediators/experts is obtained.

9 The availability of that mediator/expert/referee is confirmed.

10 A date is set for a preliminary conference between the parties, the mediator/expert/referee and ACDC staff member.

11 Position statements are provided by both sides.

12 Preliminary conference held to outline the issues and set a date for meeting on the issues in dispute.

13 Mediation/? held on the appropriate day supported by ACDC staff.

ACDC AND THE COURTS

ACDC sees itself as an adjunct to and expansion of the court system. In NSW Part 72 of the Supreme Court procedures allows the court to appoint an arbitrator or referee. Lawyers for clients wanting a person to arbitrate or act as referee have approached ACDC for suggestions as to an appropriate person. What often happens is:

1 The lawyers or the judge will suggest a Part 72 order application.

2 The lawyers or the judge may suggest that an approach be made to ACDC for a suggestion of a suitable person.

3 Once an approach has been made ACDC often suggests that the person to be chosen with the consent of the parties attempts first to resolve the dispute by mediation.

4 Mediation with ACDC professional staff support is successful in a short period and terms of settlement are handed up to the court without the necessity for arbitration or referee's report.

Here ACDC offers these main benefits:

• advice on how to custom design a structured negotiation process for that dispute
• access to the mediators ACDC has trained
• staff support to ensure the mediation is successful.

It is even simpler for ACDC to provide this assistance to the courts whereas with the Queensland Supreme Court there is power to refer a case to an outside mediator.

ACDC is most willing to provide this assistance on a trial programme basis to any court for commercial matters so that the success of our assistance can be experienced and evaluated. We are confident that significant court delays would be prevented by such a programme.

THE FUTURE

It is becoming accepted wisdom that consensual ADR processes will be increasingly used in preference to traditional adjudicative and adversarial dispute resolution methods. There is every reason to believe this will also be the case in Australia and throughout the Pacific Rim as companies and businesses seek more cost-effective and expeditious dispute settlement methods.

Part IV
Training, research and futures

Introduction

If we are to contemplate an extension of dispute resolution methods and practice in the future, the three elements in this part are necessary concomitants of that. First, a need to find ways of training third parties for the skills of intervention. Second, a research programme to evaluate the various techniques and practices. Finally, a strategy for raising awareness of ADR methods and practice, and for encouraging initiatives and action.

David Cruickshank (Chapter 17) provides an overview and case study of the design of a training course in mediation. His story links in to the work of the British Columbia International Commercial Arbitration Centre, whose development has been described by Bonita Thompson (Chapter 14). He articulates the complex elements that make up skilled performance and the need to integrate these in designing a course of instruction. Two courses are described, for personal injury and commercial mediators, and some of the strengths and weaknesses of alternative models of course design described. An important element in Cruickshank's argument is the need for an interaction between research and mediation teaching programmes, and between teaching and learning. Neil Gold (Chapter 18) takes this one stage further into an analysis of research needs in ADR. He reviews developments in ADR and some of the tentative conclusions on ADR from existing research programmes. However, given the unsystematic nature of much of the early research, he suggests the need for a more rigorous research base 'to temper the over-optimistic and silence the sceptics'. The sort of programme that he has in mind is one that would draw on a co-ordinated interdisciplinary approach reflecting the values behind ADR approaches and the wider social interest in finding effective community mechanisms of dispute resolution, an interest which may not be in harmony with adversarial modes of dispute resolution. The social value of this area, he suggests, should be reflected in a national governmental commitment to supporting this type of research endeavour.

Karl Mackie (Chapter 19) also pursues a similar theme in his concluding review of ADR and its potential for development.

17 Training mediators: moving towards competency-based training

David A. Cruickshank

This chapter explores the development of mediation functions at the British Columbia International Commercial Arbitration Centre and the training programmes associated with these new functions.[1] Using the brief experience in British Columbia, the literature on skills training, and our instructional design experiences in the Professional Legal Training Course, I will suggest the elements of a sound, competency-based training programme for mediators.[2] Mediators, like many others practising professional skills, have strong debates about their role and tactics in dispute resolution.[3] The flow of these debates spills over into training. Some observations about the relationship between the role of mediators and strategies for training will be necessary.

COMPETENCY-BASED TRAINING

It is now commonplace for those active in legal skills training to begin a discussion of training strategies by emphasizing the holy trinity: knowledge, skills and attitudes (see e.g. Ayling and Constanzo 1984). Using what we have learned about competency-based training in interviewing, advocacy and negotiation, combined with legal transactions, a reasonable working hypothesis suggests that effective mediators would be able to demonstrate competence in these general dimensions:

1 *Knowledge*
- of negotiation theory and mediation theory (knowledge of theory)
- of strategies, stages and tactics in both negotiation and mediation (process knowledge)
- of the rules applicable to the legal dispute (substantive and procedural knowledge – context knowledge)

2 *Skills*
- the actions and intellectual processes of mediators from pre-mediation to settlement by the parties including analytical skills, communication skills, organizational skills and planning skills

3 *Attitudes*
- the ethics, values and professionalism exhibited by the

mediator in relationship to personal values and established codes of professional conduct.

This is a tall order for a training programme, especially one of short duration; however, instructional designers must address all of these elements, even if they must be content with skimping on some elements and leaving the more comprehensive learning to self-directed study and on-the-job experience. Most working instructional designers are faced with less time and fewer resources than they would like. The decisions about what to cut from the 'ideal' training programme are often more important than decisions on what to save. When the editing decisions are made, this general framework of knowledge, skills and attitudes must be combined with a thorough understanding of the target audience in order to achieve a compromise that will make the investment of time and training dollars worthwhile.

But I am getting two steps ahead of myself. To achieve the goal of 'becoming an effective mediator' we must know how to define effectiveness in a mediator. As Gold (1987: 65–6) and Moore (1986: 297, n. 2) have noted, we have little research about what constitutes effectiveness in mediation or the skills of good mediators. Nevertheless, until the research base is developed to respond to these questions, the practical truth is that there is a current demand for mediators and many training resources are being directed toward that demand. The issue for instructional designers becomes: How can we make the best of what we do know about effectiveness in relation to the knowledge, skill and attitudes of mediators?

The constraints of an inadequate research base, time and money are all worthy excuses for not mounting effective formal training programmes in mediation. But a practical trainer can feel somewhat more optimistic when it comes to the principles of adult education that contribute to good skills training programmes. Andragogy, the art and science of helping adults learn, has been referred to often in the skills training literature (see e.g. Hathaway 1987: 389). For constructing a mediation training programme, the adult education criteria outlined by Tobin (1987) are most useful:

1 That as a person matures, his or her self-concept moves from one of being a dependent personality towards one of being a *self-directing* human being.
2 That the adult accumulates a growing reservoir of *experience* that becomes an increasing resource for learning.
3 That the adult's readiness to learn becomes increasingly oriented to the development of his or her social role.
4 The adult's time perspective changes from one of postponed application of knowledge to *immediacy of application of knowledge*.
5 Accordingly, the adult's orientation towards learning shifts from one of subject-centredness to one of *problem-centredness*.

(Tobin 1987: 56, referring to Knowles 1970, emphasis added)

These criteria speak to the kinds of skill exercises one might develop in mediation training. At the same time, the criteria do not provide us with the menu of 'process knowledge', the context (family law, commercial law, etc.) or the ethical gridwork for competency training for mediators. I question whether problem-centred methods can be the 'broad shoulders' for these other elements of competency (though some would argue that problem methods are adequate). The training strategy for mediation must include *integration* of knowledge, skill and attitudes and criteria-referenced *performance*.[4] In Table 17.1 I have set up a matrix to demonstrate the intersection of skills, knowledge and attitudes with the six main criteria for effective training. In the intersecting boxes, I have suggested some instructional methods that would meet the individual criteria. More complex exercises and cumulative instructional strategies would be able to address all the criteria, thus leading to performance which can be classified as competent. For example, a mediation fact pattern for a simulation might be the final exercise in an instructional strategy that can be represented by a pyramid (see Figure 17.1).

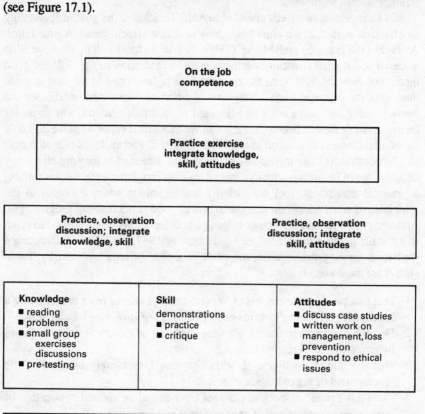

Figure 17.1 Instructional strategy pyramid

Table 17.1 Effective training matrix

	Independent	Experience	Immediate application	Problem centred	Performance related to criteria	Integration
Skill	• work in pairs • peer critiques • several levels of practice available	• pre-test in negotiation skills • take inventory of similar tasks	• simulations • group critique exercises • video replay	• problems from 'real practice' • 'outsider' • 'clients'	• short simulations • videotape and replay • critique tied to criteria • isolate areas for improvement	• simulation of real transaction and critique complete performance • address knowledge, • focus on areas where integrated performance weak (e.g. can student assess and advise on 'value' of personal injury case?)
Knowledge process and context	• pre-reading of skill materials • brainstorm to assemble key elements • call on participant experts	• ask small group to 'research' their experience and report • use participant experts • use participant experts	• next day use of readings • narrow context for simulation fact patterns	• brainstorming • circle of knowledge • buzz groups All aimed at concrete problems		
Attitudes	• seek individual written responses to short problems • short overnight assignments	• set up analogies to negotiation, litigation for discussion	• stop demonstrations, simulations to discuss ethical issues; re-start	• use problems with 'embedded' ethical issues • assign weight to performance criteria		

Within each of the blocks in Figure 17.1 there is a full agenda for teacher and participant. In the British Columbia trial-and-error experience, we have tried to design exercises and simulations which move to the integration level very quickly. In sharp contrast to our early design efforts, we rarely use a 'subskill hierarchy' to build up legal skills. We believe that an understanding of the underlying skills is important; it contributes to 'process knowledge'. At the same time, most adults are unwilling to spend time on subskills such as 'questioning', 'listening', 'fact-investigating', 'responding to others' – even though they may desperately need some of these subskills. They want to interview, negotiate or mediate right away. Why is there this gap between 'needs' and 'wants' in the development of a skill? It goes back to the design criteria suggested earlier. Adults want

1 credit for their experience (in life as well as law practice)
2 immediate application of the skill which relates to on-the-job circumstances, not isolated elements of the skill
3 problems which challenge or even exceed their reach.

With these background principles and training experiences in mind, I shall turn to a description and evaluation of the recent mediation training efforts in British Columbia (BC).

BC INTERNATIONAL COMMERCIAL ARBITRATION CENTRE (BCICAC): MEDIATION TRAINING EFFORTS

The BCICAC has undertaken two training programmes: one in personal injury mediation (offered twice) and the other in commercial mediation skills. The Justice Institute of British Columbia, a training centre for police, sheriffs, para-legals, court workers and other law-related occupations, was instrumental in designing or coaching in both programmes. They led the way in developing a personal injury mediation programme. The commercial mediation skills course was taught by American Arbitration Association instructors and sponsored by the Continuing Legal Education Society of BC and the BCICAC.

The demand for personal injury mediators was created by the Centre itself. The early years of the Centre's operation have not produced weekly volumes of international clients. Therefore the Centre worked with the Insurance Corporation of British Columbia (ICBC) to promote negotiated or mediated settlement of automobile injury cases. The corporation is the exclusive provider of automobile insurance in the province and operates as a Crown corporation. There is a public interest in keeping insurance rates low and considerable motivation for preventing the costs of litigation. Furthermore, an agreement with ICBC means that the volume of potential mediations could be very high indeed. In 1987, for example, ICBC assigned over 10,000 cases to defence counsel to defend on behalf of the corporation. A further 1,000 were handled internally. Since even a 10 per cent rate of litigated cases would overwhelm ICBC and the courts, there was a clear incentive for ICBC and the BCICAC to reach an agreement to mount a voluntary programme for mediation or arbitration of personal injury claims arising from motor vehicle accidents. This is a pilot project but it has already attracted many cases. Lawyers for ICBC or the plaintiff may choose mediation or arbitration, although the Centre is strongly encouraging the parties to try mediation first.

The mediation process requires that a mediator meet with lawyers representing each side. In addition, the clients are expected to be available in an adjacent room. On occasion, all parties will meet together. On the defence side, it is expected that the insurance adjuster will have full authority to reach an agreement. Likewise, counsel for the plaintiff and the defendant are asked to come with full authority.

The fee for a four-hour mediation is $450.00 (Canadian) including administrative expenses, a meeting room at the Centre and a fee for the mediator. Arbitrations can be arranged within six to twelve weeks and can range from $2,300.00 to $5,000.00 or more.[5]

In addition to working directly with ICBC, the Centre will be attempting to expand its mediation services to personal injury claimants and private insurance companies in other types of disputes. There is an expansion of services taking place in domestic commercial disputes also. Promoting the services of the Centre makes sense from a business point of view. Those who are converts to alternative dispute resolution know that it makes sense from a professional practice point of view. It remains to be seen whether the litigation-minded lawyers can be educated and reassured that this service makes sense from the client's point of view.

The BCICAC strategy for training mediators got to the heart of this latter problem. They went to the community of personal injury lawyers, commercial lawyers and trained family mediators to find their mediators. They have, in the case of personal injury mediation training, selected individuals for training. They looked for individuals who had experience in negotiation and mediation and a solid reputation in the legal profession. A premium was placed on negotiation and mediation skills rather than specific expertise in personal injury law. The Centre made the judgment that early in the programme, generic mediation skills outweighed knowledge of the specific context in which mediation was to operate.

In the case of commercial mediation, the marketing effort was aimed at senior lawyers who had negotiated commercial deals frequently. In fact, most of the forty participants were very experienced and few had less than ten years at the bar. There was no screening as to experience, although most had commercial law knowledge and little in the way of a background in mediation.

In some respects, the two training programmes provided a laboratory for observation about the background that participants should have upon entering mediation training. Is it more important to have baseline skills and process knowledge or context knowledge? Ideally trainers would like to have both. But when there are so few lawyers with mediation skills in the community, we probably must learn to expect that most participants will have more context knowledge than process knowledge or skills in mediation.

Personal injury mediation skills training: evaluation

The personal injury training programme is outlined in Table 17.2 and the criteria for performance (based on a mediation model) shown in Table 17.3. By looking at this outline and applying the 'pyramid' for effective skills training (see Figure 17.1), some evaluative comments can be made.

Table 17.2 Personal injury training programme

Day 1	
3:00	Overview of insurance mediation issues and terms: questions and discussion
5:00	Dinner break
7:00	Overview of mediation process; role of the mediator
7:40	Stages 1 and 2: Introduction; opening statements; agenda
	Case study 1: 'The Olympics'
9:45	Debrief
Day 2	
8:30	Objective criteria
	Stages 3 and 4; skills lecturette
	Case Study 1: continued through Stages 3 and 4
11:40	Debrief
12:00	Lunch
1:00	Case Study 2: 'Leaky Roofing'
3:45	Regroup; debrief; closure
4:30	Adjourn

Table 17.3 Mediation model

Preparation

1   agree on roles, responsibilities, use of caucusing, handling disagreements
2   variation: plaintiff available for consultation on-site, but not present in mediation session
3   mediator to have background information from each side, plus a one-page summary (which has also been exchanged between the two sides)
4   review of one-page summaries

Stage one: introduction

1   establish rapport and set climate
2   clarify process: voluntary; use of caucusing
3   review guidelines for mediation

4   describe roles and responsibilities
5   agree to time-limit for session – possible future session
6   confirm fees (if appropriate)
7   seek commitment to mediation (BATNA);* necessity of moving from positions
8   seek written agreement not to subpoena the mediator at a later date should the case go to court

Stage two: opening statements

1   presentation of one-page summaries by each counsel
2   clarification and summary
3   ensure understanding by all parties
4   listen for common ground
5   manage the climate

Stage three: exploring the issues

1   separate and prioritize the issues
2   determine and specify common ground
3   determine interests beneath positions
4   establish objective criteria
5   ensure understanding
6   manage the climate
7   write down areas of agreement

Stage four: create the agreement

1   generate options for mutual gain (brainstorm)
2   reinforce objective criteria
3   refer to BATNAs*
4   seek areas of agreement and list them
5   encourage empathic reasoning
6   write down agreement on each issue
7   probe for realism
8   summarize key points

Note: *'BATNA' is Fisher and Ury's (1982) term for the Best Alternative To a Negotiated Agreement. They recommend developing these alternatives in preparing for a negotiation.

Strengths

1 Participants were selected for their experience in mediation or personal injury law and negotiation, but not all had both.[6] This meant that process knowledge and skill were high for some but context knowledge was low for them. For others, the reverse was true. With calculated arrangement of

subgroups for teaching and simulation (mediators together with a teaching personal injury lawyer; personal injury lawyers with a teaching mediator) it would be possible to raise the competence of both types of participants.

2 The skills teaching cycle had three important elements: a demonstration of the skill, structured practice in chronological sequence, and feedback at each stage of practice.

3 There was a brief exposure to context knowledge of personal injury law and the litigation process (two hours), although feedback was aimed more at skills than knowledge.

4 A model of mediation and a theory of negotiation (Fisher and Ury's principled negotiation theories) were presented.

5 Audio-visual demonstrations were used effectively.

6 Performance was critiqued in relation to the stages of the mediation model; however, the performance criteria were not very specifically defined.

7 After a day and a half of formal training, there was follow-up training for those who had less previous mediation experience. This was on-the-job training using co-mediation, with the experienced mediator taking the lead, then reviewing the session with the other mediator after the session. This is an outstanding feature of the Centre's commitment to mediation training; it is a step normally omitted from other skills training programmes.

8 The simulation problems were realistic, simple enough and well-organized. Therefore, the training was problem-centred.

9 There was follow-up training in personal injury law and procedure some weeks after the programme (three hours).

Weaknesses (and areas for improvement)

1 The presentation of process knowledge and context knowledge were on the right track, but far too thin to prepare participants for integrated learning. In future, pre-assigned readings from texts like Fisher and Ury (1982) and Moore's *The Mediation Process* (1986) would permit the instructors to get on with the active learning agenda. For those with mediation experience and little personal injury background, continuing legal education readings or courses might be prerequisites. If the training programme leads to a credential (e.g. getting on an approved list of mediators), I would have no hesitation in using the following: assigned readings in advance, a brief written or oral pre-test on process and context knowledge, and teaching geared at assumed knowledge from the readings.[7]

2 There was an inadequate base of negotiation theory and training for the participants. While experience may have taught them negotiation skills, experience did not teach them how to observe negotiations with a more analytical, critical perspective. Since 'mediation is essentially negotiation that includes a third party who is knowledgeable in effective negotiation procedures' (Moore 1986: 14, n. 2), it is vital to build a common foundation

of negotiation skills. This probably requires at least a full day of prior training in negotiation.

3 The criteria for performance of mediators were not adequately described. The more detailed criteria used by the American Arbitration Association might serve as a starting-point for improved criteria (see Table 17.5).

4 More attention could be paid to integration of knowledge, skill and attitudes in the design of case study 2 of the programme. This puts an onus on the critiquer to review strengths and weaknesses of performance in all dimensions of competence. There is great potential for a focus on integration during the on-the-job co-mediation that follows formal training. Of course, the training mediator would have to target the feedback to those tasks requiring most integration.

5 During the training programme, non-participant observers were assessing the skills of the trainee mediators in order to decide who would be invited to be on the panel of paid mediators in the Centre's programme. While expedience may have prompted this procedure, it is antithetical to the objectives of basic skills training. Less experienced participants must have an unthreatening environment, one in which they can make mistakes without serious consequences. The introduction of performance evaluation (for purposes of granting credentials) too early in the training sequence could seriously damage the credibility and effectiveness of the training programme.

On the other hand, trained mediators who are told that the programme has a performance evaluation component should be able to deal with those pressures. Although some may object to the artificiality of simulation, they would all face a common problem and the evaluators would be able to make fairer comparative judgments.

Commercial mediation skills training: evaluation

The three-day programme in commercial mediation skills was designed and principally taught by the Department of Education and Training of the American Arbitration Association.[8] The course was open to all British Columbia lawyers, but a large number of senior lawyers and judges enrolled. Their evaluations of the course were very positive, so criticism of the programme is a risky business. On the other hand, most of the lawyers had never experienced formal skills training or simulations as a teaching method and they may have lacked a basis for comparison. The programme is outlined in Table 17.4 and the criteria for feedback (observer's sheet) are shown in Table 17.5.

Table 17.4 Commercial mediation skills training programme*

Day 1	
9:00	*Introduction and welcome*
	• Introduction of participants and staff
	• Programme orientation
	• Review of programme agenda and programme plan
9:30	*Introduction to alternative dispute resolution processes*
	• Overview of dispute resolution processes
	• Comparisons between the procedures of ADR
	• Relationship between negotiation and mediation
	• Use and application of the mediation process
10:30	*The mediation process*
	• Stages in the process
	• Establishing credibility
	• Techniques and tools of mediation
	• Role of the opening statement
	• Establishing support
	• Maintaining control
12:00	*Lunch*
1:15	*Introduction to case study exercises*
	Explanation of the case studies and their role in mastering the skills and techniques of the mediator.
1:30	*Mock mediation exercise: case study 1*
	Participants will be divided into groups of three to engage in the first of three mock mediation sessions.
3:15	*Critique and evaluation of case study*
	Mediation simulation exercise will be critiqued by the participants and faculty/observer with specific focus on the skill and techniques used by the 'mediator' in Case Study 1.
4:45	*Adjournment*
Day 2	
9:00	*Negotiating mediated settlements:* a video case study
	Film and discussion of an insurance mediation case study with a detailed analysis of the skills and techniques used by the mediator.
10:30	*Mediating a commercial or insurance dispute*
	(Class will be divided into three subgroups to focus their attention on either the commercial, construction or the insurance area. Subsequent discussions and exercises will use case studies from the three areas for the mock mediation simulations.)
	• Unique aspects of commercial, construction and insurance disputes

- Applying the mediation process to the commercial, construction and insurance areas
- Mediating multi-party disputes

12:00   *Lunch*

1:15   *Mock mediation exercise: case study 2*

Participants working in groups of three, either on a commercial, construction or insurance case, will engage in a mock mediation simulation.

3:00   *Critique and evaluation of case study 2*

Exercise will be critiqued by the participants and faculty/observer with specific focus on the skill and techniques used by the 'mediator' in Case Study 2.

4:30   *Wine and cheese party*

Sponsored by the BC International Commercial Arbitration Centre

Day 3

9:00   *Potential problems in mediating a dispute*

- Confronting an impasse
- Techniques for resolving an impasse
- Dealing with the parties' failure
- Maintaining communication
- Use of alternative processes

10:45   *The role of a central agency in facilitating use of the process*

- Responsibilities to the parties
- Support of mediators and the mediation process
- The educational function
- Working with the business and legal community
- Policing/protecting the process

12:00   *Lunch*

1:15   *Mock mediation exercise: case study 3*

Participants working in groups of three, either on a commercial or insurance case, will engage in a mock mediation simulation.

2:45   *Critique and evaluation of case study 3*

Exercise will be critiqued by the participants and faculty/observer with specific focus on the skill and techniques used by the 'mediator' in Case Study 3.

3:45   *Review and summary of workshop*

Evaluation of programme and final review of the mediation process.

4:30   *Adjournment*

Note: *These materials are the sole property of the American Arbitration Association and may not be used or reproduced without the express permission of the Department of Education and Training, American Arbitration Association, 140 West 51st Street, New York, NY 1020, USA.

Table 17.5 Evaluation of mediator's skills: strategies and techniques of mediation*

Stage one   initiate meeting with parties

1   open channels of communication
2   establish credibility
3   establish control of proceedings
4   maintain order
5   gain acceptance and respect

Stage two   identify issues and positions

1   initiate discussion on unresolved problem
2   clarify what is said
3   organize information
4   initially identify parties' needs and priorities
5   gain trust of parties

Stage three   prepare for movement

1   caucus and re-caucus with parties
2   reduce level of scepticism
3   determine real priorities and positions
4   translate and transmit information
5   increase parties' perception and awareness
6   encourage movement and avoid escalation of additional issues
7   set the pace of the negotiations
8   clarify and verify positions
9   maintain confidence of parties

Stage four   get movement

1   test the validity of parties' positions
2   create doubts in minds of parties
3   explore alternatives and seek trade-offs
4   communicate possibilities of movement
5   deflate unrealistic or extreme positions
6   develop habits of agreement
7   narrow differences between parties
8   reinforce trust with parties

Stage five   approach closure

1   emphasize progress and rate of movement
2   stress the consequences of no agreement

continued/

3   exert pressure
4   make specific suggestions
5   achieve an overlap in parties' positions
6   receive commitment

Stage six   get closure

1   have parties negotiate closure in joint session
2   make final suggestions
3   use leverage
4   make recommendations
5   recess
6   close discussions

Stage seven   finalize agreement

1   verify and re-state specifics of agreement
2   reduce to writing

Note: *See note to Table 17.4

Strengths

1 The materials on process knowledge for mediators were succinct and well organized. They were designed for a generic course with busy practitioners in mind.
2 The model for mediation and the criteria for performance were much better articulated than in the personal injury programme, both orally and in written form.
3 Presenters used audio-visual aids, including a videotaped demonstration, to good advantage.
4 The design model of explanations, demonstration, practice and feedback was followed.
5 There was a faculty–participant ratio of 3 to 1 and the faculty providing critique all had mediation experience, extensive skills training experience, or both.
6 All participants had an opportunity to role-play protagonist in negotiations, antagonist and mediator. Feedback was directed to the mediator only.
7 The wrap-up at the conclusion of each simulation drew on the experience and questions of the participants.
8 The presenter with extensive case experience related well to the on-the-job experience of the senior lawyers. His concrete illustrations of resolving logjams in mediation were extremely helpful.

Weaknesses (and areas for improvement)

1 From the viewpoint of an instructional designer, the main flaw in the programme arose from a hotly disputed issue in skills training: can we train for generic skills (e.g. in mediation) or must skills training always have a solid base of context knowledge? In the commercial mediation skills course, the presentation and design were primarily targeted to generic skills even though the advance billing was 'commercial mediation'. The evidence for finding fault with the generic approach is based on these features of the programme:

   (a) the morning presentations (except for those of the commercial mediator) focused on process knowledge and there was little ability to respond to the context knowledge of the participants

   (b) the simulations, in order of presentation, were a contract dispute (very basic commercial law), a construction dispute, and a motor vehicle, personal injury insurance claim

   (c) faculty assigned to provide feedback had little or no specific context knowledge or experience in commercial law and dispute resolution.

   In my judgment, the relative absence of context knowledge and the lack of simulations rooted in commercial law meant that participants achieved much less integrated learning compared to the learning potential in the audience.

2 No theory of negotiation was presented, nor were negotiation skills given much attention. The comments under the personal injury training programme are relevant here.

3 All presenters used assumptions about US law and procedure that were frequently inappropriate and irrelevant to Canadian legal practice.

4 The videotaped demonstration, conducted on the morning of the second day, portrayed a personal injury case. It was out of the commercial law context and little was done to transfer its lessons to commercial mediation.

FUTURE DIRECTIONS: TRAINING THE NEXT GENERATION OF MEDIATORS

Concluding observations

In my view, most successful mediation training programmes for lawyers will have to be based in single legal context. The context, be it Family Law, Commercial Law or Insurance Law, is essential because

1 it draws on existing experience

2 there is an immediate source of relevant, realistic problems for discussion or simulation

3 'off-the-shelf' materials, courses and tests are already available in the substantive areas

4 we know that the substantive title, not the skill, is the better drawing card for marketing skill programmes.

Mediation skill trainers must do a better job of defining competent performance of all the functions and tasks of a mediator. This will lead to better 'skill guides' for teaching and performance evaluation purposes. Moore's (1986) outline of mediation functions would be a good starting-point for a more detailed articulation:[9]

- The *opener of communications* channels who initiates communication or facilitates better communication if the parties are already talking.
- The *legitimizer* who helps all parties recognize the right of others to be involved in negotiations.
- The *process facilitator* who provides a procedure and often formally chairs the negotiation session.
- The *trainer* who educates novice, unskilled, or unprepared negotiators in the bargaining process.
- The *resource expander* who provides procedural assistance to the parties and links them to outside experts and resources, such as lawyers, technical experts, decision makers, or additional goods for exchange, that may enable them to enlarge acceptable settlement options.
- The *problem explorer* who enable people in dispute to examine a problem from a variety of viewpoints, assists in defining basic issues and interests, and looks for mutually satisfactory options.
- The *agent of reality* who helps build a reasonable and implementable settlement and questions and challenges parties who have extreme and unrealistic goals.
- The *scapegoat* who may take some of the responsibility or blame for an unpopular decision that the parties are nevertheless willing to accept. This enables them to maintain their integrity and, when appropriate, gain the support of their constituents.
- The *leader* who takes the initiative to move the negotiations forward by procedural, or on occasion, substantive suggestions.

(Moore 1986: 18, n. 2)

Two neglected areas in the spectrum of competency-based training deserve more attention from instructional designers. They are the experience base of the participants and the opportunities for follow-up training during actual mediation performance. The BCICAC training programmes have demonstrated promise in addressing both of these issues.

We need to develop research projects that will give us a feedback loop from lasting settlements to mediation training. These projects would not have to be all-encompassing studies of competency or effectiveness in mediation. They could focus on a handful of desirable mediator skills (i.e. thought by theorists and educators to be desirable) and correlate those skills to lasting settlements. The feedback loop would look like Figure 17.2.

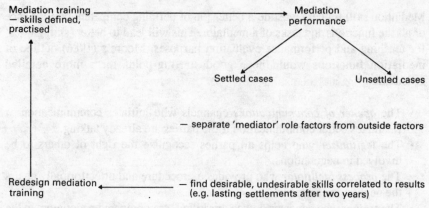

Figure 17.2 Feedback loop from lasting settlements to mediation training

A basic instructional design outline for mediation training

Combining principle, practice and pragmatism isn't easy and it rarely works the first time. Nevertheless, fundamental mistakes in instructional design could be avoided by following these steps.

1 Define mediation skills and tasks and create educational objectives for the programme.
2 Choose a substantive context for the programme and define the kind of entry-level knowledge you want the participants to have.
3 Provide alternate routes, available in advance, for gaining process knowledge and context knowledge (e.g. questionnaires on experience, readings, self-testing instruments). Follow through by assuming that knowledge, not lecturing on it, in the formal programme. This step goes to the self-directed criterion for adult learning.
4 One-quarter to one-third of the programme should be devoted to negotiation theory and skills. I would tie this to mediation by conducting simulated negotiations and selecting those cases which don't settle. In phase two of the training programme, the unsettled cases could be referred to mediation. This kind of continuity reinforces process knowledge and motivates participants to find a solution before the deadline (end of the course).
5 Demonstrations should be brief, but they should touch all main stages of mediation. Ideally, they should be in the legal context announced for the programme.
6 Simulations should be sequenced from least complex to most complex, with integrated learning objectives planned for the last one or two simulation exercises (e.g. on the basis of the pyramid presented earlier). They should all be in the same legal context area so that at least one piece of the learning equation remains constant. Furthermore, if the problems are based on an actual case that went on to litigation, the teaching potential in comparing mediated vs. litigated outcomes is tremendous.[10]

7 Ethical issues should be embedded in both negotiation and mediation simulation problems. This helps to integrate 'attitude' training and discussion.

8 Trained critiquers should provide feedback. If they have only process knowledge and mediation skills, that background is preferable to those who have only legal context knowledge.

9 Primary presenters should have skill and credibility as mediators in the specific legal field chosen as the context.

10 Even if the training programme leads to a credential, the credential-testing performances should be clearly separated from the training segments. Participants will not feel free to learn from their mistakes otherwise.

11 Send the participants away with good self-education learning tools: skill guides, summaries of process knowledge and updated context knowledge, further reading, reference lists, etc.

12 Put in place a follow-up phase of training: a refresher course, co-mediation, or a post-training performance test.

If you can accomplish all of this, you may well be exhausted. But you will be advancing mediation training an important step forward. Instead of repeating the mistakes of others, you will be in a position to overcome those problems and contribute more to your audience and to other instructional designers. The chief reward of teaching mediation skills, like many other skills, is that the distinction between teaching and learning is constantly eroding. As we teach competence to others, we learn more about the competencies involved in both mediation and teaching.

NOTES

1 The author acknowledges the helpful comments of Bonita J. Thompson, QC, in the preparation of this chapter.

2 The British Columbia course is a ten-week, full-time post-degree programme. The course is skills-based and uses full-time faculty, small classes and simulations to replicate legal skills in realistic settings. The curriculum and its objectives are more fully discussed in Cruickshank (1985).

3 Christopher Moore (1986: 39–43ff.) explores the debate between procedurally oriented mediators and substantively oriented mediators. He also raises many of the ethical dilemmas confronted by mediators.

4 Tobin (1987: 61) acknowledges the need for performance criteria in educational objectives; likewise, what he describes as the need for 'a theory of legal practice' may coincide with my call for 'integration' in teaching and learning legal skills.

5 The mediation and arbitration programmes are more fully described in the Centre's newsletter, *Arbitration Canada* 1988, Fall, 1.

6 In fact, the first group of sixteen trainees all had mediation experience, but less personal injury expertise; the second group included more lawyers with personal injury practices but fewer with mediation skills.

7 All of these techniques are employed successfully in the Professional Legal Training Course.

8 Allan Silberman, Department Director, and Neil Blacker of the Seattle Regional Office of the AAA were principal leaders. Don Logerwell, an experienced Seattle commercial mediator, also led plenary sessions.
9 Moore credits the American Arbitration Association for the description of functions.
10 The BCICAC personal injury programme used this method very successfully.

18 Considering dispute resolution: a research prospectus[1]

Neil Gold

INTRODUCTION TO THE PROBLEM

It has been suggested that an important measure of a civilization is the quality of justice received by its citizens. In the past decade there has been an increasing concern that the traditional adversary system is not adequate to handle effectively all the disputes currently being placed before it. A number of factors have combined to create this concern. The increasing complexities of modern life have increased considerably the number of potential disputes. The capacities of traditional, informal dispute resolution institutions to resolve disputes, such as the family, neighbourhood or church, seem to have diminished. The expansion of the role of government in the lives of its citizens has brought with it an increasing number of controversies between citizen and state. There is a perception too that as a people we have become more litigious. All this has resulted in an increase in litigation, aggravating the problems within the current judicial structure, causing delays from the ensuing backlog of cases, higher costs to the parties and the taxpayer, the bureaucratization of dispute-processing systems and exaggeration of minor disputes as a result of regulations, delays and costs. Furthermore, both court congestion and high cost are used as bargaining tools to extract settlements which may otherwise be unacceptable.

For many, however, the concern runs deeper. There is a growing awareness that the corner-stone of our judicial structure, the adversary system itself, is not the most appropriate for the effective resolution of all forms of disputes; it may not be capable of resolving a problem to *both* parties' satisfaction and may easily cause disputes to escalate to more serious levels. Moreover, even though the vast majority of disputes are 'resolved' outside the courtroom, they are still resolved 'under the shadow' of this adversary mentality (see Mnookin and Kornhauser 1979); for instance, the threat of instituting court proceedings may be enough to exact an inappropriate settlement. It is often unfortunate that the adversary mentality permeates all resolution processes, polarizing the parties and exacerbating their disaffection. Still, negotiated or 'lumped' settlements far exceed in number those resolved through other means. On many occasions the 'threat' of suit is therapeutic where otherwise stubbornness might prevail.

The basic philosophy of the adversary system is that it is the best means to find the truth through the testing of the various versions of the disputants by putting each to the proof of his or her claim. Correlatively the burden of establishing legal entitlement rests with the litigants. The system is based on individualistic premises: each party is presumed to be equally motivated and competent to investigate the facts and to present his or her case to a passive, neutral and independent court and each is presumed to have equal opportunity to pursue the claim. Implicitly the system presumes adequate resources in both time and money in order to do so. Each party confronts the other, as an adversary, before the court, each having an opportunity to present her or his story, to a judge, whose business is to decide the dispute under law. Eventually so the theory goes, the truth will emerge – at least to the extent it can be discovered.

However, it is generally accepted that the practice does not work nearly as well as the theory, despite an absence of empirical evidence either way. Each party will usually not have equal or even adequate time, money, motivation or ability to present his or her case properly. Furthermore, because the system is in part predicated on competitiveness, combativeness and confrontation, the emphasis is less on the best resolution of conflict but rather, oftentimes it seems, on 'winning at all costs'. It is little wonder that this system has been labelled 'the sporting theory of justice' (Pound 1906). The end results include a lot of wasted time and money and a perceived lack of fairness in the justice system as a whole. In the final analysis to be efficacious a legal system must be perceived as both fair and just. To the extent that users of the legal system feel dissatisfied there is a strong likelihood of disaffection and loss of faith. There have even been fears that the system might collapse under its own weight.

In the United States, where the adversary system can be said to have achieved its 'most rigorous purity' (McKay 1983: 361) and greater acceptance, this concern has also been strongly felt. It has been recognized by Chief Justice Warren Burger of the Supreme Court of the United States who recently noted that:

> [The US legal system] must move away from total reliance on the adversary contest for resolving all disputes. For some disputes, trial will be the only means, but for many claims, trials by the adversarial contest must in time go the way of the ancient trial by battle and blood. Our system is too costly, too painful, too destructive, too inefficient for a truly civilized people. To rely on the adversarial process as the principal means of resolving conflicting claims is a mistake that must be corrected.
>
> (Burger 1984: 17)

Needless to say, the Chief Justice is not alone.

This is not to argue that adjudication in the context of the adversary system is *always* ineffective and inappropriate, but rather to state that it may not be the most effective nor appropriate for every type of human conflict currently being dealt with by our courts. Given the judicial system's reliance on the adversary approach and its criticisms, it follows that a citizen's access to justice through the judicial system may not be the most effective.

THE ISSUE

The central question, therefore, is how to increase a citizen's access to and satisfaction from the justice system, both procedurally and substantively, by reducing the costs and delays in the resolution of conflict and by eliminating unwarranted confrontation and bureaucratic or procedural complication. In short, how can justice best be done?

POSSIBLE RESPONSES TO THE PROBLEM

This proposal suggests, then, that we are seeking processes which provide a fairer, more efficient, more humane and more just system of justice. To this end three basic options on their own or in combination have been proposed:

1 expand existing court resources, through the increase of court personnel and courtrooms
2 improve the existing court resources and refine procedures
3 promote and institute the use of alternative procedures in place of or in combination with traditional dispute resolution mechanisms.

(Kane 1982: 4)

The first two options aim at improving the performance of the existing system. However, there are many limits as to what can be accomplished by these means. Governments just do not have the resources to continue appointing more judges and other personnel, building more courtrooms and jails, improving court administration, restructuring the courts and amending rules of practice. Furthermore, such reforms do not generally address the more serious underlying concerns about the appropriateness, utility and fairness of the adversary system itself. None the less serious research into dispute processing in the courts is necessary to verify assumptions and point to reforms within the judicial system where possible.

The third option of providing alternatives may also be used to improve the performance of the traditional justice system on the hypothesis that if a dispute can be effectively resolved *before* it reaches the courts at all or at least before trial, such a dispute does not then contribute as greatly to the costs and delays in the administration of justice (Kane 1982: 48–9; in fact this has been a motivation behind many alternatives programmes). However, cases which are settled in the shadow of adjudication are often affected by pre-trial manoeuvres, including motions, discovery, and so on. More importantly, however, alternative procedures do not need to be based upon the adversarial premise and, hence, may be used more effectively and appropriately in these areas where such an approach is neither the most appropriate nor necessary to ensure the public establishment of legal rights. Alternatives may even prove a means through which to attempt to shift the emphasis of our judicial system away from the confrontational and combative toward a more co-operative attitude (Linden 1983: 23). For all the above reasons and many others too numerous to mention here, there has been a growing interest in alternatives to adjudication as a means in which to provide a fairer, more efficient, more humane and more just justice system.

ALTERNATIVE DISPUTE RESOLUTION PROCESSES

The idea of providing alternatives is not new – the development of the Court of Equity in thirteenth- and fourteenth-century England was based on a desire to find ways of ameliorating the then existing structure. In fact, the King's own common law courts were developed as a promise of better justice than that provided by the manorial courts of early England. The rapid growth of administrative tribunals in the twentieth century, now entrenched within the legal system, were created in many instances to provide an alternative means to resolve conflicts, usually in specialized areas. However, in light of the recent concerns about adjudication in an adversarial setting there has been a resurgence of interest in alternatives within the last few decades and a number of significant developments have taken place. This is especially true in the United States in which probably over 200 alternative dispute resolution programmes have now been instituted. Moreover, this number does not include a much greater number of specialized applications in areas such as divorce mediation, consumer arbitration and environmental mediation (Pearson 1982: 423).

In Canada this development has been much more modest. Much of the work has been done in the criminal justice system area; in particular juvenile and summary conviction pre-trial diversion. However, some work has been done in the civil law area, especially in the area of family law, where several community-based mediation programmes have been instituted.

GOALS OF DISPUTE RESOLUTION ALTERNATIVES

In light of the foregoing discussion, four separate goals can be ascertained from the literature on the subject of the amelioration of dispute processing:

1 to relieve court backlog, undue cost and delay
2 to increase community involvement in the dispute-resolution process
3 to increase a citizen's access to justice
4 to provide more effective, efficient and satisfying dispute resolution, thereby improving the quality of justice and citizen perception of it.

(Goldberg *et al.* 1985: 5)

It should be noted that these goals overlap and conflict. Much of the current controversy over criteria for evaluating the success of an alternative initiative can be attributed to a lack of consensus over its goals. Therefore, a first step in any research activity must be the clarification of goals and the values upon which they are predicated.

Table 18.1 Dispute processing options

I	**Unilateral actions on the part of a disputant**	
	A	Inaction
	B	Active avoidance (move, terminate relationship, etc.)
	C	Self-help
		1 redefinition of the problem
		2 elimination of the deficit
		3 use of social service agencies and other assistance
II	**Dyadic options – contacts between the disputing parties**	
	A	Coercion (threats and use of force)
	B	Negotiation
III	**Third-party resolution techniques**	
	A	Conciliation (bringing parties together for negotiation)
	B	Mediation (structured communication, recommendations)
		1 general mediational projects
		2 projects mediating limited disputes for the general public
		3 projects mediating general disputes for a limited segment of the population
		4 projects mediating a limited range of disputes for an institutional population
	C	Arbitration
		1 general arbitration projects
		2 arbitration of small claims matters
		3 consumer arbitration projects
		4 contractually based arbitration
	D	Fact-finding
		1 media action lines
		2 trade association projects
		3 government ombudsmen
	E	Administrative procedures
		1 court-oriented processing
		2 informal court operated processing
		3 routine administrative processing
		4 measures reducing or eliminating the need for adjudication
		5 measures simplifying adjudication
	F	Adjudication

Source: McGillis and Mullen 1977: 5.

RANGE OF AVAILABLE ALTERNATIVES

Table 18.1 provides an overview of dispute processing options starting from the most informal to the most formal. (Goldberg *et al.* 1985: 8–9 describe another model of the variety of dispute resolution processes and their characteristics: see Table I.1, p. 14.) The most commonly used techniques are as follows. (There are many varied definitions of negotiation, mediation and arbitration; these are offered as descriptions, not prescriptions.)

1 *Negotiation* A process through which the parties either directly or through their affiliates exchange information and seek to persuade the other to change their position.
2 *Mediation* A form of negotiation in which a neutral third party is actively involved in helping the parties with or without affiliates to reach a compromise to the resolution of their dispute.
3 *Arbitration* A process in which a neutral third party settles a dispute with varying amounts of control over the process in the hands of the arbitrator. Rules of procedure and evidence may be relaxed. This decision is usually, but may not be, binding.

There are a variety of hybrid or combination approaches which will be briefly described later.

TYPES OF INITIATIVES

Types of dispute resolution initiatives can be divided into specialized dispute resolution and general dispute resolution processes.

Specialized dispute resolution

So far, most of the initiatives have developed in specialized areas responding to specific problems and needs. Accordingly in the context of dispute resolution as a whole, this gives a rather disjointed perspective as some areas are much more developed (e.g. labour law and family law areas) than others (e.g. environmental law). Still others remain almost totally without alternatives (e.g. personal injury claims). It should also be noted that not just one, but several techniques may be employed in conjunction, usually seriatim. For example both mediation and arbitration can be used under collective bargaining agreements in the labour law area. Negotiation and adjudication almost always coexist.

General dispute resolution

These types of initiatives can be divided into alternatives developed *within* or in close relation to the court system and those developed *outside* the system. The former includes the small claims court, new minor offences procedures, amendments to practice procedures (pre-trials, offers to settle, etc.) and recent developments in the United States such as 'rent-a-judge' (retired judges who arbitrate), mini-hearings and court-annexed arbitration. These initiatives are primarily designed to decrease the demand on judicial resources, thereby reducing costs and delay, but still premised, to a greater or lesser extent, upon the adversary process.

Those generalized dispute resolution initiatives developed outside the traditional legal system tend to be community-based mediation centres designed to resolve relatively minor interpersonal disputes. In the United States the most well known are the Neighbourhood Justice Centres created by the US Department of Justice in 1977. In Canada, at least three community-based projects have been developed in Halifax, Kitchener-Waterloo and (recently closed) in Windsor.

RESEARCH INTO DISPUTE RESOLUTION

While there has been a lot written on the subject of alternative means of processing disputes, surprisingly enough there is a dearth of rigorous empirical research (see the discussion in Edelman 1984: 137–9). Only a limited number of US studies have employed an experimental design, attempting to compare alternative means, using the traditional court process as a control group.[2] Most studies have merely consisted of descriptions of project caseload, referral sources, average time per case, average cost per case and other 'performance' data. Moreover the bases for these analyses are far from uniform thereby rendering it difficult, if not impossible, to compare one analysis with another in any useful or accurate way (see Pearson 1982: 423; Mandelbaum 1984: 28).

In Canada, this lack of empirical research is even more marked. Furthermore, assuming Canadians have a way of approaching conflict including various cultural norms and values, which are different from Americans, the US studies should be accepted with even more caution.

SUMMARY OF THE FINDINGS

For the USA see evaluation of valuations in Pearson (1982), Mandelbaum (1984: 16–40) and Tomasic and Feeley (1982). For Canada see ARA Consultants (1983; 1984a; 1984b). Despite the limitations in the currently available research there has been enough experimentation and evaluation to provide a suggestion of whether alternative means to the traditional dispute processing mechanisms serve a useful purpose. Some of the findings include the following.

1 The rate of participation of disputants in alternatives seems to depend upon the degree of programme coercion. Programmes with high participation tend to be compulsory, while voluntary programmes tend to fail to attract a substantial number of participants.
2 The chance of reaching an agreement, once both disputants have *chosen* an alternative technique, is quite good, though the data relating to mediation, in particular, are variable and are hence equivocal and difficult to interpret.
3 Non-traditional approaches seem to promote more compromise than the traditional systems.
4 Alternatives uniformly report a high level of user satisfaction.
5 Mediated and arbitrated agreements seem to result in higher rates of participant compliance with the resolution and the amount of 'relitigation'

seems to be less frequent than in decisions resulting from more traditional dispute resolution processes.

6 Alternatives do not significantly alleviate court congestion.
7 Alternatives do not save substantial sums of money.
8 Alternatives tend to save time for the disputants, although these savings vary according to programme format and outcome.
9 The highest rate of use has been by low-income participants (though this may be because most of the programmes have been located in low-income areas and/or connected with the criminal justice system).

Basically the studies show that alternatives fail to achieve, to any significant extent, many of the *performance goals* one might posit for them, such as decreasing court time and court costs. It should be noted, however, that most of the evaluations, upon which these tentative findings have been based, were focused on experimental projects concentrating only on the first two years of their operations. It is clear that the initial period of a project's life is far from typical of its routine operations, especially where it is experimental. Accordingly evaluations are needed, even from a performance goals perspective, to assess the longer range operations and impact.

On the other hand, with regard to the *quality of services* and *client satisfaction*, alternatives fare much better. The evaluations almost invariably show high levels of user satisfaction, better perceptions of fairness, compliance with outcomes and reduced levels of relitigation.

RESEARCH NEEDS: DEVELOPING THE PROSPECTUS

See Edelman (1984), Goldberg *et al.* (1985: 13–14), Mandelbaum (1984), Pearson (1982) and Tomasic (1982). Given the current wave of enthusiasm for dispute resolution programmes, it is vital to examine rigorously the nature and appropriateness of these programmes as early as possible to avoid waste and ensure the implementation of the best options across the board. The earlier the limitations of alternatives are shown, the earlier improvements and refinements can be instituted. This will avoid the possible disenchantment resulting from overselling. At the moment there is an acute need for *accurate* and *independent* assessments of the effectiveness of dispute resolution programmes, especially *vis-à-vis* the existing dispute resolution procedures. In particular a research programme should include the following items.

1 Examination of the *existing* structures, both formal and informal, of dispute resolution to determine (a) their legitimacy; (b) their efficiency; (c) their effectiveness; (d) participant satisfaction; and (e) compliance with results.
2 Ascertaining and subjecting the basic assumptions of our current structure and of the reforms to critical and independent analysis and evaluation.
3 Analysis of theories of human conflict and the role of conflict.

4 Determination of the scope of the public interest in the public processing of disputes whether major or minor, and the role of the judicial system in this regard.

5 Determination of the appropriate balance and relationship amongst the various types of dispute resolution process.

6 Determination of analysis to evaluate the efficiency and effectiveness of dispute resolution techniques, to take into account not only economic and financial aspects, but also psychological, sociological, cultural and jurisprudential factors.

7 Development of a systematic analysis of disputes to try to match a type of dispute with the appropriate resolution process in accordance with dispute processing typologies or taxonomies.

8 Examination of the possible consequences of large-scale expansion and replication of alternative programmes were they to be developed. In particular, can the negative consequences of bureaucratization and professionalization be avoided or minimized?

9 Determination as to whether alternative methods should be institutionalized. If so, would they provide more procedural and substantive *justice*? To what extent can and should they be integrated into or related to the existing justice system?

10 Determination as to whether the institutionalization of alternatives simply becomes a means for the state to exert more social control. If so, is it in the individual's interest or, ultimately, in the public's interest for the state to do so? To what degree should the state intervene to 'control' or channel the behaviour of its citizens?

11 Determination of whether alternatives merely provide 'second-class' justice for low-income groups, weakening their rights through lessened access to the courts, and thereby allowing the issue of the high cost of entry into the court system to be deferred.

12 Determination of whether alternative procedures should be developed through a general approach or a more case-type specialized approach.

13 Ascertaining the extent to which alternatives require new practitioners with skills different from those who practise in the judicial system, and what changes in the judicial system and educational system are required. For example should mediators belong to a separate profession with its own training, certification and regulation? Should mediators be able to claim some sort of legal privilege?

14 Determination of which case types should be left to be resolved as they now are.

15 Determination of what cases ought to be eliminated from all formal processes.

16 Evaluation of all forms of alternatives not only with regard to performance goals, but also with regard to substantive goals, such as quality of service, appropriateness of process and client satisfaction.

A NEED FOR A COMPREHENSIVE APPROACH: A RESEARCH PROSPECTUS

A comprehensive approach to dispute resolution not only will require research into substantive law and procedure, but also must involve aspects of philosophy, jurisprudence, sociology, anthropology, economics, administration, psychology, statistics, history, political science and social work. In addition to the sixteen matters listed on pp. 274–75, the issues that such a comprehensive approach will be concerned with include:

1 establishment of a priority list of goals for use in the evaluation of the effectiveness, efficiency and appropriateness of various dispute resolution programmes
2 establishment of objective criteria for evaluation research on all forms of dispute resolution, either traditional or proposed, formal or informal
3 establishment of criteria to assess the cost of reforms on the justice system and society as a whole, both in terms of performance and substantive goals
4 establishment of a monitoring system of all the dispute resolution programmes throughout the country
5 establishment of a clearing-house to facilitate the dissemination of information on dispute resolution and to provide advice and expertise concerning the establishment, operation and evaluation of dispute resolution programmes throughout the country
6 implementation of needed reforms of dispute resolution process on the federal level and assistance in their implementation on the provincial level and with private organizations
7 provision of citizen education regarding alternative dispute systems and regarding the resolution of conflict in general.

CONCLUSIONS

At the beginning of this chapter it was stated that a measure of a civilization is the quality of justice received by its citizens. It follows that a society's justice system should reflect its society's values. Modern nation-states seek to develop, by and large, through reconciling diversity peaceably, without revolution or undue civil confrontation. It can be argued, however, that a justice system based upon the adversary process does not totally reflect this spirit. In this respect, the growth of interest in alternative techniques of resolving disputes, as a way to promote more co-operation and compromise, less confrontation and combativeness and more acceptable, personally just results, may be seen as arising out of a desire to have a dispute resolution system reflect more legitimately the values of the wider society (Linden 1983: 23–4).

This growth of interest in alternatives during the 1980s has been extraordinarily rapid. Though these techniques have been shown to be effective, there is an urgent need for continuing objective empirical research in order to temper the over-optimistic and silence the sceptics. Moreover, this research should be done on a comprehensive level, so that the needs of and impact on the legal structure and society as a whole can be adequately assessed. Only by this means can there be developed a co-ordinated judicial system, which offers the most efficient, effective and just resolution for all the different types of human conflict, in the public interest.

NOTES

1 This chapter was originally written at the request of the Law Reform Commission of Canada, Shilton Allen M. Linden, President. Frederick Kingston assisted in the research. It has been revised for publication here. I am grateful to the President for his permission to publish it here and to Mr Kingston for his tremendous assistance.
2 See David (1982) concerning an evaluation of a programme involving mediation or criminal adjudication of crimes arising from interpersonal disputes; and Pearson (1979) concerning a programme comparing mediation and adjudication of contested custody and visitation matters.

19 Conclusion: dispute resolution futures

Karl J. Mackie

Democratization is taking place everywhere, acquiring acute forms at times. . . . Emotional outbursts are an inevitable part of any complicated endeavour. This has always been the case in revolutionary times. Today it is as if we are going through a school of democracy again. We are learning. We still lack political culture. We do not even have the patience to hear out our friends. All this is sure to pass. We will master this science, too. The thorniest issues have to be discussed with due respect for one another. Even the most extreme viewpoint contains something valuable and rational, for the person who upholds it honestly and who cares for the common cause in his own way reflects some real aspects of life. For us this is not an antagonistic, class struggle; it is a quest, a debate on how we can really get going with the restructuring effort and make our progress solid and irreversible. So I don't see any drama in polemics, in comparing viewpoints. This is normal.

(Gorbachev 1988: 81)

The expression of dispute is an essential part of a healthy and vigorous democracy or, indeed, of any community whether workplace or local community or family. On its own, however, knowledge of this fact is not enough. Societies and social institutions evolve their own 'science' – theories, customs, rules of law and procedure – of dispute-expression and dispute-handling techniques in order to ensure both that points of view can be fairly expressed and that disputes do not spill over into 'destructive' forms and directions. Ultimately our survival as a species depends on how we can thus manage our (inevitable) conflicts of interests and ideas. History tells us that our common interest in survival is not necessarily, or even frequently, our most salient concern, whether one applies this to ideological conflicts or to conflicts between the desire for economic growth and our interest in conservation of our planet's resources. Our common interest in effective dispute resolution mechanisms is therefore often less prominent than our concerns with the substantive issues that divide us.

The strength of the ADR movement has been to reawaken a vigorous interest in the question of dispute resolution *per se*. Despite its vagueness and difficulties of definition, it has succeeded in drawing together very different interests and motivations in order to expand awareness of the variety of models of dispute resolution mechanism which are available for experimentation and analysis, from mediation and conciliation through mini-trials and fact-finding to the concept of the Multi-Door Courthouse. In stimulating this new awareness, it has also generated a new confidence for experimentation and action. It has mobilized academics and practitioners to rethink and challenge anachronistic, unsatisfactory and unchallenged dispute resolution processes, to seek new means to extend access to justice and in the process to explore anew definitions and forms of justice. This handbook has demonstrated the richness of such efforts that are taking place in the UK and elsewhere in the field of dispute resolution.

If one can identify a weakness of ADR, it perhaps lies in the comments I have just made, but 'translated' into a sceptic's viewpoint. If the process is so rich and so variable in its aptness for disputes, couldn't a sceptic now turn round and re-describe this field not as an exciting portent of the future but as merely an unhelpful mishmash of vague schemes and half-baked optimism with little substantial merit or applicability, and little likelihood of permanence? Couldn't the sceptic ignore the volcanic eruption of dispute resolution centres in the United States – commercial, charitable, academic, legal – and dismiss this as merely a typical example of the crazy swings of fashion in a somewhat crazy culture (one which, after all, manages to combine a statistic of more psychotherapists and more lawyers per head of the population than any other country)? Hot AIR rather than hot ADR, so to speak?

I have detected elements of this viewpoint amongst many practitioners and academics. And, of course, all dispute resolution professionals worth their salt will appreciate, with Mikhail Gorbachev, that there are always two sides (at least) to a story. The real weakness of the ADR movement has perhaps been its stress on the adjective 'alternative'. Take that away, however, and examine the evidence and one thing is clear. We are witnessing an era where dispute resolution *per se*, defined as systems of third-party intervention of all kinds traditional and new, has been finding significant new sources of inspiration and energy. Wherever one looks one finds evidence of developing debates *and* action: the world-wide re-discovery of arbitration as a genuine alternative to litigation (rather than imitation of, or prelude to, litigation); the growth of the conciliation movement in family law work; the spread of new models of dispute settlement in industrial relations along the lines of 'final-offer' arbitration and med-arb; the growth of offender reparation and mediation schemes in criminal justice; the expansion of arbitration and ombudsmen systems in the consumer disputes field; the extension of ombudsmen into the media, pension scheme and legal services disputes; the suggestions in the Lord Chancellor's Civil Justice Review of a major extension of the small claims arbitration system, and further reforms anticipated in legal practice and litigation; the resurgence of the concept of the rule of law in a number of the socialist countries.

The upsurge of ADR has been compared to the development of equity in the history of English law – a new system with more justice and flexibility emerged to compensate for an earlier system of dispute resolution that had become fettered by tradition and institutionalization. However, the analogy breaks down in terms of the fact that current developments do not admit of one easy label or theoretical underpinning. What we are witnessing is the increasing sophistication of dispute settlement procedures as appropriate to a much more complex society. A consumer analogy is more appropriate than the historical legal one – the corner shop (court or Dispute Resolution Store) with its limited stock of products is being overtaken by the Dispute Resolution Supermarket with an array of prices, labels and products.

However, there are also cautions against this optimism. The widespread enthusiasm for, and knowledge of, ADR, alongside relatively limited use, testifies to a degree of consumer confusion. It is not yet clear which systems give best value for money (nor how best to define value), and there is a degree of caution amongst consumers as to whether to try new products as against the tested-and-tried systems of negotiation, arbitration and litigation. The traditionalism of lawyers and legal training also contributes to the slowness of change, resisting 'ADR-literacy' as they once resisted computer-literacy. This is nowhere clearer than in the world of inter-business disputes, where schemes of outside mediation, mini-trials, etc. are only slowly making headway. Many of the developments that have taken place are the result more of pragmatism and the internal dialectic of debate in a particular sector of dispute, rather than through a better, more *strategic* sense of dispute resolution procedure as a 'science' (in Gorbachev's words) to master in its own right. Thus our consumer analogy also breaks down in that our Dispute Resolution Supermarket does not appear to have a single roof or a common management, but appears more as a collection of stall-holders unsure how much to share marketing, products and costs with their fellow stall-holders. Part of the development of ADR techniques will involve the forming of a common consciousness and purpose, albeit that a common roof may be premature or undesirable.

If we do believe, therefore, that there is still considerable scope to develop more effective dispute resolution systems, how to achieve this? The future development of ADR, I suggest, lies in the following developments taking place.

1 An educational campaign to make users and practitioners more widely aware of the flexibility that can be brought into dispute settlement techniques. This should not detract, however, from attempts to see that those who are currently deprived of real opportunities for access to the courts, can obtain such access. Nor in turn should it detract from a search to reform and renew current litigation practice where it fails to meet acceptable standards of procedural justice or efficiency.

2 A call for users and dispute resolution professionals to be ready to experiment within their own sectors, to demonstrate a degree of courage in their activities and advice in this area, and in their readiness to learn from others' experiences. Legal practices in particular need to rethink the philosophy and tools available to their 'litigation departments' (towards a concept of 'settlement departments' – Fisher 1985); the courts need to rethink whether to continue their aversion to involvement in active

settlement procedures; businesses and their in-house corporate counsel could act more proactively (Mackie 1989), replacing abhorrence for litigation costs with positive ADR 'pledges' and the use of extended ADR clauses in contracts.

3 I believe developments will also depend on a degree of institutional support for initiatives in research and practice, from professional associations, from governments, business and community groups, the Office of Fair Trading, consumers' associations and others. Part of such support in the UK could involve the Lord Chancellor's Department in ranging more widely than reviews of existing litigation practice, with a brief to allow the Lord Chancellor to initiate limited experiments in new forms of procedural mechanism (e.g. inquisitorial procedures, court-annexed mediation, a review of the payment into court system and other active settlement programmes), and a responsibility to review on a regular basis the range of dispute resolution mechanisms being used to handle social disputes (on a parallel with the Council on Tribunals?). There is perhaps even a need to give a clearer signal of support for settlement by a new statute designed to encourage settlement efforts (R. Williams 1989). On a more international plane, the signs of a major shift in European political structures including an end to the competing camps of Cold War thinking may also assist with a desire to innovate and experiment with new forms of dispute resolution within and between societies.

4 There is an important role for research in refining our knowledge of the various procedures, their effectiveness, efficiency and appropriateness in different contexts. (For example when should an arbitration system be used in preference to an ombudsman system in consumer disputes? Are there features of inquisitorial civil law systems from which we can benefit, given greater integration within Europe?)

5 There is a need too for more education in the theory and skills of dispute resolution mechanisms. A starting-point would be our schools. Our children are made well aware of conflict in the world through the news media and they experience it directly themselves in family, school and community settings. But they are given little education in the dispute resolution mechanisms and skills which underpin conflict resolution. (For an example of US schools material on ADR, see Kestner 1988.) At a later educational stage, our law faculties and law schools have a particular responsibility in this area given their primacy as the academic discipline for the study of the architecture of dispute-handling mechanisms. On exercising this they also need to give greater thought to the insights of their social science colleagues. It is to be hoped that this handbook will contribute to the development of that discipline. Finally, some of these educational, research and policy strands need to meet in practical training programmes for mediators, conciliators and others involved in third-party roles, in the skills of dispute intervention and resolution.

Dispute procedures have long been recognized – by diplomats, labour negotiators and lawyers – as a significant factor for negotiation in addition to negotiation over substantive issues. Procedures matter to disputants both in terms of their process and participative value, and in terms of the way they can help influence outcomes – thus the support for the rule of law itself as a concept within political systems. As dispute resolution professionals, we need to spend more time articulating the options and their implications. The process of fashioning a new culture and strategy for dispute resolution to match the growing complexity of our life as a species, will itself spawn disputes of interest and values between those with different perspectives on dispute resolution and different stakes in old and new procedures. Such tension and conflict, however, are an integral part of the search to define, to establish and to renew justice in its many forms and forums.

Postscript – ADR in action

In November 1990 the Centre for Dispute Resolution (CEDR) was launched in London at the headquarters of the Confederation of British Industry. CEDR aims to promote more effective resolution of commercial disputes in Europe by use of ADR techniques, thus filling a gap I identified when this handbook was compiled in 1989. Even in its first few months it has generated a significant membership among UK businesses.

The intriguing link between ADR and the practice of law continues – it was two solicitors, Eileen Carroll and David Miles, who took the initiative in forming a steering committee to establish CEDR as a non-profit making organisation funded by membership subscriptions from business and professional firms. I was initially involved as one of a small group of individuals with whom they consulted and communicated; my appointment as the first CEDR Chief Executive means that I have the fortunate task of helping put ADR theory into action and of testing Tony Gibson's comment in this volume that an ounce of practice is worth a ton of talk.

Nor is the launch of CEDR the only sign of a potential sea-change in developments in dispute resolution. In the same year, apart from the onward march of the Ombudsman concept as a mechanism to handle individual grievances (now extended into legal services and pension schemes), the Bar Council has issued a paper calling for court-annexed conciliation in UK county courts, while a number of other UK organisations, such as the Chartered Institute of Arbitrators, the Scottish Council of Arbitration, IDR (Europe) and the British Academy of Experts, have all announced ADR initiatives. A leader in *The Times* on Access to Justice on 13 December 1990 went so far as to state that 'ADR is sorely needed on every High Street in Britain'.

What was marginal only a year earlier thus looks dangerously like becoming fashionable. However, such a level of interest seems certain to translate soon into significant reform in dispute resolution practice. For those of us who have been involved in ADR study, Robert Rice writing on CEDR in the *Financial Times* (12 November 1990) summed up well a sense of the change taking place, in the words of Victor Hugo: 'An invasion of armies may be resisted, but not an idea whose time has come.'

Karl Mackie
December 1990

References

Abel, R.L. (ed.) (1982a) *The Politics of Informal Justice*, New York: Academic Press.
—— (1982b) 'The contradictions of informal justice', in R.L. Abel (ed.) *The Politics of Informal Justice*, Vol. 1, New York: Academic Press.
Abel-Smith, B. and Stevens, R. (1970) *Lawyers and the Courts*, London: Heinemann.
Adler, J.W., Hensler, D. and Nelson, C.E. (1983) *Simple Justice: How Litigants Fare in the Pittsburg Court Arbitration Program*, Santa Monica, Calif.: Institute for Civil Justice, Rand Corporation.
Advertising Standards Authority (ASA) (1983–6) *Annual Reports* 1983–6, London: ASA.
Applebey, G. (1978) *Small Claims in England and Wales*, Institute of Judicial Administration, University of Birmingham.
—— (1979) 'Small claims in England and Wales', in M. Cappelletti and J. Weisner (eds) *Access to Justice* vol. 2, Alphen aan den Rijn: Sijthoff.
ARA Consultants (1984b) *Couples in Crisis II: The Kingston Mediation Model*, Kingston, Ontario: Frontenac Family Referral Service.
Australian Commonwealth Ombudsman (1985) *Annual Reports 1984–85*, Canberra: Australian Government Publishing Service.
Australian Law Reform Commission (1988) *Grouped Proceedings in the Federal Court*, Report no. 46, Canberra: Commonwealth Government.
Ayling, R. and Constanzo, M. (1984) 'Towards a model of education for competent practice', *Journal of Professional Legal Education* 2, 94–127.
Baldwin, J. and McConville, M. (1977) *Negotiated Justice: Pressures on Defendants to Plead Guilty*, London: Martin Robertson.
Beale, H. and Dugdale, T. (1975) 'Contracts between businessmen: planning and the use of contractual remedies', *British Journal of Law and Society* 2(1), 45–60.
Beer, J.E., Stief, E.M. and Walker, C.C. (1982) *Mediator's Handbook*, Philadelphia, Pa: Friends Mediation Service.
Birds, J. and Graham, C. (1988) 'Complaints mechanisms in the financial services industry', *Civil Justice Quarterly* 7, 313–28.
Birkinshaw, P. (1985) *Grievances, Remedies and the State*, London: Sweet & Maxwell.
—— (1987) 'Consumers and ratepayers', in M. Parkinson (ed.) *Reshaping Local Government*, Berkshire: Policy Journals.
—— (1988) 'Corporatism and accountability', in A. Cox and N. O'Sullivan (eds) *The Corporate State*, Aldershot: Edward Elgar.
—— (1989) 'Freedom of information – the US experience', unpublished paper.
Blankenburg, E. (1980) 'Recht als Gradualisiertes Konzept: Begriffsdimensionen der Diskussion um Verrechtlichung und Entrechtlichung', in E. Blankenburg, E. Klausa and H. Rottleuthner (eds) *Alternative Rechtsformen und Alternativen zum Recht*, Jahrbuch für Rechtssoziologie und Rechtstheorie, vol. 6, Opladen: Westdeutscher Verlag.

Blankenburg, E. and Taniguchi, Y. (1987) 'Informal alternatives to and within formal procedures', summary report presented at the 8th International Congress on Procedural Law at Utrecht, 24–27 August.

Blankenburg, E., Klausa, E. and Rottleuthner, H. (eds) (1980) *Alternative Rechtsformen und Alternativen zum Recht*, Jahrbuch für Rechtssoziologie und Rechtstheorie, vol. 6, Opladen: Westdeutscher Verlag.

Blankenburg, E., Gottwald, W. and Strempel, D. (eds) (1982) *Alternativen in der Ziviljustiz – Berichte, Analysen, Perspektiven*, Köln: Bundesanzeiger.

Booth Committee (1985) *Report of the Matrimonial Causes Procedure Committee*, London: HMSO.

Building Societies Association (BSA) (1983) *The Future Constitution and Powers of Building Societies*, London: BSA.

Building Societies Ombudsman Bureau (BSOB) (1987) *Ombudsman Scheme under Part IX of the Building Societies Act 1986*, London: BSOB.

—— (1987–8) *Annual Report*, London: BSOB.

Burger, W.E. (1984) Speech to American Bar Association Midyear Meeting, 12 February.

Butler-Sloss, A.E.O. (1988) *Report of the Inquiry into Child Abuse in Cleveland*, Cm 412, London: HMSO.

Caesar-Wolf, B. (1985) ' "Professionalized" lawyer–client-interaction: an exemplary case study of a divorce-consultation', paper presented at the workshop on Lawyer–Client-Interaction, Groningen, 24–27 October (published in German in *Zeitschrift für Rechtssoziologie* (1987) 8, 167–92).

Canaroff, J.L. and Roberts, S. (1981) *Rules and Processes: The Cultural Logic of Dispute in an African Context*, Chicago: University of Chicago Press.

Casper, J., Tyler, T.R. and Fisher, B. (1988) 'Procedural justice in felony cases', *Law and Society Review* 22, 483–507.

Chiasson, E.C., QC (1986) 'Canada: no man's land no more', *Journal of International Arbitration* 67 (June).

Cocks, R. (1988) *New Law Journal* 730.

Cohen, J.A. (1968) *The Criminal Process in the People's Republic of China, 1949–1963: An Introduction*, Cambridge, Mass.: Harvard University Press.

Consumer Council (1970) *Justice Out of Reach*, London: HMSO.

Coulson, R. (1987) *Business Mediation: What You Need to Know*, New York: American Arbitration Association.

Council of the Banking Ombudsman (1989) *Response to the Report of the Review Committee on Banking Services Law*, London: OBO.

Council on the Role of Courts (1984) *The Role of Courts in American Society*, St Paul, Minn.: West Publishing.

Cruickshank, D. (1985) 'The professional legal training course in British Columbia, Canada', *Journal of Professional Legal Education* 3, 111–32.

Danzig, R. (1973) 'Towards the creation of a complementary, decentralised, system of criminal justice', *Stanford Law Review* 1–26.

David, R.C. (1982) 'Mediation: the Brooklyn experiment', in R. Tomasic and M.M. Feeley (eds) *Neighbourhood Justice: Assessment of an Emerging Idea*, New York: Longman.

Davis, G. (1987) 'Public issues and private troubles: the case of divorce', *Family Law* 17, 299–308.

—— (1988) 'The halls of justice and justice in the halls', in R. Dingwall and J. Eekelaar (eds) *Divorce Mediation and the Legal Process*, Oxford: Oxford University Press.

Davis, G. and Roberts, M. (1988) *Access to Agreement*, Milton Keynes: Open University Press.

Davis, K.C. (1971) *Discretionary Justice*, Chicago: University of Illinois Press.

Demant, B., Dotterweich, J., Morasch, H. and Reichelt, P. (1984) 'Ergebnisse aus einer Umfrage über die Praxis der Schieds- und Schlichtungsstellen', in H. Morasch (ed.)

Schieds- und Schlichtungsstellen in der Bundesrepublik, Praxisanalysen und Perspektiven aus einem Kolloquium der GMD, Köln: Bundesanzeiger.

Denning, Lord (1947) *Committee on Procedure on Matrimonial Causes*, Cmd. 7024, London: HMSO.

Denti, V. and Vigoriti, V. (1983) 'Le rôle de la conciliation comme moyen d'éviter le procès et de résoudre le conflit', in W. Habscheid (ed.) *Effektiver Rechtsschutz und verfassungsmässige Ordnung*, Bielefeld: Gieseking.

Dienel, P. (1989) 'The citizen as assessor: planning public services – social services', in J. Epstein (ed.) *Providing Public Services that Serve the Public*, London: Anglo-German Foundation.

Dingwall, R. and Eekelaar, J. (eds) (1988) *Divorce Mediation and the Legal Process*, Oxford: Oxford University Press.

Director-General of Telecommunications (1988) *Annual Report 1987*, HC 432 1987–88, London: HMSO.

DoT (1980) *The Self-Regulatory System of Advertising Control – Report of the Working Party*, London: Department of Trade.

Ebener, P. and Betancourt, D. (1985) *Court-Annexed Arbitration: The National Picture*, Santa Monica, Calif.: Institute for Civil Justice, Rand Corporation.

Eberhardt, L. (1988) *Selbstverständnis, Anspruch und Verfahrenspraxis der ärztlichen Gutachterkommissionen und Schlichtungsstellen*, Frankfurt: Peter Lang.

Edelman, P.B. (1984) 'Institutionalizing dispute resolution alternatives', *Justice System Journal* 9, 134.

Eidmann, D. (1988) 'Schiedsstellen greifen ein: Rekonstruktion der Handlungslogik von Schieds- und Schlichtungsstellen', paper presented at the congress 'Kultur und Gesellschaft' of the West German, Austrian and Swiss sociological associations, Zurich, 4–7 October.

—— (1989) 'Rekonstruktion der Handlungslogik von Schieds- und Schlichtungsstellen anhand exemplarischer Fallstudien', unpublished paper.

Eisenberg, M.A. (1976) 'Private ordering through negotiation: dispute settlement and rule making', *Harvard Law Review* 89(4), 637–81.

Falckenstein, R.v. (1977) *Die Bekämpfung unlauterer Geschäftspraktiken durch Verbraucherverbände*, Köln: Bundesanzeiger.

Falke, J. and Gessner, V. (1982) 'Konfliktnahe als Masstab für gerichtliche und aussergerichtliche Streitbehandlung', in E. Blankenburg, W. Gottwald and D. Strempel (eds) *Alternativen in der Ziviljustiz – Berichte, Analysen, Perspektiven*, Köln: Bundesanzeiger.

Falke, J., Hörmann, G., Holzscheck, K., Plett, K. and Schumann, C. (1983) *Aushandeln und Recht: Formen und Foren der Konfliktaustragung*, Bremen: Zentrum für Europäische Rechtspolitik (ZERP DP 11/83).

Ferguson, R.B. (1980) 'The adjudication of commercial disputes and the legal system in modern England', *British Journal of Law and Society* 7(2), 141–57.

Financial Intermediaries, Managers and Brokers Regulatory Association (FIMBRA) (1987) *FIMBRA's Approach to its Regulatory Responsibilities as a Self-Regulating Organisation*, London: FIMBRA.

Finer, M. (1974) *Report of the Committee on One-Parent Families*, Cmnd. 5629, London: HMSO.

FIRM (1988) *What is FIRM and What Does it Aim to Do?*, Beaconsfield: FIRM.

—— (1989) *Working through Conflict: Annual Report 1988–89*, Beaconsfield: FIRM.

Fisher, R. (1985) 'He who pays the piper', *Harvard Business Review* March–April, 150–9.

Fisher, R. and Ury, W. (1982) *Getting to Yes: Negotiating Agreement without Giving in*, London: Hutchinson.

Fiss, O. (1984) 'Against settlement', *Yale Law Journal* 93, 1,071.

Franks Committee (1957) *Report of the Committee on Administrative Tribunals and Enquiries*, Cmnd. 218, London: HMSO.

Fuller, L. (1971) 'Mediation – its forms and functions', *Southern California Law Review* 44, 305–28.

—— (1978) 'The forms and limits of adjudication', *Harvard Law Review* 92, 353.

Galanter, M. (1974) 'Why the "Haves" come out ahead . . .', *Law and Society Review* 9, 95–160.

—— (1984) 'World of deals: using negotiation to teach about legal process, *Journal of Legal Education* 34.

Gartner, A. and Riessman, F. (1974) *The Service Society and the Consumer Vanguard*, New York: Harper & Row.

Garwood, F. (1989) *Children in Conciliation*, Edinburgh: Scottish Association of Family Conciliation Services.

Gellhorn, W. (1967) *Ombudsman and Others: Citizen Protectors in Nine Countries*, Cambridge, Mass.: Harvard University Press.

Genn, H. (1987) *Hard Bargaining: Out of Court Settlement in Personal Injury Actions*, Oxford: Clarendon Press.

Gessner, V. and Plett, K. (forthcoming) 'Informal justice in German legal development', in C. Meschievitz and K. Plett (eds) *Beyond Disputing*, Baden-Baden: Nomos.

Gold, N. (1987) 'Taking skills seriously: a research prospectus', *Journal of Professional Legal Education* 5, 64–71.

Gold, N., Mackie, K.J. and Twining, W. (eds) (1989) *Learning Lawyers' Skills*, London: Butterworths.

Goldberg, S.B., Green, E.D. and Sander, F.E.A. (1985) *Dispute Resolution*, Boston, Mass.: Little, Brown.

Gorbachev, M. (1988) *Perestroika: New Thinking for Our Country and the World*, London: Fontana.

Gosling, J. (1989) 'The role of outreach in conciliation and mediation work', *FIRMNEWS* 2(1), 2–3.

Gottwald, W. (1981) *Streitbeilegung ohne Urteil – Vemittelende Konfliktregelung Alltäglicher Streitigkeiten in den Vereinigten Staaten aus rechtsvergleichender Sicht*, Tubingen: J.C.B. Mohr.

—— (1987) 'Informelle Verfahrensangebote in der Ziviljustiz', in *Informal Alternatives to and within Formal Procedures*, reports presented at the eighth international Congress on Procedural Law, Utrecht 24–27 August, Amsterdam: Institute for Socio-Legal Studies, Free University (xeroxed), 84–115.

Gower, L.C.B. (1988) 'Big Bang and city regulation', *Modern Law Review* 51, 1–22.

Guo Xiang, Xu Qian, Li Chunli *et al.* (eds) (1986) *Renmin Tiaojie Zai Zhongguo* (People's Mediation in China), Tianjin: Huazhong Shifan Daxue Chubanshe (Central China Teacher's Training University Press).

Hahndorf, R. (1983) 'Schonung der Rechtsgewährungsresourcen Konfliktregelung durch den Anwalt', in W. Gottwald *et al.* (eds) *Der Prozessvergleich – Möglichkeiten, Grenzen, Forschungsperspektiven*, Köln: Bundesanzeiger.

Hanel, E. (1985) *Rechtsfragen der Kfz-Werkstatt*, Munich: Bartsch.

Harden, I., Lewis, N. and Birkinshaw, P. (1990) *Government by Moonlight: The Hybrid Parts of the Constitution*, London: Unwin-Hyman.

Harlow, C. and Rawlings, R. (1984) *Law and Administration*, London: Weidenfeld & Nicolson.

Harris, D.R., Maclean, M., Genn, H., Lloyd-Bostock, S., Fenn, P., Corfield, P. and Brittan, Y. (1984) *Compensation and Support for Illness and Injury*, Oxford: Clarendon Press.

Hathaway, J.C. (1987) 'A structured approach to clinical legal education', in R. Matas and D. McCawley (eds) *Legal Education in Canada*, Montreal: Federation of Law Societies of Canada.

Henry, J.F. (1985) 'Mini-trials: an alternative to litigation', *Negotiation Journal* January, 13–17.

Henry, J.F. and Lieberman, J.K. (1985) *The Manager's Guide to Resolving Legal*

Disputes: Better Results Without Litigation, New York: Harper & Row.

Hensler, D. (1984) *Reforming the Civil Litigation Process: How Court Arbitration Can Help*, Santa Monica, Calif.: Institute for Civil Justice, Rand Corporation.

Herrmann, G. (1987) 'The British Columbia enactment of the UNCITRAL Model Law', in R. Paterson and B.J. Thompson (eds) *UNCITRAL Arbitration Model in Canada*, Agincourt, Ontario: Carswell.

Hiltrop, J.M. (1987) 'Hiltrop Report: survey of ACAS Collective Conciliation', unpublished paper, University of Bradford.

Hippel, E.v. (1986) *Verbraucherschutz*, 3rd edn, Tübingen: J.C.B. Mohr.

Home Office (1983) *Inter-Departmental Committee on Conciliation*, London: HMSO.

—— (1984) *The Statement of National Objectives and Priorities*, London: HMSO.

Hughes Committee (1980) *Report of the Royal Commission on Legal Services in Scotland*, Chairman Lord Hughes, Cmnd. 7846, London: HMSO.

Institute of Directors (1984) *Settling Disputes Peacefully*, Position Paper, London: Institute of Directors.

Institute of Law Research and Reform (1987) *Towards a New Arbitration Act for Alberta*, Issues Paper no. 1, Edmonton, Alberta: Institute of Law Research and Reform.

Insurance Ombudsman Bureau (IOB) (1981, 1982, 1983, 1984, 1985, 1986, 1987, 1988) *Annual Report*, London: IOB.

Investment Management Regulatory Organization (IMRO) (1987) *Bulletin no. 3*, London: IMRO.

Jack Committee (1989) *Report of the Review Committee on Banking Services Law and Practice*, Chairman Prof. R.B. Jack CBE, Cm 622, London: HMSO.

Jansen, D. with G. Schwarz (1987) 'Das Güteverfahren vor dem Schiedsmann – ein alternatives Vermittlungsverfahren in zivilrechtlichen Streitigkeiten?', in K.F. Röhl (ed.) *Das Güteverfahren vor dem Schiedsmann*, Köln: Heymanns.

Jiang Fuyuan and Chen Cuiyin (1982) 'Minshi susongshong de renmin tiaojie weiyuanhui', (People's mediation committees in civil litigation), in Zhonggua Shehui Kexueyuan Yanjiusuo Tushu Ziliaoshi (The Books and Reference Materials Office of the Legal Research Institute of the Chinese Academy of Science) (eds) *Renmin Tiaojie Ziliao Xuanbian* (A Collection of Selected Materials on People's Mediation), Beijing: Qunzhong Chubanshe (The Masses Publishing House).

JUSTICE (1977) *Our Fettered Ombudsman*, London: JUSTICE.

—— (1988) *Administrative Justice: Some Necessary Reforms*, Oxford: Clarendon Press.

Kane, T. (1982) 'Delays and costs in the administration of justice: a survey of the Canadian response', Presentation to the Civil Litigation Section of the Canadian Bar Association's 1982 Annual Meeting, 30 August.

Kestner, P.B. (1988) *Education and Mediation: Exploring the Alternatives*, Chicago: American Bar Association.

Knowles, M. (1970) *The Modern Practice of Adult Education*, New York: Association Press.

Law Commission (1980) *Insurance Law: Non-Disclosure and Breach of Warranty*, Cmnd. 8064, London: HMSO.

Lax, D.A. and Sebenius, J.K. (1986) *The Manager as Negotiator: Bargaining for Cooperation and Competitive Gain*, New York: Free Press.

Lewis, N., Seneviratne, M. and Cracknell, S. (1987) *Complaints Procedures in Local Government* 2 vols, University of Sheffield, Centre for Criminological and Socio-Legal Studies.

Life Assurance and Unit Trust Regulatory Organization (LAUTRO) (1987) *LAUTRO's Approach to its Responsibilities as an SRO*, London: LAUTRO.

Lind, E.A. and Tyler, T.R. (1988) *The Social Psychology of Procedural Justice*, New York: Plenum.

Lind, E.A., Lissak, R. and Conlon, D. (1983) 'Decision control and process control effects on procedural fairness', *Journal of Applied Social Psychology* 4, 338–50.

Lind, E.A., MacCoun, R.J., Ebener, P.A., Felstiner, W.L.F., Hensler, D.R., Resnik, J. and Tyler, T.R. (1988) *Perceptions of Justice: Tort Litigants' Views of Settlement Conferences, Court-Annexed Arbitration and Trials*, Santa Monica, Calif.: Institute of Civil Justice, Rand Corporation.

Linden, A.M. (1983) 'In praise of settlement: towards cooperation, away from confrontation', *Canadian Commercial Law Journal*, 6, 4.

Lord Chancellor's Department (1986) *Civil Justice Review – Small Claims*, London: HMSO.

—— (1987) *Civil Justice Review: General Issues*, London: HMSO.

—— (1988) *Report of the Review Body on Civil Justice*, Cm 394, London: HMSO.

—— (1989a) *The Work and Organisation of the Legal Profession*, Cm 570, London: HMSO.

—— (1989b) *Report of the Conciliation Project Unit on the Costs and Effectiveness of Conciliation in England and Wales* (Ogus, A., Walker, J., Jones-Lee, M., Cole, W., Corlyon, J., McCarthy, P., Simpson, R. and Wray, S.) London: HMSO.

Lubman, S. (1967) 'Mao and mediation: politics and dispute resolution in Communist China', *California Law Review* 55, 1,284–359.

Macaulay, S. (1963) 'Non-contractual relations in business: a preliminary study', *American Sociological Review* 28, 55–67.

—— (1986) 'Private government', in L. Lipson and S. Wheeler (eds) *Law and the Social Sciences*, New York: Russell Sage Foundation.

MacCoun, R.J., Lind, E.A., Hensler, D.R., Bryand, D.L. and Ebener, P.A. (1988) *Alternative Adjudication: An Evaluation of the New Jersey Automobile Arbitration Program*, Santa Monica, Calif.: Institute of Civil Justice, Rand Corporation.

Macdougall, D.J. (1984) 'Negotiated settlement of family disputes', in J. Eekelaar and S.N. Katz (eds) *The Resolution of Family Conflict: Comparative Legal Perspectives*, Toronto: Butterworths.

McEwen, C.A. and Maiman, R.J. (1981) 'Small claims mediation in Maine: an empirical assessment', *Maine Law Review* 33, 237.

—— (1984) 'Mediation in small claims court: achieving compliance through consent', *Law and Society Review* 18, 11–49.

McGillis, D. and Mullen, J. (1977) *Neighborhood Justice Centers: An Analysis of Potential Models*, National Institute of Law Enforcement and Criminal Justice, Washington, DC: US Government Printing Office.

McKay, R.B. (1983) 'Civil litigation and the public interest', *Kansas Law Review* 31, 355.

Mackie, K.J. (1987) 'Lessons from Down-Under: conciliation and arbitration in Australia', *Industrial Relations Journal* 18(2), 100–16.

—— (1989) *Lawyers in Business and the Law Business*, London: Macmillan.

Mandelbaum, L. (1984) *Alternative Justice: The Potential for Local Mediation Centers in the State of Washington*, Olympia: Washington State Institute for Public Policy.

Mao Zedong (1977) *MaoZedong Xuanji* (Collected Works of Mao Zedong), vol. 5, Beijing: Beijing Renmin Chubanshe (Beijing People's Publishing House).

Marshall, T.F. (1985) *Alternatives to Criminal Courts*, Aldershot: Gower.

—— (1988) 'Informal justice: the British experience', in R. Matthews (ed.) *Informal Justice?*, London: Sage.

Marshall, T.F. and Walpole, M. (1985) *Bringing People Together*, London: Home Office Research and Planning Unit paper 33.

Matthews, R. (ed.) (1988) *Informal Justice?*, London: Sage.

Mental Health Act Commission (1987) *Second Biennial Report 1985–87*, London: HMSO.

Merrills, J.G. (1984) *International Dispute Settlement*, London: Sweet & Maxwell.

Merry, S.E. (1982) 'Defining "success" in the Neighborhood Justice Movement', in R. Tomasic and M.M. Feeley (eds) *Neighborhood Justice: Assessment of an Emerging Idea*, New York: Longman.

Micklitz, H.W. (1983) 'Schieds- und Schlichtungsstellen für Verbraucher: Eine kritische Bestandsaufnahme', *Deutsche Richterzeitung* 61, 119–27.

Miller, E.J. (1986) *Conflict and Reconciliation*, Occasional Paper no. 9, London: Tavistock Institute.

Mnookin, R.H. and Kornhauser, L. (1979) 'Bargaining in the shadow of the law: the case of divorce', *Yale Law Journal* 88, 950–97.

Molony Committee (1962) *Report of the Committee on Consumer Protection*, Chairman Mr J.T. Molony QC, Cmnd. 1781, London: HMSO.

Moore, C.W. (1986) *The Mediation Process: Practical Strategies for Resolving Conflict*, San Francisco, Calif.: Jossey-Bass.

Moran, M. (1988) 'Thatcherism and the Constitution: the case of financial regulation', in C. Graham and T. Prosser (eds) *Waiving the Rules: The Constitution under Thatcherism*, Milton Keynes: Open University Press.

Morasch, H. (ed.) (1984) *Schieds- und Schlichtungsstellen in der Bundesrepublik, Praxisanalysen und Perspektiven aus einem Kolloquium der GMD*, Köln: Bundesanzeiger.

Morris, B.E. (1987) 'The Banking Ombudsman', *Journal of Business Law* 131(6), 199–200.

Morrison, C. (1981) *Policy Holder Insurance Journal* 3 April.

Morton Committee (1956) *Royal Commission on Marriage and Divorce*, Cmd. 9678, London: HMSO.

Mullen, T. (1989) 'The Social Fund – cash limiting social security', *Modern Law Review* 52, 64–92.

Nader, L. and Shugart, Ch. (1980) 'Old solutions for old problems', in L. Nader (ed.) *No Access to Law – Alternatives to the Judicial System*, New York: Academic Press.

NAO (National Audit Office) (1986–87) *Incorrect Payments of Social Security Awards*, HC 319 1986–87, London: HMSO.

—— (1987–88a) *Quality of Clinical Health-Care in NHS Hospitals*, HC 736 1987–88, London: HMSO.

—— (1987–88b) *Quality of Service to the Public at DHSS Local Offices*, HC 451 1987–88, London: HMSO.

—— (1987–88c) *Management of Family Practitioner Services*, HC 498 1987–88, London: HMSO.

National Center for State Courts (1978) *Small Claims Courts: A National Examination*, Washington: NCSC.

National Consumer Council (NCC) (1970) *Justice Out of Reach*, London: NCC.

—— (1979) *Simple Justice*, London: NCC.

—— (1983) *Banking Services and the Consumer*, London: Metheun.

—— (1985) *In Dispute with the Solicitor*, London: NCC.

—— (1987) *Evidence to the Review Committee on Banking Services Law*, London: NCC.

—— (1989) *Ordinary Justice – Legal Services and the Courts in England and Wales: A Consumer View*, London: HMSO.

Nothdurft, W. and Spranz-Vogasy, Th. (1986) 'Der kulturelle Kontext von Schlichtung: Zum Stand der Schlichtungsforschung in der Rechts-Anthropologie', *Zeitschrift für Rechtssoziologie* 7, 31–52.

Oevermann, U. (1979) 'Re- oder Deprofessionalisierung von Juristen', lecture held at University of Hannover, Department of Law.

Office of the Banking Ombudsman (OBO) (1985–6, 1986–7, 1987–8) *Annual Report*, London: OBO.

—— (no date) *The Banking Ombudsman Scheme: Terms of Reference*, London: OBO.

Office of Fair Trading (OFT) (1980) *Redress Procedures under Codes of Practice – Consultative Document*, London: OFT.

—— (1981) *Redress Procedures under Codes of Practice – Report*, London: OFT.

—— (1984) *I'm Going to Take it Further*, London: OFT.

—— (1986) *Consumer Dissatisfaction*, London: OFT.

—— (1988) *Annual Report of the Director General of Fair Trading for 1988*, HC 544, London: HMSO.

Ogus, A., McCarthy, P. and Wray, S. (1987) 'Court annexed mediation programmes in England and Wales', in J. McCrory (ed.) *The Role of Mediation in Divorce Proceedings: A Comparative Perspective (United States, Canada and Great Britain)*, Vermont Law School.

Page, A. (1987) 'Financial services: the self-regulatory alternative?', in R. Baldwin and C. McCrudden (eds) *Regulation and Public Law*, London: Weidenfeld & Nicolson.

Palmer, M. (1987) 'The People's Republic of China: new marriage regulations', *Annual Survey of Family Law 1986* 10: 39–57.

—— (1988) 'The revival of mediation in the People's Republic of China: (1) Extra-judicial mediation', in W.E. Butler (ed.) *Yearbook on Socialist Legal Systems 1987*, Dobbs Ferry, NY: Transnational Books.

—— (1989) 'The revival of mediation in the People's Republic of China: (2) Judicial mediation', in W.E. Butler (ed.) *Yearbook on Socialist Legal Systems 1989*, Dobbs Ferry, NY: Transnational Books.

Parkinson, L. (1983) 'Conciliation – pros and cons', *Family Law* 13 (1 and 6), 22–5 and 183–6.

—— (1986) *Conciliation in Separation and Divorce*, London: Croom Helm.

Parks, R.B. (1976) 'Police responses to victimization: effects on citizen attitudes and perceptions', in W. Skogan (ed.) *Sample surveys of the Victims of Crime*, Cambridge, Mass.: Ballinger.

Parliamentary Commissioner for Administration (1985–6) *Second Report from the Select Committee on the Parliamentary Commissioner for Administration*, HC 312 1985–86, London: HMSO.

—— (1986) *Annual Report*, HC 248 1986–87, London: HMSO.

—— (1987) *Annual Report*, HC 363 1987–88, London: HMSO.

Partington, M. (1985) in P. McAuslan and J.F. McEldowney (eds) *Law, Legitimacy and the Constitution*, London: Sweet & Maxwell.

Paterson, R. and Thompson, B.J. (eds) (1987) *UNCITRAL Arbitration Model in Canada*, Agincourt, Ontario: Carswell.

Pearson, J. (1979) 'The custody mediation project', *Colorado Lawyer* 8, 7.

—— (1982) 'An evaluation of alternatives to court adjudication', *Justice System Journal* 7, 420.

Pearson, J. and Thoennes, N. (1988) 'Divorce mediation: an American picture', in R. Dingwall and J. Eekelaar (eds) *Divorce Mediation and the Legal Process*, Oxford: Oxford University Press.

Pearson Commission (1978) *Royal Commission on Civil Liability and Compensation for Personal Injury*, Cmd. 7054, London: HMSO.

Peng Zhen (1987) 'Explanations of the Seven Draft Laws', in *The Laws of the People's Republic of China 1979–1982*, compiled by the Legislative Affairs Commission of the Standing Committee of the National People's Congress of the People's Republic of China, Beijing: Foreign Languages Press.

Plett, K. (1988–9) 'Civil justice and its reform in West Germany and the United States', *Justice System Journal* 13, 186–201.

—— (1989) 'Die Bau-Schlichtungsstelle in Frankfurt als Verfahrensalternative für Baustreitigkeiten – Forschungsbericht', Bremen: xeroxed paper.

Plett, K. and Eidmann, D. (1987) 'Schieds- und Schlichtungsstellen in der Bundesrepublik Deutschland: Ein Gutachten zur Frage des Verhältnisses zwischen vor- und aussergerichtlicher und gerichtlicher Beilegung von Verbraucherstreitigkeiten', Bremen: xeroxed paper.

Poggi, G. (1978) *The Development of the Modern State*, London: Hutchinson.

Police Complaints Authority (1987–88) *Triennial Report*, HC 466 1987–88, London: HMSO.

Pound, R. (1906) 'The causes of popular dissatisfaction with the administration of justice', *American Bar Association Reports* 29, 395; repr. in the Pound *Conference: Perspectives on Justice in the Future*, Proceedings of the National Conference on Justice, 1980, 337 ff.

—— (1913) 'The administration of justice in the modern city', *Harvard Law Review* 26, 302.

Prosser, T. (1986) *Nationalised Industries and Public Control*, Oxford: Basil Blackwell.

Public Accounts Committee (PAC) (1987–88) *Quality of Service to the Public at DHSS Local Offices*, HC 491 1987–88, London: HMSO.

Purdue, M. (1987) 'Current topics', *Journal of Planning Law* 82–3.

Raiffa, H. (1982) *The Art and Science of Negotiation*, Cambridge, Mass.: Harvard University Press.

Ramsay, I. (1987) 'Courts, corporation and bureaucracy', paper presented at the Law and Society Annual Meeting, 11–14 June, and the Conference on Dispute Resolution Research in Europe, 15 June, Washington, DC.

Rawlings, R. (1986) 'Parliamentary redress of grievance', in C. Harlow (ed.) *Public Law and Politics*, London: Sweet & Maxwell.

Redfern, A. and Hunter, M. (1986) *Law and Practice of International Commercial Arbitration*, London: Sweet & Maxwell.

Reich, N. (1982) 'Alternativen zur Ziviljustiz im Verbraucherschutz – Überlegungen zur Bedeutung von Schieds- und Schlichtungsverfahren', in E. Blankenburg, W. Gottwald and D. Strempel (eds) *Alternativen in der Ziviljustiz – Berichte, Analysen, Perspektiven*, Köln: Bundesanzeiger, pp. 219–29.

Reide, C.T. (1986) 'The ombudsman's cousin: the procuracy in socialist states', *Public Law* 311–26.

Riskin, L.L. (1982) 'Mediation and lawyers', *Ohio State Law Journal* 43, 29.

Riskin, L.L. and Westbrook, J.E. (1987) *Dispute Resolution and Lawyers*, St Paul, Minn.: West Publishing.

Roberts, S. (1986) 'Toward a minimal form of alternative intervention', *Mediation Quarterly* 2, 25–41.

Robinson, P.D. (1983) *Report of the Inter-Departmental Committee on Conciliation*, London: HMSO.

Rolph, E. (1984) *Introducing Court-Annexed Arbitration: A Policymaker's Guide*, Santa Monica, Calif.: Institute for Civil Justice, Rand Corporation.

Rosenthal, D.E. (1974) *Lawyer and Client: Who's in Charge?*, New Jersey: Transaction Books.

Ruffat, M. (1987) *Le contre-pouvoir consommateur aux états-unis*, Paris: Presses Universitaires de France.

Sander, F.E.A. (1984) 'Towards a functional analysis of family process', in J. Eekelaar and S.N. Katz (eds) *The Resolution of Family Conflict: Comparative Legal Perspectives*, Toronto: Butterworths.

Scott Committee (1973) *Linked Life Assurance: Report of the Committee on Property Bonds and Equity-Linked Life Assurance*, Cmnd. 5281, London: HMSO.

Scottish Consumer Council (1982) *Class Actions in the Scottish Courts*, Edinburgh, Scottish Consumer Council.

Securities and Investments Board (SIB) (1986) *Proposed Ombudsman Arrangements*, London: SIB.

—— (1987) *SIB's Approach to its Regulatory Responsibilities*, London: SIB.

Seeling, E.R. (1984) 'Die neuere Entwicklung der Gebrauchtwagen-Schiedsstellen', in H. Morasch (ed.) *Schieds- und Schlichtungsstellen in der Bundesrepublik, Praxisanalysen und Perspektiven aus einen Kolloquium der GMD*, Köln: Bundesanzeiger.

Shepherd, G. and Howard, J. (1985) 'Theft of conciliation? The thieves reply', *Probation Journal* 32, 59–60.

Sheppard, B.H. and Lewicki, R.J. (1987) 'Toward general principles of managerial fairness', *Social Justice Research* 1, 161–76.

Shonholtz, R. (1987) 'The citizen's role in justice', *Annals of the American Academy of Political and Social Science*, 494, 42–52.

—— (1988) Report of a talk, *FIRMNEWS* May, 1, 2.

Stacey, B. (1978) *Ombudsmen Compared*, Oxford: Clarendon Press.

Stein, P. (1984) *Legal Institutions: The Development of Dispute Settlement*, London: Butterworths.

Stewart, R. (1984) 'Reform of administrative law: the academic agenda vs. the political agenda', unpublished paper.

Streeck, W. and Schmitter, Ph.C. (1985) 'Community, market, state – and associations? The prospective contribution of interest governance to social order', in W. Streeck and Ph.C. Schmitter (eds) *Private Interest Government – Beyond Market and State*, London: Sage.

Sun Zhenming (1985) 'Ershen fayuan nengfou tiaojie jingji jiufen anjian?' (Can an appellate court mediate economic cases?), *Faxue* (Jurisprudence) 9, 29.

Sunkin, M. (1987) 'What is happening to applications for judicial review', *Modern Law Review* 432–67.

Taylor, R.W. (1986) 'Redress of grievances in the USA: shy power', *Parliamentary Affairs* 197.

Thibaut, J. and Walker, L. (1975) *Procedural Justice: A Psychological Analysis*, Hillsdale, NJ: Erlbaum Associates.

Thomas, R. (1982) 'A code of procedure for small claims', *Civil Justice Quarterly* 2, 52.

—— (1988) 'Alternative dispute resolution – consumer disputes', *Civil Justice Quarterly* 7, 206–19.

—— (1990) 'Civil justice review – treating litigants as consumers', *Civil Justice Quarterly* 9, 51–60.

Thompson, B.J. (1987a) 'Commercial arbitration: a new look at a new era', *The Advocate* 45(2) March: 185.

—— (1987b) 'The marriage of the UNCITRAL Model Arbitration Law and the UNCITRAL Arbitration Rules', in R. Paterson and B.J. Thompson (eds) *UNCITRAL Arbitration Model in Canada*, Agincourt, Ontario: Carswell.

Tobin, A. (1987) 'Criteria for the design of legal training programmes', *Journal of Professional Legal Education* 5, 55–63.

Tomasic, R. (1982) 'Mediation as an alternative to adjudication: rhetoric and reality in the neighborhood justice movement', in R. Tomasic and M.M. Feeley (eds) *Neighborhood Justice: Assessment of an Emerging Idea*, New York: Longman.

Tomasic, R. and Feeley, M.M. (eds) (1982) *Neighborhood Justice: Assessment of an Emerging Idea*, New York, Longman.

Tottenham Neighbourhood Law Centre (TNLC) (1982) *Annual Report 1982*, London: TNLC.

Townley, B. (1987) 'Union recognition: a comparative analysis of the pros and cons of a legal procedure', *British Journal of Industrial Relations* 25(2), 177–99.

Tyler, T.R. (1984) 'The role of perceived injustice in defendants' evaluations of their courtroom experience', *Law and Society Review* 18: 51–74.

—— (1987) 'Conditions leading to value expressive effects in judgements of procedural justice: a test of four models', *Journal of Personality and Social Psychology* 52, 333–44.

—— (1988) 'What is procedural justice: criteria used by citizens to assess the fairness of legal procedures', *Law and Society Review* 22, 301–55.

—— (1989a) 'The quality of dispute resolution processes and outcomes: measurement problems and possibilities', *Denver University Law Review* 66, 419–36.

—— (1989b) 'The psychology of procedural justice: a test of the group value model', *Journal of Personality and Social Psychology* 57, 830–38.

—— (1990) *Why People Obey the Law: Procedural Justice, Legitimacy and Compliance*, New Haven, Conn.: Yale University Press.

Tyler, T.R. and Bies, R. (1990) 'Interpersonal aspects of procedural justice', in J.S. Carroll (ed.) *Applied Social Psychology in Business Settings*, Hillsdale, NJ: Erlbaum.

Tyler, T.R., Rasinski, K. and Spodick, N. (1985) 'The influence of voice on satisfaction with leaders: exploring the meaning of process control', *Journal of Personality and Social Psychology* 48, 72–81.

Tyler, T.R., Casper, J. and Fisher, B. (1989) 'Maintaining allegiance toward political authorities: the role of prior attitudes procedures', *American Journal of Political Science* 33, 629–52.

Vroom, P., Fasset, D. and Wakefield, R.A. (1981) 'Mediation: the wave of the future?', *American Family* 4 (June/July), 8–13.

Walker, J.A. (1987) 'Divorce mediation: an overview from Great Britain', in J. McCrory (ed.) *The Role of Mediation in Divorce Proceedings: A Comparative Perspective (United States, Canada and Great Britain)*, Vermont Law School.

—— (1989) 'Family conciliation in Great Britain: from research to practice to research', *Mediation Quarterly* 24, 29–55.

Walker, J.A. and Wray, S. (1987) *Current Alternatives to Litigation in England and Wales*, Swindon, Wilts: National Family Conciliation Council.

Weekes, B.C.M., Mellish, M., Dickens, L. and Lloyd, J. (1975) *Industrial Relations and the Limits of the Law: The Industrial Effects of the Industrial Relations Act 1971*, Oxford: Basil Blackwell.

Weller, S., Ruhnaka, J. and Martin, J. (1981) 'Compulsory arbitration: the Rochester answer to court backlogs', *Judges Journal* Summer, 36.

Whelan, C. (1987) 'The role of research in civil justice reform: small claims in the county court', *Civil Justice Quarterly* 6, 237–47.

Which? (1988) 'BT – still out of order?', *Which?* June, 266–70.

Widdicombe, D. (1986) *The Conduct of Local Authority Business*, Cmnd. 9797, London: HMSO.

Wikeley, N. (1988) 'Conciliation in English family law', *Civil Justice Quarterly* 7, 194.

Wilkinson, M. (1981) *Children and Divorce*, Oxford: Basil Blackwell.

Williams, G. (1983) *Legal Negotiation and Settlement*, St Paul, Minn.: West Publishing Co.

Williams, R. (1989) 'Eliminating cost and delay in civil litigation', *Law Society's Gazette* 26 April (16), 28–32.

Woolf, L.J. (1986) 'Public law – private law: why the divide?', *Public Law* 220–38.

Yardley, D.C.M. (1986) *Principles of Administrative Law*, 2nd edn, London: Butterworths.

Yngvesson, B. and Hennesey, P. (1975) 'Small claims: complex disputes: a review of the small claims literature', *Law and Society Review* 9, 2197–274.

Zeng Fangwen (1987) 'Tamen wei schenme qijia chuzou?' (Why do they abandon their families and run away?), *Shehui* (Sociology) 6, 37–9.

Zheng Tianxing (1986) 'Zuigao Renmin fayuan gongzuo baogao' (Report on the work of the Supreme People's Court), *Xinhua Yeukan* (New China Monthly) May, 71–5.

Name index

Subject index